Arabia: The Cradle of Islam

A TYPICAL ARAB OF YEMEN

Arabia: The Cradle of Islam

Studies in the Geography, People and Politics of the Peninsula with an account of Islam and Mission-work

BY

REV. S. M. ZWEMER, F.R.G.S.

INTRODUCTION BY

REV. JAMES S. DENNIS, D.D.

DARF PUBLISHERS LTD
LONDON
1986

FIRST PUBLISHED 1900
NEW IMPRESSION 1986

ISBN 1 85077 111 1

Printed and bound in Great Britain
by A. Wheaton & Co. Ltd, Exeter, Devon

DEDICATED

The " Student Volunteers " of America

IN MEMORY OF

THE TWO AMERICAN VOLUNTEERS WHO LAID DOWN THEIR
LIVES FOR ARABIA

PETER J. ZWEMER

AND

GEORGE E. STONE

And Jesus said unto him : This day is salvation come to this house, for-asmuch as he also is a son of Abraham.   For the Son of Man is come to seek and to save that which was lost.—LUKE xix. 9, 10.

Introductory Note

THE author of this instructive volume is in the direct line of missionary pioneers to the Moslem world. He follows Raymond Lull, Henry Martyn, Ion Keith-Falconer, and Bishop French, and, with his friend and comrade the Rev. James Cantine, now stands in the shining line of succession at the close of a decade of patient and brave service at that lonely outpost on the shores of the Persian Gulf. Others have followed in their footsteps, until the Arabian Mission, the adopted child of the Reformed Church in America, is at present a compact and resolute group of men and women at the gates of Arabia, waiting on God's will, and intent first of all upon fulfilling in the spirit of obedience to the Master the duty assigned them.

These ten years of quiet, unflinching service have been full of prayer, observation, study, and wistful survey of the great task, while at the same time every opportunity has been improved to gain a foothold, to plant a standard, to overcome a prejudice, to sow a seed, and to win a soul. The fruits of this intelligent and conscientious effort to grasp the situation and plan the campaign are given to us in this valuable study of "Arabia, the Cradle of Islam." It is a missionary contribution to our knowledge of the world. The author is entirely familiar with the literature of his subject. English, German, French, and Dutch authorities are at his command. The less accessible Arabic authors are easily within his reach, and he brings from those mysterious gardens of spices into his clear, straightforward narrative, the local coloring and fragrance, as well as the indisputable witness of original medieval sources. The ethnological, geographical, archeological, commercial, and

1

political information of the descriptive chapters brings to our hands a valuable and readable summary of facts, in a form which is highly useful, and will be sure to quicken an intelligent interest in one of the great religious and international problems of our times.

His study of Islam is from the missionary standpoint, but this does not necessarily mean that it is unfair, or unhistorical, or lacking in scholarly acumen. Purely scientific and academic study of an ethnic religion is one method of approaching it. It can thus be classified, labelled, and put upon the shelf in the historical museum of the world's religions, and the result has a value which none will dispute. This, however, is not the only, or indeed the most serviceable, way of examining, estimating and passing a final judgment upon a religious system. Such study must be comparative; it must have some standard of value; it must not discard acknowledged tests of excellence; it must make use of certain measurements of capacity and power; it must be pursued in the light of practical ethics, and be in harmony with the great fundamental laws of religious experience and spiritual progress which have controlled thus far the regenerative processes of human development.

The missionary in forming his final judgment inevitably compares the religion he studies with the religion he teaches. He need not do this in any unkind, or bitter, or abusive spirit. On the contrary, he may do it with a supreme desire to uncover delusion, and make clear the truth as it has been given to him by the Great Teacher. He may make a generous and sympathetic allowance for the influence of local environment, he may trace in an historic spirit the natural evolution of a religious system, he may give all due credit to every worthy element and every pleasing characteristic therein, he may regard its symbols with respect, and also with all charity and consideration the leaders and guides whom the people reverence; yet his own judgment may still be inflexible, his own allegiance unfaltering, and he may feel it to be his duty to put into plain, direct, and vigorous prose his irreversible verdict that Christianity being true, Islam is not, Buddhism is not, Hinduism is not.

There he stands ; he is not afraid of the issue. His Master is the one supreme and infallible judge, who can pronounce an unerring verdict concerning the truth of any religion. He has ventured to bear witness to the truth which his Master has taught him. Let no one lightly question the value of the contribution he makes to the comparative study of religion.

The spirit in which our author has written of Islam is marked by fairness, sobriety, and discrimination, and yet there is no mistaking the verdict of one who speaks with an authority which is based upon exceptional opportunities of observation, close study of literary sources and moral results, and undoubted honesty of purpose.

It may not be out of place to note the hearty, outspoken satisfaction with which the author regards the extension of British authority over the long sweep of the Arabian coast line. His admiration and delight can only be fully understood by one who has been a resident in the East, and has felt the blight of Moslem rule, and its utter hopelessness as an instrument of progress.

Let this book have its hour of quiet opportunity, and it will broaden our vision, enlarge our knowledge, and deepen our interest in themes which will never lose their hold upon the attention of thoughtful men.

JAMES S. DENNIS.

Preface

THERE are indications that Arabia will not always remain
in its long patriarchal sleep and that there is a future in
store for the Arab. Politics, civilization and missions have all
begun to touch the hem of the peninsula and it seems that soon
there will be one more land—or at least portions of it—to add
to "the white man's burden." History is making in the Persian Gulf, and Yemen will not forever remain, a tempting prize,
—untouched. The spiritual burden of Arabia is the Mohammedan religion and it is in its cradle we can best see the fruits
of Islam. We have sought to trace the spiritual as well as the
physical geography of Arabia by showing how Islam grew out
of the earlier Judaism, Sabeanism and Christianity.

The purpose of this book is especially to call attention to
Arabia and the need of missionary work for the Arabs. There
is no dearth of literature on Arabia, the Arabs and Islam, but
most of the books on Arabia are antiquated or inaccessible to
the ordinary reader; some of the best are out of print. The
only modern work in English, which gives a general idea of
the whole peninsula is Bayard Taylor's somewhat juvenile
"*Travels in Arabia.*" In German there is the scholarly compilation of Albrecht Zehm, "*Arabie und die Araber, seit
hundert jahren,*" which is generally accurate, but is rather dull
reading and has neither illustrations nor maps. From the
missionary standpoint there are no books on Arabia save the
biographies of Keith-Falconer, Bishop French and Kamil Abd-
ul-Messiah.

This fact together with the friends of the author urged their
united plea for a book on this "Neglected Peninsula," its people, religion and missions. We have written from a missionary

5

viewpoint, so that the book has certain features which are intended specially for those who are interested in the missionary enterprise. But that enterprise has now so large a place in modern thought that no student of secular history can afford to remain in ignorance of its movements.

Some of the chapters are necessarily based largely on the books by other travellers, but if any object to quotation marks, we would remind them that Emerson's writings are said to contain three thousand three hundred and ninety three quotations from eight hundred and sixty-eight individuals! The material for the book was collected during nine years of residence in Arabia. It was for the most part put into its present form at Bahrein during the summer of 1899, in the midst of many outside duties and distractions.

I wish especially to acknowledge my indebtedness to W. A. Buchanan, Esq., of London, who gave the initiative for the preparation of this volume and to my friend Mr. D. L. Pierson who has generously undertaken the entire oversight of its publication.

The system for the spelling of Arabic names in the text follows in general that of the Royal Geographical Society. This system consists, in brief, in three rules: (1) words made familiar by long usage remain unchanged; (2) vowels are pronounced as in Italian and consonants as in English; (3) no redundant letters are written and all those written are pronounced.

We send these chapters on their errand, and hope that especially the later ones may reach the hearts of the Student Volunteers for foreign missions to whom they are dedicated; we pray also that the number of those who love the Arabs and labor for their enlightenment and redemption may increase.

S. M. ZWEMER.

Bahrein, Arabia.

Table of Contents

7

Bahrein occupied—Lines of work—Muscat—Journey through Yemen—The mission transferred to the Reformed Church—Troubles at Muscat and Busrah—Dr. Worrall—Journeys in Oman—Scripture-sales—First-fruits—Reinforcements.

XXXIV

XXXV

The general problem of missions to Moslems—The Arabian problem—What part of Arabia is accessible—Turkish Arabia—Its accessibility—Limitations—The accessibility of independent Arabia—Climate—Moslem fanaticism—English influence—Illiteracy—The Bedouins—The present missionary force—Its utter inadequacy—Methods of work—Medical missions—Schools—Work for women—Colportage—Preaching—Controversy—What should be its character—The attitude of the Moslem mind—Fate of converts—Thoughtless and thoughtful Moslems—The Bible as dynamite—The right men for the work.

XXXVI

Two views of work for Moslems—Christian fatalism—Results in Moslem lands—India—Persia—Constantinople—Sumatra and Java—Other signs of progress—The significance of persecution—Character of converts—Promise of God for victory over Islam—Christ or Mohammed—Missionary promises of the Old Testament—The Rock of Jesus' Sonship—Special promises for Arabia—Hagar and Ishmael—The prayer of Abraham—The sign of the covenant with Ishmael—The third revelation of God's love—The sons of Ishmael—Kedar and Nebaioth—The promises—Seba and Sheba—The spiritual boundaries of Arabia—Da Costa's poem—Faith like Abraham—O that Ishmael might live before thee.

List of Illustrations

VIEW OF MECCA AND THE SACRED MOSQUE

THE REPUTED TOMB OF EVE AT JIDDAH

I

THE NEGLECTED PENINSULA

" Intersected by sandy deserts and vast ranges of mountains it presents on one side nothing but desolation in its most frightful form, while the other is adorned with all the beauties of the most fertile regions. Such is its position that it enjoys at once all the advantages of hot and of temperate climates. The peculiar productions of regions the most distant from one another are produced here in equal perfection. What Greek and Latin authors mention concerning Arabia proves by its obscurity their ignorance of almost everything respecting the Arabs. Prejudices relative to the inconveniences and dangers of travelling in Arabia have hitherto kept the moderns in equal ignorance."—*M. Niebuhr* (1792).

WHAT Jerusalem and Palestine are to Christendom this, and vastly more, Mecca and Arabia are to the Mohammedan world. Not only is this land the cradle of their religion and the birthplace of their prophet, the shrine toward which, for centuries, prayers and pilgrimage have gravitated; but Arabia is also, according to universal Moslem tradition, the original home of Adam after the fall and the home of all the older patriarchs. The story runs that when the primal pair fell from their estate of bliss in the heavenly paradise, Adam landed on a mountain in Ceylon and Eve fell at Jiddah, on the western coast of Arabia. After a hundred years of wandering they met near Mecca, and here Allah constructed for them a tabernacle, on the site of the present Kaaba. He put in its foundation the famous stone once whiter than snow, but since turned black by the sins of pilgrims! In proof of these statements travellers are shown the Black stone at Mecca and the tomb of Eve near Jiddah. Another accepted tradition says that Mecca stands on a spot exactly beneath God's throne in heaven.

Without reference to these wild traditions, which are soberly

set down as facts by Moslem historians, Arabia is a land of
perpetual interest to the geographer, and the historian.

Since Niebuhr's day many intrepid travellers have surveyed
the coasts and penetrated into the interior, but his charge that
we are ignorant of the real character of the vast peninsula is
still true as far as it relates to the southern and southeastern
districts.   No traveller has yet crossed the northern boundary
of Hadramaut and explored the Dahna desert, also called the
Roba-el-Khali, or "empty abode."   The vast territory between the peninsula of Katar and the mountains of Oman is also
practically a blank on the best maps.   Indeed the only note-
worthy map of that portion of the peninsula is that of Ptolemy
reproduced by Sprenger in his "Alte Geographie Arabiens."

Arabia has well-defined boundaries everywhere except on the
north.   Eastward are the waters of the Persian Gulf, the Strait
of Ormuz and the Gulf of Oman.   The entire southern coast is
washed by the Indian Ocean which reaches to Bab-el-Mandeb
"The Gate-of-tears," from which point the Red Sea and the
Gulf of Akaba form the western boundary.   The undefined
northern desert, in some places a sea of sand, completes the
isolation which has led the Arabs themselves to call the
peninsula their "Island" (Jezirat-el-Arab).   In fact the northern boundary will probably never be defined accurately.   The
so-called "Syrian desert," reaching to about the thirty-fifth
parallel might better be regarded as the Arabian desert, for in
physical and ethnical features it bears much greater resemblance
to the southern peninsula than to the surrounding regions of
Syria and Mesopotamia.   Bagdad is properly an Arabian city
and to the Arabs of the north is as much a part of the peninsula
as is Aden to those of the southwest.   The true, though shifting, northern boundary of Arabia would be the limit of Nomad
encampments, but for convenience and practical purposes a
boundary line may be drawn from the Mediterranean along the
thirty-third parallel to Busrah.

Thus the shores of Arabia stretch from Suez to the Euphrates delta for a total length of nearly 4,000 miles. This coast-line has comparatively few islands or inlets, except in the Persian Gulf. The Red Sea coast is fringed by extensive coral reefs, dangerous to navigation, but from Aden to Muscat the coast is elevated and rocky, and contains several good harbors. Eastern Arabia has a low, flat coast-line made of coral-rock with here and there volcanic headlands. Farsan, off the Tehamah coast, famous as the centre for Arab slave-dhows; Perim, where English batteries command the gate of the Red Sea; the Kuria-Muria group in the Indian Ocean; and the Bahrein archipelago in the Persian Gulf, are the only important islands. Socotra, although occupied by an Arab population and historically Arabian, is by geographers generally attached to Africa. This island is however under the Indian government, and, once Christian, is now wholly Mohammedan.

The greatest length of the peninsula is about 1,000 miles, its average breadth 600, and its area somewhat over 1,000,000 square miles. It is thus over four times the size of France or larger than the United States east of the Mississippi River.

Arabia, until quite recently, has generally been regarded as a vast expanse of sandy desert. Recent explorations have proved this idea quite incorrect, and a large part of the region still considered desert is as yet unexplored. Palgrave, in his "Central Arabia" gives an excellent summary of the physical characteristics of the whole peninsula as he saw it. Since his time Hadramaut has been partially explored and the result confirms his statements: "The general type of Arabia is that of a central table-land surrounded by a desert ring sandy to the south, west and east, stony to the north. This outlying circle is in its turn girt by a line of mountains low and sterile for the most, but attaining in Yemen and Oman considerable height, breadth and fertility; while beyond these a narrow rim of coast is bordered by the sea. The surface of the midmost table-land equals somewhat less than one-half of the entire peninsula; and its special demarkations are much affected,

nay often absolutely fixed, by the windings and inrunnings of the
Nefud (sandy desert). If to these central highlands or *Nejd*,
taking that word in its wider sense, we add whatever spots of
fertility belong to the outer circles, we shall find that Arabia
contains about two-thirds of cultivated or at least of cultivata-
ble land, with a remaining third of irreclaimable desert, chiefly
on the south."

From this description it is evident that the least attractive
part of the country is the coast. This may be the reason that
Arabia has been so harshly judged, as to climate and soil and
so much neglected by those who only knew of it from the captains who had touched its coast in the Red Sea and the Persian Gulf. Nothing is more surprising, than to pass through
the barren cinder gateway of Aden up the mountain passes
into the marvellous fertility and delightful climate of Yemen.
Arabia like the Arab, has a rough, frowning exterior but a
warm, hospitable heart.

From the table-land of Nejd, which has an average elevation
of about 3,000 feet above the sea, there is a gradual ascent
southward to the highlands of Yemen and Oman where there
are mountain peaks as high as 8,000 and 10,000 feet. This
diversity of surface causes an equal diversity of climate. The
prevailing conditions are intense heat and dryness, and the
world-zone of maximum heat in July embraces nearly the entire peninsula. On the coast the heat is more trying because
of the moisture from the enormous evaporation of the land-
locked basins. During part of the summer there is scarcely
any difference in the register of the wet-and dry-bulb thermometer. In the months of June, July and August, 1897, the
averages of maximum temperature at Busrah were 100°, 103½°
and 102° F. ; and the minimum 84°, 86½° and 84° F. Nejd
has a salubrious climate, while in Yemen and Oman on the
highlands the mercury even in July seldom rises above 85°.
In July, 1892, I passed in one day's journey from a shade temperature of 110° F. on the coast at Hodeidah to one of 55° at

Menakha on the mountains. At Sanaa there is frost for three months in the year, and Jebel Tobeyk in northwest Arabia is covered with snow all winter. In fact, all northern Arabia has a winter season with cold rains and occasional frosts.

The geology of the peninsula is of true Arabian simplicity. According to Doughty it consists of a foundation stock of plutonic (igneous) rock whereon lie sandstone, and above that limestone. Going from Moab to Sinai we cross the strata in the reverse order, while in the depression of the gulf of Akaba the three strata are in regular order although again overtopped by the granite of the mountains. Fossils are very rare, but coral formation is common all along the coast. Volcanic formations and lava (called by the Arabs, harrat) crop out frequently, as in the region of Medina and Khaibar. In going by direct route from the Red Sea (Jiddah) to Busrah, we meet first granite and trap-rock, overtopped in the Harrat el-Kisshub by lavas, and further on at Wady Gerir and Jebel Shear by basalts; at the Nefud el Kasim (Boreyda) sandstones begin until we reach the limestone region of Jebel Toweyk. Thence all is gravel and sand to the Euphrates.

Arabia has no rivers and none of its mountain streams (some of which are perennial) reach the seacoast. At least they do not arrive there by the *overland* route, for it is a well-established fact that the many fresh water springs found in the Bahrein archipelago have their origin in the uplands of Arabia. At Muscat, too, water is always flowing toward the sea in abundance at the depth of ten to thirty feet below the wady-bed; this supplies excellent well-water. In fact the entire region of Hasa is full of underground water-courses and perennial springs. Coast-streams are frequent in Yemen during the rain-season and often become suddenly full to overflowing dashing everything before them. They are called *sayl*, and well illustrate Christ's parable of the flood which demolished the house built upon the sand.

The great wadys of Arabia are its characteristic feature,

celebrated since the days of Job, the Arab. These wadys, often full to the brim in winter and black by reason of frost but entirely dried up during the heat of summer, would never be suspected of giving nourishment to even a blade of grass. They are generally dry for nine and ten months in the year, during which time water is obtained from wells sunk in the wady-bed. Wady Sirhan runs in a southeasterly direction from the Hauran highlands to the Jauf district on the edge of the great Nefud; it is fed by the smaller Wady er-Rajel. Wady Dauasir which receives the Nejran streams drains all of the Asir and southern Hejaz highlands northward to Bahr Salumeh, a small lake, the only one known in the whole peninsula. The Aftan is another important wady running from the borders of Nejd into the Persian Gulf. This wady-bed is marked on some maps as a river, flowing into the Persian Gulf apparently by two mouths. It does not exist to-day. The most important water-bed in Arabia is the celebrated Wady er-Ruma, only partly explored, which flows from Hejaz across the peninsula for nearly 800 miles in a northwesterly direction toward the Euphrates. Were there a more abundant rainfall this wady would reach the Shat-el-Arab and give unity to the now disjointed water-system of Mesopotamia and north Arabia.[1] For obvious reasons the caravan routes of Arabia generally follow the course of the wadys.

Arabia is also a land of mountains and highlands. The

---

[1] May not this wady have been once a noble stream perhaps, as Glaser conjectures, the fourth of the Paradise rivers? (Gen ii. 10–14.) Upon the question as to where the ancient Semites located Paradise Glaser says that it was in the neighborhood of the confluence of the Euphrates and Tigris, on the Arabian side. There the sacred palm of the city of Eridu grew; there according to the view of the ancient Arabs the two larger wadys of Central Arabia opened. The one is the Wady er-Ruma or the Gaihan; and the other is the Wady ed-Dauasir, *a side wady* of which in the neighborhood of Hamdani still bears the name of Faishan (Pishon).—See " Recent Research in Bible Lands," by H. V. Hilprecht, (Philadelphia, 1897). See also *The Sunday-School Times*, Vol. XXXIII., No. 49.

most clearly developed system is the extensive range skirting
the Red Sea at a distance of from one to three days' journey
from the coast. South of Mecca there are peaks of over 8,000
feet; and beyond, the range broadens out to form the Yemen
highlands, a corner of the peninsula worthy of its old name
"Arabia Felix." The mountains along the south coast are
more irregular and disconnected until they broaden out a second time between Ras el Had and Ras Mussendum to form the
highlands of Oman. Along the gulf coast there are no mountains except an occasional volcanic hill like Jebel Dokhan in
Bahrein and Jebel Sanam near Zobeir.

The Nejd is crossed by several ridges of which the best
known is Jebel Shammar running nearly east and west at an
altitude of about 6,000 feet. Jebel Menakib, Jebel Aared,
Jebel Toweyk and Jebel Athal are other ranges south of Jebel
Shammar and also running in a similar direction toward the
southwest and northeast. The Sinai peninsula is a rocky limestone plateau intersected by rugged gorges and highest toward
the south in the region of Sinai proper.

Next to its wadys and mountains Arabia is characterized
chiefly by the so-called *Harrat* or volcanic tracks already
mentioned. These black, gloomy, barren regions occupy a
much wider extent of north Arabia than is generally supposed.
The largest is *Harrat Khaibar*, north of Medina, the old centre of the Jews in the days of Mohammed. It is over 100
miles in length and in some parts thirty miles wide. A wilderness of lava and lava-stones with many extinct crater heads,
craggy, and strewn with rough blocks of basalt and other igneous rocks. In some places the lava beds are 600 feet deep.
Signs of volcanic action are still seen at Khaibar, smoke issuing
from crevices and steam from the summit of Jebel Ethnan.
A volcanic eruption was seen at Medina as late as 1256 A. D.[1]
and the hot and sulphur springs of Hasa and Hadramaut seem
to indicate present volcanic action.

[1] Samhudi's History of Medina. (Arabic text p. 40, sqq.)

The sandy-tracts of the so-called Arabian deserts are termed by the Arabs themselves *nefud* (drained, exhausted, spent), the name given on most maps. The general physical features of this "desert" are those of a plain clothed with stunted, aromatic shrubs of many varieties, but their value as pasture is very unequal, some being excellent for camels and sheep, others absolutely worthless. Some nefuds abound in grasses and flowering plants after the early rains, and then the desert "blossoms like the rose." Others are without rain and barren all year; they are covered with long stretches of drift-sand, carried about by the wind and tossed in billows on the weather side of the rocks and bushes.[1] Palgrave asserts that some of the nefud sands are 600 feet deep. They prevail in the vast unexplored region south of Nejd and north of Hadramaut including the so-called "Great Arabian Desert." Absolute sterility is the dominant feature here, whereas the northern nefuds are the pasture lands for thousands of horses and sheep.

[1] These wastes are also termed *Dakhna*, *Ahkaf*, and *Hamad* according to the greater or less depth or shifting nature of the sands or the more or less compact character of the soil.

very suggestive that in the present revolt some of the Arabs made use of the English flag to secure sympathy.

In Hasa, the real sovereignty of Turkey only exists in three or four towns while all the Bedouin and many of the villagers yield to the Dowla, neither tribute, obedience nor love. Irak alone is actually Turkish and yields large revenue. But even here Arab-uprisings are frequent. Nominally, however, Turkey holds the fairest province on the south, the religious centres on the west and the fertile northeast of Arabia,—one-fifth of the total area of the peninsula.

The remainder of Arabia is independent of Turkey. Petty rulers calling themselves Sultans, Ameers or Imams have for centuries divided the land between them. The Sultanate of Oman and the great Nejd-kingdom are the only important governments, but the former lost its glory when its seat of power and influence was transferred to Zanzibar. Nejd in its widest sense is governed to-day by Abd-el-Aziz bin Mitaab the nephew of the late Mohammed bin Rashid, King Richard of Arabia, who gained his throne by the massacre of seventeen possible pretenders. The territory of this potentate is bordered southward by Riad and the Wahabi country. Northward his influence extends beyond the Nefud, right away to the Oases of Kaf and Ittery in the Wady Sirhan (38° E. Long., 31° N. Lat.) east of the Dead Sea. The inhabitants of these oases acknowledge Abd-el-Aziz as their suzerain paying him a yearly tribute of four pounds ($20.00) for each village. The people of the intervening district of Jauf also acknowledge his rule which reaches westward to Teima. He also commands the new pilgrim-route from the northeast which formerly passed through Riad but now touches Hail, the capital of Nejd. The Wahabi movement has collapsed and their political power is broken, although their influence has extended to the furthest confines of Arabia.

The only foreign power dominant in Arabia, beside Turkey, is England. Aden became a British possession in 1838 and since then British influence has extended until it now embraces a district 200 miles long by forty broad and a population of 130,000. The Island of Perim in the Strait of Bab-el-Mandeb, the Kuria-Muria Islands on the south coast, and Socotra are also English. All the independent tribes on the coast from Aden to Muscat and from Muscat to Bahrein have made exclusive treaties with Great Britian, are subsidized by annual payments or presents and are "protected." Muscat and Bahrein are in a special sense protected states since England's settled policy is to have sole dominion in the Persian Gulf. She has agencies or consulates everywhere; the postal system of the Persian Gulf is British; the rupee has driven the piastre out of the market and as ninety-eight per cent. of the commerce is in English hands the Persian Gulf may yet become an English lake.

Arabia has no railroads, but regular caravan routes take their place in every direction. Turkish telegraph service exists between Mecca and Jiddah in Hejaz; between Sanaa, Hodeidah and Taiz in Yemen; and along the Tigris-Euphrates between Bagdad and Busrah connecting at Fao (at the delta) with the submarine cable to Bushire and India.

Of the fauna and flora of Arabia we will not here speak at length. The most characteristic plants are the date-palm of which over 100 varieties are catalogued by the Arab peasantry, and which yields a staple food. Coffee, aromatic and medicinal plants, gums and balsams, have for ages supplied the markets of the world. Yemen is characterized by tropical luxuriance, and in Nejd is the *ghatha* tree which grows to a height of fifteen feet, and yields the purest charcoal in the world.

Among the wild animals were formerly the lion and the panther, but they are now exceedingly rare. The wolf, wild boar, jackal, gazelle, fox, monkey, wild cow (or white antelope) ibex, horned viper, cobra, bustard, buzzard and hawk are also found. The ostrich still exists in southwest Arabia but is not common.   The chief domestic animals are the ass, mule, sheep, goats, but above all and superior to all, the camel and the horse.

The exact population of a land where there is no census, and where women and girls are never counted is of course unknown. The Ottoman government gives exaggerated estimates for its Arabian provinces, and travellers have made various guesses. Some recent authorities, omitting Irak, put the total population of Arabia as low as 5,000,000.   A. H. Keane, F. R. G. S., gives the following estimate : [1]

Turkish Arabia :

Hejaz,	3,500,000
Yemen,	2,500,000

Independent Arabia :

Oman,	1,500,000
Shammar, Bahrein, etc.,	3,500,000
	11,000,000

Albrecht Zehm in his book " Arabien seit hundert Jahren," arrives at nearly the same result :

Yemen and Asir,	2,252,000
Hadramaut,	1,550,000
Oman and Muscat,	1,350,000
Bahrein Katif, Nejd,	2,350,000
Hejaz, Anaeze, Kasim, and Jebel Shammar,	3,250,000
	10,752,000

But undoubtedly both of these estimates, following Turkish authorities, are too high, especially for Hejaz and Yemen.   A conservative estimate would be 8,000,000 for the entire peninsula in its widest extent.   The true number of inhabitants will remain unknown until further explorations disclose the real character of southeastern Arabia, and until northern Hadramaut yields up its secrets.   In this, as in other respects, the words of Livingstone are true : " The end of the geographical feat is the beginning of the missionary enterprise."

[1] Geography of Asia (Vol II., p. 460), 1896.

III

THE HOLY LAND OF ARABIA—MECCA

" The Eastern world moves slowly—*eppur si muove*. Half a generation
ago steamers were first started to Jiddah: now we hear of a projected railway from that port to Mecca, the shareholders being all Moslems. And
the example of Jerusalem encourages us to hope that long before the end
of the century a visit to Mecca will not be more difficult than a trip to
Hebron."—*Burton* (1855).

" Our train of camels drew slowly by them: but when the smooth
Mecca merchant heard that the stranger riding with the camel men was a
Nasrany, he cried ' Akhs! A Nasrany in these parts!' and with the hor-
rid inurbanity of their jealous religion he added, ' Ullah curse his father!'
and stared on me with a face worthy of the Koran."—*Doughty* (1888).

IT is a rule laid down in the Koran and confirmed by many
traditions that the sacred territory enclosing the birthplace and the tomb of the prophet shall not be polluted by the
visits of infidels. " O believers! only those are unclean who
join other gods with God! Let them not therefore after this
their year come near the Sacred Mosque." (Surah ix. 27.)
Mohammed is reported to have said of Mecca, " What a
splendid city thou art, if I had not been driven out of thee by
my tribe I would dwell in no other place but in thee. It is not
man but God who has made Mecca sacred. My people will be
always safe in this world and the next as long as they respect
Mecca." (Mishkat book XL., ch. xv.)
The sacred boundaries of Mecca and Medina not only shut
out all unbelievers, but they make special demands of " purity
and holiness" (in the Moslem sense) on the part of the true
believers. According to tradition it is not lawful to carry
weapons or to fight within the limits of the *Haramein*. Its

MOHAMMEDAN PILGRIMS AT MECCA

THE SACRED WELL OF ZEMZEM AT MECCA

grass and thorns must not be cut nor must its game be molested. Some doctors of law hold that these regulations do not apply to Medina, but others make the burial-place of the prophet equally sacred with the place of his birth. The boundaries of this sacred territory are rather uncertain. Abd ul Hak says that when, at the time of the rebuilding of the Kaaba, Abraham, the friend of God, placed the black stone, its east, west, north and south sides became luminous, and wherever the light extended, became the boundaries of the sacred city! These limits are now marked by pillars of masonry, except on the Jiddah and Jairanah road where there is some dispute as to the exact boundary.

The sacred territory of Medina is ten or twelve miles in diameter, from Jebel 'Air to Saoor. Outside of these two centres all of the province of Hejaz is legally accessible to infidels, but the fanaticism of centuries has practically made the whole region round Mecca and Medina forbidden territory to any but Moslems. In Jiddah Christians are tolerated because of necessity, but were the Mullahs of Mecca to have their way not a Frankish merchant or consul would reside there for a single day.

Despite these regulations to shut out "infidels" from witnessing the annual pilgrimage and seeing the sacred shrines of the Moslem world, more than a score of travellers have braved the dangers of the transgression and escaped the pursuit of fanatics to tell the tale of their adventures.[1] Others have lost

[1] The first account of a European visiting Mecca is that of Ludovico Bartema, a gentleman of Rome, who visited the city in 1503; his narrative was published in 1555. The first Englishman was Joseph Pitts, the sailor from Exeter, in 1678; then followed the great Arabian traveller, John Lewis Burckhardt, 1814; Burton in 1853 visited both Mecca and Medina; H. Bicknell made the pilgrimage in 1862 and T. F. Keane in 1880. The narratives of each of these pilgrims have been published, and from them, and the travels of Ali Bey, and others, we know something of the Holy Land of Arabia. Ali Bey was in reality a Spaniard, called Juan Badia y Seblich, who visited Mecca and Medina in 1807 and left a

their life in the attempt even in recent years.   Doughty[1] tells
of a Christian who was foully murdered by Turkish soldiers
when found in the limits of Medina in the summer of 1878.
Burton at one time barely escaped being murdered because
they suspected him of being an unbeliever.

Jiddah, the harbor of Mecca, is distant from the sacred city
about sixty-five miles, and is in consequence the chief port of
debarkation and embarkation for pilgrims.   It has a rather
pretty and imposing appearance from the sea, the houses being
white and three or four stories high, surrounded by a wall and
flanked by a half dozen lazy windmills of Dutch pattern !   Its
streets are narrow, however, and indescribably dirty, so that
the illusion of an Oriental picture is dispelled as soon as you
set foot on shore.   The sanitary condition of this port is the
worst possible ; evil odors abound, the water supply is precarious and bad, and a shower of rain is always followed by
an outbreak of fever.   The population is not over 20,000 of
every Moslem nation under heaven, Galilee of "the believers."
Its commercial importance, which once was considerable, has
altogether declined.   The opening of the Suez canal and the
direct carrying of trade by ocean steamers dealt the deathblow
to the extensive coast-trade of both Jiddah and the other Red
Sea ports.   The people of Jiddah, like those of Mecca, live
by fleecing pilgrims, and when the traffic is brisk and pilgrims
affluent they grow rich enough to go to Mecca and set up a
larger establishment of the same sort.   There are hotel-keepers,
drummers, guides, money-changers, money-lenders, slave-deal-

long account of his travels in two volumes illustrated by many beautiful
engravings.   Burton's account of his pilgrimage is best known, but Burckhardt's is more accurate and scholarly.   Of modern books, that of the
Dutch scholar, Snouck Hurgronje, who resided in Mecca for a long time,
is by far the best.   His *Mekka*, in two volumes, is accompanied by an
atlas of photographs and gives a complete history of the city as well as a
full account of its inhabitants and of the Java pilgrimage.

[1] Vol. II., p. 157.

ers and even worse characters connected with the annual transfer of the caravans of *hajees* (pilgrims) from the coast inland. The number of pilgrims arriving at Jiddah by sea in 1893 was 92,625. In 1880 Mr. Blunt collected some interesting statistics of the total numbers attending the pilgrimage at Mecca,[1] and his investigations prove that the overland caravans are steadily becoming smaller.

Before any pilgrims are allowed to enter Jiddah harbor they are compelled to undergo ten days' quarantine at Kamaran, an island on the west coast of Arabia; this is the first woe. At Jiddah they remain only a few days and then having secured their *Mutawwaf* or official guide they proceed to Mecca. The

[1] *TABLE OF MECCA PILGRIMAGE, 1880.*
(From Blunt's " Future of Islam.")

NATIONALITY OF PILGRIMS.	Arriving by Sea.	Arriving by Land.	Total Moslem Pop. represented.
Ottoman Subjects (excluding Arabia)	8,500	1,000	22,000,000
Egyptians	5,000	1,000	5,000,000
From " Barbary States "	6,000	——	18,000,000
Yemen Arabs	3,000	——	2,500,000
Oman and Hadramaut	3,000	——	3,000,000
Nejd, etc., Arabs	——	5,000	4,000,000
Hejaz (including Mecca)	——	22,000	2,000,000
Negroes from Sudan	2,000	——	10,000,000
" " Zanzibar	1,000	——	1,500,000
Malabari from Cape of G. Hope .	150	——	
Persians	6,000	2,500	8,000,000
Indians (British Subjects)	15,000	——	40,000,000
Malays and Javanese	12,000	——	30,000,000
Chinese	100	——	15,000,000
Mongols . . . . ⎱	——	——	6,000,000
Russians, Tartars, etc. . . . . ⎬	——	——	5,000,000
Afghans and Baluchis . . . . ⎰	——	——	3,000,000
(included in Ottoman Haj.)			
	61,750	31,500	
	93,250		
Total pilgrims present at Arafat .			175,000,000

road is barren and uninteresting in the extreme. Halfway to
Mecca is El Had where the road divides; one branch leads
to Taif, the only fertile spot in this wilderness province, and
the other proceeds to Mecca, the ancient name of which was
Bakkah.

Were we to believe one half of what is said by Moslem
writers in praise of Mecca it would prove the Holy City to be
a very paradise of delights, a centre of learning and the paragon of earthly habitations. But the facts show it to be far
otherwise. The location of the city is unfortunate. It lies in
a hot sandy valley absolutely without verdure and surrounded
by rocky barren hills, destitute of trees or even shrubs. The
valley is about 300 feet wide and 4,000 feet long, and slopes
toward the south. The Kaaba or Beit Allah is located in the
bed of the valley and all the streets slope toward it, so that it
is almost closed in on every side by houses and walls, and
stands as it were in the pit of the theatre. The houses are
built of dark stone and are generally lofty in order to accommodate as many pilgrims as possible in the limited space. The
streets are nearly all unpaved and in summer the sand and
dust are as disagreeable as is the black mud in the rainy season. Strangely enough, although the city itself and even the
Kaaba have more than once suffered from destructive floods
that have poured down the narrow valley, Mecca is poorly
provided with water. There are few cisterns to catch the
rains and the well water is brackish. The famous well of
Zemzem has an abundance of water but it is not fit to drink.[1]
The best water is brought by an aqueduct from the vicinity of
Arafat six or seven miles distant and sold for a high price by a
water-trust which annually fills the coffers of the Shereef of

[1] Professor Hankin in the *British Medical Journal* for June, 1894, published the result of his analysis of Zemzem water as follows: "Total
solid in a gallon, 259; Chlorine, 51.24; Free ammonia, parts per million, 0.93; Albuminoid ammonia, .45. It contains an amount of solids
greater than that in any well water used for potable purposes."

PILGRIMS AROUND THE KAABA IN THE SACRED MOSQUE AT MECCA

Mecca. This official is the nominal and often the real governor of the city. He is chosen from the *Sayyids* or descendants
of Mohammed living in Hejaz or secures the high office by
force. His tenure of office is subject to the approval and authority of the Turkish Sultan, whose garrisons occupy the fort
near the town.

The Sacred Mosque, (Mesjid el Haram) containing the
Kaaba or Beit Allah is the prayer-centre of the Mohammedan
world and the objective point of thousands of pilgrims every
year. According to Moslem writers it was first constructed in
heaven, 2,000 years before the creation of the world. Adam,
the first man, built the Kaaba on earth exactly under the spot
occupied by its perfect model in heaven. The 10,000 angels
appointed to guard this house of God seem to have been very
remiss in their duty for it has often suffered at the hands of
men and from the elements. It was destroyed by the flood and
rebuilt by Ishmael and Abraham. The legends connected with
its construction and history fill many pages of the Moslem traditions and commentaries. The name Kaaba means a *cube ;*
but the building is not built true to line and is in fact an unequal trapezium.[1] Because of its location in a hollow and its
black-cloth covering these inequalities are not apparent to the
eye.

The Kaaba proper stands in an oblong space 250 paces long
by 200 broad. This open space is surrounded by colonnades
used for schools and as the general rendezvous of pilgrims. It
is in turn surrounded by the outer temple wall with its nineteen
gates and six minarets. The Mosque is of much more recent
date than the Kaaba which was well known as an idolatrous
Arabian shrine long before the time of Mohammed. The
Sacred Mosque and its Kaaba contain the following treasures :
the Black-Stone, the well of Zemzem, the great pulpit, the
staircase, and the *Kubattein* or two small mosques of Saab and

[1] Its measurements, according to Ali Bey, are 37 ft. 2 in., 31 ft. 7 in.,
38 ft. 4 in., 29 ft. and its height is 34 ft. 4 in.

Abbas.   The remainder of the space is occupied by pavements and gravel arranged to accommodate and distinguish the four orthodox sects in their devotions.

The Black-Stone is undoubtedly the oldest treasure of Mecca. Stone-worship was an Arabian form of idolatry in very ancient times and relics of it remain in many parts of the peninsula. Maximus Tyrius wrote in the second century, " the Arabians pay homage to I know not what god which they represent by a quadrangular stone."   The Guebars or ancient Persians assert that the black stone was an emblem of Saturn and was left in the Kaaba by Mahabad.   We have the Moslem tradition that it came down snow-white from heaven and was blackened by the touch of sin—according to one tradition, that of an impure woman, and according to another by the kisses of thousands of believers.   It is probably an aerolite and owes its reputation to its fall from the sky.   Moslem historians do not deny that it was an object of worship before Islam, but they escape the moral difficulty and justify their prophet by idle tales concerning the stone and its relation to all the patriarchs beginning with Adam.

The stone is a fragment of what appears like black volcanic rock sprinkled with irregular reddish crystals worn smooth by the touch of centuries.   It is held together by a broad band of metal, said to be silver, and is imbedded in the southeast corner of the Kaaba five feet from the ground.   It is not generally known that there is a second sacred stone at the corner facing the south.   It is called Rakn el Yemeni or Yemen pillar and is frequently kissed by pilgrims although according to the correct ritual it should only be saluted by a touch of the right hand.

The well of Zemzem is located near the Makam Hanbali, the place of prayer of this sect.   The building which encloses the well was erected in A. H. 1072 (A. D. 1661) and its interior is of white marble.   Mecca perchance owes its origin as an old Arabian centre to this medicinal spring with its abundant supply of purgative waters for the nomads to-day go long distances

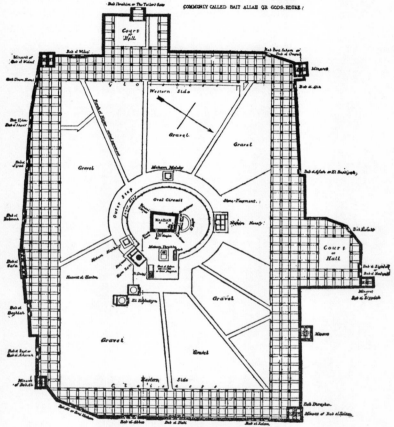

ALI BEY'S PLAN OF THE PROPHET'S MOSQUE AT MECCA

to visit sulphur and other springs in various parts of Arabia. The well of Zemzem is one of the great sources of income to the Meccans.   The water is carried about for sale on the streets and in the mosques in curious pitchers made of unglazed earthenware.   They are slightly porous so as to cool the water, which is naturally always of a lukewarm temperature, and are all marked with certain mystical characters in black wax. Crowds assemble around the well during the pilgrimage and many coppers fall to the share of the lucky Meccans who have the privilege of drawing the water for the faithful.

The pilgrimage to Mecca should be performed in the twelfth lunar month of the calendar called *Dhu el Haj*.   It is incumbent on every believer except for lawful hindrance because of poverty or illness.   Mohammed made it the fifth pillar of religion and more than anything else it has tended to unify the Moslem world.   The Koran teaching regarding the duties of pilgrims at the Sacred Mosque, is as follows :   " Proclaim to the peoples a Pilgrimage.   Let them come to thee on foot and on every fleet camel arriving by every deep defile."   (Surah xxii. 28.)   " Verily As Safa and Al Marwa are among the signs of God : whoever then maketh a pilgrimage to the temple or visiteth it shall not be to blame if he go round about them both." (ii. 153.)   " Let the pilgrimage be made in the months already known and who so undertaketh the pilgrimage therein let him not know a woman, nor transgress nor wrangle in the pilgrimage.   .   .   .   It shall be no crime in you if ye seek an increase from your Lord (by trade) ; and when ye pass swiftly on from Arafat then remember God near the holy Mosque. .   .   .   Bear God in mind during the stated days ; but if any haste away in two days it shall be no fault to him, and if any tarry it shall be no fault in him."   (Surah ii. passim.)

From the Koran alone no definite idea of the pilgrim's duties can be gleaned ; but fortunately for all true believers the Prophet's perfect example handed down by tradition leaves nothing in doubt and prescribes every detail of conduct with ridiculous minuteness. The orthodox way is as follows : arrived within a short distance of Mecca the pilgrims, male and female, put off their ordinary clothing and assume the garb of a *hajee*. It consists of two pieces of white cloth one of which is tied around the loins and the other thrown over the back ; sandals may be worn but not shoes and the head must be left uncovered. (In idolatrous days the Arabs did not wear any clothing in making the circuit of the Kaaba.) On facing Mecca the pilgrim pronounces the *niyah* or " intention " :

> " Here I am, O Allah, here I am ;
> No partner hast Thou, here I am ;
> Verily praise and riches and the kingdom are to Thee ;
> No partner hast Thou, here am I."

After certain legal ablutions the pilgrim enters the Mosque by the Bab-el-salam and kisses the Black-Stone making the circuit, running, around the Kaaba seven times. (In idolatrous days the Arabs did this in imitation of the motions of the planets ; a remnant of their Sabean worship.) Another special prayer is said and then the pilgrim proceeds to Makam Ibrahim, where Abraham is said to have stood when he rebuilt the Kaaba. There the *hajee* goes through the regular genuflections and prayers. He drinks next from the holy well and once more kisses the Black-Stone. Then follows the running between Mounts Safa and Merwa. Proceeding outward from the Mosque by the gate of Safa he ascends the hill reciting the 153d verse of the Surah of the Cow. " Verily Safa and Merwa are the signs of God." Having arrived at the summit of the mount he turns to the Kaaba and three times recites the words :

> " There is no god but God !
> God is great !
> There is no god save God alone !
> He hath performed His promise
>   and hath aided His servant and
>   put to flight the hosts of in-
> fidels by Himself alone ! "

He then runs from the top of Safa through the valley to the summit of Merwa seven times repeating the aforesaid prayers each time on both hills.   This is the sixth day, on the evening of which the pilgrim again encompasses the Kaaba.   On the next day there is a sermon from the grand pulpit.   On the eighth day the pilgrim goes three miles distant to Mina, where Adam longed for his lost paradise (!) and there spends the night.   The next morning he leaves for Arafat, another hill about eleven miles from Mecca, hears a second sermon, returning before nightfall to Muzdalifa, a place halfway between Mina and Arafat.

The following day is the great day of the pilgrimage.   It is called the day of Sacrifice and is simultaneously celebrated all over the Moslem world.[1]   Early in the morning the pilgrim proceeds to Mina where there are three pillars called, the " Great Devil," the " Middle Pillar" and the " First One."   At these dumb idols the " monotheist" flings seven pebbles and as he throws them says : " In the name of Allah and Allah is mighty, in hatred of the devil and his shame, I do this."   He then performs the sacrifice, a sheep, goat, cow or camel according to the means of the pilgrim.   The victim is placed facing the Kaaba and a knife plunged into the animal's throat with the cry, *Allahu Akbar*.   This ceremony concludes the pilgrimage proper ; the hair and nails are then cut and the *ihram* or pilgrims' garb is doffed for ordinary clothing.   Three days more are sometimes counted as belonging to the pilgrimage, the eleventh, twelfth and thirteenth days, called *Eyyam-u-tashrik*, or days of drying flesh, because during them the flesh of the sacrifices is cut into slices and dried in the sun to be eaten on the return journey.

After the Meccan pilgrimage most Moslems go to Medina to visit the tomb of Mohammed ; the Wahabees however consider

---

[1] This religion which denies an atonement and teaches that Christ was not crucified yet has for its great festival a feast of sacrifice to commemorate the obedience of Abraham and the substitute provided by God !

this "infidelity" and honor of the creature more than of the
Creator.   Other Moslems base their conduct on the saying of
the prophet himself, *Man yuhajja wa lam ye-zurni fakad
jefani*, "who goes on Haj and does not visit me has insulted
me!"   The Meccans call themselves "neighbors of God" and
the people of Medina "neighbors of the prophet."   For long
ages a hot rivalry has existed between the two cities, a rivalry
which, beginning in the taunt or jest, often ends in bloodshed.

The pilgrim, having completed all legal requirements, is
sure to visit the proper authorities and secure a *certificate* to
prove to his countrymen that he is a real Hajee and to sub-
stantiate his religious boasting in days to come.   The certificate is also required when one goes on pilgrimage for a
deceased Moslem or a wealthy Moslem who is bedridden.   In
such a case the substitute has all the pleasures (!) of the journey at the expense of his principal but the merit goes to the
man who pays the bills and who naturally craves the receipt.
The certificate is of various forms and contains crude pictures
of the holy places and verses from Koran.

Needless to relate these certificates cost money, as does
everything at Mecca save the air you breathe.   No honest
Moslem ever spoke with praise of the citizens of Mecca; many
are their proverbs to prove why wickedness flourishes in the
courts of Allah.   And European travellers agree that of all
Orientals the Meccans take the palm for thoroughgoing rascal-
ity.   Ali Bey dilates on the lewdness of the men and the loose-
ness of the women of Mecca.   Hurgronje unblushingly lifts the
veil that hides the corruption of the sacred temple service with
its army of eunuch police, and pictures the slave-market in full
swing within a stone's throw of the Kaaba.   Burton thus characterizes the men who live on their religion and grow fat
(figuratively) by unveiling its mysteries to others:

"The Meccan is a covetous spendthrift.   His wealth, lightly
won, is lightly prized.   Pay, pensions, stipends, presents, and
the 'Ikram' here, as at Medina, supply the citizen with the

age of Jesus and an Evangelist." Of course, the women
themselves are in total ignorance of the inscription and character of the coin.

There is a great abundance of schools at Mecca but no
education. Everything is on the old lines, beginning and end-

A CHRISTIAN COIN USED AS AN AMULET BY MECCAN WOMEN.[1]

ing with the Koran, that Procrustean bed for the human intellect. "The letter killeth." And it is the *letter* first, foremost
and always that is the topic of study. The youth learn to
read the Koran not to understand its meaning, but to drone it
out professionally at funerals and feasts, so many chapters for
so many shekels. Modern science or history are not even
mentioned, much less taught, at even the high-schools of
Mecca. Grammar, prosody, calligraphy, Arabian history, and
the first elements of arithmetic, but chiefly the Koran commentaries and traditions, traditions, traditions, form the curric-
ulum of the Mohammedan college. Those who desire a post-
graduate course devote themselves to Mysticism (*Tassawaf*)
or join an order of the Derwishes who all have their representative sheikhs at Mecca.

The method of teaching in the schools of Mecca, which can
be taken as an example of the best that Arabia affords, is as
follows. The child of intellectual promise is first taught his
alphabet from a small wooden board on which they are written

[1] This coin is called *Mishkash* and is a Venetian coin of Duke Aloys
Mocenigo I. (1570–77 A. D.). On one side the Duke is kneeling before
St. Mark the patron saint of Venice and on the other is the image of
Christ surrounded by stars.

by the teacher; slates are unknown. Then he learns the *Abjad* or numerical value of each letter—a useless proceeding at present as the Arabic notation, originally from India, is everywhere in use. After this he learns to write down the ninety-nine names of Allah and to read the first chapter of the Koran; then he attacks the last two chapters, because they are short. The teacher next urges him through the book, making the pupil read at the top of his voice. The greatest strictness is observed as to pronunciation and pauses but nothing whatever is said to explain the meaning of the words. Having thus *finished* the Koran, that is, read it through once, the pupil takes up the elements of grammar, learning rules by rote both of *sarf* (inflection) and *nahw* (syntax). Then follow the liberal sciences, *al-mantik* (logic), *al-hisab* (arithmetic), *al-jabr* (algebra), *al-ma'ana wa'l beyan* (rhetoric and versification), *al-fikh* (jurisprudence), *al-akäid* (scholastic theology), *at-tafsir* (exegetics), *ilm ul-usul* (science of sources of interpretation) and lastly, the capstone of education, *al-ahadith* (traditions). Instruction is given by lectures; text-books are seldom used; lessons begin in the morning and continue for a few hours; in the afternoon they are interrupted by prayer-time. Even at Mecca the favorite place for teaching is in the Mosque-court where constant interruptions and distractions must make it pleasant for a lazy pupil.

A MECCAN WOMAN IN HER BRIDAL COSTUME

A WOMAN OF MECCA

IV

THE HOLY LAND OF ARABIA—MEDINA

" Within the sanctuary or bounds of the city all sins are forbidden; but the several schools advocate different degrees of strictness. The Imam Malik, for instance, allows no latrinæ nearer to El Medina than Jebel Ayr, a distance of about three miles. He also forbids slaying wild animals, but at the same time he specifies no punishment for the offence. All authors strenuously forbid, within the boundaries, slaying man, (except invaders, infidels and the sacrilegious) drinking spirits and leading an immoral life. In regard to the dignity of the sanctuary there is but one opinion; a number of traditions testify to its honor, praise its people and threaten dreadful things to those who injure it or them."—*Burton.*

ABOUT seventy miles southeast of Mecca is the small but pleasant town of Taif, to which the pashas condemned for the murder of Abdul Aziz Sultan were banished. It is one of the most interesting and attractive towns of all Arabia, being surrounded by gardens and vineyards from which Mecca has been supplied for ages. The tropical rains last from four to six weeks at Taif, and good wells abound to water the gardens when the rains cease, so that the place is famous for its garden-produce. In close proximity to the barren Mecca district Taif is a paradise for the pilgrim and a health resort for the jaundiced, fever-emaciated Meccan. At Taif Doughty saw three old stone idols of "the days of ignorance"; *El Uzza,* a block of granite some twenty feet long; another called *Hubbal,* with a cleft in the middle, "by our Lord Aly's sword-stroke"; and *El Lat,* an unshapely crag of grey granite. These were earlier stone-gods of the Arab, and now lie forsaken in the dirt, while their brother-god, the famous Black-Stone, receives the reverence of millions!

The road from Mecca to El Medina—"*the* city"—so called because the prophet chose it as his home in time of persecution—leads nearly due north. It is an uninteresting, and for the most part, a forsaken country that separates the rival cities. Burton writes that it reminded him of the lines,

> " Full many a waste I've wandered o'er,
>   Clomb many a crag, crossed, many a shore,
>   But, by my halidome
>   A scene so rude, so wild as this,
>   Yet so sublime in barrenness,
>   Ne'er did my wandering footsteps press,
>   Where'er I chanced to roam."

There are two caravan-routes, both of which are used by the pilgrims, but the eastern road is used most frequently.[1]

The region between Mecca and Medina is the home of the ancient poets of Arabia and is classic ground. The seven Moallakat or suspended poems find their scene in this region. Lebid wrote :

> " Deserted is the village—waste the halting place and home,
>   At Mina, o'er Rijam and Ghul wild beasts unheeded roam,
>   On Rayyan hill the channel lines have left their naked trace,
>   Time-worn as primal writ that dints the mountain face."

El Medina, formerly called *Yathrib*, is now also called *El Munowera*, the "illuminated," and devout Moslems commonly claim to see, on approaching the city, a luminous haze hanging over its mosques and houses. The legends and superstitions that cluster around the last resting-place of the Prophet are not less in number nor less credible than those that glorify the place of his birth, although the town is only about

---

[1] The western or coast route goes by Koleis, Rabek, Mastura, and near Jebel Eyub (Job's Mountain) over Jebel Subh, then to Suk-es-Safra and Suk el Jedid to Medina. The eastern road was the one taken by Burton, and goes by way of El Zaribah, El Sufena, El Suerkish, etc., a distance 248 miles.

half the size and contains 16,000 inhabitants. It consists of three principal divisions: the town proper, the fort and the suburbs. It is surrounded by a wall forty feet high; the streets are narrow and unpaved; the houses are flat-roofed and double-storied.

The current dispute, however, for many centuries has been regarding the relative sanctity and importance of the two cities, Mecca and Medina. A visit to Medina is called *Ziyarat*, as that to Mecca is called *Haj;* the latter is obligatory by order of the Koran, while the former is meritorious on the authority of tradition. The orthodox further stipulate, that circumambulation around the prophet's tomb at Medina is not allowed as around the Kaaba at Mecca nor should men wear the *ihram*, nor kiss the tomb. On the other hand, to spit upon it or treat it with contempt, as the Wahabees did, is held to be the act of an infidel. To quote again from Burton: "The general consensus of Islam admits the superiority of the Beit Allah at Mecca to the whole world; and declares Medina to be more venerable than every part of Mecca, and consequently all the earth, except only the Beit Allah. This last is a *juste milieu* view by no means in favor with the inhabitants of either place."

The one thing that gives Medina claim to sanctity is the prophet's tomb, and yet there is some doubt as to whether he is really buried in the mosque raised to his honor; of course every Moslem, learned or ignorant, believes it, but there are many arguments against the supposition.[1] One of these argu-

---

[1] These arguments may be stated briefly as follows:

1. A tumult followed the announcement of the prophet's death, and Omar threatened destruction to any one who asserted it. Is it probable that a quiet interment took place?

2. Immediately after Mohammed's death a dispute about the succession arose, in the ardor of which, according to the Shiahs, the house of Ali and Fatima, near the present tomb, were threatened by fire.

3. The early Moslems would not be apt to *reverence* the grave of the

ments alone would have little value against so old a tradition and practice, but their cumulative force cannot be denied, and throws serious doubt on the question whether the present mosque of the prophet contains any trace of his remains.   On the other hand pious Moslems affirm that the prophet is not

prophet, as do those of later date, when tradition has exalted him above the common humanity.   The early Moslems were indifferent as to the exact spot.

4.   The shape of the prophet's tomb was not known in early times, nor is it given in the traditions ; so that we find convex graves in some lands and flat in others.

5.   The accounts of the learned among the Moslems are discrepant as to the burial of Mohammed.

6.   Shiah schismatics had charge of the sepulchre for centuries, and because of its proximity to the graves of Abubekr and Omar, it was in their interest to remove the body.

7.   Even the present position of the grave, with relation to other graves, is in dispute, because the tomb-chamber (*Hujrah*) is closely guarded by eunuchs, who do not allow any one to enter.

8.   The tale of the blinding light which surrounds the prophet's tomb seems a plausible story to conceal a defect.

9.   Mohammed el Halebi, the Sheikh-el Ulema of Damascus, assured Burton that he was permitted to pass the door leading into the tomb-chamber, and that he saw no trace of a sepulchre.

10.   Moslem historians admit that an attempt was made in A. H. 412 to steal the bodies of Mohammed and the two companions by the third Fatimite Caliph of Egypt; they relate marvels connected with the failure of the attempt, and assert that a trench was dug deep all around the graves and filled with molten lead to prevent the theft of the body.

11.   In A. H. 654 the mosque was destroyed by a volcanic eruption, according to the Moslem historians, but the tomb-chamber escaped all damage!   Again in A. H. 887 it was struck by lightning.   " On this occasion," says El Samanhudi (quoted by Burckhardt) " the interior of the Hujrah (tomb-chamber) was cleared and three deep graves were found in the inside full of rubbish, but the author of this history, who himself entered it, saw no trace of tombs."   The same author declared that the coffin containing the dust of Mohammed was cased with silver.

12.   Lastly the Shiah and Sunni accounts of the prophet's death and burial are contradictory as to the exact place of burial.

really dead, but "eats and drinks in the tomb until the day of resurrection," and is as much alive as he ever was.

The Mesjid-el-Nebi or prophet's mosque at Medina is about 420 feet long by 340 broad. It is built nearly north and south and has a large interior courtyard, surrounded by porticoes. From the western side we enter the *Rauzah* or prophet's garden. On the north and west it is not divided from the rest of the portico ; on the south side runs a dwarf wall and on the east it is bounded by the lattice-work of the *Hujrah*. This is an irregular square of about fifty feet separated on all sides from the walls of the Mosque by a broad passage. Inside there are said to be three tombs carefully concealed inside the iron railing by a heavy curtain arranged like a four-post bed. The Hujrah has four gates, all kept locked except the fourth which admits only the officers in charge of the treasure, the eunuchs who sweep the floor, light the lamps and carry away the presents thrown into the enclosure by devotees. It is commonly asserted that many

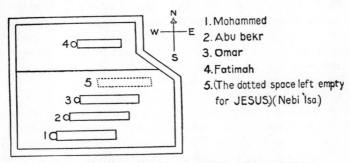

1. Mohammed
2. Abu bekr
3. Omar
4. Fatimah
5. (The dotted space left empty for JESUS)(Nebi 'Isa.)

REPORTED ARRANGEMENT OF THE INTERIOR OF THE HUJRAH.

early Moslem saints and warriors desired the remaining space for their grave, but that by Mohammed's wish it is reserved for 'Isa on his second coming and death. The story of a coffin suspended by magnets has of course no foundation in fact and may have arisen from the crude drawings of the tombs.

The *ziyarah* at the Mosque consists in prayers and alms-giving with silent contemplation on the sacred character of Mohammed. The following sample " prayer " offered at the shrine of Fatima, gives some idea of what is to Christian ears a blasphemous service : " Peace be upon thee, O daughter of the apostle of Allah ! Thou mother of the excellent seed. Peace be upon thee thou Lady amongst women. Peace be upon thee, O Fifth of the people of the Prophet's garment ! A pure one, O virgin ! Peace be on thee, O spouse of our Lord, Ali el Murtaza, O mother of Hasan and Hussein, the two Moons, the two Lights, the two Pearls, the two princes of the youth of Heaven, the Coolness of the eyes of true believers ! etc., etc." The prayers offered at the prophet's grave are more fulsome in their praise and of much greater length. What would the camel-driver of Mecca say if he heard them ?

As at Mecca so at Medina the townspeople, one and all, live on the pilgrims. The keeper of the Mosque is a Turkish Pasha with a large salary and many perquisites; there are treasurers and professors and clerks and sheikhs of these eunuchs kept on salary. Sweepers and porters, all eunuchs, and guides as at Mecca who live by backsheesh or extortion. Water-carriers here too peddle about the brackish fluid by the cupful to thirsty pilgrims. Those who are not in the service of the Mosque usually keep boarding-houses, or sell prayers which are to be made once a year at the prophet's tomb, for the absent pilgrim. Most of the officials receive their salaries from Constantinople and Cairo.

The population of Medina is not less a mixed multitude than that of Mecca ; here also the observation of Zehm holds true, " every pilgrimage brings new fathers." Burton testifies, " It is not to be believed that in a town garrisoned by Turkish troops, full of travelled traders, and which supports itself by plundering *Hajis* the primitive virtues of the Arab could exist. The Meccans, a dark people, say of the Madani, that their hearts are as black as their skins are white. This is of course exaggerated; but it is not too much to assert that pride, pugnacity, a peculiar point of honor, and a vindictiveness of wonderful force and patience, are the only characteristic traits of Arab character which the citizens of El Medina habitually display." Intoxicating liquors are made at Medina and sold, although not openly.

There are two colleges with "libraries" at Medina and many mosque-schools. In Burckhardt's day he charged the town with utter ignorance and illiteracy, but now they devote themselves apparently to literature, at least in a measure.

The climate of Medina is better than that of Mecca and the winters are cold and rigorous. Mohammed is reputed to have said, "he who patiently endures the cold of El Medina and the heat of Mecca, merits a reward in paradise."

Returning from the lesser pilgrimage to Medina the traveller can retrace his steps to Mecca, and thence to Jiddah, or go to the nearer port of Yanbo (Yembo) and thence return home by steamer or sailing-vessel. The distance by camels' route, between Medina and the port is 132 miles, six stages, although a good dromedary can make it in two days. At Yanbo the sultan's dominions in Arabia begin, for the coast northward pertains to Egypt. The town resembles Jiddah in outward appearance, has 400 or 500 houses built of white coral rock, dirty streets and a precarious water supply. Sadlier, (1820) after his journey across the peninsula, visited Yanbo, and describes it as " a miserable Arab seaport surrounded by a wall"; Yanbo has, however, a good harbor, and was in earlier days, a large and important place; it has been identified with Iambia village on Ptolemy's map a harbor of the old Nabateans.

Thus ends our pilgrimage through the Holy Land of Arabia. Let us in conclusion ponder the words of Stanley Lane Poole as to the place which Mecca and the pilgrimage holds in the Mohammedan religion. " It is asked how the destroyer of idols could have reconciled his conscience to the circuits of the Kaaba and the veneration of the Black-Stone covered with adoring kisses. The rites of the pilgrimage cannot certainly be defended against the charge of superstition; but it is easy to see why Mohammed enjoined them. . . . He well knew the consolidating effect of forming a centre to which his followers should gather, and hence he reasserted the sanctity of the Black-Stone that 'came down from heaven'; he ordained that everywhere throughout the world the Moslem should pray looking toward the Kaaba, and enjoined him to make the pilgrimage thither. Mecca is to the Moslem what Jerusalem is to the Jew. It bears with it all the influence of centuries of associations. It carries the Moslem back to the cradle of his faith and the childhood of his prophet. . . . And, most of all, it bids him remember that all his brother Moslems are worshipping toward the same sacred spot; that he is one of a great company of believers united by one faith, filled with the same hopes, reverencing the same thing, worshipping the same God."

V

ADEN AND AN INLAND JOURNEY

"Aden is a valley surrounded by the sea; its climate is so bad that it turns wine into vinegar in the space of ten days. The water is derived from cisterns and is also brought in by an aqueduct two farsongs long."
—*Ibn-el-Mojawir*. (A. D. 1200.)

ARABIA is unfortunate because, like a chestnut-burr, its exterior is rough and uninviting. In scenery and climate, Yemen fares worst of all the provinces. The two gateways to Arabia Felix are very *infelix*. What could be more dreary and dull and depressing than the " gloomy hills of darkness " that form the background to Aden as seen from the harbor? There is no verdure, no vegetation visible; everywhere there is the same appearance of a cinder heap. And where can one find a more filthy, hot, sweltering, odorous native town than Hodeidah? Yet these two places are the gateways to the most beautiful, fertile, populous and healthful region of all Arabia.

Yemen is best known of all the provinces, and has been quite thoroughly explored by a score of intrepid travellers.[1] Most people, however, travelling in a P. and O. Steamer, calling at Aden for coal, remain in total ignorance of the fair highlands just beyond the dark hills that hide the horizon.

---

[1] Niebuhr, 1763; Seetzen, 1810; Cruttenden, 1836; Dr. Wolff, 1836; Owen, 1857; Botta, 1837 ; Passama, 1842; Arnaud, 1843; Van Maltzan, 1871; Halvéy, 1870; Millingen, 1874; Renzo Manzoni, 1879; Glaser, 1880; Defler, 1888; Haig, 1889 ; Harris, 1892; and later travellers. Defler is the authority on the flora, Glaser on the antiquities, Manzoni on the Turks and their government, Haig on the agricultural population, and Harris tells of the recent rebellions. Niebuhr's magnificent volumes are still good authority on the geography and natural history of Yemen.

Yemen extends from Aden to Asir on the north and eastward into Hadramaut for an indefinite distance. On the earlier maps Arabia Felix stretched as far as Oman—a great mountainous region with a temperate climate. An Arabian author, describing Yemen as it was before the time of Mohammed, wrote : " Its inhabitants are all hale and strong, sickness is unknown, nor are there poisonous plants or animals ; nor fools, nor blind people, and the women are ever young ; the climate is like paradise and one wears the same garment summer and winter."

The massive rock promontory of volcanic basalt called Aden, has from time immemorial been the gateway and the stronghold for all Yemen. It is generally agreed that Ezekiel, the prophet, referred to Aden when he wrote : " Haran and Canneh and *Eden*, the merchants of Sheba, Asshur and Chilmad, were thy merchants." The place was fortified and its wonderful rock cisterns were probably first constructed by the early Himyarites. A Christian church was erected at Aden by the embassy of the Emperor Constantius, A. D. 342, and Aden was for a long time in the hands of the Christian kings of Yemen. Then it fell a prey to the Abyssinians and next to the Persians, about the time when Mohammed was born. Albuquerque in 1513 with his Portuguese warriors laid siege to Aden for four days, but in spite of scaling-ladders and gunpowder could not take the town. The Mameluke Sultans of Egypt also failed to capture this fortress. In 1838 the English took it by storm and have held the place ever since.

Aden is now a British settlement, a commercial-centre, a coaling-station and a fortress; the last most emphatically. All the latest improvements in engineering and artillery have been put to use in fortifying the place. The ride from Steamer-Point to " the crater " or from the telegraph-station to the " Crescent " gives one some idea of the vast amount of money and labor expended to shape this Gibraltar and make it impregnable from land and sea. The isthmus is guarded by

massive lines of defence, strengthened by a broad ditch cut
out of the solid rock; bastions, casements and tunnels all serve
one purpose; batteries, towers, arsenals, magazines, barracks;
mole-batteries toward the sea, mines in the harbor, obstruction
piers and subservient works;—everything tells of military
strength, and the town has always a warlike aspect in perfect
accord with its forbidding physical geography.

The inhabited peninsula is an irregular oval about fifteen
miles in circumference; it is in reality a large extinct crater
formed of lofty precipitous hills the highest peak of which,
Shem Shem, has an altitude of nearly 1,800 feet. The
varieties of rock are numerous, and vary in color from
light brown to dark green. Pumice and tufas are very common; the former is an article of export. Water is very scarce,
and there is almost no rainfall during some years. When
there is a shower, the nature of the soil and the immense water-
shed for so small an area cause heavy torrents to pour down
the valleys. These rare occasions are utilized to fill the huge
tanks near Aden camp. The tanks were built as early as 600
A. D. by the Yemenites who built besides the celebrated dam at
Marib, and the many similar structures in various parts of
Yemen. Water is also brought by an aqueduct from Sheikh
Othman, seven miles distant, but the majority of the population is supplied from the government condensers. In spite of
the desert character of the soil and the aridity of the climate
Aden is not entirely without natural vegetation. Thomas
Anderson of the Bengal Medical Service enumerates ninety-
four species of plants found on the Aden peninsula, some of
which are entirely unique. Most of the plants, however, are
desert-dwellers with sharp thorns, an aromatic odor, and yield
gums and resins.

The Aden settlement has four centres of population; Steamer-
Point, the Crescent, the town of Maala and the " Camp " or
Aden proper. A road, the only road in fact, extends from
Steamer-Point on the west to Aden proper on the east, and no

one can boast of having seen Aden who has not taken the ride in a *geri* from the landing-pier to the tanks.   The Aden horses are of all creatures most miserable for the geri-drivers whip their horses much, but feed them little.   The Crescent is a semi-circular range of houses and shops crowded against the mountain side ; with a Hotel de l'Univers and a Hotel de l'Europe (both equally " Grand ") ; cafés, shops, banks, and offices.   The post office, hospital, churches and barracks are further we t toward the telegraph-station.   A drive of about two mile brings us to the native town of Maala.   Here the road forks, the lower one leading to the barrier-gate and Sheikh Othman, and the upper ascending the mountain through the gate of the fortifications and by a sharp declivity leading down to the town of Aden.   It is not an Oriental town in its administration, but it has all the motley character of Port Said on its streets. Europeans, Americans, Africans, Asiatics and mixed races are all represented in the crowd of the market or the loungers in the streets.   The total population is 30,000, including Chinese, Persians, Turks, Egyptians, Somalis, Hindus, Parsees, Jews and Arabs from every part of the peninsula.   Aden is a great centre for native shipping, and the dhows and buggalows that sail every year from the Persian Gulf to Yemen and Jiddah alway call at Aden *en route*.   Also from Oman and Hadramaut the modern Sinbads run their craft into Aden to exchange produce or to lay in supplies for their voyages to the coast of Africa.

The distance from Aden to Yemen's old capital, Sana is nearly 200 miles in a direct line, but on my second journey thither, in 1894, I was obliged to take a roundabout journey to Taiz, because of an Arab uprising.   This and the mountainous character of the country made the distance over 250 miles.   This route passes through, or near, all the important towns of Yemen south of Sana.

With my Bedouin companion, Nasir, I left Sheikh Othman early on the second morning of July.   We reached a small

TRAVELLING IN SOUTHERN ARABIA

THE KEITH FALCONER MEMORIAL CHURCH IN ADEN

village, Wahat, at noon, the thermometer registering 96° in the shade. After a short rest we mounted the camels at seven o'clock in the evening for an all-night journey. Our course was through a barren region, and at daylight we entered Wady Mergia, with scanty vegetation, resting at a village of the same name under a huge acacia tree. The next day we entered the mountains, where rich vegetation showed a cooler climate. We passed several villages, Dar El Kadim, Khoteibah, Suk-el-Juma and others. As this was said to be a dangerous part of the road all the caravan, which we joined at Wahat, was on the look-out, with lighted rope-wicks for their flint-locks swinging from their shoulders and looking in the dark like so many fireflies. At three A. M. we had ascended to the head of the wady and rested for the day at Mabek. All the houses here are of stone, the booths of date-mats and twigs being only found on the maritime plain of Yemen. During the night there had been talk among the wild Arabs of the village of holding me as a hostage to obtain money from the English at Aden ! But Nasir quieted them with a threefold Bedouin oath that I was not a government official nor an Englishman, but an American traveller.

The day after leaving Mabek brought us to the beginning of the happy valleys of Yemen, very different from the torrid coast. A country where the orange, lemon, quince, grape, mango, plum, apricot, peach, apple, pomegranate, fig, date, plantain and mulberry, each yield their fruit in season ; where wheat, barley, maize, millet and coffee are staple products and where there is a glorious profusion of wild flowers—called "grass" by the unpoetic camel-drivers. A land whose mountains lift up their heads over 9,000 feet, terraced from chilly top to warm valley with agricultural amphitheatres, irrigated by a thousand rills and rivulets, some of them peren-nial, flowing along artificial channels or leaping down the rocks in miniature falls. A land where the oriole hangs her nest on the dark acacia, the wild doves hide in clefts of the rock and the chameleon sports his colors by the wayside under the tall

flowering cactus. Such is Yemen. The vegetation of Arabia
Felix begins just before reaching Mufallis, on this route, where
a Turkish castle and customhouse proclaim the boundary of
Ottoman aggression.

Beautiful was the air and scenery on our march. Arab
peasants were at work in the fields, plowing [1] with oxen, repair-
ing the walls of the terraces and opening the water-courses.
The women were all unveiled and had the picturesque costume universal in southern Yemen ; their narrow trousers were
fastened at the waist and ankles, while over their shoulders
hung long mantle-like garments, low in the neck, girded, and
fringed at the bottom with embroidered cloth of green or red.
Here they wear a kind of light turban, but on the Hodeidah
coast broad-brimmed straw hats cover the heads of the Yemen
belles as they urge their donkeys to market.

At sunrise we were in sight of the highest peaks to the left of
the wady-bed. One of them is crowned by a *walli* or saint's-
tomb of Saled bin Taka. These tombs are common in Yemen
and thousands of people visit them annually to ask intercession,
each saint having a special day in the Moslem calendar. At
Mocha the grave of the Arab sheikh Abu-el-Hassan Shadeli,
who first discovered the use of coffee, is highly honored by distant pilgrims.

At eight o'clock on the morning of July fourth we reached
the *burj* called Mufallis and had our first experience of Turkish
rule in Yemen. Unexpectedly we here stumbled upon a
Turkish customhouse, which I had thought was located at
Taiz, as the boundary of Turkish Yemen on my maps did not
extend further south. An unmannerly negro, calling himself
Mudeer of Customs, looked out of a port-hole and demanded
my ascent. Through dirt and up darkness I reached his little
room and stated my errand and purpose. No kind words or

---

[1] The Yemen plow is shaped like an English plow in many respects ;
although it has only one handle its coulter is broad and made of iron, a
great improvement over the crooked stick of Mesopotamia.

offered backsheesh would avail; "*all* the baggage must be opened and *all* books were forbidden entrance into Yemen by a recent order," so he affirmed. First, therefore, I unscrewed the covers of the two boxes with an old bowie-knife. The books, after having been critically examined by eyes that could not read, were seized; next my saddle-bags were searched, and every book and map was also confiscated. I was refused even a receipt for the books taken, and to every plea or question the only reply was, to go on to Taiz and appeal to the Governor.

Despoiled of our goods, we left the "customhouse" at eleven A. M., taking an old man on a donkey armed with a spear, as guide and defence, because Nasir heard that there was disturbance in this quarter. At two o'clock we rested for half an hour under the shade of a huge rock in the bed of the wady, and then warned by peals of thunder, we hastened on, hoping to reach Hirwa before dark. In less than an hour, however, the sky was black, rain fell in torrents, and we found it hopeless to attempt to urge the slow camels on through the wady. There was no shelter in sight, so we crouched under a small tree halfway up the mud bank. The rain turned to hail —large stones that frightened the camels so that they stampeded—and we became thoroughly chilled.

When the storm ceased, our donkey man came with looks of horror to tell us that his poor beast had fallen down the slope and was being swept away by the torrent! What had been a dry river bed half an hour before, was now a rushing rapids. We decided to climb up the terraces to a house which we saw on the mountain side. The camels had preceded us, and after a vigorous climb over mud-fields and up the rocks we reached the house and hospitality of Sheikh Ali. Over the charcoal fire, after drinking plenty of *kishr*, (made from the *shell* of the coffee bean,) we had to listen to a long discussion concerning the lost donkey. Finally, matters were smoothed over by my offering to pay one-half the price of the animal on condition that our guide should proceed with us to *Hirwa*.

The next day we were off early. Because of the steep ascents I was obliged to walk most of the way, and I sprained my ankle severely. It did not pain me until night, when it was swollen and kept me "on crutches" for several days. *Hirwa* is a small Arab village with a weekly market, and we found shelter in the usual coffee-shop characteristic of Yemen. The following day we reached *Sept Ez zeilah*, where we found cleaner quarters than the night before. At about midnight a war party of Bedouins came and frightened the peaceful villagers with demands for food, etc. They had just returned from setting fire to a small castle, and, numbering sixty hungry men, were not to be intimidated. They were about to force their way into our quarters when Nasir and the women promised to give them food. Within, I kept quiet and listened to the noise of grinding and baking and coffee-pounding. Without, some of the Arabs seized a cow belonging to a poor woman and butchered it for their feast. At this there was a crying of women and barking of dogs and swearing of oaths by the Great Allah, such as I hope never to hear again. Finally, the Arabs went away with full stomachs, and we slept a broken sleep for fear they might return. The next day we proceeded to Taiz, and arrived at noon, one week after leaving Aden.

The Mutasarrif Pasha, or Governor, was satisfied with my passports, and expressed his regrets that the books had been seized at Mufallis, but such was the law. He would, however, allow me to send for them for inspection. What is written here in four lines was the work and patience of four weary days! A soldier was sent to Mufallis; I was obliged to entrust him with money to pay the custom dues; to hire a camel to carry the books; finally to pay for two sticks of sealing wax (price in Taiz one rupee) with which to ʀeal the books and maps lest they be tampered with—all this at the order of the enlightened government of the Sublime Porte! The first messenger never reached Mufallis; on the road he was attacked by Arabs, stabbed in the neck, robbed of his rifle, and carried back to the military hospital at Taiz. Then there was more delay to find and send a second soldier with the same camel and money and sealing wax, but with a new rifle. He returned with the books safely after five days! No Turk could set a value on a book, and so the law is that books are taxed by weight, boxes included. The customs receipt was attached for "200 kilograms Jewish books (at twenty piastres a kilo.), value, 4,000 piastres, and custom dues amounting to 288 piastres." In the same document I was spoken of as "the Jew, Ishmail, Dhaif Ullah,"—a rather curious combination of names. I was called a "Jew" because of the case of Hebrew New Testaments; Ishmail was the equivalent for Samuel; and Dhaif Ullah, my Arabic cognomen.

VI

YEMEN : THE SWITZERLAND OF ARABIA

"If the Turks would clear out of Yemen, a wonderful field for commerce would be thrown open, for the Turkish government is vile and all cultivators are taxed to an iniquitous extent."—*Ion Keith Falconer.*

WHILE waiting at Taiz I had an opportunity to study Yemen town life and the system of government, as well as to learn a little about the cultivation of coffee and kaat, the two chief products of this part of Yemen.

Taiz has not often been visited by travellers from the occident, and is a most interesting place. It is a large fortified village of perhaps 5,000 inhabitants, the residence of a Mutasarrif whose authority extends from the province of Hodeidah to the Aden frontier including Mocha and Sheikh Seyyid on the coast, recently abandoned by France. The place has five gates, one of which has been walled up, and five large mosques in Byzantine style. The largest Mosque is called El Muzafer, and has two large minarets and twelve beautiful domes. Taiz was once a centre of learning and its libraries were celebrated all over Arabia. Firozabadi, the Noah Webster of the Arabic language, taught in Taiz and edited his "Ocean" dictionary there. He died at the neighboring town of Zebid, in 1414 A. D., and his grave is honored by the learned of Yemen.

The bazaar is not large, but the four European shops kept by Greek merchants are well supplied with all ordinary articles of civilization. One public bath, in splendid condition, and a military hospital show Ottoman occupation. The fort holds perhaps 1,300 soldiers and the residence of the Mutasarrif is in a beautiful and comfortable little building outside of the town.

The mosques were once grand but are now ruined and a home for bats; the famous libraries have disappeared and the sub-terannean vaults of the largest Mosque formerly used as porticoes for pupils are now Turkish horse-stables. There is a post office and telegraph; the post goes once a week to Hodeidah via Zebid and Beit el Fakih, and the telegraph in the same direction a little more rapidly when the wires are in order.

Taiz is girt around by Jebel Sobr, the highest range of mountains in southern Yemen. Hisn Aroos peak, near the town, has an elevation of over 7,000 feet. According to Niebuhr and Defler, on a clear day one can look from the summit of this peak across the lowlands and the Red Sea into Africa. I was unable to reach the summit as my Arab guide failed me and the days were misty and frequent rains fell.

Taiz is the centre of kaat-culture for all Yemen, and coffee comes here on its way to Hodeidah or Aden. Amid all the wealth of vegetation and fruitage every plant seems familiar to the tourist save kaat. It is a shrub whose very name is unknown outside of Yemen, while there it is known and used by every mother's son, as well as by the mothers and daughters themselves. Driving from Aden to Sheikh Othman, one first learns the *name*. Why are those red flags hoisted near the police stations, at intervals on the road, and why are they hauled down as soon as those camels pass? Oh, they are taking loads of kaat for the Aden market, and the flags are to prevent cheating of the customs. Over 2,000 camel loads come into Aden every year, and each load passes through English territory by " block-signal " system, for it is highly taxed. As to its *use*, step into a kahwah in any part of Yemen shortly before sunset, and you will see Arabs each with a bundle of green twigs in his lap, chewing at the leaves of kaat.

At Taiz I first had an opportunity to meet the Jews of the interior of Yemen. Altogether they number perhaps 60,000 in the whole province. They live mostly in the large towns and very few are agriculturists. They are a despised and down-trodden race, but they say at Sana, that their condition is not so bad under the Turks as it was under the Arab rulers before 1871. The accounts of their origin are discrepant. Some say they are descended from the Jews of the Dispersion, but others hold that they were immigrants from the North over 900 years ago. They are more cleanly, more intelligent and more trustworthy than the Arabs; and although they are out of all communication with the rest of the world and in ignorance of their European countrymen they are not ignorant of Hebrew and rabbinic learning. Their synagogue near Taiz is a low stone building, twenty-five by fifteen feet. For furniture it has only a few curtains of embroidered texts, a printed diagram of the ancient candlestick, with the names of the twelve tribes, and a high reading-desk. Such are all the synagogues of Yemen.

At Taiz the Jews seemed to have grown content under long centuries of oppression and taxation. Many of the old Moslem laws against infidels, such as those forbidding them to *ride*, to carry weapons or wear fine clothes in public, are still rigorously enforced by custom if not by the government. The Jew is universally despised, yet he cannot be spared, for nearly all artisan work is in Jewish hands. The Moslem Arab has learned nothing from the Jew outside of the Koran ; but, alas! the Jew has imbibed many foolish customs and superstitions foreign to his creed from Islam.

When the Hebrew Scriptures reached Taiz I was again disappointed, for the Governor would not permit the boxes to be opened, but they were to be sent sealed and under guard to Sana. I afterward learned that the "guard" was for me as well as the books, and that the soldier carried a letter with this accusation written : "This is a converted Jew, who is corrupting the religion of Islam, and sells books to Moslems and Jews." I had no alternative but to proceed to Sana ; taking a Damar Arab as servant, having dismissed the Aden camels.

I left Taiz on a mule July 26th, and arrived at Seyanee the

same day. The following night we reached Ibb. Here I was forced to lodge outside of the town, as the guard had instructions not to let me "see things." I endured this impatiently, until I learned that our servant had been imprisoned on our arrival because he told me the names of the villages on the route ! I then appealed to the Mayor, and on virtue of my passports demanded the right of going about the town and the release of my servant. After some delay, both requests were granted. The incident is one of many to show the suspicion with which a stranger is regarded by the authorities in Yemen. On Saturday the soldier and I hastened on to reach the large town of Yerim before Sunday, and rest there, waiting for the baggage camel. It was a long ride of twelve hours, but through a delightful country everywhere fertile and terraced with coffee plantations and groves of kaat.

Yerim, with perhaps 300 houses, lies in a hollow of the Sumara range of mountains. It has a fortress and some houses of imposing appearance, but the general aspect of the town is miserable. A neighboring marsh breeds malaria, and the place is proverbially unhealthy in this otherwise salubrious region. Niebuhr's botanist, Forskal, died here on their journey in 1763. The road from Ibb to Yerim has perhaps the finest scenery of any part of Yemen; never have I seen more picturesque mountains and valleys, green with verdure and bright with blossoms. Scabiosa, bluebells, forget-me-nots, golden-rod, four-o'clocks and large oleander-trees —

> "All earth was full of heaven
> And every bush afire with God."

The cacti-plants were in full bloom, and measured twenty feet against the mountain passes. Two thousand feet below one could hear the sound of the water rushing along the wady-bed or disappearing under the bridges that span the valleys. While high above, the clouds were half concealing the summit of the "Gazelle Neck" (Unk el-Gazel).

Sunday, July 29th, was a cold day at Yerim; early in the
morning the temperature went down to 52°, and at night two
blankets were needed. Not until nine o'clock was it warm
enough for the Yerim merchants to open their shops.

A Jewish family, en route for Taiz, were stopping with us at
the caravansari, and at night I spoke for over two hours with
them and the Arabs about Christ.   There was no interruption,
and I was impressed to see the interest of a Jew and Arab
alike in what I told them from Isaiah liii., reading it in Arabic
by the dim candle light, amidst all the baggage and beasts of
an Oriental inn.   At the little village of Khader, eight miles
from Waalan, angry words arose from the "guard" because I tried to speak to a Jew.   When I spoke in protest
they began to strike the Jew with the butt end of their rifles,[1]
and when the poor fellow fled, my best defence was silence.
On my return journey, I inadvertently raised trouble again, by
mentioning that Jesus Christ and Moses were *Jews*—which the
Arabs considered an insult to the prophets of God.

On the road beyond Yerim we passed a large boulder with
an irregular impression on one side.   This is called Ali's foot-
print, and the Arabs who pass always anoint it with oil.   The
steep ascents and descents of the journey were now behind
us.   From Yerim on to Sana the plateau is more level.   Wide
fields of lentils, barley and wheat take the place of the groves
of kaat and coffee; camels were used for ploughing, and
with their long necks and curious harness, were an odd sight.

The next halt we made was at Damar, 8,000 feet above sea-
level.   It is a large town, with three minaret-mosques and a
arge bazaar; the houses are of native rock, three and four-
stories high, remarkably clean and well-built.   Inside they are
whitewashed, and have the Yemen translucent slabs of gypsum

---

[1] It was not pleasant for an American to notice that nearly all the
Turkish rifles in Yemen were "Springfield 1861." The same weapons
that were employed to break the chains of slavery in the southern states,
are now used to oppress the peaceful Yemenites.

for window-panes. From Damar the road leads northeast over Maaber and the Kariet en-Nekil pass to Waalan; thence, nearly due north, to Sana. From Damar to Waalan is thirty-five miles, and thence to the capital, eighteen miles more. The roads near the city of Sana are kept in good repair, although there are no wheeled vehicles, for the sake of the Turkish artillery.

On Thursday, August 2d, we entered Sana by the Yemen gate. Three years before I had entered the city from the other side, coming from Hodeidah; then in the time of the Arab rebellion and now myself a prisoner. I was taken to the Dowla and handed over to the care of a policeman until the Wali heard my case. After finding an old Greek friend from Aden, who offered to go bail for me, I was allowed liberty, and for nineteen days was busy seeing the city and visiting the Jews.[1]

Sana, anciently called Uzal, and since many centuries the chief city of Yemen, contains some 50,000 inhabitants and lies stretched out in a wide, level valley between Jebel Nokoom and the neighboring ranges. It is 7,648 feet above sea-level. The town is in the form of a triangle, the eastern point consisting of a large fortress, dominating the town, and built upon the lowest spur of Nokoom. The town is divided into three walled quarters, the whole being surrounded by one continuous wall of stone and brick. They are respectively the city proper, in which are the government buildings, the huge bazaars, and the residences of the Arabs and Turks; the Jews' quarter; and Bir-el-azib, which lies between the two, and contains gardens and villas belonging to the richer Turks and Arabs. The city had once great wealth and prosperity, and to-day remains, next to Bagdad, the most flourishing city in all Arabia. The shops are well supplied with European goods, and a large

---

[1] Of the work among the latter, and my experiences in distributing the New Testament, a report was published by the Mildmay Mission; we therefore omit reference to it here.

manufacture of silk, jewelry and arms is carried on. The government quarter, with its cafés, billiard-rooms, large Greek shops, carriages, bootblacks, and brass-band reminds one of Cairo. Sana has forty-eight mosques, thirty-nine synagogues, twelve large public-baths, a military hospital with 200 beds, and is the centre of trade for all northern Yemen and northwestern Hadramaut, as well as for the distant villages of Nejran and fertile Wady Dauasir. Arabs from every district crowd the bazaars, and long strings of camels leave every day for the Hodeidah coast.

On August 14th I took an early morning walk to Rhoda, a village about eight miles north of Sana, and in the midst of beautiful gardens. From Roda the direct caravan route leads to Nejran, and from the outskirts of the village, looking north, an inviting picture met the eye. A fertile plateau stretched out to the horizon, and only two days' journey would bring one into the free desert beyond Turkish rule. But this time the way across the peninsula was closed by my bankruptcy; robbed at Yerim in the coffee-shop, and already in debt at Sana, it would have been impossible to proceed, except as a dishonest dervish.

On the 21st of August I left Sana for Hodeidah, receiving a loan of twenty dollars from the Ottoman government, to be paid back at the American consulate. We followed the regular postal route, the same which I had travelled on my first journey.

The plateau or table-land between Sana'a and Banàn is a pasture country. The Bedouins live in the stone-built villages and herd their immense flocks on the plain; camels, cows and sheep were grazing by the hundreds and thousands. After Banàn begins the difficult descent to the coast down breakneck mountain *stairways* rather than roadways, over broken bridges, and through natural arches. Fertile, cultivated mountain slopes were on every side, reminding one of the valleys of Switzerland. In one district near Suk-el-Khamis the whole mountain-side for a height of 6,000 feet was terraced from top to bottom. General Haig wrote of these terraces : " One can hardly realize the enormous amount of labor, toil and perseverance which these represent. The terraced walls are usually from five to eight feet in height, but toward the top of the mountain they are sometimes as much as fifteen or eighteen feet. They are built entirely of rough stone, laid without mortar. I reckon on an average that each wall retains a terrace not more than twice its own height in width, and I do not think I saw a single breach in one of them unrepaired." [1]

In Yemen there are two rainy seasons, in spring and in autumn, so that there is generally an abundance of water in the numerous reservoirs stored for irrigation. Yet, despite the extraordinary fertility of the soil and the surprising industry of the inhabitants, the bulk of the people are miserably poor, ill-fed and rudely clothed, because they are crushed down by a heartless system of taxation. Every agricultural product, implement and process is under the heavy hand of an oppressive administration and a military occupation that knows no law. The peasantry are robbed by the soldiers on their way to market, by the custom-collector at the gate of each city, and by the tax-gatherer in addition. On the way to Sana my soldier-companion stopped a poor peasant who was urging on a little donkey loaded with two large baskets of grapes ; he emptied the best of the grapes into his saddle-bags, and then beat the man and cursed him because some of the grapes were unripe ! No wonder we read of rebellions in Yemen, and no wonder that intense hatred lives in every Arab against the very name of Turk.

From Suk-el-Khamis, a dirty mountain village,[2] with an elevation of over 9,500 feet, the road leads by Mefak and Wady Zaun to the peculiarly located village of Menakha. At an altitude of 7,600 feet above sea-level, it is perched on a narrow ridge between two mountain ranges. On either side of the one

---

[1] Geog. Soc. Proceedings, 1887, p. 482.

[2] Defler says in his diary that this place has " une odeur atroce et des legions de puces et de punaises." I also had an all-night's battle.

street that forms the backbone of the summit are precipices
2,000 feet deep. So narrow is the town that there are places
where one can stand and gaze down both sides of the abyss at
the same time. To reach it from the west there is only one
path zigzagging up the mountain-side, and from the east it can
only be approached by a narrow track cut in the face of the
precipice and winding up for an ascent of 2,500 feet. Menakha is the centre of the coffee trade ; it has a population of
10,000 or more, one-third of which are Jews. There are four
Greek merchants, the Turks had 2,000 troops garrisoned in the
town, and the bazaars were equal to those of Taiz. Its exact
elevation is given by Defler, after eighteen observations, as
7,616 feet above sea-level.

From Menakha to the coast is only two long days' journey ; three by camel. The first stage is to Hejjeila, at the
foot of the high ranges ; thence to Bajil, a village of 2,000 people, and along the barren, hot plain to Hodeidah. At Bajil
the people are nearly all shepherds, and the main industry is
dyeing cloth and weaving straw. Here one sees the curious
Yemen straw hats worn by the women, and here also the peas-
ant-maidens wear no veils. Yet they are of purer heart and
life than the black-clouted and covered women of the Turkish
towns.

Hodeidah by the sea is very like Jiddah in its general appearance. The streets are narrow, crooked and indescribably
filthy. The " Casino " is a sort of Greek hotel for strangers,
and the finest house in the city is that of Sidi Aaron, near the
sea, with its fine front and marble courtyard. The population
is of a very mixed character ; east of the city in a separate
quarter live the *Akhdam* Arabs, whose origin is uncertain, but
who are considered outcasts by all the other Arabs. They are
not allowed to carry arms and no Arab tribe intermarries with
them.

From Hodeidah there is a regular line of small steamers to
Aden, and the Egyptian Red Sea coasting steamers also call

here fortnightly.   The trade of Hodeidah was once flourishing, but here too Turkish misrule has brought deadness and dullness into business, and taxation has crushed industrial enterprise.

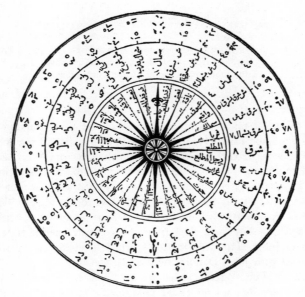

AN ARABIAN COMPASS.

VII

THE UNEXPLORED REGIONS OF HADRAMAUT

> " As when to them who sail
> Beyond the Cape of Hope, and now are past
> Mozambic, off at sea northeast winds blow
> Sabean odors from the spicy shore
> Of Araby the blest."—*Milton.*

WE must take at least a glimpse of the almost unknown region called Hadramaut.[1] This is a strip of territory stretching between the great desert and the sea from Aden eastward to Oman. Our knowledge of the interior of this region was almost a perfect blank until some light was thrown on it by the enterprising traveller A. Von Wrede in 1843. The coast is comparatively well known, at least as far as Makalla and Shehr. The land rises from the coast in a series of terraces to Jebel Hamra (5,284 feet), which is connected on the northeast with Jebel Dahura, over 8,000 feet high.

Adolph Von Wrede sailed from Aden to Makalla and thence penetrated inland as far as Wady Doan the most fertile spot of all South Arabia. This wady flows northward through the land of the Bni Yssa and the district is bordered on the west by Belad-el-Hasan and on the east by Belad-el-Hamum. But how far this region extends northward and whether the sandy desert of El Ahkaf (quicksands) really begins with the Wady Rakhia, a branch of the Doan are points on which Von Wrede throws no light and which are still uncertain. In 1870

---

[1] Hadramaut is a very ancient name for this region. Not only does Ptolemy place here the *Adramitæ* in his geography, but there seems little doubt that Hadramaut is identical with Hazarmaveth, mentioned in the tenth chapter of Genesis.

the French Jew, Joseph Halévy, made a bold attempt to penetrate into Hadramaut from Yemen.   Since then little was
added to our knowledge of Hadramaut until 1893 when Shibam,
the residence of the most powerful Sultan of Hadramaut was
visited by Theodore Bent and his wife.   In 1897 they made a
second journey into the same region which cost Mr. Bent his
health and afterward his life.   From the account of these journeys we quote a few paragraphs which set forth clearly the interesting character of this almost unknown country.[1]

"Immediately behind Makalla rise grim arid mountains of a
reddish hue, and the town is plastered against this rich-tinged
background.   By the shore, like a lighthouse, stands the white
minaret of the Mosque, the walls and pinnacles of which are
covered with dense masses of seabirds and pigeons; not far
from this the huge palace where the Sultan dwells reminds one
of a whitewashed mill with a lace-like parapet; white, red and
brown are the dominant colors of the town, and in the harbor
the Arab dhows with fantastic sterns rock to and fro in the
unsteady sea, forming altogether a picturesque and unusual
scene.

"Nominally Makalla is ruled over by a Sultan of the Al
Kaiti family, whose connection with India has made them very
English in their sympathies, and his Majesty's general appearance, with his velvet coat and jewelled daggers, is far more
Indian than Arabian.   Really the most influential people in the
town are the money-grubbing Parsees from Bombay, and it is
essentially one of those commercial centres where Hindustani
is spoken nearly as much as Arabian.   We were lodged in a
so-called palace hard by the bazaar, which reeked with mysterious smells and was alive with flies; so we worked hard to
get our preparations made and to make our sojourn in this un-
congenial burning spot as short as possible.   . . .

[1] "The Hadramaut: a Journey" by Theodore Bent. *Nineteenth
Century,* September, 1894.   Also Mrs. Bent's "Yafei and Fadhli
countries." *Geographical Journal,* July, 1898.

" Leaving these villages behind us, we climbed rapidly higher and higher, until, at an elevation of over 5,000 feet, we found ourselves at last on a broad level plateau, stretching as far as the eye could reach in every direction, and shutting off the Hadramaut from the coast. This is the ' mons excelsus ' of Pliny ; here we have the vast area where once flourished the frankincense and the myrrh. Of the latter shrub there is plenty left, and it is still tapped for its odoriferous sap ; but of the former we only saw one specimen on the plateau, for in the lapse of ages the wealth of this country has steadily disappeared ; further east, however, in the Mahra country, there is, I understand, a considerable quantity left.

" Near Hajarein are many traces of the olden days when the frankincense trade flourished, and when the town of Doani, which name is still retained in the Wady Doan, was a great emporium for this trade. Acres and acres of ruins, dating from the centuries immediately before our era, lie stretched along the valley here, just showing their heads above the weight of superincumbent sand which has invaded and overwhelmed the past glories of this district. The ground lies strewn with fragments of Himyaritic inscriptions, pottery, and other indications of a rich harvest for the excavator, but the hostility of the Nahad tribe prevented us from paying these ruins more than a cursory visit, and even to secure this we had to pay the Sheikh of the place nineteen dollars ; and his greeting was ominous as he angrily muttered, ' Salaam to all who believe Mohammed is the true prophet.'

" At Assab they would not allow us to dip our vessels in their well, nor take our repast under the shadow of their Mosque : even the women of this village ventured to insult us, peeping into our tent at night, and tumbling over the guys in a manner most aggravating to the weary occupants.

" Our troubles on this score were happily terminated at Haura, where a huge castle belonging to the Al Kaiti family dominates a humble village surrounded by palm groves. With-

out photographs to bear out my statement, I should hardly dare
to describe the magnificence of these castles in the Hadramaut.
That at Haura is seven stories high, and covers fully an acre
of ground beneath the beetling cliff, with battlements, towers,
and machicolations bearing a striking likeness to Holyrood.
But Holyrood is built of stone, and Haura, save for the first
story, is built of sun-dried bricks; and if Haura stood where
Holyrood does, or in any other country save dry, arid Arabia,
it would long ago have melted away. . . .

"One of the most striking features of these Arabian palaces
is the wood-carving. The doors are exquisitely decorated with
intricate patterns, and with a text out of the Koran carved on
the lintel; the locks and keys are all of wood, and form a study
for the carver's art, as do the cupboards, the niches, the sup-
porting beams and the windows, which are adorned with fret-
work instead of glass. The dwelling-rooms are above, the
ground floor being exclusively used for merchandise, and the
first floor for the domestics."

Concerning the chief town of the interior of Hadramaut Mr.
Bent writes as follows :

"Then he sent us to reside for five more days in his capital
of Shibam, which is twelve miles distant from Al Katan, and
is one of the principal towns in the Hadramaut valley. It is
built on rising ground in the centre of the narrowest point of
the valley, so that no one can pass between it and the cliffs of
the valley out of gunshot of the walls. This rising ground has
doubtless been produced by many generations of towns built of
sun-dried bricks, for it is the best strategical point in the neighborhood. Early Arab writers tell us that the Himyarite population of this district came here when they abandoned their
capital at Sabota, or Shabwa, further up the valley, early in our
era, but we found evident traces of an earlier occupation than
this—an inscription and a seal with the name 'Shibam' engraved on it, which cannot be later than the third century,
B. C. And as a point for making up the caravans which started

from the frankincense-growing district, Shibam must always have been very important.

"The town of Shibam offers a curious appearance as you approach ; above its mud-brick walls with bastions and watch towers appear the tall whitewashed houses of the wealthy, which make it look like a large round cake with sugar on it. Outside the walls several industries are carried on, the chief of which is the manufacture of indigo dye. The small leaves are dried in the sun and powdered and then put into huge jars— which reminded us of the Forty Thieves—filled with water. Next morning these are stirred with long poles, producing a dark blue frothy mixture ; this is left to settle, and then the indigo is taken from the bottom and spread out on cloths to drain ; the substance thus procured is taken home and mixed with dates and saltpetre. Four pounds of this indigo to a gallon of water makes the requisite and universally used dye for garments, the better class of which are calendered by beating them with wooden hammers on stones."

Of the coast town of Shehr and its ruler Mr. Bent says :

"Shehr is a detestable place by the sea, set in a wilderness of sand. Once it was the chief commercial port of the Hadramaut valley, but now Makalla has quite superseded it, for Shehr is nothing but an open roadstead and its buildings are now falling into ruins. Ghalib, the eldest son and heir of the chief of the Al Kaiti family, rules here as the viceregent of his father, who is in India as jemadar or general of the Arab troops, chiefly all Hadrami, in the service of the Nizam of Hyderabad. Ghalib is quite an Oriental dandy, who lived a life of some rapidity when in India, so that his father thought it as well to send him to rule in Shehr, where the capabilities for mischief are not so many as at Bombay. He dresses very well in various damask silk coats and faultless trousers ; his swords and daggers sparkle with jewels ; in his hand he flourishes a golden-headed cane ; and, as the water is hard at Shehr, he sends his dirty linen in dhows to Bombay to be washed."

The Arabs of Hadramaut have been still more in contact with Java than with India. Large colonies of Hadramis emigrated to the Dutch Archipelago more than a century ago; intermarriage between the Javanese and the Arabs is very common; and the Mohammedanism of the Dutch East Indies is entirely of the Hadramaut type. These interesting facts were first brought to light by Van den Berg, a Dutch scholar in his elaborate work on this province of Arabia and the Arab colonies in Java.[1] His account of Hadramaut is a compilation from the lips of the Arab immigrants, but the description of the manners and customs of the people and their religious peculiarities is from personal observation. Altogether, in spite of minor geographical inaccuracies, the book is the best single volume on Southern Arabia and tells the story of Islam in the Dutch Archipelago as it is to-day. The Arabs have always been a strong race at colonizing but it is well to note that the influence of Hadramaut on Java and Sumatra to-day is not less than that of Oman on Zanzibar and East Africa in the last century. Even Hadramaut will not always remain undiscovered and unremembered. The incense-country of antiquity has a future before it even as it has had a glorious past.

A CASTLE IN HADRAMAUT.

[1] Le Hadramont et les Colonies Arabes dans le Archipel Indien par L. W. C. Van den Berg. Batavia, 1886. By order of the Government.

VIII

" Oman is separated from the rest of Arabia by a sandy desert. It is, in fact, as far as communication with the rest of the world is concerned, an island with the sea on one side and the desert on the other. Hence its people are even more primitive, simple and unchanged in their habits than the Arabs generally. Along the coast, however, especially at Muscat they are more in contact with the outer world."—*General Haig.*

IN Arab nomenclature Oman applies only to a small district in the vicinity of Muscat, but the name is generally given to the entire southeastern section of the Arabian peninsula, including everything east of a line drawn from the Kuria-Muria islands to the peninsula of Katar, anciently called Bahrein. Thus defined it is the largest province of Arabia and in some respects the most interesting. Historically, politically and geographically Oman has always been isolated from the other provinces. Turkish rule never extended this far nor did the later caliphs long exercise their authority here. The whole country has for centuries been under independent rulers called Imams or Seyyids. The population, which is wholly Arab and Mohammedan, (save in the coast towns) was derived originally from two different stocks known to the Arabs as Kahtani and Adnani or the Yemeni and Muadi. These names have changed since the beginning of the eighteenth century to Hinani and Ghaffiri. The Yemen tribes came first and are most numerous. The two rival races have been in open and continuous feud and antagonism and have kept the country in perpetual turmoil. They even inhabit separate quarters in some of the towns, according to Colonel Miles. In Somail, about fifty miles inland from Muscat a broad road marks the division between the two clans. These two parent stocks are subdivided into some 200 different tribes and these again into sub-tribes or "houses." Each family-group has its own Sheikh, a hereditary position assumed by the eldest male in the family.

Very few of the tribes of Oman are nomadic; the greater part live in towns and villages along the wady-beds. With the exception of fruits of which there is a great variety and abundance, dates are the sole food product and the chief export of the province. Rice is imported from India. The total population of Oman is estimated by Colonel Miles not to exceed 1,500,000. There are numerous towns of 5,000 to 10,-000 inhabitants; Muscat and Mattra are the chief towns on the coast, and are practically united as they are only two miles apart. The climate of Oman on the coast is excessively hot and moist during a large part of the year, although the rainfall here is only six to ten inches annually; in the interior the heat is greatly tempered by the elevation, the rainfall is much greater and the climate as pleasant as in the highlands of Yemen.

The Omanese state was at its greatest height of power at the beginning of the present century. Then the Sultans of Muscat exercised rule as far as Bahrein to the northwest, had possession of Bunder Abbas and Linga in Persia, and called Socotra and Zanzibar their own. At this time the Oman Arabs began their extensive journeys in Africa and, urged by the enormous profits of the slave-trade, explored every corner of the great interior of the Dark Continent. At present the authority of the Sultan at Muscat, Seyyid Feysul bin Turki, does not extend far beyond the capital and its suburbs.

In the early years of the Oman Sultanate, Nizwa was the capital, afterward Rastak became the seat of government, but since 1779, Muscat has been at once the capital and the key, the gateway and the citadel of the whole country. On approaching Muscat in a British India steamer, the land is first sighted, looming up in one mass of dark mountain ranges;

closer, one portion of this mass directly over the town of Muscat is seen to be of a dark brown color, crag on crag, serrated and torn in a fantastic manner and giving the harbor a most picturesque appearance.   The town itself shows white against the dark massive rocks, on the summits of which are perched numerous castles and towers.   But, though presenting a pleasing prospect from a distance, a nearer view reveals the usual features of large Oriental towns,—narrow, dirty streets, unattractive buildings, and masses of crumbling walls under the torrid heat of a burning sun and amid all the sweltering surroundings of a damp climate.

The heat of Muscat is proverbial.   John Struys, the Dutchman, who visited this town in 1672, wrote that it was " so incredibly hot and scorching that strangers are as if they were in boiling cauldrons or sweating tubs."   A Persian, named Abd-er-Razak, being a Persian, was able to surpass all others in exaggerated description and wrote of Muscat in 1442, " The heat was so intense that it burned the marrow in the bones, the sword in its scabbard melted like wax, and the gems that adorned the handle of the dagger were reduced to coal.   In the plains the chase became a matter of perfect ease, for the desert was filled with roasted gazelles ! "   It is said that a black bulb thermometer has registered 189° F. in the sun at Muscat and 107° even at night, is not unusual during the hottest part of the year.   The bare rocks form a parabolic mirror to the sun's rays from the south and west; add to this the facts that the hills shut off the breezes and that Muscat lies on the Tropic of Cancer in the zone of greatest heat.   According to the witness of a resident, " the climate of Muscat is bad beyond all description.   For about three months in the year, from December to March, it is tolerably cool at night but after the latter month the heat becomes intense and makes Muscat rank but little after the Infernal Regions.   There is a short break in the hot weather about the middle of July which generally lasts a month."

THE HARBOR AND CASTLE AT MUSCAT

READY FOR A CAMEL RIDE IN THE DESERT

The most conspicuous buildings of Muscat are the two forts, the relics of the Portuguese dominion, which stand out boldly on each side of the town about 100 feet above the sea. They command not only the sea-approach, but the town itself and are only accessible by a fine stairway cut out of the natural rock. The guns that bristle from the forts are nearly all old and comparatively harmless. Several of them are of brass and· bear the royal arms of Spain ; one is dated 1606. In the fort to the right of the harbor, one can still see the ruins of a Portuguese chapel. When Pelly visited it in 1865 the following inscription was legible :

AVE MAR. GRASA P._EA ☐s ‾ECUM Etc. . . .

Its translation given by him reads: "Hail Mary full of grace, the Lord is with thee. Don Phillip III., King of Spain, Don Juan de Acuna of his council of war and his captain-general of the artillery in the year 1605, in the eighth year of his reign in the crown of Portugal, ordered through Don Quarte Menezes, his commissioner of India, that this fortress should be built."

The Sultan has also a town residence in half decay like all the other stone-built but mud-cemented houses of the natives. The only residences well-built and durable are those of the British resident and the American consul. The former occupies the choice location, in a rock cleft, where breezes blow from two directions. The bazaar of Muscat has little to boast of ; one of the chief industries is the manufacture of *Hilawi* or Muscat candy-paste, which to the acquired taste is delicious, but to the stranger smells of rancid butter and tastes like sweet wagon-grease.

The town is cut off from the plain behind by a substantially built wall which stretches from hill to hill. This wall is pierced with two gates which are always guarded and closed a couple of hours after sunset. The moat outside the wall is dry. Beyond it are houses and hundreds of mat huts principally inhabited by Beluchis and Negroes. The American mission house is also outside of the wall, in this quarter. About a third of a mile beyond are the gardens of Muscat and the wells, protected by a tower and guard. "The gardens" are always visited at sunset by the strollers for exercise, but they are hardly large enough "to supply a week's food for 100 self-respecting locusts of normal appetite."

The population of Muscat is of very mixed character, Arabs, Beluchis, Banian-Traders, Negroes, Persians, and every other nation that frequents this port of transit. The Arabic spoken in all Oman is a dialect quite different from that of Nejd or Yemen but the Arabic of Muscat is full of pigeon-English and pigeon-Hindustani. The extensive and long intercourse with Zanzibar and East Africa has also had its influence on the speech and habits of the Muscat Arab trader. The present trade is still very considerable, although less than a century ago. It is mostly with India, there being little direct trade with England. The chief exports are dates, fruit, shark-fins, fish, and salt; the imports, rice, sugar, piece-goods, coffee, silk, petroleum and arms. The largest export is of dates which nearly all go to the American Market. Besides the large number of steamers which call at this port, the native merchants own several old British sailing vessels, some of them noted clippers in their day, which make one or two voyages a year and bring profit to their owners. Native boats also transport cargoes landed at Muscat, to the less frequented ports. This adds to the importance of Muscat as an *entrepôt* for Oman. Mattra is the terminus of the caravan-routes from the interior and is in communication with Muscat by a narrow mountain path and by sea.

The so-called Pirate coast stretches along the northern boundary of Oman on the Persian Gulf from El Katar to Ras Musendum and was, even as early as Ptolemy's day, inhabited by wild, lawless Arabs. On his map of Arabia they are named *Ichthiophagoi*, or fish-eaters. Niebuhr wrote of this part of Oman, "Fishes are so plentiful upon the coast and so easily caught, as to be used not only for feeding cows, asses, and other domestic animals, but even as manure for the fields." Sir John Malcolm, in his quaint sketches of Persia wrote forty years ago: "I asked who were the inhabitants of the barren shore of Arabia that we saw. He answered with apparent alarm, 'they are of the sect of Wahabees and are called Jowasimee. But God preserve us from them, for they are monsters. Their occupation is piracy, and their delight murder, and to make it worse they give you the most pious reasons for every villainy they commit. They abide by the letter of the sacred volume, rejecting all commentaries and traditions. If you are their captive and offer all to save your life they say, No! It is written in the Koran that it is not lawful to plunder the living; but we are not prohibited from stripping the dead —so saying they knock you on the head.'"

Thanks to English commerce and gunboats these fanatic Wahabis have become more tame, and most of them have long given up piracy and turned to pearl-diving for a livelihood. Hindu traders have settled among them, foreign commerce reaches their bazaars, and the black tent is making room for the three or four important towns of Dabai, Sharka, Abu Thubi and Ras-el-Kheima, with growing population and increasing wealth.

The cape of Musendum and the land back of it, called Ras-el-Jebel is very mountainous, but beyond Ras-el-Kheima, the coast is low and flat all the way up the gulf. The villages are all built near the entrance of salt-water creeks or marshes, which serve as harbors at high-tide. For the most part the coast is unfertile, but near Sharka there are palmgroves, and further inland are oases. The islands off this coast are most of them uninhabited.

The Batina coast is the exception to all the maritime plains that surround so large a part of the peninsula; in western and eastern Arabia these low sandy plains are nearly barren of all vegetation, but here extensive date plantations and gardens extend almost to the very ocean beach. Back of the rising plain are the lofty ranges of Jebel Akhdar. This fertile coast begins at Sib, about twenty-five miles from Muscat, and extends for 150 miles to the neighborhood of Khor Kalba with an average width of about twelve miles. It has many towns and villages; the principal ones are the following. Sib is a scattered town chiefly built of mat-huts with two small detached forts. It has a very small bazaar, but extensive date-groves and gardens. Back of Sib on the way up the coast one sees the great bluff of Jebel Akhdar, 9,900 feet high, and visible over 100 miles out at sea. Barka has a lofty Arab fortress, but for the rest mat-huts among date-plantations characterize its general appearance. Large quantities of shell fish are collected and sent inland; the bazaar is good and some Banian traders are settled here. Passing several islands the next town is Suaik. After it the larger town of Sohar, with perhaps 4,000 people. This town is walled with a high fort in the middle, the residence of the Sheikh. A high conical peak, of light color, rises conspicuously about twelve miles west of the town, and with the surrounding date gardens and other trees makes a pretty picture, altogether more green than one would expect on Arabian coasts. Beyond Sohar the chief villages are, in order, Shinas, Al Fujaira, Dibba. The two latter are already beyond the Batina and are between the high cliffs and the deep sea.

Going from southeast Muscat down the coast toward Ras-el-Had we first pass the little village of Sudab and Bunder Jissa. The latter is of interest as the place the French were trying to acquire for a coaling-station from the Sultan of Muscat last year. It has a good anchorage, is only five miles from Muscat, and an island precipice, 140 feet high, guards the entrance. After this, Karyat, Taiwa, Kalhat and smaller villages passed, we reach Sur. This large, double town is situated on a khor or backwater, with two forts to the westward. The in-

habitants, numbering perhaps 8,000, consist of two clans of
the Bni Bu Ali and the Bni Janaba, often at feud with each
other.   The country inland is partly cultivated and date
groves abound.   Sur has always been a place of trade and
enterprise and its buggalows visit India, Zanzibar and the
Persian Gulf.   The people are all bold sailors since many
generations.   But Sur also has the unenviable reputation of
being even now the centre of illicit slave-trading.   Beyond
Sur is the headland of Jebel Saffan and Ras-el-Had, the east-
ernmost point of Arabia, almost reaching the sixtieth degree
of longitude.

For a knowledge of the coast beyond Ras-el-Had we are indebted to the papers of Assistant Surgeon H. J. Carter in the
journal of the Bombay branch of the Royal Asiatic Society.[1]
The two great Arab tribes that dwell on this coast are the
Mahrah and the Gharah; the former really belong to Hadramaut, but the boundaries drawn on the maps are purely artificial and have no significance.   Neither tribe is dependent on
the Oman Sultan or acknowledges any allegiance to him.   The
Mahrah are descended from the ancient Himyarites and occupy
a coast-line of nearly 140 miles from Saihut to Ras Morbat;
their chief town is Damkut (Dunkot) on Kamar bay.   In
stature the Mahrahs are smaller than most Arabs, and by no
means handsome; in their peculiar mode of Bedouin saluta-
tion they put their noses side by side and breathe softly!
They subsist by fishing and are miserably poor; their plains,
mountains and valleys, except close to Damkut, are sandy and
barren.   Religion they have scarcely any, and Carter says that
they do not even know the Moslem prayers, and are utterly
ignorant of the teachings of Mohammed.   Their dialect is soft
and sweet, and they themselves compare it to the language of
the birds; it is evidently a corrupted form of the ancient

[1] Notes on the Mahrah Tribe with vocabulary of their language; notes
on the Gharah tribe; geography of the southeast coast of Arabia;—July,
1845, July, 1847; and January, 1851, in the journal of the Society.

Himyaric and therefore of great importance in the study of philology.[1]

The Gharah tribe inhabit the coast between Moseirah island and the Kuria-Muria islands.   Their country is mountainous and cavernous and consists of a white stratified limestone formation 4,000 or 5,000 feet above the sea-level.   The upper part of the mountains are covered with good pasturage and their slopes with a dense thicket of small trees among which frankincense and other gum trees are plentiful.   The whole tribe are *troglodytes*, "cave-dwellers," since nature gives them better dwellings than the best mud-hut, and cooler than the largest tent of Kedar.   They are largely nomadic, however, and shift from cave to cave in their wanderings.   Their wardrobe is not an incumbrance as it consists of a single piece of coarse blue cotton wrapped around the loins like a short kilt. The women wear a loose frock of the same texture and color with wide sleeves, reaching a little below the knee in front and trailing on the ground behind ; the veil is unknown.   Children go about entirely naked.   Both men and women tattoo their cheeks.   For weapons they have swords, spears, daggers, and matchlocks.   Their food consists of milk, flesh and honey with the wild fruits of the mountains.

This entire region has been justly celebrated for honey since the days of the Greek geographers who enumerate honey and frankincense as its chief products.   The wild honey of South Arabia collected from the rocks and packed in large dry gourds, is fit for an epicure.   On Ptolemy's map of Arabia the region inland from this coast is called *Libanotopheros Regio*, the place of incense ; and by Pliny is termed *regio thurifera*, the region of frankincense.   From the earliest times this has been the country that produces real frankincense in abundance.   Once its export was a source of wealth to the inhabitants, for incense was used in the temples of Egypt and India as well as by the

[1] The most characteristic difference between Mahri and Arabic is the substitution of *Shin* (sh) for *Kaf* (k) in many words.

Jews, and by all the nations of antiquity. So important was this commerce in the early history of the world that Sprenger devotes several pages in his Ancient Geography of Arabia to describing the origin, extent, and influence of frankincense on civilization. The Arabs were then the general transport agents between the east and the west, *i. e.*, India and Egypt. The Queen of Sheba's empire grew rich in frankincense-trade; she brought to Solomon "spices in abundance," nor was there "any such spice" or brought in "such abundance" as that which Queen Sheba gave to Solomon. (B. C. cir. 992.)

The rise of Islam, the overthrow of the old Himyarite kingdom, the discovery of the passage round the Cape of Good Hope, all these coöperated to destroy the ancient importance and prosperity of Southern Arabia. At present, frankincense is still exported, but not in large quantities. The gum is procured by making incisions in the bark of the shrub in May and December. On its first appearance it comes forth white as milk, but soon hardens and discolors. It is then collected by men and boys, employed to look after the trees by the different families who own the land on which they grow.

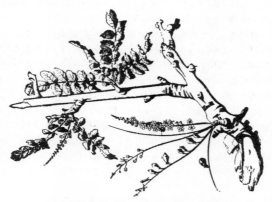

A BRANCH OF THE INCENSE TREE.

IX

THE LAND OF THE CAMEL

"To see real live dromedaries my readers must, I fear, come to Arabia, for these animals are not often to be met with elsewhere, not even in Syria; and whoever wishes to contemplate the species in all its beauty, must prolong his journey to Oman, which is for dromedaries, what Nejd is for horses, Cashmere for sheep, and Tibet for bulldogs."—*Palgrave.*

ALL Oman, but especially the region just described, is called among the Arabs *Um-el-ibl*, "mother of the camel." Palgrave, Doughty and other Arabian travellers agree that the Oman dromedary is the prince of all camel-breeds, and Doughty says they are so highly esteemed at Mecca as to fetch three times the price of other camels.

Unless one knows something about the camel one can neither understand the Arab nor his language; without the camel, life in a large part of Arabia would at present be impossible; without the camel the Arabic language would be vastly different. According to Hammer Purgstall, the Arabic dictionaries give this animal 5,744 different names; there is not a page in the lexicon but has some reference to the camel.

The Arabs highly value the camel, but do not admire its form and shape. There is an Arab tradition, cited in Burton's "Gold Mines of Midian," to the effect that when Allah determined to create the horse, He called the South Wind and said, "I desire to draw from thee a new being, condense thyself by parting with thy fluidity." The Creator then took a handful of this element, blew upon it the breath of life, and the noble quadruped appeared. But the horse complained against his Maker. His neck was too short to reach the distant grass blades on the march; his back had no hump to steady a saddle; his hoofs were sharp and sank deep into the sand; and

88

he added many similar grievances. Whereupon Allah created the camel to prove the foolishness of his complaint. The horse shuddered at the sight of what he wanted to become, and this is the reason every horse starts when meeting its caricature for the first time. The camel may not be beautiful, (although the Arabic lexicon shows that the words for "*pretty*" and "*camel*" are related) but he is surpassingly useful.

This animal is found in Persia, Asia Minor, Afghanistan, Beluchistan, Mongolia, Western China, Northern India, Syria, Turkey, North Africa and parts of Spain, but nowhere so generally or so finely developed as in Arabia. The two main species, not to speak of varieties, are the Southern, Arabian one-humped camel and the Northern, Bactrian two-humped camel. Each is specially adapted to its locality. The Bactrian camel is long-haired, tolerant of the intense cold of the steppes and is said to eat snow when thirsty. The Arabian species is short-haired, intolerant of cold, but able to endure thirst and extreme heat. It is incredible to Arabs that any camel-kind should have a double hump. A camel differs from a dromedary in nothing save blood and breed. The camel is a pack-horse; the dromedary a race-horse. The camel is thick-built, heavy-footed, ungainly, jolting; the dromedary has finer hair, lighter step, is easy of pace and more enduring of thirst. A caravan of camels is a freight-train; a company of Oman *thelul*-riders is a limited express. The ordinary caravan travels six hours a day and three miles an hour, but a good dromedary can run seventy miles a day on the stretch. A tradesman from Aneyza told Doughty that he had ridden from El Kasim to Taif and back, a distance of over 700 miles, in fifteen days ! Mehsan Allayda once mounted his dromedary after the Friday midday prayer at El-Aly and prayed the next Friday in the great Mosque at Damascus about 440 miles distant. The Haj-road post-rider at Ma'an can deliver a message at Damascus, it is said, at the end of three days; the distance is over 200 miles.

The Arabs have a saying that "the camel is the greatest of all blessings given by Allah to mankind." One is not surprised that the meditative youth of Mecca who led the camels of Khadiyah, to Syria and back by the desert way, should appeal to the unbelievers in Allah and His prophet in the words, "*And do ye not look then at the camel how she is created?*" (Surah lxxxviii. 17 of the Koran.)

To describe the camel is to describe God's goodness to the desert-dwellers. Everything about the animal shows evident design. His long neck, gives wide range of vision in desert marches and enables him to reach far to the meagre desert shrubs on either side of his pathway. The cartilaginous texture of his mouth, enables him to eat hard and thorny plants—the pasture of the desert. His ears are very small, and his nostrils large for breathing, but are specially capable of closure by valve-like folds against the fearful Simoon. His eyes are prominent, but protected by a heavy overhanging upper-lid, limiting vision upward thus guarding from the direct rays of the noon sun. His cushioned feet are peculiarly adapted for ease of the rider and the animal alike. Five horny pads are given him to rest on when kneeling to receive a burden or for repose on the hot sand. His hump is not a fictional but a *real* and acknowledged reserve store of nutriment as well as nature's packsaddle for the commerce of ages. His water reservoirs in connection with the stomach, enable him when in good condition to travel for five days without water. Again, the camel alone of all ruminants has incisor-teeth in the upper jaw, which, with the peculiar structure of his other teeth, make his bite, the animal's first and main defence, most formidable. The skeleton of the camel is full of proofs of design. Notice, for example, the arched backbone constructed in such a way as to sustain the greatest weight in proportion to the span of the supports; a strong camel can bear 1,000 pounds' weight, although the usual load in Oman is not more than 600 pounds.

The camel is a *domestic* animal in the full sense of the word,

for the Arabian domicile is indebted to the camel for nearly all
it holds.   All that can be obtained from the animal is of value.
Fuel, milk, excellent hair for tents, ropes, shawls and coarser
fabrics are obtained from the living animal; and flesh-food,
leather, bones and other useful substances from the dead.
Even the footprints of the camel though soon obliterated, are
of special value in the desert.   A lighter or smaller foot would
leave no tracks, but the camel's foot leaves data for the Bedouin
science of *Athar*—the art of navigation for the ship of the
desert.   Camel tracks are gossip and science, history and
philosophy to the Arab caravan.   A camel-march is the standard
measure of distance in all Arabia; and the price of a milch-
camel the standard of value in the interior.   When they have
little or no water the miserable nomads rinse their hands in
camel's water and the nomad women wash their babes in it.
Camel's-milk is the staple diet of thousands in Arabia even
though it be bitter because of wormwood pasturage.

As to the character of the camel and its good or evil nature
authorities differ.   Lady Ann Blunt considers the camel the
most abused and yet the most patient animal in existence.
Palgrave, on the other hand, thus describes the stupidity and
ugly temper of the beast: " I have, while in England, heard
and read more than once of the docile camel.   If docile means
stupid, well and good ; in such a case the camel is the very
model of docility.   But if the epithet is intended to designate
an animal that takes an interest in its rider so far as a beast can,
that obeys from a sort of submissive or half fellow-feeling with
its master, like the horse and elephant, then I say that the
camel is by no means docile, very much the contrary.   He
will never attempt to throw you off his back, such a trick being far beyond his limited comprehension ; but if you fall off,
he will never dream of stopping for you ; and if turned loose
it is a thousand to one he will never find his way back to his
accustomed home or pasture.   One only symptom will he give
that he is aware of his rider, and that is when the latter is

about to mount him, for on such an occasion, instead of ad-
dressing him in the style of Balaam's more intelligent beast,
'Am not I thy camel upon which thou hast ridden ever since
I was thine unto this day?' he will bend back his long snaky
neck toward his master, open his enormous jaws to bite, if he
dared, and roar out a tremendous sort of groan, as if to complain of some entirely new and unparalleled injustice about to be
done him.   In a word he is from first to last an undomesticated
and savage animal rendered serviceable by stupidity alone.
Neither attachment nor even habit can impress him; never
tame, though not wide-awake enough to be exactly wild."
We can bear witness that the camels we have ridden in
Hassa and Yemen were altogether more kindly than the ugly
creature of Palgrave.

The chief authorities on the interior of Oman were, until
recent date, Niebuhr, Wellsted (1835), Whitelock (1838),
Eloy (1843) and Palgrave, (1863).   Palgrave, however, only
visited the coast and his account of the interior and its history
is pure romance.   Later travellers have visited the chief cities
of Jebel Achdar and corroborated the accuracy of Lieutenant
Wellsted in his "Travels in Arabia."   Unfortunately Wellsted's acquaintance even with colloquial Arabic was very
limited and he frankly avows that he encountered serious difficulties in understanding the people.   "Wellsted's map," says
Badger, "is the only one of the province which we possess
drawn up from personal observation and   .   .   .   it affords little
or no certain indication of the numerous towns and villages
beyond the restricted routes of the travellers.   It is remarkable
and by no means creditable to the British Government in India,
that, notwithstanding our intimate political and commercial
relations with Oman, for the last century, we know actually
less of that country beyond the coast than we do of the Lake
districts of Africa." [1]   Badger wrote in 1860, but although
Colonel Miles and others have visited the region of Jebel

[1] " History of Oman."

Achdar, all the country beyond is still largely *terra incognita*. No one has ever made the journey beyond the range of mountains or solved the mystery of Western Oman, which is still a blank on the best maps; nor do we know anything of the land 100 miles southwest of Muscat, save by Arab hearsay.

The highlands of Oman may be divided into three districts; *Ja'alan* from Jebel Saffan to Jebel Fatlah on the east. *Oman* proper on the Jebel Achdar, and *Ez-Zahirah* on the eastern slopes of Jebel Okdat. The most populous and fertile district is that of Jebel Achdar which is also the best known. The fertility of the whole region is wonderful and in striking contrast with the barren rocks of so large a part of the coast. With a semi-tropical climate, an elevation of 3,000 to 5,000 feet and abundant springs the wadys and oases of Oman have awakened the delight and amazement of every traveller who has ventured to explore them. Water, the one priceless treasure in all Arabia, here issues in perennial streams from many rocky clefts and is most carefully husbanded by the ingenuity of the people, for wide irrigation, by means of canals or watercourses called *faluj*. Wellsted thus describes these underground aqueducts : "They are as far as I know peculiar to this country, and are made at an expense of labor and skill more Chinese than Arabian. The greater part of the surface of the land being destitute of running streams on the surface, the Arabs have sought in elevated places for springs or fountains beneath it. A channel from this fountain-head is then, with a very slight descent, bored in the direction in which it is to be conveyed, leaving apertures at regular distances to afford light and air to those who are occasionally sent to keep it clean. In this way the water is frequently conducted for a distance of six or eight miles, and an unlimited supply is thus obtained. These channels are about four feet broad and two feet deep and contain a clear, rapid stream. Most of the large towns or oases have four or five of these rivulets or *falj* (plural *faluj*) running into them. The isolated spots to which water is thus conveyed, possess a soil so fertile that nearly every grain, fruit or vegetable, common to India, Arab or Persia, is produced almost spontaneously ; and the tales of the oases will be no longer regarded as an exaggeration, since a single step conveys the traveller from the glare and sand of the desert into a fertile tract, watered by a hundred rills, teeming with the most luxurious vegetation.''

The chief caravan routes inland start from the coast, at Sohar through Wady-el-Jazy, at Suaik through Wady Thala, at Barka or Sib through Wady Mithaal and Wady Zailah (alternative routes) at Matra, by the same, and at Sur through Wady Falj. On the eastern side of the mountain range the chief towns are Rastak, Nakhl and Someil. On the farther side we have Tenoof, Behilah and Nezwa, all large towns well-watered. "Between these fertile oases one travels [1] sometimes an entire day through stony wady, or over volcanic rock, climbing a difficult mountain pass, or crossing a wide sea-like desert, without seeing a habitation or meeting a fellow-creature except an occasional caravan. Their rifles are swung over the shoulders of the riders, and their wild song keeps time with the slow tread of the camels. . . .

"From Nakhl it is a long day's journey to Lihiga at the foot of Jebel Achdar. Two other beautifully situated mountain villages, Owkan and Koia are in close proximity. Here, as well as on the mountains, dwells a tribe of hardy mountaineers, the Bni Ryam. In features and habits this tribe is quite distinct from the other Oman tribes. All over these mountains the people lead a peaceful life, and the absence of fire-arms was noticeable in comparison with the valley tribes, where each man carries his rifle, often of the best English or German pattern.

"From Lihiga we began the ascent, and after a half-a-day

---

[1] The remainder of the chapter is quoted from the letters of my brother, Rev. P. J. Zwemer, and the sketch of Tenoof was drawn by him on one of his journeys.

of most difficult climbing, reached the top of the pass at noonday, my barometer registering 7,050 feet. Here on a level
projecting rock, which afforded a splendid extended view of
the Wady Mestel, where dwell the Bni Ruweihah, we had our
lunch, and were glad to slake our thirst out of the goatskin
the guide carried on his shoulder. From the top of the pass
we descended to the level table-land at a height of 6,200 feet,
and at sunset reached the ideally beautiful village of Sheraegah.
It is in a circular ravine several hundred feet in depth, and like

TENOOF FROM THE EAST.
From a pencil sketch by Peter J. Zwemer.

a huge amphitheatre where grow in terraces, apples, peaches,
pomegranates, grapes and other temperate products in rich
profusion. Ice and snow are frequently seen here during the
winter, and in summer the temperature registers no higher than
80° F. In March we had a temperature of 40°, and enjoyed
a huge fire in the guest-room where a hundred Arabs came to
visit us, and entertained us with the recitation of Arabic
poetry. Such an opportunity was not to be neglected, and
they, as an agricultural people, were interested in the parable of
the Sower and the explanation. . . .

"We pressed on over the most difficult mountain roads to Tenoof, at the foot of the mountains on the further side. Nizwa, the old capital of Oman, is but three hours' journey from Tenoof. It has a large circular fort about 200 feet in diameter, built of rough hewn stone and cement. We intended to return to Muscat along the valley road via Someil, but the state of affairs at Nezwa made roads through hostile territory unsafe, and we decided to recross the mountains, enjoying again their cool climate and the friendliness of the people. By riding long camel-stages and taking short rests, we were able to reach Muscat from the top of the mountains in four days, having been absent on the journey twenty-one days."

X

THE PEARL ISLANDS OF THE GULF

"'We are all from the highest to the lowest slaves of one master—Pearl,' said Mohammed bin Thanee to me one evening; nor was the expression out of place. All thought, all conversation, all employment, turns on that one subject; everything else is mere by-game, and below even secondary consideration."—*Palgrave*.

HALF way down the Persian Gulf, off the east Arabian coast, between the peninsula of El Katar and the Turkish province of El Hassa, are the islands of Bahrein.[1] This name was formerly applied to the entire triangular projection on the coast between the salt-sea of the gulf and the fresh water flood of the Euphrates; hence its name *Bahr-ein* "the two seas." But since the days of Burckhardt's map the name is restricted to the archipelago. The larger island is itself often called Bahrein, while the next in size is named Moharrek—"place of burning." The Arabs say that this was so named because the Hindu traders used it for cremating their dead.

The main island is about twenty-seven miles in length from

---

[1] These islands are identified by Sprenger and others with Dedan of the Scriptures, (*Ezekiel* xxvii. 15), and were known to the Romans by the name of Tylos. Pliny writes of the cotton-trees, "*arbores vocant gossympinos fertiliore etiam Tylo minore.*"—(xii. 10). Strabo describes the Phœnician temples that existed on the islands, and Ptolemy speaks of the pearl-fisheries which from time immemorial flourished along these coasts. The geographer, Juba, also tells of a battle fought off the islands between the Romans and the Arabs. Ptolemy's ancient map shows how little was known as to the size or location of the group. Even Niebuhr's map, which is wonderfully correct in the main, makes a great error in the position of the islands; in his day the two principal islands were called Owal and Arad, names which still linger.

MAP OF THE
ISLANDS OF
BAHREIN.

north to south, and ten miles in breadth. Toward the centre
there is a slightly elevated table-land, mostly barren. Twelve
miles from the northern end is a clump of dark volcanic hills,
400 feet high, called Jebel Dokhan, "Mountain of Smoke."
The northern half of the island is well watered by abundant
fresh-water springs, always luke-warm in temperature. This
part of the island is covered with beautiful gardens of date-

palms, pomegranate, and other trees. The coast is everywhere low, and the water shallow for a long distance. There is no pier or jetty anywhere, so that, except at high water, boats anchor nearly a quarter of a mile from the shore.

The total population of the islands is estimated at nearly 60,000, all of them Moslems with the exception of about 100 Banian traders from Sindh, India. Menamah, the large town on the northeast point of the island, with perhaps 10,000 inhabitants, is built along the shore for about a mile ; the houses are mostly poor, many being mere mat-huts. This town is the market-place and commercial centre for the whole group. Here is the post office and custom-house and here the bulk of the trade is carried on for the whole island. A short distance from Menamah is the old town of Belad le Kadim, with ruins of better buildings and a fine mosque with two minarets. The mosque is of very early date, for the older Cufic character is on all its inscriptions, covered over in some places by more recent carving and inscriptions in later Arabic.

The largest spring on the islands is called El Adhari, "the virgins." It issues from a reservoir thirty yards across, and at least thirty feet deep, flowing in a stream six or eight feet wide and two feet deep. This is remarkable for Arabia, and gives some idea of the abundant supply of water. Under the sea, near the island of Moharrek, are fresh-water springs always covered with a fathom of salt water. The natives lower a hollow, weighted bamboo through which the fresh water gushes out a few inches above sea-level. The source of these fresh-water springs of Bahrein must be on the mainland of Arabia, as all the opposite coast shows a similar phenomena. Apparently the *River Aftan* marked on old maps of the peninsula as emptying into the Persian Gulf near Bahrein was an *underground river*, known to the older geographers.

If Egypt is the gift of the Nile, Bahrein may well be called the gift of the pearl-oyster. Nothing else gave the islands their ancient history, and nothing so much gives them their

present importance.   The pearl-fisheries are the one great industry of Bahrein.   They are carried on every year from June
until October, and even for a longer period, if hot weather sets
in earlier.   Nearly all the island population are engaged in the
work in some way, and during the season there is only one
topic of conversation in the coffee-shops and the evening-
mejlis,—PEARLS.   The pearl has this distinction above all
other precious stones, that it requires no human hand to bring
out its beauties.   By modern scientists, pearls are believed to
be the result of an abnormal secretion, caused by the irritation
of the mollusk's shell by some foreign substance—in short, a
disease of the pearl-oyster.   But it is not surprising that the
Arabs have many curious superstitions as to the cause of pearl-
formation.   Their poets tell of how the monsoon rains falling
on the banks of Ceylon and Bahrein find chance lodgment in
the opened mouth of the pearl-oyster.   Each drop distills a
gem, and the size of the raindrop determines the luck of the
future diver.   Heaven-born and cradled in the deep blue sea,
it is the purest of gems and, in their eyes, the most precious.

Not only in its creation, but in its liberation from its prison-
house under ten fathoms of water the pearl costs pain and sacrifice.   So far as this can be measured in pounds, shillings and
pence, this cost is easy of computation.   The total value of
pearls exported from Bahrein in 1896 was £303,941 sterling
($1,500,000).   The number of boats from Bahrein engaged
in the fisheries is about nine hundred and the cost of bringing
one boat's share to the surface is 4,810 rupees (about $1,600).[1]
Hundreds of craft also come to the oyster-banks from other
ports on the gulf.   It is scarcely necessary to say that the
pearl divers do not receive the amount fairly due them for their
toil.   They are one and all victims of the " truck-system " in
its worst form, being obliged to purchase all supplies, etc.,

---

[1] This cost is divided as follows: Fishing smack *r.* 400; wages of 10
divers *r.* 2,000; wages of 12 rope-holders *r.* 2,400; apparatus *r.* 40.
Total *rupees* 4,810.

THE VILLAGE OF MENAMAH, BAHREIN ISLANDS

A BAHREIN HARBOR BOAT

from their masters.   They are consequently so much in debt
to him as often to make them practically his slaves.   The boats
are generally owned by the merchants, and the crew are paid
at a low rate for a whole year's work, only receiving a small
extra allowance when they bring up pearls of special size or
brilliancy.   In the winter season these divers are out of work,
and consequently incur large debts which are charged to the
next season's account.   By force of circumstances and age-
long practice the islanders are also much given to the vice of
gambling on the market.   Even the poorest fisherman will lay
his wager—and lose it.   It is not the thirty thousand fishermen
of the gulf with their more than five thousand boats who grow
rich in the pearl-fishing business; the real profit falls to those
who remain on shore—the Arab and Hindu brokers of Bombay
who deal direct with Berlin, London and Paris.   A pearl often
trebles in value by changing hands, even before it reaches the
Bombay market.

The divers follow the most primitive method in their work.
Their boats are such as their ancestors used before the Portuguese were expelled from Bahrein in 1622.   Even Sinbad the
sailor might recognize every rope and the odd spoon-shaped
oars.   These boats are of three kinds, very similar in general
appearance, but differing in size, called *Bakāret, Shua'ee* and
Bateel.[1]   All of the boats have good lines and are well-built
by the natives from Indian timber.   For the rest, all is of
Bahrein manufacture except their pulley-blocks, which come
from Bombay.   Sailcloth is woven at Menamah and ropes are
twisted of date-fibre in rude rope-walks which have no machinery worth mentioning.   Even the long, soft iron nails that
hold the boats together are hammered out on the anvil one by
one by Bahrein blacksmiths.

Each boat has a sort of figure-head, called the *kubait*, generally covered with the skin of a sheep or goat which was

[1] The *Mashooah* is a much smaller boat, like the English jolly-boat, and
is used in the harbor and for short journeys around the islands.

sacrificed when the boat was first launched.   This is one of the
Semitic traits which appear in various forms all over Arabia—
blood-sacrifice—and which has Islam never uprooted.   All the
fishermen prefer to go out in a boat which has cut a covenant
of blood with Neptune.   The larger boats used in diving hold
from twenty to forty men, less than half of whom are divers,
while the others are rope-holders and oarsmen.   One man in
each boat is called *El Müsülly*, *i. e.*, the one-who-prays, because his sole daily duty is to take charge of the rope of any
one who stops to pray or eat.   He has no regular work, and
when not otherwise engaged vicariously mends ropes and sails
or cooks the rice and fish over charcoal embers.   He is therefore also called *El Gillās*, "the sitter," very suggestive of his
sinecure office.

  The divers wear no elaborate diving-suit, but descend
clothed only in their *fitaam* and *khabaat*.   The first is a true
pince-nez or clothespin-like clasp for their nostrils.   It is
made of two thin slices of horn fastened together with a rivet
or cut out whole in a quarter circle so as to fit the lower
part of the nose and keep out the water.   It has a perforated
head through which a string passes and which suspends it from
the divers neck when not in use.   *Khabaat* are "finger-hats"
made of leather and thrice the length of an ordinary thimble.
They are worn to protect the fingers in gathering the pearl-
shells from the sea-bottom; at the height of the pearl season
large baskets full of all sizes of these finger-caps are exposed
for sale in the bazaar.   Each diver uses two sets (*twenty*) in a
season.   A basket, called *dajeen*, and a stone-weight complete
the diver's outfit.   This stone, on which the diver stands when
he plunges down feet-first, is fastened to a rope passing between his toes and is immediately raised; another rope is attached to the diver and his basket by which he gives the signal
and is drawn up.   The best divers remain below only two or
three minutes at most, and when they come up are nine-tenths
suffocated.   Many of them are brought up unconscious and

often cannot be brought to life.   Deafness, and suppuration of
the ear, due to carelessness or perforated ear-drums, caused by
the enormous pressure of the water at such depths, are common among divers.   Rheumatism and neuralgia are universal
and the pearl-fishers are the great exception among the Arabs
in not possessing beautiful teeth.

Sharks are plentiful and it is not a rare thing for them to attack divers.   But the Bahrein divers are more fearful of a
small species of devil-fish which lays hold of any part of the
body and draws blood rapidly.   Against this monster of the
sea they guard themselves by wearing an "overall" of white
cloth during the early part of the season when it frequents the
banks.   Their tales of horror regarding the devil-fish equal
those of Victor Hugo in his "Toilers of the Sea."

The divers remain out in their boats as long as their supply
of fresh water lasts, often three weeks or even more.   Sir
Edwin Arnold's lines are thus not as correct as they are beautiful :

> "Dear as the wet diver to the eyes
> Of his pale wife who waits and weeps on shore
> By sands of Bahrein in the Persian Gulf ;
> Plunging all day in the blue waves ; at night,
> Having made up his tale of precious pearls,
> Rejoins her in their hut upon the shore."

When the pearl-oysters are brought up they are left on deck
over night and the next morning are opened by means of a
curved knife, six inches long, called *miflaket*.   Before the days
of English commerce the mother-of-pearl was thrown away as
worthless.   Now it has a good market-value and (after being
scraped free of the small parasites that infest the outer shell) is
packed in wooden crates and exported in large quantities.   The
total value of this export in 1897 was £5,694 ($28,000).
The Arabs have asked me in amazement what in the world the
"Franks" do with empty sea-shells; and some tell idle tales of

how they are ground up into pearl dust and pressed into artificial gems, or are used as a veneer to cover brick houses.

On shore the pearls are classified by the merchants, according to weight, size, shape, color and brilliancy. There are button-pearls, pendants, roundish, oval, flat, and perfect pearls; pearls, white, yellow, golden, pink, blue, azure, green, grey, dull and black; seed-pearls the size of grains of sand and pearls as large as an Arab's report, emphasized with frequent *wallahs*, can make them. I have seen a pendant pearl the size of a hazelnut worth a few thousand rupees but there are Arabs who will swear by the prophet's beard (each hair of which is sacred !) that they have brought up pearls as large as a pigeon's egg. The pearl brokers carry their wares about tied in bags of turkey-red calico; they weigh them in tiny brass scales and learn their exact size by an ingenious device consisting of a nest of brass sieves, called *taoos*, six in number, with apertures slightly differing in size. The pearls are put into the largest sieve first; those that do not fall through its pea-sized holes are called, *Ras*, "chief"; such are generally pearls of great price, although their value depends most on weight and perfection of form. The second size is called *Batu* "belly," and the third *Dhail*, "tail." Color has only a fashion-value; Europe prefers white and the Orient the golden-yellow; black pearls are not highly esteemed by Orientals.

Before they are shipped the large pearls are cleaned in *reeta* a kind of native soap-powder, and the smaller ones in soft brown sugar; then they are tied up in calico and sold in lots by weight, each bundle being supposed to contain pearls of average equal value. How it is possible to collect custom dues on *pearls* among a people whose consciences rival their wide breast-pockets in concealing capacity, surpasses comprehension. But the thing is done, for the farmer of the custom dues grows rich and the statistics of export are not pure guess-work.

The Bahrein islands also produce quantities of dates, and there is an export trade in a remarkably fine breed of asses, celebrated all over the Persian Gulf. A good Bahrein donkey is easy to ride and almost as good a roadster as an average horse. The only manufactures, beside sail-sheeting, are coarse cloth for turbans, and reed-mats of very fine texture. The chief imports are rice, timber and piece-goods for which Bahrein is the depot for all eastern Arabia. Three sights are shown to the stranger-tourist to the islands of Bahrein : the pearl-fisheries, the fresh-water springs, and the ancient ruins of an early civilization at the village of Ali. These ruins are the " *bayoot el owalin* " the dwellings of the first inhabitants, who are believed to have been destroyed by Allah because of their wickedness. An hour's ride through the date gardens and past the minarets brings us to the village of Ali. It can generally be seen from a good distance because of the smoke which rises from the huge ovens where pottery is baked. The potter turns his wheel to-day and fashions the native water-jars with deft hand utterly ignorant and careless of the curious sepulchral tumuli which cast their shade at his feet. South and west of the village the whole plain is studded with mounds, at least three hundred of them, the largest being about forty feet in height. Only two or three have ever been opened or explored. Theodore Bent in company with his wife explored these in 1889, with meagre results, but no further investigations have been made though it is a field that may yet yield large results. M. Jules Oppert, the French Assyriologist, and others regard the island as an extremely old centre of civilization and it is now well known that the first settlements from ancient Babylonia were in the Persian Gulf which then extended as far north as Mugheir, near Suk-es Shiukh. But those first settlers probably went to the coasts of Africa and to the kingdoms of Southern Arabia, in which case Bahrein was on their line of travel. It must always have been a depot for shipping because of its abundant water-supply in a region where fresh-water is generally scarce. The mounds at Ali probably date from this very early period ; although no corroboration in the shape of cylinders or bricks bearing inscriptions has yet been found, the character of the structures found in the mounds is undoubted proof of their great antiquity.

The larger mound opened by Bent, now consists of two rock-built chambers of very large stones, square masonry, and no trace of an arch or a pillar. The lower chamber is twenty-eight feet in length, five feet in width, and eight feet high ; it has four niches or recesses about three feet deep, two at the end of the passage and two near its entrance. The upper chamber is of the same length as the lower, but its width is six inches less, and its height only four feet eight inches. The lower passage is hand plastered as an impression of the mason's hand on the side wall still proves. If diggings were made *below* the mounds or other mounds were opened better results might follow, and perhaps inscriptions or cylinders would be discovered. A year or two ago a jar containing a large number of gold coins was found near Ali by some native workmen ; these however were Cufic and of a much later period than the mounds. Near Yau and Zillag, on the other side of the island there are also ruins and very deep wells cut through solid rock with *deep* rope-marks on the curbing; perhaps these also are of early date. On the island of Moharrek there is a place called *Ed Dair*, "the monastery" with ruins of what the Arabs call a church; whether this is of Portuguese date like the castle or goes back to a much earlier period before Mohammed, we cannot tell.

The climate of Bahrein is not as bad as it is often described by casual visitors. No part of the Persian Gulf can be called a health resort, but neither is the climate unhealthful at all seasons of the year. In March and April, October, November and December the weather is delightful, indoor temperatures seldom rising above 85° F., or falling below 60° F. When north winds blow in January and February it is often cold enough for a fire ; these are the rainy months of the year and least healthful, especially to the natives in their badly-built mat-huts. From May to September inclusive is the hot season, although the nights remain cool and the heat is tempered by sea-breezes (called, *El Barih*), until the middle of June. Heavy dews at night are common and make the atmosphere murky and oppressive when there is no sea-breeze. Land-breezes from the west and south continue irregularly throughout the entire summer. When they fail the thermometer leaps to over one hundred and remains there day and night until the ripples on the stagnant, placid sea proclaim a respite from the torture of sweltering heat. A record of temperature, kept at Menamah village in the summer of 1893, shows a minimum indoor temperature of 85° and a maximum of 107° F., in the shade. The prevailing wind at Bahrein, and in fact all over the Gulf, is the *shemmāl* or Northwester changing its direction slightly with the trend of the coast. The air during a shem-māl is generally very dry and the sky cloudless, but in winter they are sometimes at first accompanied by rain-squalls. In winter they are very severe and endanger the shipping. The only other strong wind is called *kaus*; it is a southeaster and blows irregularly from December to April. It is generally accompanied by thick, gloomy weather, with severe squalls and falling barometer. The saying among sailors that "there is always too much wind in the Gulf or none at all," is very true of Bahrein.

This saying holds true also of the political history of the Gulf. Bahrein, because of its pearl-trade has ever been worth contending for and it has been a bone of contention among the neighboring rulers ever since the naval battle fought by the early inhabitants against the Romans. After Mohammed's day the Carmathians overran the islands. Portuguese, Arabs from Oman, Persians, Turks and lastly the English have each in turn claimed rule or protection over the archipelago. It is sufficient to note here that in 1867, 'Isa bin Ali (called *Esau* in Curzon's "Persia," as if the name came from Jacob's brother instead of the Arab form of Jesus!) was appointed ruling

Sheikh by the British who deposed his father Mohammed bin Khalifa for plotting piracy.

The present Sheikh is a typical Arab and spends most of his time in hawking and the chase; the religious rule, which in a Moslem land means the judicial and executive department, rests with the *Kadi* or Judge.   There is no legislature as the law was laid down once for all in the Koran and the traditions. The administration of *justice* is rare.   Oppression, black-mail and bribery are universal; and, except in commerce and the slave-trade, English protection has brought about no reforms on the island.   To be "protected" means here strict neutrality as to the internal affairs and absolute dictation as to affairs with other governments.   To "protect" means to keep matters in *status quo* until the hour is ripe for annexation. Sometimes the process from the one to the other is so gradual as to resemble growth; in such a case it would be correct to speak of the growth of the British Empire.

Contact with Europeans and western civilization has, however, done much for Bahrein in the matter of disarming prejudice and awakening the sluggish mind of the Arab to look beyond his own "Island of the Arabs."   Even as early as 1867, Palgrave could write: "From the maritime and in a manner central position of Bahreyn my readers may of themselves conjecture that the profound ignorance of Nejd regarding Europeans and their various classifications is here exchanged for a partial acquaintance with those topics; thus, English and French, disfigured into the local *Ingleez* and *Francees* are familiar words at Menamah, though Germans and Italians, whose vessels seldom or never visit these seas, have as yet no place in the Bahreyn vocabulary; while Dutch and Portuguese seem to have fallen into total oblivion.   But Russians or *Moskop*, that is Muscovites, are alike known and feared, thanks to Persian intercourse and the instinct of nations.   Beside the policy of Constantinople and Teheran are freely and at times sensibly discussed in these coffee-houses no less than the stormy diplomacy of Nejd and her dangerous en-croachments.''

To the Bahrein Arabs Bombay is the centre of the world of civilization, and he who has seen that city is distinguished as knowing all about the ways of foreigners. So anxious are the boys for a trip on the British India steamer to this Eldorado of science and mystery that they sometimes run from home and go as stowaways or beg their passage. This close contact with India has had its effect on the Arabic spoken on the island which, although not a dialect, is full of Hindustani words. Of late years there has been a considerable Persian immigration into Bahrein from the coast between Lingah and Bushire, and next to Arabic, Persian is the language most in use.

XI

THE EASTERN THRESHOLD OF ARABIA

BEYOND Bahrein the mainland stretches westward for eight hundred miles across the province of Hassa and lower Nejd and Hejaz to the Red Sea. As Jiddah is the western port, Bahrein is the eastern port for all Arabia. It is the gateway to the interior, the threshold of which is Hassa. Draw a line from Menamah to Katif, then on to Hofhoof (or El Hassa) and thence back to Menamah, and the triangle formed will include every important town or village of Eastern Arabia. North of that triangle on the coast is the inhospitable barren, thinly populated, country of the Bni Hajar; south of it is the peninsula of El Katar; westward stretches the sandy desert for five days' marches to Riad and the old Wahabi country. The region thus bounded is really the whole of Hassa, although on maps that name is given to the whole coast as far as Busrah. But neither the authority of the Turkish government nor the significance of the word *Hassa* (low, moist ground) can be said to extend outside of the triangle.

The peninsula of El Katar, about 100 miles long and fifty broad, is unattractive in every way and barren enough to be called a desert. Palgrave's pen-picture cannot be improved upon: "To have an idea of Katar my readers must figure to themselves miles on miles of low barren hills, bleak and sun-scorched, with hardly a single tree to vary the dry monotonous outline; below these a muddy beach extends for a quarter of a mile seaward in slimy quicksands, bordered by a rim of sludge and seaweed. If we look landwards beyond the hills we see what by extreme courtesy may be called pasture land, dreary downs with twenty pebbles for every blade of grass;

110

NEIBUHR'S MAP OF THE PERSIAN GULF

and over this melancholy ground scene, but few and far between, little clusters of wretched, most wretched earth cot-
tages and palm-leaf huts, narrow, ugly and low; these are the
villages, or 'towns' (for so the inhabitants style them) of
Katar. Yet poor and naked as is the land it has evidently
something still poorer and nakeder behind it, something in
short even more devoid of resources than the coast itself, and
the inhabitants of which seek here by violence what they cannot find at home. For the villages of Katar are each and all
carefully walled in, while the downs beyond are lined with
towers and here and there a castle, huge and square with its
little windows and narrow portals."

The population of Katar is not large; its principal town is
Bedaa'. All the inhabitants live from the sea by pearl-diving
and fishing, and in the season send out two hundred boats.
The whole peninsula with its wild Bedouin population is
claimed by Turkey and is the dread of the miserable soldiers
who are sent there to preserve peace and draw precarious pay
while they shake with malaria and grow homesick for Bagdad.
The Arabs are always at feud with the government and it is
very unsafe outside the walls after sunset.

The usual route from Bahrein to the interior of Hassa is to
cross over by boat to Ojeir on the mainland, and thence to
travel by caravan to Hofhoof. In October, 1893, I took this
route, returning from the capital to Katif and thence back to
Menamah. Embarking at sunset we landed at Ojeir before
dawn the next day and I found my way to a Turkish custom-
house officer to whom I had a friendly letter from a Bahrein
merchant. Ojeir, although it has neither a bazaar nor any
settled population, has a mud-fort, a dwarf flagstaff and an imposing custom-house. The harbor although not deep is protected against north and south winds and is therefore a good
landing-place for the immense quantity of rice and piece-goods
shipped from Bahrein into the interior. A caravan of from
two to three hundred camels leaves Ojeir every week. For

although the Jebel Shammar country is probably supplied overland from Busrah and Bagdad, the whole of Southern Nejd receives piece-goods, coffee, rice, sugar and Birmingham wares
by way of Bahrein and Ojeir.

The whole plain in and about the custom-house was piled
with bales and boxes and the air filled with the noise of load-
ing seven hundred camels.   I struck a bargain with Salih, a
Nejdi, to travel in his party and before noon-prayers we were
off.   The country for many hours was bare desert, here and
there a picturesque ridge of sand, and in one place a vein of
greenish limestone.   When night came we all stretched a
blanket on the clean sand and slept in the open air ; those who
had neglected their water-skins on starting now satisfied thirst
by scooping a well with their hands three or four feet deep and
found a supply of water.   During the day the sun was hot and
the breeze died away; but at night, under the sparkling stars
and with a north wind it seemed, by contrast, bitterly cold.
On the second day at noon we sighted the palm-forests that
surround Hofhoof and give it, Palgrave says, "the general
aspect of a white and yellow onyx chased in an emerald rim."
As we did not reach the "emerald rim" until afternoon I
concluded to remain at Jifr, one of the many suburb villages.
Here Salih had friends, and a delicious dinner of bread, butter, milk and dates, all fresh, was one of many tokens of hospitality.   At sunset we went on to the next village, Menazeleh,
a distance of about three miles through gardens and rushing
streams of tepid water.   The next morning early we again rode
through gardens and date-orchards half visible in the morning
mist.   At seven o'clock the mosques and walls of Hofhoof appeared right before us as the sun lifted the veil ; it was a beautiful sight.

El Hofhoof can claim a considerable age.   Under the
name of Hajar, it was next to Mobarrez, the citadel town of the
celebrated Bni Kindi and Abd El Kais (570 A. D.).   Both of
these towns, and in fact every village of Hassa, owe their

existence to the underground watercourses, which are the
chief characteristic of the province; everywhere there is the
same abundance of this great blessing.   A land of streams and
fountains,—welling up in the midst of the salt sea, as at
Bahrein; flowing unknown and unsought under the dry desert
at Ojeir; bubbling up in perennial fountains as at Katif; or
bursting out in seven hot springs that flow, cooling, to bless
wide fields of rice and wheat at Mobarrez.   The entire region

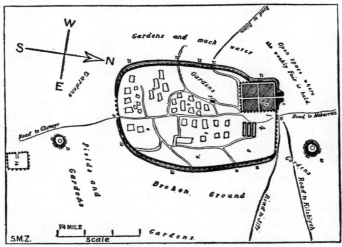

PALGRAVE'S PLAN OF HOFHOOF.

is capable of rich cultivation, and yet now more than half of it
is desert.   There is not a man to till the ground, and paradise
lies waste except near the villages.   Elsewhere Bedouin robbers
and Turkish taxes prevent cultivation.   *These two are the
curse of agriculture all over the Ottoman provinces of Arabia.*

Hofhoof itself is surrounded by gardens, and its plan gives
a good idea of the general character of the towns of Arabia.
A castle or ruler's house; a bazaar with surrounding dwellings
and a mud-wall built around to protect the whole.   The moat

is now dry and half filled in with the débris of the walls, which are not in good repair. The town is nearly a mile and a-half across at its greater diameter, but the houses are not built as close together as is the custom in most Oriental towns; here is the pleasant feature of gardens *inside* the walls. The date-palm predominates, and indeed comes to wonderful perfection, but the nabak, the papay, the fig and the pomegranate are also in evidence. Indigo is cultivated, and also cotton, while all the region round about is green with fields of rice and sugar-cane and vegetables,—onions, radishes, beans, vetches, and maize.

The population of the city is entirely Moslem, except one Roman Catholic Christian, who is the Turkish doctor, and a half dozen Jews. The three Europeans who have previously visited and described Hofhoof are, Captain Sadlier (1819), Palgrave (1863), and Colonel Pelly (1865). The first gives the population at 15,000 and Palgrave speaks of 20,000 to 30,000. In 1871 when the Turkish expedition against Nejd took the city, they reported it to have 15,000 houses and 200 suburb villages (!) This shows the absolute uncertainty of most statistics in regard to Arabia.

El Hassa (Hofhoof) is the first stage on the direct caravan route from east Arabia to Mecca and Jiddah. Abd Er Rahman bin Salama, the Arab Sheikh, under the Turkish governor of the Rifa'a quarter of the town gave me the following information regarding this route. From Hassa to Riad is six days by camel; from Riad to Jebel Shammar nine days; to Wady Dauasir seven; and from Riad to Mecca eighteen days. That would be *twenty-eight days* to cross the peninsula, not including stops on the road and travelling at the rate of an ordinary caravan, *i. e.*, three miles an hour.

The Kaisariyeh or bazaar of Hofhoof is well supplied with all the usual requirements and luxuries of the Levant; weapons, cloth, gold embroidery, dates, vegetables, dried fish, wood, salted locusts, fruit, sandals, tobacco, copper-ware and piece-goods—in irregular confusion as enumerated. Public auctions are held frequently in the square or on the plain outside the walls. Here, too, the barbers ply their trade, and blacksmiths beat at their anvils under the shade of a date-hut. The Rifa'a quarter has the *best* houses, while the Na'athal has the largest number; the "East-end" in Hofhoof being for the rich and the "West-end" for the poor, as is proper in a land of paradoxes.

Hassa is celebrated for two sorts of manufacture; cloaks or *abbas*, with rich embroidery in gold and colored thread, delicately wrought and of elegant pattern, the gayest and costliest garments of Arabia; and brass coffee-pots of curious shape and pretty form, which, with the cloaks, are exported all over Eastern Arabia, even as far as Busrah and Muscat. Once trade flourished and the merchants grew rich in this land of easy agriculture and fertile soil. But intestine wars, Wahabi fanaticism and Turkish indolence, extortion and taxation have taken away prosperity, and Hassa's capital is not what it was in the days of old, when the Carmathians held the town.

One remnant of its former glory remains; a unique and entirely local coinage called the *Toweelah* or "long-bit." It consists of a small copper-bar, mixed with a small proportion of silver, about an inch in length, split at one end and with a fissure slightly opened. Along one or both of its flattened sides run a few Cufic characters, nearly illegible in most specimens, but said to read: *Mohammed-al-Saood*, *i.e.*, "Mohammed of the Saood family." The coin has neither date nor motto, but was undoubtedly made by one of the Carmathian Princes about the year 920 A. D. This Moslem sect owed its origin to a fanatic and enthusiast born at Cufa, called Carmath, who first had a following about the year 277 of the Hejira. He assumed the lofty titles, Guide, Director, the Word, the Holy Ghost, the Herald of the Messiah, etc. His interpretation of the Koran was very lax in the matters of ablution, fasting, and pilgrimage, but he increased the number of prayers to fifty daily. He had twelve apostles among the Bedouins, and his sect grew so rapidly that they could muster in the field 107,000 fanatical warriors. Cufa and Busrah were pillaged and Bagdad taken. In 929 Abu Taher stormed the Holy City of Mecca and the Carmathians took away the black stone in triumph to Katif. The centre of their power remained at Hassa for some years. Here the coin was struck, which is the only remnant of their power and fanaticism. And while the Carmathian doctrines are held in abhorrence, their little bars of copper still buy rice and dates and stick to the hands of the money-changer in the bazaar.

In former days there were gold and silver coins of similar shape. Some in silver can yet be found occasionally inscribed with the noble motto in Arabic: *" Honor to the sober man, dishonor to the ambitious."* When I was in Hofhoof that strange, two-tailed copper-bar was worth half an anna and disputed its birthright in the market with rupees and Indian paper and Maria Theresa dollars and Turkish coppers. But how changed the bazaar itself would appear to the ghost of some Carmathian warrior of the ninth century who first handled a "long-bit." Even the Wahabis have disappeared and tobacco, silk, music and wine are no longer deadly sins. Of these Moslem Puritans many have left for Riad, and the few that remain stroke their long white beards in horror at Turkish Effendis in infidel breeches smoking cigarettes, while they sigh for the golden days of the Arabian Reformer.

There is a military hospital at Hofhoof with a surgeon and doctor, but at the time of my visit there was a dearth of medicines and an abominable lack of sanitation. Few soldiers submit to hospital treatment, preferring to desert or seek furlough elsewhere, and nothing is done for the Arab population. Before my coming cholera raged here as well as on the coast, and during my short visit smallpox was epidemic and carried off many, many children. Thrice awful are such diseases in a land where a practical fanaticism, under the pious cloak of religion, scorns medicine or preventive measures.

The government of the province of Hassa is as follows. The *Sandjak* (Turkish for administrative division) is divided into three *cazas*, Nejd, Katar and Katif and a small garrison holds each of these cazas; 600 men at Hofhoof, and 300 at Katar and Katif. The governor, called Mutaserrif Pasha, resides at the capital and. *kaimakams* or sub-governors at the other two centres. There are the usual Turkish tribunals and each Arab tribe has a representative or go-between to arrange its affairs with the governor. The principal tribes which at present acknowledge Turkish occupation and submit to their rule are: El Ajeman, El Morah, Bni Hajar, Bni Khaled, Bni Hassam, El Motter, El Harb, and El Ja'afer. The Turkish government has opened three schools in the province; the total number of pupils according to the Turkish official report is 3,540. The same report puts the entire population of the province at 250,000; this gives a fair idea of the backwardness of education even in this province which has always been re-markable for book-learning. The large mosque with its twenty-four arches and porticoes, smooth-plastered and with a mat-spread floor is always full of mischievous youth learning the mysteries of grammar and the commonplaces of Moslem theology; but the days of poetry and writing of commentaries on the Koran are in the past; even the Wahabi merchants talk of Bombay and are glad to get hold of an English primer or an atlas of the new world which is knocking at their door for admittance.

After four days spent in the city I accepted an opportunity to return northward with a caravan; I was not allowed to go, however, until after I had signed a paper, which, because of the unsafety of the road disclaimed all responsibility on the part of the Government should I come to lose life, limb or luggage. A copy of this document is in my possession, but the only foe I met in the desert was—fever. On Tuesday noon our small party set out, not going through the large town of Mobarrez as I had hoped, but turning east and reaching Kilabeejeh at two o'clock.

We passed fountains and streams and fields of rice and swamps,—everything very unlike Arabia of the school-geography. In four hours, however, we were again in the midst of desert where the sun proved too hot for me and I was taken with a fever which did not leave me until I returned to Bahrein. The road continued desert all the way to Katif. On Wednesday we rode all night under the stars (because of a false alarm of robbers) until nine o'clock next morning. Then we rested at a place called, with bitter irony, Um El Hammam; there are no *baths*, no trees, no grass, only a shallow pit of dirty water and small shrubbery of dates. Here we spent a hot day. On Friday morning we came to the borders of Katif,—palm-groves, wells, and ancient aqueducts with curious towers and air-holes at intervals. Through gardens and around by the large square fort we came to the sea. At the custom-house, again, I found rest and refreshment.

Katif has no good name among Hassa Arabs; its location is low and marshy; "its inhabitants are mostly weak in frame, sallow in complexion, and suffer continually from malaria. The town itself is badly built, woefully filthy, damp and ill-favored in climate. Yet it has a good population and brisk trade. The inhabitants are mostly Shiahs of Persian origin and are held in abhorrence by the Wahabis and the Turks alike as little better than infidels. The present location of Katif corresponds to the very ancient settlement of the *Gerrha* of the Greek geographers but no exploration for ruins has ever been made. A Portuguese castle marks *their* occupation of this coast also during their supremacy in the gulf. Katif was taken by the Turks in 1871 and has been occupied by them ever since.

The Arabian coast north of Katif, all the way to Kuweit is without a single large settlement. Mostly barren and in the hands of the predatory and warlike tribe of Bni Hajar, it is very uninteresting and entirely unproductive.

XII

THE RIVER-COUNTRY AND THE DATE-PALM

"The rich plains of Mesopotamia and Assyria which were once cultivated by a populous nation and watered by surprising efforts of human
industry, are now inhabited, or rather ravaged by wandering Arabs. So
long as these fertile provinces shall remain under the government, or
rather anarchy of the Turks they must continue deserts in which nature
dies for want of the fostering care of man."—*Niebuhr* (1792).

WHAT changes of history have left their records in ruins
and names and legends on the great alluvial plains
of Northeastern Arabia! The two rivers still bear their
Bible names, the Euphrates and *Dijleh*, or Hiddekel, but
nothing else is left which could be called paradise. What
impresses the traveller first and most is that so large an extent
of this fertile region lies waste and unproductive under an
effete rule. The splendor of the past can scarcely be believed
because of the ruin of the present. Everywhere are traces of
ancient empires and yet it seems incredible as we watch the
half-naked Arabs ploughing through the mud-banks with their
wild cattle and primitive implements.

Was this the cradle of the human race? Babylon and Nineveh are here for the archæologist; Ctesiphon, Kufa and Zobeir
for the historian; Bagdad and Busrah (or Bassorah) for old
Arabian romance; and Ur of the Chaldees for the Bible student. Since Haroun Rashid went about in disguise how many
yet stranger Arabian nights has Bagdad seen! How surprised
Sinbad the sailor would be to see the decay of Busrah, yet
with a dozen "smoke-ships" in its harbor!

Mesopotamia, called by the Arabs *El Jezira*, was formerly
limited to the land lying between the two rivers and south of

the old wall by which they were connected above Bagdad. From this point to the Persian Gulf the district was and is still known as Irak-Arabi, to distinguish it from the Irak of Persia. Commonly, however, the name of Mesopotamia (Mid-River-Country) is given to the whole northeastern part of Arabia. It has a total area of 180,000 square miles and presents great uniformity in its physical as well as its ethnical characteristics. Arabs live and Arabic is spoken for three hundred miles beyond Bagdad as far as Diarbekr and Mardin; but we limit our description to the region between Busrah and Bagdad including the delta at the mouth of the rivers.

Near Bagdad the two giant rivers, after draining Eastern Asia Minor, Armenia and Kurdistan, approach quite near together; from thence the main streams are connected by several channels and intermittent watercourses, the chief of which is the Shatt-el Hai. At Kurna the two rivers unite to form the Shatt-el-Arab which traverses a flat, fertile plain dotted with villages and covered with artificially irrigated meadow-lands and extensive date groves. As far up as Bagdad the river is navigable throughout the year for steamers of considerable size. It is entirely owing to the enterprise of English commerce and the Bagdad-Busrah steamship line that the country, so gloomily described by Niebuhr, in 1792, and even by Chesney in 1840, has been developed into new life and prosperity. Even Turkish misrule and oppression cannot do away utterly with natural fertility and productiveness; and if ever a good government should hold this region it would regain its ancient importance and double its present population.

Two features are prominent in the physical geography of this region. First the flat almost level stretches of meadow without any rise or fall except the artificial ancient mounds.[1] The

---

[1] The only remarkable exception is the Jebel Sinam—a rough hill of basaltic rock that crops out in the midst of the alluvial delta near Zobeir; a peculiar phenomenon, but proving Doughty's general scheme for the Arabian geology correct even here.

second is the date-palm.   The whole length of the country from Fao and Mohammerah to the country of the Montefik Arabs above Kurna is one large date plantation, on both sides of the wide river.   Everywhere the tall shapely trees line the horizon and near the lower estuary of the Shatt-el-Arab they are especially luxuriant and plentiful.   Formerly every palm-tree on the Nile, was registered and taxed ; but to count every such tree on the Shatt-el-Arab would be an unending task.

The proper coat-of-arms for all lower Mesopotamia would be a date-palm.   It is the " banner of the climate " and the wealth of the country.   There may be monotony in these long groves and rows of well-proportioned columns with their tops hidden in foliage, but there certainly is nothing wearisome.   A date garden is a scene of exceeding beauty, varying greatly accord-ing to the time of the day and the state of the weather.   At sunrise or sunset the gorgeous colors fall on the gracefully pend-ant fronds or steal gently through the lighter foliage and re-flect a vivid green so beautiful that once seen, it can never be forgotten.   At high-noon the dark shadows and deep colors of the date-forests refresh and rest the eye aching from the brazen glare of sand and sky.   But the forest is at its best, when on a dewy night the full moon rises and makes a pearl glisten on every spiked leaf and the shadows show black as night in con-trast with the sheen of the upper foliage.

It was an Arab poet who first sang the song of the date-palm so beautifully interpreted by Bayard Taylor :

"Next to thee, O fair Gazelle !
O Bedowee girl, beloved so well,—
Next to the fearless Nejidee
Whose fleetness shall bear me again to thee—
Next to ye both I love the palm
With his leaves of beauty and fruit of balm.
Next to ye both, I love the tree
Whose fluttering shadows wrap us three
In love and silence and mystery.

Our tribe is many, our poets vie
With any under the Arab sky
Yet none can sing of the palm but I.
The noble minarets that begem
Cairo's citadel diadem
Are not so light as his slender stem.
He lifts his leaves in the sunbeam glance
As the Almehs lift their arms in dance ;
A slumberous motion, a passionate sigh
That works in the cells of the blood like wine.
O tree of love, by that love of thine
Teach me how I shall soften mine."

Mark Twain compared the palm-tree to " a liberty-pole with a haycock " on top of it. The truth lies between the poet and the " Innocent " traveller, for the date-tree is both a poem and a commercial product ; to the Arab mind it is the perfection of beauty and utility.

The date palm-tree is found in Syria, Asia Minor, nearly all parts of Arabia and the southern islands of the Mediterranean, but it attains to its greatest perfection in upper Egypt and Mesopotamia.[1] Some idea of the immense importance of this one crop in the wealth of Mesopotamia may be gained from the statement of an old English merchant at Busrah, that " the entire annual date-harvest of the River-country might conservatively be put at 150,000 tons."

The date-tree consists of a single stem or trunk about fifty to eighty feet high, without a branch, and crowned at the summit by a cluster of leaves or " palms " that drop somewhat in the shape of a huge umbrella. Each of these palms has long lanceolate leaves spreading out like a fan from the centre stem which often attains a length of ten or even twelve feet. In a wild state the successive rows of palms, which mark the annual growth of the tree, wither and contract but remain upon the trunk, producing with every breath of wind the creaking sound

[1] The dates of Hassa and Oman may equal those of Busrah but the gardens are inferior and the quantity produced is not so large.

DATES GROWING ON A DATE-PALM

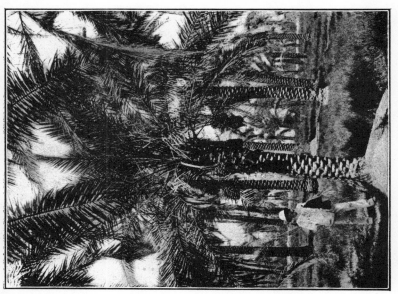

A DATE ORCHARD NEAR BUSRAH

so often heard in the silence of the desert-night. But where the palms are cultivated the old stems are cut away as fast as they dry and are put to many different uses. The trunk of the palm-tree therefore presents the appearance of scales which enable a man, whose body is held to the tree by a rope noose, to climb to the top with ease and gather the fruit. At a distance, these annual *rings* of the date-palm appear as a series of diagonal lines dividing the trunk. Palm-trees often reach the age of a hundred years. The date-palm is diœcious ; but in Mesopotamia the pistilate-palms far exceed in number the staminate. Marriage of the palms takes place every spring and is a busy time for the husbandman as it is no small task to climb all the trees and sprinkle the pollen.

Arabs have written books and Europeans have composed fables on the thousand different uses of the palm-tree. Every part of this wonderful tree is useful to the Arabs in unexpected ways. To begin at the top :—The pistils of the date-blossom contain a fine curly fibre which is beaten out and used in all Eastern baths as a sponge for soaping the body. At the extremity of the trunk is a terminal bud containing a whitish substance resembling an almond in consistency and taste, but a hundred times as large. This is a great table delicacy. There are said to be over one hundred varieties of date-palm all distinguished by their fruit and the Arabs say that " a good housewife may furnish her husband every day for a month with a dish of dates differently prepared." Dates form the staple food of the Arabs in a large part of Arabia and are always served in some form at every meal. Syrup and vinegar is made from old dates ; and by those who disregard the Koran, even a kind of brandy. The date-pit is ground up and fed to cows and sheep so that nothing of the precious fruit may be lost. Whole pits are used as beads and counters for the Arab children in their games on the desert-sand. The branches or palms are stripped of their leaves and used like rattan, to make beds, tables, chairs, cradles, bird-cages, reading-stands, boats,

crates, etc., etc.   The leaves are made into baskets, fans and
string and the *bast* of the outer trunk forms excellent fibre for
rope of many sizes and qualities.   The wood of the trunk,
though light and porous, is much used in bridge-building and
architecture and is quite durable.   In short, when a date-
palm is cut down there is not a particle of it that is wasted.
This tree is the "poor-house" and asylum for all Arabia;
without it millions would have neither food nor shelter.
For one half of the population of Mesopotamia lives in date-
mat dwellings.

Although everywhere the date-culture is an important industry, Busrah is the centre of the trade, for here is the principal depot for export.   The three best varieties of dates known
at Busrah are the *Hallawi, Khadrawi* and *Sayer*.   These are
the only kinds that will stand shipping to the European markets.
They are packed in layers in wooden boxes, or in smaller car-
ton boxes.   The average export to London and New York
from Busrah for the past five years has been about *20,000 tons,*
nearly one half of which was for the American market.   Other
important varieties are *Zehdi, Bérem, Dery* and *Shukri*.   These
are packed more roughly in matting or baskets, and are sent
along the whole Arabian coast, to India, the Red Sea littoral
and Zanzibar.   There are over thirty other varieties cultivated
near Busrah for local consumption.   Some of them have curious names such as: "Mother of Perfume," "Sealed-up,"
"Red Sugar," "Daughter of Seven," "Bride's-finger,"
"Little Star," "Pure Daughter"; others have names which
it is better not to translate.

Palgrave and others, with whose verdict I agree, pronounced
the *Khalasi* date of El Hassa superior to all other kinds.   It
has recently been introduced into Mesopotamia.   Palgrave
says, "the literal and not inappropriate translation of the name
is 'quintessence' —a species peculiar to Hassa and easily the
first of its kind."   The fruit itself is rather smaller than
the usual *Hallawi* date, but it is not so dry and far more

luscious. It is of a rich dark amber color, almost ruddy, and translucent; the kernel is small and easily detached; the date tastes sweet as sugar and is as far superior to the date bought in the American market as a ripe Pippin is to dried apple-rings.

At Busrah the date season opens in September and keeps every one busy until the vast harvest is gathered and shipped. The dates for export to Europe and America are of prime quality; a box of half a hundred-weight on board the steamer is worth about three or four shillings wholesale. All poor, wet, and small dates are packed separately in mats or bags, and are sent to India as second-quality. The poorest lot are sent in mass to the distilleries in England. Thus nothing is lost. Date-packers, who put the fruit in layers, receive three or four *kameris* for packing a box. The best packers can only pack four boxes a day, so that their wages are about a *kran* (about ten cents) per day. They live cheaply on the fruit, and bring all their family, babes and greybeards with them to lodge for the season in the date-gardens. The date season in Busrah begins in the early or middle part of September and lasts for six or eight weeks. The price of the date-crop varies. It is usually fixed at a meeting held in some date-garden where the growers and buyers play the bull and the bear until an agreement is reached. The prices in 1897 were, in the language of the trade: " 340 Shamis for Hallawis, 280 Shamis for Khadrawis, and 180 Shamis for Sayer." Seventeen *Shamis* are equal to about one pound sterling, and the prices quoted are for a *kara*, about fifty hundred-weights.

The culture of the date has steadily increased for the past fifteen years. In 1896 the greater part of the country was inundated by heavy floods and over a million date-trees are said to have been destroyed; new gardens are being planted continually. The Arabs of Mesopotamia display great skill and unusual care in manuring, irrigating and improving their date-plantations, for they realize more and more that this is no mean source of wealth. One recent use to which export dates are put is in the manufacture of vinegar; it would seem, since the beet-sugar industry has proved so profitable, that there must be some method by which good sugar could be manufactured from date-syrup.

Mesopotamia is rich not only in date-groves but in cereals, wool, gums, licorice root and other products. The export of wool alone in 1897 was valued at £288,700. And the total exports the same year, for the two provinces of Bagdad and Busrah, were put at £522,960. Busrah is the shipping place for all the region round about, and ocean steamers of considerable size are always in Busrah harbor; during 1897 four hundred and twenty-one sailing vessels and ninety-five steamships cleared the port, with a total tonnage of 131,846; ninety-one of the steamships were British.

The population of the two vilayets is given by Cuinet, who follows Turkish authorities, as follows:

	Moslems.	Christians.	Jews.	Total.
Bagdad Vilayet,	789,500	7,000	53,500	850,000
Busrah Vilayet,	939,650	5,850	4,500	950,000

In Bagdad vilayet nearly four-fifths of the Moslem population belongs to the Sunnite sect, while in Busrah vilayet three-fourths of them are Shiahs. The Sabeans are generally reckoned among the Christians, although these are already sufficiently divided into Latin, Greek Orthodox, Greek, Syrian, Chaldean Catholic, Armenian Gregorian, Armenian Catholic and Protestants—the last in the smallest minority possible and the others chiefly distinguished by mutual distrust and united hatred of Protestantism.

The vilayet of Bagdad is divided again into three *Sandjaks* or districts of Bagdad, Hillah and Kerbela, and that of Busrah likewise into those of Busrah, Amara Muntefik and Nejd.[1] Of these six districts that of Bagdad is the largest in area and importance and is the centre of military power for both vilayets.

[1] The last named is outside of our present subject and is a misnomer given by Turkish audacity to the region of Hassa.

The boundaries of Bagdad Sandjak go as far as Anah on the Euphrates toward the north and include Kut-el-Amara on the south with both banks of the Tigris. Hillah and Kerbela are along the Euphrates with irregular boundaries while the Muntefik Sandjak with its provincial town of Nasariya separates them from that of Busrah. The Sandjak of Amara begins a few miles north of the junction of the two rivers, and the whole frontier toward Persia is entirely undefined or at least "*in litigation*," as the Turkish official maps have it.

The two Turkish provinces have all the involved machinery of Turkish civil and military administration. There are plenty of offices and office-holders and constant changes in both. Each province has a governor-general or *Wali* and (outside of the governor's sandjak) each district has its *mutaserrif-pasha* either of the first or second class—those one has to deal with generally prove to be of the latter. Then there are *Kaimakams* for smaller districts or cities, and finally *mudirs* for villages. At the seat of government, called the *Serai*, there is an administrative council, including the *Näib* or *kadi*, corresponding to chief-justice ; the *defterdar* or secretary of finance ; the *mufti* or public interpreter of Moslem law ; the *nakib*, etc., etc., etc. There are several courts of justice of different rank ; the custom-house administration is on the *e pluribus unum* plan and *ne plus ultra* system. Besides these there are the "Regie des tabacs" or the tobacco-monopoly, the post and telegraph administration, the sanitary offices, the salt-inspectors, and, at Kerbela, the Tarif of corpses levied on imported pilgrims. To describe all these satisfactorily would require a volume.

XIII

THE CITIES AND VILLAGES OF TURKISH-ARABIA

KUWEIT,[1] on the gulf a little south of the river delta, will in all probability—before long, rise in importance and be as well known as Suez or Port Said. It has the finest harbor in all Eastern Arabia, and is an important town of from 10,000 to 12,000 inhabitants. Here will probably be the terminus of the proposed railroads to bind India and the gulf to Europe by the shortest route. The whole country round about being practically desert, the place is entirely dependent on its trade for support. It possesses more bagalows (sailing-vessels) than any port in the gulf; is remarkably cleanly; has some very well-built houses and an extensive dockyard for boat building. The town and tribe are nominally under Turkish subjection, although protection is the better word, and it is rumored that Kuweit will soon be as much in the hands of the English as is Bahrein.

The Bedouin tribes of Northern Hassa, and even from Nejd, bring horses, cattle and sheep to this place to barter for dates, clothing and fire-arms. There is nearly always a large encampment of Bedouins near the town. The route overland from Kuweit to Busrah is across the desert until we come to an old artificial canal; leaving Jebel Sinam to the left the second march brings us to Zobeir, a small village on the site of ancient Busrah, and only a few hours to the present site. At Zobeir is

[1] Kuweit is the Arabic diminutive of *Kut* a walled-village; the place is called Grane on some maps—evidently a corruption of *Kurein* or " little horn," a name given to an island in the harbor.

the tomb of the Moslem leader for whom the town is named. The village contains about 400 houses; and the population is rich and fanatical. In the vicinity are gardens where a kind of melon is raised, which is celebrated in all the region round about for sweetness and delicacy of flavor. The journey from Kuweit to Busrah is generally made, even by natives, in bugalows; while the Persian Gulf steamers, not calling at Kuweit, proceed direct from Bushire to Fao, at the mouth of the Shatt-el-Arab. A great hindrance to commerce is the bar formed by the alluvial deposit of the immense river as it reaches the gulf. At low tide there is only ten feet of water in the deepest part of the channel, and even at flood tide large steamers must plow their way through the mud to reach Busrah.

Fao is of no importance except as the terminus of the cable from Bushire. A British telegraph station was established here in 1864. The Turkish telegraph system from up the rivers terminates at Fao, and here too they have a representative to govern the place and enforce stringent quarantine. The Shatt-el-Arab winds motononously between the vast date-orchards or desert banks for about forty miles, until we reach the Karun river and the Persian town of Mohammerah. Busrah is sixty-seven miles from the bar and between it and Fao there are many important villages on each bank of the river. Aboo Hassib is perhaps the most important and is a great centre for date-culture and packing.

Busrah consists of the native city—containing the principal bazaars, the government house, and the bulk of the population—and the new town on the river. The native town is about two miles from the river on a narrow creek, called *Ashar ;* a good road runs along the bank, and this road really unites the two parts of the city into one as it is lined with dwelling-houses for a large part of the way. Busrah has seen better days, but also worse. In the middle of the eighteenth century it numbered upward of 150,000 inhabitants. In 1825, it had diminished to 60,000; the plague of 1831 reduced it further by nearly

one-half, and after the plague of 1838, scarcely 12,000 inhabitants remained.   In 1854, it is said to have had only
5,000 inhabitants.   At present the place is growing yearly in
population and importance in spite of misgovernment and
ruinous taxation.   It has every natural advantage over Bagdad, except climate, and will yet outstrip the city of the old
caliphs, if Turkey's rule mends or ends.   The present population
of the city proper is given by Ottoman authorities at 18,000.
Many ruins all over the plains and in the surrounding gardens tell
of its former extent and splendor.   At present the native town
looks sadly dilapidated, and tells the story of neglect and decay.   The unexampled filthiness of the streets and the un-
drained marshes in the environs make the place proverbially
unhealthy.   This unhygienic condition is not improved by the
Ashar Creek being at the same time the common sewer and the
common water supply for over one-half of the population.   The
wealthy classes send out boats to bring water from the river,
but all the poorer people use the creek.   Such are the results of
an imbecile government which could easily drain the marshes
and supply every one with great abundance of pure water.

Ancient Busrah, near the present site of Zobeir, was founded
in 636 A. D., by the second Caliph Omar as a key to the
Euphrates and Tigris.   It reached great prosperity, and was
the home of poetry and grammatical learning, as Bagdad was
the centre of science and philosophy.   After the twelfth century the city began to decay, and at the conquest of Bagdad
by Murad IV., in 1638, this entire stretch of country fell into
the hands of the Turks.   Then the present city took the name
of Busrah.   Later it was in the hands of the Arabs and Persians, and from 1832 to 1840, Mohammed Ali was in possession.
Under the rule of Midhat Pasha, governor-general of Bagdad,
the city of Busrah arose in importance partly because of the
Turkish Steam Navigation Company which he promoted.   But
it was a dream-life.   English commerce and enterprise aroused
the place thoroughly, and the whistle of steamships has kept it

awake ever since the Suez canal opened trade with Europe by way of the gulf.[1]

In making the journey from Busrah to Bagdad the traveller has choice of two lines of river-steamers : the Ottoman service has six steamers and the English company three, but the latter are only allowed to use two by the Turkish government. For romance, discomfort and tediousness, choose the former ; for all other reasons select the latter. I have tried both. The English steamers carry the mails to Bagdad and make weekly trips ; four or five days being required for the journey up stream, and three days down, although when the water is low the journey may be long delayed. In bad or shallow places the steamers often discharge a part of their cargo, heave over the shallow part and load up again. Of course trade suffers and vast quantities of merchandise often lie for weeks at Busrah awaiting shipment. No steps are ever taken by the Ottoman government to counteract the great waste of water which flows into the marshes. In course of time, unless prevented, this waste will lead to the closing up of the main channel of the Tigris even as the Euphrates below Suk-es-Shiukh has become a marsh for lack of use.

The good Steamship *Mejidieh* with its kindly Captain Cowley, or the sister ship *Khalifah* lies at anchor just off the English Consulate, the blue-peter flies overhead and the decks are over-crowded with all sorts and conditions of men—Persians, Turks, Indians, Arabs, Armenians, Greeks ;—baggage, bales, boxes, water-bottles—chickens, geese, sheep, horses, not to speak of the insect-population on which it is impossible to collect freight-charges. The steamers are somewhat after the type of the American river-steamers on the Mississippi ; but no Mark Twain has yet arisen to immortalize them, although they afford an even more fertile theme. With a double deck and broad

[1] For the interesting history of the cities that occupied the site of Busrah before the days of Islam, and as far back as Nebuchadnezzar, see Ainsworth's " Personal narrative of the Euphrates expedition."

of beam they carry hundreds of passengers and an astonishing amount of cargo for their size. The accommodation during cool weather is excellent, and during the hot days no one travels for the sake of luxury.

The first place at which the steamer calls is Kurna at the junction of the rivers, and from whence the course is up the Tigris to Bagdad. The Tomb of Ezra, about nine hours from Busrah, is a great place for pilgrimages by the Jews. It is a pretty spot on the river bank and picturesque with its crowd of embarking and disembarking Jews and Jewesses. The tomb is a domed cloister enclosing a square mausoleum, and paved with blue tiles. Over the doorway are two tablets of black marble with Hebrew inscriptions attesting to the authenticity of the tomb. It is not improbable that Ezra is buried here, for the Talmud states that he died at Zamzuma, a town on the Tigris. He is said to have died here on his way from Jerusalem to Susa to plead the cause of the captive Jews. Josephus says that he was buried at Jerusalem, but no Jew of Bagdad doubts that Ezra's remains rest on the Tigris.

Ten hours beyond, we pass also on the west bank, Abu Sadra, a tomb of an Arab saint marked only by a reed-hut and a grove of poplars. Next is Amara, a large and growing village with a coaling-depot and an enterprising population. This place was founded in 1861, and promises to become a centre of trade. After passing Ali Shergi, Ali Gherbi, and Sheikh Saad, small villages, without stopping, the steamer calls at Kut-el-Amara, a larger place even than Amara, on the east bank, with over 4,000 inhabitants.

All the way from Busrah to Bagdad, but especially along this part of the river, we pass Bedouin tribes, encamped in the black tents of Kedar, engaged in the most primitive agriculture or irrigation of their land, or rushing along the banks to hail the passing steamer. A hungry, impudent, noisy, cheerful lot they are; filling the merciful with pity and moving the thoughtless to laughter, as they scramble up and down the

THE REPUTED TOMB OF EZRA ON THE TIGRIS RIVER

RUINS OF THE ARCH OF CTESIPHON NEAR BAGDAD

banks into the water to catch a piece of bread or a few dates
thrown to them.

Meanwhile we steam along passing Bughela, Azizieh, Bag-
dadieh and reach Bustani Kesra, or the arch of Ctesiphon.
The little village of Soleiman-Pak is named for the pious man
who was the private barber of Mohammed the prophet. After
various wanderings, poor pious Pak was buried here, only a
short distance from the great arch. A village sprang up near
the tomb, pilgrims come from everywhere and miracles are
claimed to be wrought by him who when alive only handled
the razor. The whole region of Mesopotamia is more rich in
saints, tombs and pilgrim-shrines than any other part of Arabia.

The arch of Ctesiphon is not a shrine but it is well worth a
visit. It is the only prominent object that remains of the vast
ruins of Ctesiphon on the east bank of the Tigris, and Seleucia
on the west. The arch is now almost in ruins but must once
have been the façade of a magnificent building. Its length is
275 feet, and its height is given variously as eighty-six or one
hundred feet; the walls are over twelve feet thick and the
span of the magnificent arch is nearly eighty feet. What
Ctesiphon was in the days of the Sassanian kings we read in
Gibbon. Now its glory has departed and the tomb of the
Barber has more visitors than the ancient throne of the Chos-
roes. Eight hours after leaving Ctesiphon's ruins, our steamer
is in full sight of the city of Haroun Rashid.

Bagdad is a familiar name even to the boy who reads the
Arabian tales rather than his geography. It is one of the chief
cities of the Turkish empire and has a history much older than
the empire itself. Founded by the Caliph Mansur about the
year 765 A. D., it was the capital of the Mohammedan world
for five hundred years, until it was destroyed by Halakn,
grandson of Jengiz Khan. Situated in the midst of what was
once the richest and most productive region of the old world
it is now no longer queen of the land but rather reminds us of
decay and dissolution. Its present beauties are only the ruins

of former glory. The untidy soldiers slouching about the streets, the evil-smelling bazaars and ruined mosques, the rotten bridge of boats that spans the river, the faces of the poor and the miserable who go begging through the streets, indicate the curse of Turkish inanition and oppression.

On the west bank of the river is the old town enclosed by extensive orange and date-groves. On the east bank is New-Bagdad, which also looks old enough. Here are the government offices, consulates, and the chief commercial buildings as well as the custom-offices. Bagdad is still an important city on many accounts. No other city of the Turkish empire is influenced so much by the desert and Arabia as is Bagdad ; and no other stands in such direct contact with the towns in the interior of the peninsula. The Arabic spoken is comparatively pure, and Bedouin manners still prevail in many ways in the social life of the people. The city has a very motley population, because of commerce on the one hand and the number of pilgrim-shrines on the other. The tombs of Abd-ul-Kadir, and Abu Hanifah and the gilded domes and minarets which mark the resting-places of two of the Shiah Imams—all draw their annual concourse of visitors from many lands and peoples. All the languages of the Levant are spoken on its streets although Arabic prevails over all. Dr. H. M. Sutton remarks, "I have been at the bedside of a patient where in a company of half-a-dozen people we had occasion to use five languages, and on another occasion we were in a company of about forty people in a room where no less than fourteen languages were represented. The land of Shinar is thus still the place of the confusion of tongues." Bagdad like Busrah has suffered greatly by ravages of the plague at various times, but especially in 1830 when the plague was followed by a fearful inundation. In one night, when the river burst its banks 7,000 houses fell and 15,000 people perished.

The population of Bagdad is at present variously estimated at from 120,000 to 180,000. Nearly one-third are Jews while the Oriental Christians number about 5,000. The trade of Bagdad is large not only with the region southwards and toward Busrah but with Nejd and Northern Mesopotamia. The import trade from India and Europe to Bagdad is over £1,-000,000 every year, and the export trade to Europe alone is placed at £522,960 for 1897. The river north of Bagdad is not navigable for steamers but an immense number of *kelleks* daily arrive from the north loaded with lumber from Kurdistan and with other products. These *kelleks* are a craft made of inflated goatskins boarded over with reeds and matting. The boatmen return with the empty skins overland with the caravan companies. Still more characteristic of Bagdad is the small river-boat called a *kuffe* or coracle. It consists of a perfectly circular hull, six to eight feet in diameter, with sides curving inward like a huge basket, and covered with pitch. This type of boat is as old as Nineveh and they are pictured quite accurately on the old monuments.

Bagdad has more than sixty-eight mosques, six churches and twenty-two synagogues. Of the mosques some, like that of Daood Pasha, are in fine condition ; others are almost in ruins, and remind one of the remark of Lady Ann Blunt : " A city long past its prime, its hose a world too wide for its shrunk shanks." The feature of Bagdad is of course the river Tigris, with its swift-flowing tide ever washing the mud banks and watering the gardens for miles around. The houses come down close to the water's edge and some of them have pretty gardens almost overhanging the stream and terraces and verandas—oriental and picturesque. The British Residency is perhaps most beautiful in its location and its frontage on the river ; but the other consulates vie with it in displaying to the traveller the strength and hospitality of European States. The European community is larger than at Busrah.

XIV

THROUGH the kind assistance of Colonel Mockler, at that time the Bagdad Consul General and Resident, in the autumn of 1892, I was able to make the journey from Bagdad across to Hillah and down the Euphrates—a route not often taken by the traveller. After making necessary preparations and finding a suitable servant we hired two mules and left the city of the old Caliphs with a caravan for Kerbela. It was in July and we made our first halt four hours from Bagdad, sleeping on a blanket under the stars. An hour after midnight the pack-saddles were lifted in place and we were off again. It was a mixed company; Arabs, Persians, and Turks; merchants for Hillah and pilgrims to the sacred shrines; women in those curtained, cage-like structures called *taht-i-vans*,—two portable zenanas hanging from each beast; dervishes on foot with green turbans, heavy canes and awful visages : and to complete the picture a number of rude coffins strapped cross-wise on pack-mules and holding the remains of some "true believers," long since ready for the holy ground at Nejf (Nedjef).

The caravan travelled along the desert road mostly at night to escape the fearful heat of midday when we sought shelter in public khan. Nothing could be more uninteresting than the country between Bagdad and Babylon at this season of the year. The maps mark six khans on the route, but three of these are in ruins and the others are merely stages of a caravan rather than villages or centres of cultivation. The soil appears excellent, but there are no irrigation canals, and everything has a deserted appearance. A few low shrubs between the mounds and moles of an ancient civilization; mud-houses near the khans and some Arab encampments; camel skeletons shining white by the wayside, under a burning sun; and a troop or two of gazelle making for the river-banks—that is all you see until you reach the palm-banked Euphrates at Hillah.

The khans consist of a large enclosure with heavy walls of sun-dried or Babylonian brick. In the interior are numerous alcoves or niches, ten by six feet and four feet above ground; you seek out an empty niche and find a resting-place until the caravan starts at midnight. In the centre of the enclosure is a well and a large platform for prayer—utilized for sleeping and cooking by late arrivals who find no niche reserved as in our case. The rest of the court is for animals and baggage. Usual Arab supplies were obtainable at these resting-places, but every comfort is scarce and the innkeepers are too busy to be hospitable.

Khan el Haswa where we arrived the second day is the centre of a small village of perhaps 300 people. At three in the morning we left Haswa but it was nearly noon when we reached the river, because of a delay on the road. The bazaar and business of Hillah were formerly on the Babylonian side of the stream, but are now principally on the further side of the rickety bridge of boats four miles below the ruins of Baby-lon. After paying toll we crossed over and found a room in the Khan Pasha—a close, dirty place, but in the midst of the town and near the river. Hillah is the largest town on the Euphrates north of Busrah. Splendid groves of date-trees surround it and stretch along the river as far as the eye can reach. The principal merchandise of the town is wheat, barley and dates. Of the Moslem population two-thirds are Shiah, and the remaining Sunni are mostly Turks. There are one or two native Christians and many Jews, but it is difficult to estimate correctly the population of Hillah or of any of the towns on the Euphrates. At Hillah the river is less than 200 yards wide and has a much more gentle flow than the Tigris at

Bagdad.   A short distance northwest of the town is Kerbela. It is only a village but the spot is visited by thousands of faithful Moslems every year who venerate the twelve Imams of the Shiah sect.   Here is the tomb of Hosein the grandson of the prophet and the son of Ali whom they believe the true successor in the Caliphate.   By living or dying here the Shiah devotee has nought to fear for the next world.   So strong is this belief that many leave directions in their wills to be buried in this hallowed spot.   Thousands of corpses are imported some even from India—after proper drying and salting—and are laid to rest in the sacred ground.   Nejf, south of Hillah, is the place of Ali's martyrdom and is no less sacred for the living and the dead.

At Kerbela the manufacture of *torbas* is about the only industry.   A *torbat* is a small piece of baked clay about two inches in length, generally round or oblong, with the names of Ali and Fatima rudely engraved on it.   Made out of holyground, these are carried home by all pilgrims and are used by nearly every Shiah as a resting-place for the forehead in their prayer prostrations.   According to all reports Kerbela is similar to Mecca in its loose morals and the character of its permanent population.

On July 31st we left Hillah and sailed down the river in a native boat similar to the " bellum " of Busrah, but without awning.   The Euphrates is more muddy than the Tigris, and its course, though less sinuous, is broken here and there by shallow rapids.[1]   We sailed all night and did not stop until we arrived at Diwaniyeh the following afternoon.   Many of the villages on the way appeared to have a considerable population ; date-groves were plentiful, and we passed two or three Mathhab or tombs of Arab Sheikhs, including that reputed to be Job's, "the greatest of all the sons of the East."

[1] The following are the villages and encampments between *Hillah* and *Diwaniyeh :* El Ataj, Doulab, Dobleh, Kwaha, Saadeh, Tenhara, Bir Amaneh, Allaj, Anameh, Hosein, Khegaan Sageer and Khegaan Kebir.

At Diwaniyeh I was directed to the Serai, or government-house, where the Muttaserif Pasha of Hillah was forcing taxes from the unwilling Arabs. I was kindly received, and, probably because of my passport, was entertained at the Pasha's table. Diwaniyeh has only a small population, and its importance is due to its wealth of palms and the wheat trade, which gives another opportunity for the government to establish a toll-bridge and custom-house.

The Arabs of this region are notorious for their piracy on native craft, and in 1836 they even attacked the English surveying expedition. So I left the place with a guard of two soldiers—Saadeh and Salim, who were as happy as their names. Patching their uniforms, asleep in the bottom of the boat, eating of our bread and dates, or polishing their rifles marked " *U. S. Springfield*, Snider's Pat. 1863," we reached Samawa safely. During the day we passed the hamlets Um Nejis, Abu Juwareeb, Rumeitha, and Sheweit. But the general scene was that of narrow morass channels branching out from the river, where forests of reeds half hid mat-huts and naked Arabs. These river tribes are not true nomads,[1] but live in one place, on fish and the products of the river buffalo. It is a strange sight to see a herd of large black cattle swimming across stream, pursued by shouting, swimming and swearing herdsmen. And this was once the home of Abraham, the friend of God.

Near Rumeitha there was a large menzil of the Lamlum tribe. Here we fastened the boat for the night, as our company was afraid to cross certain rapids by starlight. Some of the Arabs came to our boat, armed with flint-locks and the Mikwar—a heavy stick knobbed with sandstone or hard bitumen—in Arab hands a formidable weapon. Most of the people

[1] The distinction between true Arabs of the nomad tribes and the *Me'dan* was made as early as 1792 by Niebuhr in his travels, and the river boatmen still answer your question with contemptuous accent: " Those are not Arabs, they are Me'dan."

were asleep, and we could get no supplies of any kind except two roast fowl from the Turkish garrison in a mud brick fort opposite. Even one of these fell to the share of a hungry jackal during the night. We left early in the morning, and after some difficulty in crossing the shallow rapids, reached Samawa in four hours. Dismissing the zaptiehs, we found a room in the Khan of Haj Nasir on the second floor and overlooking the bazaar.

It was the day before Ashera, the great day of Moharram, and the whole town was in funereal excitement. All shops were closed. Shiah were preparing for the great mourning, and Sunni sought a safe place away from the street. As soon as I came the local governor sent word that I must not leave the khan under any circumstances, nor venture in the street, as he would not be responsible for Shiah violence. I remained indoors, therefore, until the following day, and saw from the window the confusion of the night of Ashera, the tramp of a mob, the beating of breasts, the wailing of women, the bloody banners, and mock-martyr scenes, the rhythmic howling and cries of "Ya Ali! ya Hassan! ya Hussein!" until throats were hoarse and hands hung heavy for a moment, only to go at it again. A pandemonium, as of Baal's prophets on Carmel, before the deaf and dumb God of Islam,—monotheistic only in its book. "There is no god but God," and yet to the Shiah devotees of Moharram, "He is not in all their thoughts." The martyr caliphs of Nejf are their salvation and their hope, the Houris' lap.

Between Samawa and Nasariya, the next important town, we passed the villages: Zahara, El Kidr, Derj Kalat, (where there is a Turkish Mudir and a telegraph station on the Hillah-Busrah wire) Luptika El Ain Abu Tabr and El Assaniyeh. The river begins to broaden below Samawa, and its banks are beautiful with palms and willows. We were again delayed at a toll-bridge; there must be taxes everywhere in Turkey, on ships and on fishermen, on boats and on bridges, on tobacco

A PUBLIC KHAN IN TURKISH-ARABIA

ARAB PILGRIMS ON BOARD A RIVER STEAMER

and on salt ; but this taxing of the same cargo at every river port is peculiar.

Nasariya is a comparatively modern town and better built than any on the Euphrates river. Its bazaar is large and wide, and the government-houses are imposing for Arabdom. A small gunboat lies near the landing, and this floating tub, with its soldier guard and bugle-call, represents the only civilization that has yet come to the Euphrates valley, and is a thing of wonder to the Arabs. Opposite Nasariya are two large walled enclosures, wheat granaries protected from Arab robbers. Three hours west are the ruins of Mugheir—Ur of the Chaldees.

Our meheleh sailed down the river before daylight and five hours later came to Suk el Shiukh, " the bazaar of old men." Abd el Fattah, in whose Persian kahwah we found a place, is a cosmopolitan. He had seen " Franjees " before, had been to Bombay, Aden and Jiddah, knew something of books, a little less of the gospel, and spoke two English words, of which he was very proud, " Stop her " and " Send a geri." He was a model innkeeper, and had it not been for his tea and talk, the three days of stifling heat under a mat-roof would have been less tolerable.

South of Suk el Shiukh the river widens into marshes, where the channel is so shallow that part of the cargo of all river boats is transferred to smaller craft. On account of this delay, we ran short of provisions before reaching Kurna, and our boatmen were such prejudiced sectarians that it required argument and much backsheesh to bargain for some rice and the use of their cooking-pot. We were " nejis," " kafir," and what not, and the captain vowed he would have to wash the whole boat clean at Busrah from the footprints of the unbelievers. Between Suk and the junction of the two rivers to form the Shatt-el-Arab at Kurna, there are many wide, waste marshes, growing reeds and pasture for the buffalo—a breeding place for insect life and the terror of the boatmen because of the Me'dan pirates. We were three days on this part of the river, and often all of us were in the water to lift and tug the boat over some mud-bank. El Kheit is the only village of any size the whole distance, but the Bedouin of the swamp, who live half the time in the water and have not arrived at even the loin-cloth stage of civilization, are a great multitude. At length we reached Kurna and thence, by the broad, lordly, Shatt-el-Arab to the mission-house at Busrah.

What is to be the future of this great and wealthy valley, which once supported myriads and was the centre of culture and ancient civilization? Will it evermore rest under the blight of the fez and the crescent? The one curse of the land is the inane government and its ruthless taxation. The goose with the golden egg is killed every day in Turkey—at least robbed to its last *nest-egg*. The shepherd-tribes, the villagers, the nomads, the agricultural communities, all suffer alike from the same cause. When and whence will deliverance come? Perhaps a partial reply to these two questions will be found if we read between the lines in our chapter on the recent politics of Arabia. A *Turkish* railroad in the Euphrates valley would rust ; but a railroad under any other government would develop a region capable of magnificent improvement.

XV

THE INTERIOR—KNOWN AND UNKNOWN

"The central provinces of Nejd, the genuine Wahabi country, is to the rest of Arabia a sort of a lion's den on which few venture and yet fewer return."—*Palgrave.*

"A desert world of new and dreadful aspect! black camels, and uncouth hostile mountains; and a vast sand wilderness shelving toward the dire impostor's city."—*Doughty.*

THE region which, for want of a more definite name, we may call the Interior includes four large districts. Three of these have been comparatively well explored and mapped, but the fourth is utterly unknown. These districts are: Roba'-el-Khali, Nejran with Wady Dauasir, Nejd proper, and Jebel Shammar.

It is surprising that at the close of the nineteenth century there should remain so many portions of our globe still unexplored. We have better maps of the north pole and of the moon than we have of Southeastern Arabia and parts of Central Asia. A triangle formed by lines drawn from Harrara in Oman to El Harik in Southern Nejd, thence to Marib in Yemen and back to Harrara will measure very nearly 500 miles on each of its upper sides and 800 on the base. This triangle, with an area of 120,000 square miles is as utterly unknown to the world at large as if it were an undiscovered continent in some polar sea. Never has it been crossed by any European traveller or entered by an explorer. It includes all the *hinterland* of the Mahrah and Gharah tribes, all western Oman and the so-called Roba'-el-Khali (literally, "empty abode") of the Dahna desert, as well as that mysterious region of El Ahkaf to which

143

the Koran refers and which is said by the Arabs to be a sea
of quicksands, able to swallow whole caravans.

On most maps the region in question is left blank ; others
designate it as an uninterrupted desert from Mecca to Oman ;
while Ptolemy's map describes the region as producing myrrh
and abounding in Arab tribes and caravan-routes. Whatever
we know of the country at present must be the result of Arab
hearsay booked by travellers in the coast-provinces. The few
names of places given in the Roba'-el-Khali would *not* lead
one to suppose that "uninterrupted desert" was its only characteristic feature. In the north are Jebel Athal (the Tamarisk
Mountains), and Wady Yebrin. Wady Shibwan and Wady
Habuna seem to extend at least some distance into the triangle
from the west, while, in the very centre we have the very unusual names for a desert region Belad-ez-Zohur (Flower-
country) and El-Joz (the nut-trees). There is no doubt that a
large part of the region is now desert and uninhabited ; but it
may not always have been so and may hold its own secrets,
archæological and geographical.

An Arab of Wady Fatima told Doughty, what the divine
partition of the world was in the following words : "Two
quarters Allah divided to the children of Adam, the third part
He gave to Gog and Magog, a manikin people, parted from us
by a wall, which they shall overskip in the latter days ; and
then will they overrun the world. Of their kindred be the
gross Turks and the misbelieving Persians ; but you, the Eng-
leys are of the good kind with us. The fourth part of the
world is called Roba'-el-Khali, the empty quarter." Doughty
adds, "I never found any Arabian who had aught to tell,
even by hearsay, of that dreadful country. Haply it is Nefud,
with quicksands, which might be entered into and even passed
with milch dromedaries in the spring weeks. Now my health
failed me ; otherwise I had sought to unriddle that enigma."
It still awaits solution. In Oman they say it is only twenty-
seven days' caravan march overland to Mecca right through

the desert; perhaps from the Oman highlands one could more easily penetrate into the unknown and get safely to Riad if not to Yemen.

Nejran, celebrated as an ancient Christian province of Arabia and sacred by the blood of martyrs, lies north of Yemen and east of the Asir country. Together with the Dauasir-Wady region it forms a strip of territory about 300 miles long and 100 broad, well-watered and even more fertile than the best parts of Yemen.[1] The intrepid traveller, Halévy (1870) first visited this region from Yemen and found a large Jewish population in the southern part. He visited the towns Mahlaf, Rijlah and Karyet-el-Kabil, penetrated Wady Habuna but could not succeed in reaching Wady Dauasir. He describes the fertility of the Wadys and the extensive date-plantations of this part of Arabia in terms of greatest admiration. Ruins and inscriptions are plentiful. In Wady Dauasir the Arabs say that the palm-groves extend three dromedary-journeys. The people are all agricultural Arabs but, as in Oman, they live in continual feud and turmoil because of tribal jealousies and old quarrels.

The region east of Wady Dauasir is called Aflaj or Felej-el-Aflaj, two days' journey distant; here there are also palm-oases. It is six days' journey thence to Riad, but the way is rugged, without villages.[2] It was along Wady Dauasir that I

---

[1] It contains the following Wadys: Nejran, Habuna, Wanan, Moyazet, Bedr and the extensive Wady Dauasir.

[2] Aflaj has six villages: Siah, Leyta, Khurfa, Er-Rautha, El-Bedia. Wady Dauasir has these towns: El-Hammam, Es-Shotibba, Es-Soleil, Tamera, Ed-Dam, El-Loghf, El-Ferrà, Es-Showeik, and El-Ayathat. (Doughty.) Most of these towns are not given on the maps; but as some of them are, it is interesting to mention the route from Hassa to this Wady, given by Capt. Miles in a letter to Sprenger (dated Muscat, March, 1873) and quoted in his "Alte Geog. Arabiens," page 240. "Route from El Hasa to Solail: Hassa, Kharaj, Howta, Hilwa, Leilah, Kharfa, Rondha, El Sih, Bidia, Shitba, Solail. From Solail to Runniya it is three days' journey. It is a town larger than Solail. The Dosiri tribes are as fol-

had hoped to make the overland journey from Sana to Bahrein in 1894; once beyond Turkish espionage the way would have been open. According to the testimony of Halévy the inhabitants of Nejran and Wady Dauasir are not fanatical. Nowhere in Yemen are the Jews treated so kindly as by the Arabs of Nejran. This entire region must also be classed with the fertile districts of Arabia. Water is everywhere abundant coming down from the Jebel Rian, fifteen days' journey from Toweyk and from the southern ranges of Jebel Ban and Jebel Tumra. The inhabitants of Nejran and of Southern Dauasir are heretical Moslems. They belong to the Bayadhi sect like the people of Oman,[1] and are supposed to be followers of Abd-Allah-bin-Abad (746 A. D.).

Historically, Nejran is of special interest because here it was that the Roman army of 11,000 men sent by Augustus Cæsar under Ælius Gallus to make a prey of the chimerical riches of Arabia Felix came to grief. The warriors did not fall in battle but, purposely misled by the Nabateans, their allies, they marched painfully over the waterless wastes in Central Arabia six months; the most perished in misery and only a remnant returned. Strabo, writing from the mouth of Gallus himself, who was his friend and prefect of Egypt, gives a description of the Arabian desert that cannot be improved : " It is a sandy waste with only a few palms and pits of water: the acacia thorn and the tamarisk grow there ; the wandering Arabs lodge in tents and are camel graziers."

Nejd—the heart of Arabia, the genuine Arabia, the Arabia of the poets—is properly bounded,—on the east, by the Turkish province of Hasa ; on the south by the border of the desert

lows : El-Woodaieen at Solail; El Misahireh possess most camels, etc.; Al Hassan at Wasit; Beni Goweit ; El-Khutran in Shitba ; El Sherafa ; El-'Umoor, east end of Wady ; Al Saad, west of Wady ; El-Showaiej; El-Khamaseen; El Kahtan ; Hamid ; Al Amar ; El Farjan in Kharfa."

[1] A full account of their peculiar beliefs and their disputed origin is given in the Appendix to Badger's " History of Oman."

near Yemama; on the west by Hejaz in its widest extent to
Khaibar; and on the north by Jebel Shammar. Thus defined
it includes the regions of El-Kasim, El-Woshem, El-Aared,
and Yemama. The "Zephyrs of Nejd" are the pregnant
theme of many an Arab poet and in these highlands that the
air is crisp and dry and invigorating, especially to the visitors
from the hot and moist coast provinces. It was such a poet
who wrote in raptures of the Nejd climate :

"Then said I to my companion while the camels were hastening
To bear us down the pass between Menifah and Demar :
'Enjoy while thou canst the sweets of the meadows of Nejd ;
With no such meadows and sweets shalt thou meet after this evening.'
Ah! heaven's blessing on the scented gales of Nejd,
And its greensward and groves glittering from the spring showers ;
And thy dear friends when thy lot was cast in Nejd —
Months flew past, they passed and we knew not,
Nor when their moons were new nor when they waned."

As to the real and prosaic features of the country, Nejd is a
plateau of which Jebel Toweyk is the centre and backbone.
Its general height above the sea is about 4,000 feet, but there
are more lofty ledges and peaks, some as high as 5,500 feet.
These highlands are for the most clothed with fine pasture ;
trees are common, solitary or in little groups ; and the entire
plateau is intersected by a maze of valleys cut out of the sandstone and limestone. In these countless hollows is concentrated the fertility and the population of Nejd. The soil of the
valleys is light, mixed with marl sand and pebbles washed
down from the cliffs. Water is found everywhere in wells at a
depth of not much over fifteen feet and often less ; in Kasim it
has a brackish taste, and the soil is salty, but in other parts of
Nejd there are traces of iron in it. The climate of all Nejd,
according to Palgrave, is perhaps one of the healthiest in the
world. The air is dry, clear and free from all the malarial
poison of the coast ; the summers are warm but not sultry, and
the winter air is biting cold. The usual monotony of an

Arabian landscape is not only enlivened by the presence of the date-palm near the villages, but by groups of Talh, Nebaa' and Sidr, the Ithl and Ghada Euphorbia—all of them good-sized shrubs or trees.[1]

Nejd is pasture land, so that its breed of sheep are known all over Arabia ; their wool is remarkably fine, almost equal to Cashmire in softness and delicacy.   Camels abound ; according to Palgrave, Nejd is " a wilderness of camels."   The color is generally brownish white or grey ; black camels are found westward and southward in the inhospitable Harra-country toward Mecca.   Oxen and cows are not uncommon.   Game is plenty, both feathered and quadruped.   Partridges, quail, a kind of bustard ; gazelle, hares, jerboa, wild-goat, wild-boars, porcupine, antelope, and a kind of wild-ox (wathyhi) with beautiful horns.   Snakes are not common, but lizards, centipedes and scorpions abound.   The ostrich is also found in western Nejd as well as in Wady Dauasir.   The Bedouin hunt them to sell the skins to the Damascus feather merchants who come down with the Haj every year to Mecca ; forty reals (dollars) was the price paid in Doughty's time for a single skin —a small fortune to the poor nomad.   Mounted on their dromedaries they watch for the bird and then waylay it, matchlock ready to hand.   The Arabs esteem the breast of the ostrich good food ; the fat is a sovereign remedy with them and half a *finjan* (the measure of an Arab coffee-cup), is worth half a Turkish mejidie.   The ostrich is no longer as common in Arabia as formerly, and in many parts of the peninsula the bird is unknown even by name.

Nejd is a land of camels and horses.   But although a fine breed of the latter exist it is a common mistake to suppose that horses are plentiful in Central Arabia and that every Arab owns

[1] The Talh is a large tree of roundish, scanty, leafage, with a little dry berry for fruit, its branches are wide-spreading and thorny.   The Nebaa' is much smaller though of considerable height ; it has very small ovate bright green leaves.   The Sidr is a little acacia tree.

his steed. Doughty says "there is no breeding or sale of horses at Boreyda or Aneyza nor any town in Nejd." Most of the horses shipped from Busrah or Kuweit to Bombay are not from Nejd, although originally of Nejd-breed, but come from Jebel Shammar and the Mesopotamian valley. He who would know all about the beauty of the Nejd horse must visit the Hail stables with Palgrave who "goes raving mad" about the animals; or he can read Lady Ann Blunt's "Pilgrimage to Nejd" in search of horses; better still let him buy that remarkable book by Colonel Tweedie: THE ARABIAN HORSE, *His country and His people.* In this volume the horse is the hero and Arabs are grooms and stable-boys. The Arab is more kind to his horse than to any other animal. No Arab dreams of tying up a horse by the neck; a tether replaces the halter, one of the animal's hind-legs being encircled about the pastern by a light iron ring or leather strap, and connected with a chain or rope to an iron peg. Nejdi horses are specially valuable for great speed and endurance. They are all built for riding and not for draught; to the unprofessional eye they do not seem at all superior to the best horses seen in London or New York City, but I leave the matter to the authorities mentioned.[1]

[1] For our present knowledge of the government, population, cities and villages of Nejd we are chiefly indebted to the following travellers: Captain G. F. Sadlier, of the English army, who was the first European to cross the Arabian Peninsula. (1819.) George Wallin, a learned young Swedish Arabist, travelling in 1845 and 1848 as a Mohammedan doctor of law, passed through the northern desert from Jauf to Hail and visited Medina. William Gifford Palgrave, a Jesuit Roman Catholic, of English birth and scholarly tastes made his celebrated journey across Arabia from west to east in 1862-63. In 1864 the bold Italian traveller Guarmani went from Jerusalem straight to Jebel Shammar and Aneyza. In 1865 Colonel Pelly, the British Resident at Bushire made an important journey, in company with Dr. Colville and Lieutenant Dawes, from Kuweit through southeastern Nejd to Riadh, returning by Hassa to Ojeir and Bahrein. Then Charles M. Doughty (*facile princeps* among all authorities and travellers Arabian) made his long, arduous, zigzag journeys through northwestern

The government of Nejd indicates what the independent rulers of Arabia are like. Doughty testifies that the sum of all he could learn from the mouth of the Arabs themselves of Ibn Rashid's government (now in the hands of Abd-el-Aziz bin Mitaab, his nephew) was this: " He makes sure of them that may be won by gifts, he draws the sword against his adversaries, he treads down them that fear him and he were no right ruler, hewed he no heads off ! " Some of the nomads consider the prince of Nejd a tyrant, but the villagers generally are well content. Forsooth it is better for them to have *one* tyrant than *many*, as in the days before the political upheaval that unified central Arabia. Other of the more religious folk of Nejd cannot forget the bloody path by which Ibn Rashid gained his seat of power and call him " *Nejis*, (polluted), a cutter-off of his kinsfolk with the sword."

Lavish sums in the eyes of the starved Bedouin are spent on hospitality but all guests are pleased and depart from the pile of rice to praise God and the Amir of Nejd. Daily, in the guest-room, according to Doughty, one hundred and eighty messes of barley-bread with rice and butter are served to the men freely; a camel or smaller animal is killed for the first-class guests and the total expense of his famous hospitality is not over £1,500 annually. The revenues are immense and Ibn Rashid's private fortune had grown large even when Doughty visited him in 1877. He has cattle innumerable and " 40,000 camels "; some 300 blooded mares and 100 horses; over 100 negro slaves; besides private riches laid up in silver metal, land at Hail and plantations in Jauf.

Contrasted with the Turkish provinces of Arabia the subjects of the Amir of Nejd enjoy light taxation and even the Bedouin warriors who are in the service of the Nejd ruler receive better wages than the regular troops of the Sultan. From the descrip-

and northern Arabia from November, 1876, to August, 1878. Our other authority for Nejd is Lady Ann Blunt who with her husband visited the capital of Ibn Rashid's country from Bagdad in 1883,

tion of Mr. and Mrs. Blunt and Doughty at Hail, one cannot but feel that the government of Nejd is much more liberal and less fanatical than it was in the old days of the Wahabis as described by Palgrave. The old Wahabi power is now broken forever and Nejd is getting into touch with the world through commerce. Kasim already resembles the border-lands and the inhabitants are worldly-wise with the wisdom of the Bombay horse-dealers. Many of the youth of Nejd visit Bagdad, Busrah and Bahrein in their commercial ventures. Says Doughty, "all Nejd Arabia, east of Teyma, appertains to the Persian Gulf traffic and not to Syria [as does western Nejd]: and therefore the foreign color of Nejd is Mesopotamian." He marvelled at the erudition of the Nejd Arabs in spite of their isolation until he found that even here newspapers had found their way in recent years. English patent medicines are sold in the bazaar of Aneyza and the Arabs are somewhat acquainted with the wonders of Bombay and Calcutta. Palgrave found the inhabitants of Kasim and southern Nejd far more intelligent than those of the north. Except for the four large towns of Hail, Riad, Boreyda and Aneyza, Nejd has no large centres of population. Bedouin tribes are found everywhere and villagers cultivate the fertile oases even in the desert; but the population is not as dense as in Oman or Yemen nor even as in Nejran and Wady Dauasir.

Hail, the present capital of Nejd, may have a population of ten thousand within its walls. It lies east of Jebel Aja, a granite range 6,000 feet high ending abruptly at this point. The city is on a table-land 3,500 feet above the sea. The Amir's castle is a formidable stronghold occupying a position of immense natural strength in the Jebel Aja. Blunt visited this place in 1878, but does not give its exact site, "lest the information might be utilized by the Turks under possible future contingencies." We have three pen-pictures of Hail: that of Palgrave who drew a plan of the city; the description of Doughty with his plan of the Amir's residence and

guest-house ; and the sketches of Lady Ann Blunt on her pilgrimage.   It is a walled town with several gates, a large market-place, the palaces overtopping all and mosques sufficient
for the worshippers.   It is a clean, well-built town, according
to Doughty and pleasant to live in save for the awe of the
tyrant-ruler.   Its circuit may be nearly an hour ; in the centre
of the walled enclosure stands the palace ; near it the great
mosque and directly opposite the principal bazaar.   The great
coffee-hall where the Amir gives his audiences is eighty feet
long with lofty walls and of noble proportions.   It has long
rows of pillars " upholding the flat roof of ethel timbers and
palm-stalk mat-work, goodly stained and varnished with the
smoke of the daily hospitality.   Under the walls are benches
of clay overspread with Bagdad carpets.   By the entry stands
a mighty copper-tinned basin or 'sea' of fresh water with a
chained cup ; from thence the coffee-server draws and he may
drink who thirsts.   In the upper end of this princely *kahwa*
(coffee-house) are two fire-pits, like shallow graves, where
desert bushes are burned in colder weather; they lack good
fuel, and fire is blown commonly under the giant coffee-pots in
a clay hearth like a smith's furnace."

The palace castles are built in Nejd with battled towers of clay-
brick and whitened on the outside with *jiss* or plaster; this in
contrast with the palm-gardens in the walled-enclosure give the
town a bright, fresh aspect.   Outside the walls, the contrast of
the Bedouin squalor and the rusty black basalt rocks lying in
rough confusion is intense.   Hail lies in the midst of a barren
country and is an oasis not by nature but by the pluck and perseverance of its founders.   The Shammar Arabs settled here from
antiquity and the place is mentioned in the ancient poem of Antar.

Er-Riadh or Riad (the "gardens-in-the-desert") was the
Wahabi metropolis of Eastern Nejd and of all the Wahabi
empire.   The city lies in the heart of the Aared country, enclosed north and south by Jebel Toweyk and about 280 miles
southeast of Hail.   It is a large place (according to Palgrave of

30,000 population !), but nothing is known of its present state, as no European traveller has visited it since Palgrave. The general appearance of Riad, according to our guide is like that of Damascus. " Before us stretched a wide open valley, and in its foreground, immediately below the pebbly slope on whose summit we stood, lay the capital, large and square, crowned by high towers and strong walls of defence, a mass of roofs and terraces, where, overtopping all, frowned the huge but irregular pile of Feysul's royal castle, and hard by it rose the scarce less conspicuous palace, built and inhabited by his eldest son, Abdallah. All around for full three miles over the surrounding plain, but more especially to the west and south, waved a sea of palm-trees above green fields and well-watered gardens; while the singing, droning sound of the water-wheels reached us even where we had halted at a quarter of a mile or more from the nearest town-walls. On the opposite side southward, the valley opened out into the great and even more fertile plains of Yemama, thickly dotted with groves and villages, among which the large town Manhufah, hardly inferior in size to Riad itself, might be clearly distinguished. . . . In all the countries which I have visited, and they are many, seldom has it been mine to survey a landscape equal to this in beauty, and in historical meaning, rich and full alike to the eye and the mind. The mixture of tropical aridity and luxuriant verdure, of crowded population and desert tracts, is one that Arabia alone can present, and in comparison with which Syria seems tame and Italy monotonous." [1]

Undoubtedly the population of Riad has diminished since the seat of government was transferred to Hail; at present it has even less trade and importance than Hofhoof (Hassa) since the Turkish occupation.

[1] If we remember that Palgrave compares Feysul's mud-brick palace to the Tuileries of Paris, states that the great mosque of Riad can accommodate 2,000 worshippers, and gives the Wahabi ruler a standing army of 50,000, we deduct a little from the poetical description to have a balance of net facts.

JEBEL SHAMMAR and the northwestern desert, remain to be considered. The chief characteristics of this region are the extensive *Nefuds* or sandy-deserts and the nomad population. Jebel Shammar more than any part of Arabia is the tenting ground for the sons of Kedar. Everywhere are the black-worsted booths—the houses of goat-hair, so celebrated in Arabic poetry and song. Place-names on the map of this country are not villages or cities but watering-places for cattle and encampments of the tribes from year to year. From the Gulf of Akaba to the Euphrates, and as far north as their flocks can find pasture, the nomads call the land their own. Many of them are subject to the government of Nejd and pay a small annual tribute; some are nominally under Turkish rule and others know no ruler save their Sheikh and have no law save that of immemorial Bedouin custom.

Burckhardt discourses of these people like one who has dwelt among them, tasting the sweet and bitter of their hungry, homely life. He describes their tents and their simple furniture, arms, utensils, diet, arts, industry, sciences, diseases, religion, matrimony, government, and warfare. He tells of their hospitality to the stranger; their robbery of the traveller; their blood-revenge and blood-covenants; their slaves and servants; their feasts and rejoicings; their domestic relations and public functions; their salutations and language; and how at last they bury their dead in a single garment, scraping out a shallow grave in hard-burned soil and heaping on a few rough stones to keep away the foul hyenas.

Burckhardt devotes a considerable portion of his book to an enumeration of the Bedouin-tribes and their numerous sub-divisions. These will prove of great service to those who visit or cross the northern part of the Peninsula. The most important tribe is that of the *Anaeze*. They are nomads in the strictest acceptation of the word, for they continue during the whole year in almost constant motion. Their summer quarters are near the Syrian frontiers and in winter they retire into the heart of the desert or toward the Euphrates. When the tents are few they are pitched in a circle and called *dowar*, in greater numbers, they encamp in rows, one behind the other, especially along a rivulet or wady-bed ; such encampments are called *Nezel*. The Sheikh's or chief's tent has the principal place generally toward the direction whence guests or foes may be expected. The Anaeze tents are always of black goat's-hair; some other tribes have stuff striped white and black. Even the richest among them never have more than one tent unless he happen to have a second wife who cannot live on good terms with the first; he then pitches a smaller tent near his own. But polygamy is very unusual among the Bedouin Arabs, although divorce is common. The tent furniture is simplicity itself; camel-saddles and cooking utensils with carpets and provision skins, are all the Arab housewife has to look after.

Since the days of Job the Bedouin have been a nation of robbers. "The oxen were plowing and the asses feeding beside them; and the Sabeans fell upon them and took them away, yea they have slain the servants with the edge of the sword." (Job i. 14.) The Bedouin's hand is against every man in all Jebel Shammar to this day. The tribes are in a state of almost perpetual war against each other; it seldom happens, according to Burckhardt, that a tribe enjoys a moment of general peace with all its neighbors, yet the war between two tribes is not of long duration. Peace is easily made and easily broken. In Bedouin parlance a salt covenant is only binding while the salt is in their stomachs. General battles are rarely fought, and few lives are lost; to surprise an enemy by sudden attack, or to plunder a camp, are the chief objects of both parties. The dreadful effects of "blood-revenge" (by which law the kindred of the slain are in duty bound to slay the murderer or his kin) prevent many sanguinary conflicts. Whatever the Arabs take in their predatory excursions is shared according to previous agreement. Sometimes the whole spoil is equally divided by the Sheikh among his followers; at other times each one plunders for himself. A Bedouin raid is called a *ghazu*, and it is worthy of remark that the earliest biographer of Mohammed, Ibn Ishak, so designates the wars of the prophet of God with the Koreish. The Anaeze Bedouin never attack by night, for during the confusion of a nocturnal assault the women's apartments might be entered, and this they regard as treachery. The female sex is respected even among the most inveterate enemies whenever a camp is plundered, and neither men, women nor slaves are ever taken prisoners. It is war only for booty. The Arabs are robbers, seldom murderers; to ask protection or *dakheil* is sure quarter, even when the spear is lifted. Peace is concluded generally by arbitration in the tent of the Sheikh of a third tribe friendly to both combating tribes. The most frequent cause of war is quarrels over wells or watering-places and pasture grounds, just as in the days of the patriarchs.

"The Bedouins have reduced robbery," says Burckhardt, "in all its branches to a complete and regular system, which offers many interesting details." These details are very numerous, and the stories of robbery and escape given by the Arabian chroniclers, or told at the camp-fires, would fill a volume. One example will suffice us. Three robbers plan an attack on an encampment. One of them stations himself behind the tent that is to be robbed, and endeavors to excite the attention of the nearest watch-dogs. These immediately attack him; he flies, and they pursue him to a great distance from the camp, which is thus cleared of those dangerous guardians. The second robber goes to the camels, cuts the strings that confine their legs and makes as many rise as he wishes. He then leads one of the she-camels out of the camp, the others following as usual, while the third robber has all this time been standing with lifted club before the tent-door to strike down any one who might awake and venture forth. If the robbers succeed they then join their companion, each seizes the tail of a strong leading-camel and pulls it with all his might; the camels set up a gallop into the desert and the men are dragged along by their booty until safe distance separates them from the scene of robbery.   They then mount their prey and make haste to their own encampment.

Before we lightly condemn the robber we must realize his sore need.   According to Doughty and other travellers three-fourths of the Bedouin of Northwestern Arabia suffer continual famine and seldom have enough to eat.   In the long summer drought when pastures fail and the gaunt camel-herds give no milk they are in a sorry plight; then it is that the housewife cooks her slender mess of rice secretly, lest some would-be guest should smell the pot.   The hungry gnawing of the Arab's stomach is lessened by the coffee-cup and the ceaseless "tobacco-drinking" from the nomad's precious pipe.   The women suffer most and children languish away.   When one of these sons-of-desert heard from Doughty's lips of a land where "we had an abundance of the blessings of Allah, bread and clothing and peace, and, how, if any wanted, the law succored him—he began to be full of melancholy, and to lament the everlasting infelicity of the Arabs, whose lack of clothing is a cause to them of many diseases, who have not daily food nor water enough, and wandering in the empty wilderness, are never at any stay—and these miseries to last as long as their lives.   And when his heart was full, he cried up to heaven, 'Have mercy, ah Lord God, upon Thy creature which Thou createdst—pity the sighing of the poor, the hungry, the naked —have mercy—have mercy upon them, O Allah!'"

As we bid farewell to the tents of Kedar and the deserts of North Arabia let us say amen to the nomad's prayer and judge them not harshly in their misery lest we be judged.

XVI

"THE TIME OF IGNORANCE"

"The religious decay in Arabia shortly before Islam may well be taken in a negative sense, in the sense of the tribes losing the feeling of kinship with the tribal gods. We may express this more concretely by saying that the gods had become gradually more and more nebulous through the destructive influence exercised, for about two hundred years, by Jewish and Christian ideas, upon Arabian heathenism."—*H. Hirschfeld*, in the "Journal of the Royal Asiatic Society."

IN order to understand the genesis of Islam we must know something of the condition of Arabia before the advent of Mohammed. We shall then be able to discover the factors that influenced the hero-prophet and made it possible for him so powerfully to sway the destinies of his own generation and those that were to follow.

Mohammedan writers call the centuries before the birth of their Prophet *wakt-el-jahiliyeh*—"the time of ignorance"—since the Arabs were then ignorant of the true religion. These writers naturally chose to paint the picture of heathen Arabia as dark as possible, in order that the "Light of God," as the prophet is called, might appear more bright in contrast. Following these authorities Sale and others have left an altogether wrong impression of the state of Arabia when Mohammed first appeared. The commonly accepted idea that he preached entirely new truth and uplifted the Arabs to a higher plane of civilization is only half true.[1]

No part of Arabia has ever reached the high stage of civilization under the rule of Islam which Yemen enjoyed under its Christian or even its Jewish dynasties of the Himyarites.

[1] In our chapter on the Arabic language we shall see that the golden age of Arabic literature was just before the birth of Mohammed.

Early Christianity in Arabia, with all its weakness, had been a power for good. The Jews had penetrated to nearly every portion of the peninsula long before Mohammed came on the scene.[1]

In the "Time of Ignorance" the Arabs throughout the peninsula were divided into numerous local tribes or clans which were bound together by no political organization but only by a traditional sentiment of unity which they believed, or feigned to believe, a unity of blood. Each group was a unit and opposed to all the other clans. Some were pastoral and some nomadic; others like those at Mecca and Taif were traders. For many centuries Yemen had been enriched by the incense-trade and by its position as the emporium of Eastern commerce. Sprenger in his ancient geography of the peninsula says that : "The history of the earliest commerce is the history of incense and the land of incense was Arabia." The immense caravan trade which brought all the wealth of Ormuz and Ind to the West, must have been a means of civilization to the desert. The tanks of Marib spread fertility around and the region north of Sana was intersected by busy caravan-routes. W. Robertson Smith goes so far as to say that "In this period the name of Arab was associated to Western writers with ideas of effeminate indolence and peaceful opulence . . . the golden age of Yemen."

[1] "Mohammedanism had owed much to the Jewish kingdom of Sâba. The rule of the Sabean kings had extended over Mecca, and Jewish ideas and beliefs had thus made their way into the future birthplace of Mohammed. The fact is full of interest for students of the history of Islam. The epigraphic evidence which Dr. Glaser has presented to us shows that the rise of Mohammedanism was not the strange and unique phenomenon it has hitherto been thought to be. It had been prepared for centuries previously. Arabia had for ages been the home of culture and the art of writing, and for about two hundred years before the birth of Mohammed his countrymen had been brought into close contact with the Jewish faith. Future research will doubtless explain fully how great was his debt to the Jewish masters of Mecca and the Sabean kingdom of Southern Arabia."—Prof. A. H. Sayce in the *Independent*.

The Arabs had enjoyed for several thousand years, an almost absolute freedom from foreign dominion or occupation. Neither the Egyptians, the Assyrians, the Babylonians, the ancient Persians nor the Macedonians in their march of conquest ever subjugated or held any part of Arabia. But before the coming of the Prophet the proud freemen of the desert were compelled to bend their necks repeatedly to the yoke of Roman, Abyssinian and Persian rulers. In A. D. 105, Trajan sent his general, Cornelius Palma, and subdued the Nabathean kingdom of North Arabia. Mesopotamia was conquered and the eastern coast of the peninsula was completely devastated by the Romans in A. D. 116. Hira yielded to the monarchs of Persia as Ghassan did to the generals of Rome. Sir William Muir writes, "It is remarked even by a Mohammedan writer that the decadence of the race of Ghassan was preparing the way for the glories of the Arabian prophet." In other words Arabia was being invaded by foreign powers and the Arabs were ready for a political leader to break these yokes and restore the old-time independence. Roman domination invaded even Mecca itself not long before the Hegira. "For shortly after his accession to the throne, A. D. 610, the Emperor Heraclius nominated Othman, then a convert to Christianity, . . . as governor of Mecca, recommending him to the Koreishites in an authoritative letter."[1] The Abyssinian wars and invasions of Arabia during the century preceding Mohammed are better known. Their dominion in Yemen, says Ibn Ishak, lasted seventy-two years, and they were finally driven out by the Persians, at the request of the Arabs.

Arabia was thus the centre of political schemes and plots just at the time when Mohammed came to manhood ; the whole peninsula was awake to the touch of the Romans, Abyssinians and Persians, and ready to rally around any banner that led to a national deliverance.

As to the position of women in this "Time of Ignorance."

[1] Koelle's Mohammed, p. 5.

the cruel custom of female infanticide prevailed in many parts
of heathen Arabia. This was probably due, in the first instance, to poverty or famine, and afterward became a social
custom to limit population. Professor Wilken suggests as a
further reason that wars had tended to an excess of females over
males. An Arab poet tells of a niece who refused to leave the
husband to whom she had been assigned after capture. Her
uncle was so enraged that he buried all his daughters alive and
never allowed another one to live. Even one beautiful girl
who had been saved alive by her mother was ruthlessly placed
in a grave by the father and her cries stifled with earth. This
horrible custom however was not usual. We are told of one
distinguished Arab, named *Saa-Saa,* who tried to put down
the practice of "digging a grave by the side of the bed on
which daughters were born."

Mohammed improved on the barbaric method and discovered a way by which not some but *all* females could be
buried alive without being murdered—namely, the veil. Its
origin was one of the marriage affairs of the prophet with its
appropriate revelation from Allah. *The veil was unknown in
Arabia before that time.* It was Islam that forever withdrew
from Oriental society the bright, refining, elevating influence
of women. Keene says that the veil "lies at the root of all
the most important features that differentiate progress from
stagnation." The harem-system did not prevail in the days
of idolatry. Women had rights and were respected. In two
instances, beside that of Zenobia, we read of Arabian *queens*
ruling over their tribes. Freytag in his Arabian Proverbs gives
a list of female judges who exercised their office in the " time
of ignorance." According to Nöldeke, the Nabathean inscriptions and coins prove that women held an independent and
honorable position in North Arabia long before Islam ; they
constructed expensive family graves, owned large estates, and
were independent traders. The heathen Arabs jealously
watched over their women as their most valued possession and

defended them with their lives. A woman was never given away by her father in an unequal match nor against her consent. "If you cannot find an equal match," said Ibn Zohair to the Namir, "the best marriage for them is the grave." Professor G. A. Wilken[1] adduces many proofs to show that women had a right in every case to choose their own husbands and cites the case of Khadijah who offered her hand to Mohammed. Even captive women were not kept in slavery, as is evident from the verses of Hatim :

> " They did not give us Taites, their daughters in marriage ;
> But we wooed them against their will with our swords.
> And with us captivity brought no abasement.
> They neither toiled making bread nor made the pot boil ;
> But we mingled them with our women, the noblest,
> And bare us fair sons, white of face."

Polyandry and polygamy were both practiced ; the right of divorce belonged to the wife as well as to the husband ; temporary marriages were also common. As was natural among a nomad race, the marriage bond was quickly made and easily dissolved. But this was not the case among the Jews and Christians of Yemen and Nejran. Two kinds of marriage were in vogue. The *mota'a* was a purely personal contract between a man and woman ; no witnesses were necessary and the woman did not leave her home or come under the authority of her husband ; even the children belonged to the wife. This marriage, so frequently described in Arabic poetry, was not considered illicit but was openly celebrated in verse and brought no disgrace on the woman. In the other kind of marriage, called *nikah*, the woman became subject to her husband by capture or purchase. In the latter case the purchase-money was paid to the bride's kin.

The position of women before Islam is thus described in

---

[1] Het Matriarchaat bij de onde Arabieren (1884), and *Supplement* to the same, in answer to critics, (1885). The Hague.

Smith's "Kinship and Marriage in Early Arabia": "It is very remarkable that in spite of Mohammed's humane ordinances the place of woman in the family and in society has steadily declined under his law. In ancient Arabia we find . . . many proofs that women moved more freely and asserted themselves more strongly than in the modern East. . . . The Arabs themselves recognized that the position of woman had fallen . . . and it continued still to fall under Islam, because the effect of Mohammed's legislation in favor of women was more than outweighed by the establishment of marriages of dominion as the one legitimate type, and by the gradual loosening of the principle that married women could count on their own kin to stand by them against their husbands."[1]

In "the time of ignorance" writing was well known and poetry flourished. Three accomplishments were coveted—eloquence, horsemanship and liberal hospitality. Orators were in demand, and to maintain the standard and reward excellence there were large assemblies as at Okatz. These lasted a whole month and the tribes came long journeys to hear the orators and poets as well as to engage in trade. The learning of the Arabs was chiefly confined to tribal history, astrology and the interpretation of dreams; in these they made considerable progress.

According to Moslem tradition the science of writing was not known in Mecca until introduced by Harb, Father of Abu Scofian, the great opponent of Mohammed, about A. D. 560. But this is evidently an error, for close intercourse existed long before this between Mecca and Sana the capital of Yemen where writing was well known; and in another tradition Abd el Muttalib is said to have *written* to Medina for help in his younger days, *i. e.*, about 520 A. D. Both Jews and Christians also dwelt in the vicinity of Mecca for two hundred years before the Hegira and used some form of writing. For writing materials they had abundance of reeds and palm-leaves as well as

[1] Smith's " Kinship and Marriage in Early Arabia," pp. 100, 104.

the flat, smooth shoulder-bones of sheep. The seven poems
are said to have been written in gold on Egyptian silk and
suspended in the Kaaba.

In the earlier part of his mission Mohammed despised the
poets for the good reason that some, among them a poetess,
wrote satirical verses about him. The Koran says "those who
go astray follow the poets." (Surah 26 : 224) and a more
vigorous though less elegant denouncement is recorded in the
traditions (Mishkat Bk. 22, ch. 10): "A belly full of puru-
lent matter is better than a belly full of poetry." When two
of the heathen poets, Labid and Hassan embraced Islam, the
prophet became more lenient, and is reported to have said
"poetry is a kind of composition which if it is good, it is good,
and if it is bad, it is bad ! "

Concerning the religion of the heathen Arabs the Mohammedan writer Ash-Shahristani says : " The Arabs of pre-islamic
times may, with reference to religion be divided into various
classes. Some of them denied the Creator, the resurrection
and men's return to God, and asserted that Nature possesses in
itself the power of bestowing life, but that Time destroys.
Others believed in a Creator and a creation produced by Him
out of nothing but yet denied the resurrection. Others believed in a Creator and a creation but denied God's prophets
and worshipped false gods concerning whom they believed that
in the next world they would become *mediators* between themselves and God. For these deities they undertook pilgrimages,
they brought offerings to them, offered them sacrifices and approached them with rites and ceremonies. Some things they
held to be Divinely permitted, others to be prohibited. This
was the religion of the majority of the Arabs." This is remarkable evidence for a Mohammedan who would naturally be
inclined to take an unfavorable view. But his absolute silence
regarding the Jews and Christians of Arabia is suggestive.

When the Arabian tribes lost their earliest monotheism (the
religion of Job and their patriarchs) they first of all adopted

Sabeanism or the worship of the hosts of heaven.   A proof of this is their ancient practice of making circuits around the shrines of their gods as well as their skill in astrology.   Very soon however the star-worship became greatly corrupted and other deities, superstitions and practices were introduced.   Ancient Arabia was a refuge for all sorts of religious-fugitives ; and each band added something to the national stock of religious ideas.   The Zoroastrians came to East Arabia; the Jews settled at Kheibar, Medina, and in Yemen ; Christians of many sects lived in the north and in the highlands of Yemen.   For all pagan Arabia Mecca was the centre many centuries before Mohammed.   Here stood the Kaaba, the Arabian Pantheon, with its three hundred and sixty idols, one for each day in the year.   Here the tribes of Hejaz met in annual pilgrimage to rub themselves on the Black Stone, to circumambulate the Beit Allah or Bethel of their creed and to hang portions of their garments on the sacred trees.   At Nejran a sacred date-palm was the centre of pilgrimage.   Everywhere in Arabia there were sacred stones or stone-heaps where the Arab devotees congregated to obtain special blessings.   The belief in jinn or genii was well-nigh universal, but there was a distinction between them and gods.   The gods have individuality while the jinn have not; the gods are worshipped, the jinn are only feared ; the god has one form ; the jinn appear in many.   All that the Moslem world believes in regard to jinn is wholly borrowed from Arabian heathenism and those who have read the Arabian Nights know what a large place they hold in the everyday life of Moslems.

The Arabs were always superstitious, and legends of all sorts cluster around every weird desert rock, gnarled tree or intermittent fountain in Arabia.   The early Arabs therefore marked off such sacred territory by pillars or cairns and considered many things such as shedding of blood, cutting of trees, killing game, etc., forbidden within the enclosure.   This is the origin of the *Haramain* or sacred territory around Mecca and Medina.

Sacrifices were common, but not by fire. The blood of the offering was smeared over the rude stone altars and the flesh was eaten by the worshipper. First fruits were given to the gods and libations were poured out; a hair-offering formed a part of the ancient pilgrimage; this also is imitated to-day.

W. Robertson Smith tries to prove that *totemism* was the earliest form of Arabian idolatry and that each tribe had its sacred animal. The strongest argument for this is the undoubted fact that many of the tribal names were taken from animals and that certain animals were regarded as sacred in parts of Arabia. The theory is too far-reaching to be adopted at haphazard and the author's ideas of the significance of animal sacrifice are not in accord with the teaching of Scripture. It is however interesting to know that the same authority thinks the Arabian tribal marks or *wasms* were originally totem-marks and must have been tattooed on the body even as they are now used to mark property. The *washm* of the idolatrous Arabs seems related to their *wasms* and was a kind of tattooing of the hands, arms and gums. It was forbidden by Mohammed but is still widely prevalent in North Arabia among the Bedouin women.

Covenants of blood and of salt are also very ancient Semitic institutions and prevailed all over Arabia. The form of the oath was various. At Mecca the parties dipped their hands in a pan of blood and tasted the contents; in other places they opened a vein and mixed their fresh blood; again they would each draw the others' blood and smear it on seven stones set up in the midst. The later Arabs substituted the blood of a sheep or of a camel for human blood.

The principal idols of Arabia were the following; ten of them are mentioned by name in the Koran.

Hubal was in the form of a man and came from Syria; he was the god of rain and had a high place of honor.

Wadd was the god of the firmament.

Suwah, in the form of a woman, was said to be from antediluvian times,

Yaghuth had the shape of a lion.

Ya'ook was in the form of a horse, and was worshipped in Yemen. Bronze images of this idol are found in ancient tombs.

Nasr was the eagle-god.

El Uzza, identified by some scholars with Venus, was worshipped at times under the form of an acacia tree.

Allat was the chief idol of the tribe of Thakif at Taif who tried to compromise with Mohammed to accept Islam if he would not destroy their god for three years. The name appears to be the feminine of Allah.

Manat was a huge stone worshipped as an altar by several tribes.

Duwar was the virgin's idol and young women used to go around it in procession; hence its name.

Isaf and *Naila* stood near Mecca on the hills of Safa and Mirwa; the visitation of these popular shrines is now a part of the Moslem pilgrimage.

Habhab was a large stone on which camels were slaughtered.

Beside these there were numerous other gods whose names have been utterly lost and yet who each had a place in the Pantheon at Mecca. Above all these was the supreme deity whom they called ὃ θεὸς, the God, or *Allah*. This name occurs several times in the ancient pre-islamic poems and proves that the Arabs knew the one true God by name even in the "time of ignorance." To Him they also made offerings though not of the first and best; in His name covenants were sealed and the holiest oaths were sworn. Enemy of *Allah* was the strongest term of opprobrium among the Arabs then as it is to-day. Wellhausen says, " In worship *Allah* had the last place, those gods being preferred who represented the interests of a particular circle and fulfilled the private desires of their worshippers. Neither the fear of *Allah* nor their reverence for the gods had much influence. The chief practical consequence of the great feasts was the observance of a truce in the holy months; and this in time had become mainly an affair of pure practical convenience. In general the disposition of the heathen Arabs, if it is at all truly reflected in their poetry, was profane in an unusual degree. The ancient inhabitants of Mecca practiced piety essentially as a trade, just as they do now; their

trade depended on the feast and its fair on the inviolability of
the Haram and on the truce of the holy months."

There is no doubt that at the time of Mohammed's appearance the old national idolatry had degenerated. Many of the
idols had no believers or worshippers. Sabeanism had also
disappeared except in the north of Arabia ; although it always
left its influence which is evident not only in the Koran but in
the superstitious practices of the modern Bedouins. Gross
fetishism was the creed of many. One of Mohammed's contemporaries said, "When they found a fine stone they adored
it, or, failing that, milked a camel over a heap of sand and
worshipped that." The better classes at Mecca and Medina
had ceased to believe anything at all. The forms of religion
"were kept up rather for political and commercial reasons than
as a matter of faith or conviction." [1]

Add to all this the silent but strong influence of the Jews
and Christians who were in constant contact with these idolaters
and we have the explanation of the *Hanifs*. These Hanifs
were a small number of Arabs who worshipped only *Allah*, rejected polytheism, sought freedom from sin and resignation to
God's will. There were Hanifs at Taif, Mecca and Medina.
They were in fact seekers of truth, weary of the old idolatry
and the prevalent hollow hypocrisy of the Arabs. The earliest
Hanifs of whom we hear, were Waraka, the cousin of the
prophet Mohammed, and Zeid bin Amr, surnamed the Inquirer.
Mohammed at first also adopted this title of Hanif to express
the faith of Abraham but soon after changed it to Moslem.

It is only a step from Hanifism to Islam. Primary monotheism, Sabeanism, idolatry, fetishism, Hanifism, and then the
prophet with the sword to bring everything back to monotheism
—monotheism, as modified by his own needs and character and
compromises. The time of ignorance was a time of chaos.
Everything was ready for one who could take in the whole situation, social, political and religious and form a cosmos. That
man was Mohammed.

[1] Palmer's Introduction to the Koran, p. xv.

XVII

" Islam was born in the desert, with Arab Sabeanism for its mother and Judaism for its father; its foster-nurse was Eastern Christianity."—*Edwin Arnold.*

" A Prophet without miracles; a faith without mysteries; and a morality without love; which has encouraged a thirst for blood, and which began and ended in the most unbounded sensuality."—*Schlegel's Philosophy of History.*

" As we conceive God, we conceive the universe; a being incapable of loving is incapable of being loved."—*Principal Fairbairn.*

LIBRARIES have been written, not only in Arabic and Persian, but in all the languages of Europe, on the origin, character and history of Islam, the Koran and Mohammed. Views differ " as far as the east is from the west" and as far as Bosworth Smith is from Prideaux. The earlier European writers did not hesitate to call Mohammed a false prophet and his system a clever imposture; some went further and attributed even satanic agency to the success of Islam and to the words of the prophet. Carlyle, in his " Heroes and Hero-worship," set the pendulum swinging to the other side so far that his chapter on the Hero-prophet is published as a leaflet by the Mohammedan Missionary Society of Lahore. So little did Carlyle understand the true nature of Islam that he calls it "a kind of Christianity." What Carlyle said was only the beginning of a series of apologies and panegyrics which appeared soon after and placed Mohammed not only on the ped-

[1] In the order of time, and to fully grasp the extent of Christian ideas prevalent in Arabia the chapter on Early Christianity in Arabia should precede this chapter on Islam; but logically that chapter belongs with the other chapters on mission-work. The same is true, in a measure, of the chapter on the Sabeans.

estal of a great reformer but "a very prophet of God," making
Islam almost the ideal religion.   Syeed Ameer Ali succeeds in
his biography in eliminating every sensual, harsh and ignorant
trait from the character of the noted Meccan ; and the recent
valuable book of T. W. Arnold, professor in Aligarh College,
India, attempts to prove most elaborately that Mohammedanism
was propagated without the sword.

In contrast to this read what Hugh Broughton quaintly wrote
in 1662 : "Now consider this Moamed or Machumed, whom
God gave up to a blind mind, an Ishmaelite, being a poor man
till he married a widow; wealthy then and of high countenance, having the falling sickness and being tormented by the
devil, whereby the widow was sorry that she matched with
him.   He persuaded her by himself and others that his fits
were but a trance wherein he talked with the angel Gabriel.   So
in time the impostor was reputed a prophet of God and from
Judaism, Arius, Nestorius and his own brain he frameth a
doctrine."   In our day, the critical labors of scholars like
Sprenger, Weil, Muir, Koelle and others have given us a
more correct idea of Mohammed's life and character.   The
pendulum is still swinging but will come to rest between the
two extremes.

We have not space to give the story of Mohammed's life or
of the religion which he founded.   An analysis of the religion
has been attempted by means of two diagrams; one showing
its development from its creed and the other the philosophy of
its origin from outside sources.[1]   The result of a century of
critical study by European and American scholars of every
school of thought has certainly established the fact that Islam
is a composite religion.   It is not an invention but a concoc-
tion ; there is nothing novel about it except the genius of Mohammed in mixing old ingredients into a new panacea for
human ills and forcing it down by means of the sword.   These

---

[1] See pp. 177, 178 for tables showing the Elements in Islam and the
source from which they were derived.

heterogeneous elements of Islam were gathered in Arabia at a time when many religions had penetrated the peninsula, and the Kaaba was a Pantheon. Unless one has a knowledge of these elements of "the time of ignorance," Islam is a problem. Knowing, however, these heathen, Christian and Jewish factors, Islam is seen to be a perfectly natural and understandable development. Its heathen elements remain, to this day, perfectly recognizable in spite of thirteen centuries of explanation by the Moslem authorities. It is to the Jewish Rabbi Geiger that we owe our first knowledge of the extent to which Islam is indebted to the Jews and the Talmud. Rev. W. St. Clair Tisdall has recently shown how Mohammed borrowed even from the Zoroastrians and Sabeans, while as to the amount of Christian teaching in Islam, the Koran and its commentators are evidence.

There is a remarkable verse in the twenty-second chapter of the Koran, in which Mohammed seems to enumerate all the sources that were accessible to him in forming his new religion ; and at that time he seems to have been in doubt as to which was the most trustworthy source. The verse reads as follows : *" They who believe and the Jews and the Sabeans and the Christians and the Magians* (Zoroastrians) *and those who join other gods to God, verily God shall decide between them on the day of Resurrection."*

THE GOD OF ISLAM. Gibbon characterizes the first part of the Moslem's creed as "an eternal truth "—(" there is no god but God ") ; but very much depends on the character of the God, who is affirmed to displace all other gods. If *Allah's* attributes are unworthy of deity then even the first clause of the briefest of all creeds, is false. There has been a strange neglect to study the Moslem idea of God and nearly all writers take for granted that the God of the Koran is the same being and has like attributes as Jehovah or the Godhead of the New Testament. Nothing could be further from the truth.

First of all the Mohammedan conception of Allah is purely negative. God is unique and has no relations to any creature

that partake of resemblance. He cannot be defined in terms
other than negative. As the popular song has it,

> " Kullu ma yukhtaru fi balik
> Fa rabbuna mukhalifun 'an thalik—" [1]

Absolute sovereignty and ruthless omnipotence are his chief
attributes while his character is impersonal—that of a monad.
Among the ninety-nine beautiful names of God, which Edwin
Arnold has used in his poem " Pearls of the Faith," the ideas
of fatherhood, love, impartial justice and unselfishness are absent. The Christian truth " God is love " is to the learned,
blasphemy and to the ignorant an enigma. Palgrave, who certainly was not biased against the religion of Arabia and who
lived with the Arabs for long months, calls the theology of Islam
" the pantheism of force." No one has ever given a better account of *Allah*, a more faithful portrait of Mohammed's conception of deity than Palgrave. Every word of his description
tallies with statements which one can hear daily from pious
Moslems. Yet no one who reads what we quote in all its fullness will recognize here the God whom David addresses in the
Psalms or who became incarnate at Bethlehem and suffered on
Calvary. This is Palgrave's statement:

" There is no god but God—are words simply tantamount in
English to the negation of any deity save one alone; and thus
much they certainly mean in Arabic, but they imply much
more also. Their full sense is, not only to deny absolutely and
unreservedly all plurality, whether of nature or of person, in
the Supreme Being, not only to establish the unity of the Un-
begetting and Unbegot, in all its simple and uncommunicable
Oneness, but besides this the words, in Arabic and among
Arabs, imply that this one Supreme Being is also the only
Agent, the only Force, the only Act existing throughout the
universe, and leave to all beings else, matter or spirit, instinct
or intelligence, physical or moral, nothing but pure, uncon-

[1] Whatever idea your mind can conceive, God is the reverse of it.

ditional passiveness, alike in movement or in quiescence, in action or in capacity. The sole power, the sole motor, movement, energy, and deed is God ; the rest is downright inertia
and mere instrumentality, from the highest archangel down to
the simplest atom of creation. Hence, in this one sentence,
'La Ilāh illa Allāh,' is summed up a system which, for want
of a better name, I may be permitted to call the Pantheism of
Force, or of Act, thus exclusively assigned to God, who absorbs
it all, exercises it all, and to whom alone it can be ascribed,
whether for preserving or for destroying, for relative evil or for
equally relative good.   I say 'relative,' because it is clear that
in such a theology no place is left for absolute good or evil,
reason or extravagance ; all is abridged in the autocratic will
of the one great Agent : 'sic volo, sic jubeo, stet pro ratione
voluntas ' ; or, more significantly still, in Arabic, 'Kemā
yesha'o,' ' as he wills it,' to quote the constantly recurring expression of the Koran.

"Thus immeasurably and eternally exalted above, and dis-
similar from, all creatures, which lie levelled before him on one
common plane of instrumentality and inertness, God is one in
the totality of omnipotent and omnipresent action, which
acknowledges no rule, standard, or limit save his own sole and
absolute will.   He communicates nothing to his creatures, for
their seeming power and act ever remain his alone, and in return
he receives nothing from them ; for whatever they may be, that
they are in him, by him, and from him only.   And secondly,
no superiority, no distinction, no preëminence, can be lawfully
claimed by one creature over its fellow, in the utter equalization
of their unexceptional servitude and abasement; all are alike
tools of the one solitary Force which employs them to crush or to
benefit, to truth or to error, to honor or shame, to happiness, or
misery, quite independently of their individual fitness, deserts, or
advantage, and simply because he wills it, and as he wills it.

"One might at first think that this tremendous autocrat, this
uncontrolled and unsympathizing power, would be far above

anything like passions, desires or inclinations. Yet such is not the case, for he has with respect to his creatures one main feeling and source of action, namely, jealousy of them lest they should perchance attribute to themselves something of what is his alone, and thus encroach on his all-engrossing kingdom. Hence he is ever more prone to punish than to reward, to inflict than to bestow pleasure, to ruin than to build.

"It is his singular satisfaction to let created beings continually feel that they are nothing else than his slaves, his tools, and contemptible tools also, that thus they may the better acknowledge his superiority, and know his power to be above their power, his cunning above their cunning, his will above their will, his pride above their pride ; or rather, that there is no power, cunning, will, or pride save his own.

"But he himself, sterile in his inaccessible height, neither loving nor enjoying aught save his own and self-measured decree, without son, companion, or counsellor, is no less barren for himself than for his creatures, and his own barrenness and lone egoism in himself as the cause and rule of his indifferent and unregarding despotism around. The first note is the key of the whole tune, and the primal idea of God runs through and modifies the whole system and creed that centres in him.

"That the notion here given of the Deity, monstrous and blasphemous as it may appear, is exactly and literally that which the Koran conveys, or intends to convey, I at present take for granted. But that it indeed is so, no one who has attentively perused and thought over the Arabic text (for mere cursory reading, especially in a translation, will not suffice) can hesitate to allow. In fact, every phrase of the preceding sentences, every touch in this odious portrait has been taken, to the best of my ability, word for word, or at least meaning for meaning from the " Book " the truest mirror of the mind and scope of its writer. And that such was in reality Mahomet's mind and idea is fully confirmed by the witness-tongue of contemporary tradition."

The Koran shows that Mohammed had in a measure a correct knowledge of the *physical* attributes of God but an absolutely false conception of his *moral* attributes. This was perfectly natural because Mohammed had no idea of the nature of sin—moral evil—or of holiness—moral perfection.

The Imam El Ghazzali a famous scholastic divine of the Moslems says of God: "He is not a body endued with form nor a substance circumscribed with limits or determined by measure. Neither does He resemble bodies, as they are capable of being measured or divided. Neither is He a substance nor do substances exist in Him; neither is He an accident nor do accidents exist in Him. Neither is He like to anything that exists; neither is anything like to Him; nor is He determinate in quantity nor comprehended by bounds nor circumscribed by the differences of situation nor contained in the heavens. . . . His nearness is not like the nearness of bodies nor is His essence like the essence of bodies. Neither doth He exist in anything; neither does anything exist in Him." God's will is absolute and alone; the predestination of everything and everybody to good or ill according to the caprice of sovereignty. For there is no Fatherhood and no purpose of redemption to soften the doctrine of the decrees. Hell must be filled and so Allah creates infidels. The statements of the Koran on this doctrine are coarse and of tradition, blasphemous. Islam reduces God to the category of the will; He is a despot, an Oriental despot, and as the *moral*-law is not emphasized He is not bound by any standard of justice. Worship of the creature is heinous to the Moslem mind, and yet Allah punished Satan for not being willing to worship Adam. (Koran ii. 28–31.) Allah is merciful in winking at the sins of the prophet but is the avenger of all unbelievers in him.

> "A God-machine, a unit-cause
>   Vast, inaccessible
> Who doles out mercy, breaks His laws
>   And compromises ill.

" A God whose law is changeless fate,—
Who grants each prophet-wish —
For prayer and fasting opes heaven's gate,
And pardons for backsheesh."

This is *not* "the only True God" whom we know through Jesus Christ and so knowing have life-eternal. "No man knoweth the Father but the *Son* and he to whom the Son revealeth Him. He who denies the incarnation remains ignorant of God's true character. As Fairbairn says, "the love which the *Godhead* makes immanent and essential to God, gives God an altogether new meaning and actuality for religion; while thought is not forced to conceive Monotheism as the apotheosis of an Almighty will or an impersonal ideal of the pure reason." Islam knows no Godhead, and Allah is not love.

"There is no god but Allah and Mohammed is his apostle."

The Doctrine of Revelation :	The Doctrine of God
(Positive.)	(Negative.)
"Mohammed is the apostle of God."	"There is no god but God."
[The sole channel of revelation and abrogates former revelations.]	[Pantheism of Force]

ANALYSIS OF ISLAM AS A SYSTEM, DEVELOPED FROM ITS CREED.

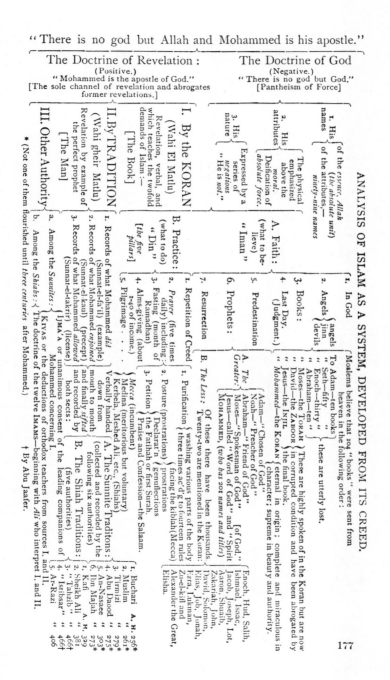

The Doctrine of God

1. His names
   - of the essence, Allah (the absolute unit)
   - of the attributes,— ninety-nine names

2. His attributes
   - The physical emphasized
   - Deification of absolute force.
   - His moral.

3. His nature
   - Expressed by a series of negations "He is not."

The Doctrine of Revelation

A. Faith: (what to believe) "Iman"

1. In God
2. Angels { angels, jinn, devils }
3. Books:
4. Last Day. (Judgment.)
5. Predestination
6. Prophets:
7. Resurrection

1. In God — Moslems believe that 104 "books" were sent from heaven in the following order:

To Adam—ten books)
" Seth—fifty "
" Enoch—thirty " } these are utterly lost.
" Abraham—ten "
" Moses—the TORAH
" David—the ZABOOR } in corrupted condition and have been abrogated by
" Jesus—the INJIL } These are highly spoken of in the Koran but are now
" Mohammed—the KORAN } eternal in origin; complete and miraculous in character; supreme in beauty and authority.

6. Prophets:

A. The Less: Of these there have been thousands; twenty-two are mentioned in the Koran: Enoch, Hud, Salih, Ishmael, Isaac, Jacob, Joseph, Lot, Aaron, Shuaib, Zakariah, John, David, Solomon, Elias, Job, Jonah, Ezra, Lukman, Zu-el-kifl and Alexander the Great, Elisha.

B. The Greater:
Adam—"Chosen of God."
Noah—"Preacher of God."
Abraham—"Friend of God."
Moses—"Spokesman of God," [of God."
Jesus—called "Word of God," and "Spirit
MOHAMMED, (who has 201 names and titles)

B. Practice: (what to do) "Din" [the five pillars]

1. Repetition of Creed
2. Prayer (five times daily) including:
3. Fasting (month of Ramadhan)
4. Alms-giving (about 1-40 of income.)
5. Pilgrimage . . . .

1. Repetition of Creed — Verbally handed down from mouth to mouth and finally sifted and recorded by both sects:

2. Prayer:
1. Purification { washing various parts of the body three times ac'd'g to fourteen rules
2. Posture (prostrations) { facing the kiblah (Mecca) Declarat'n } genuflections Petition } prostrations the Fatihah or first Surah.
3. Praise and Confession—the Salaam.

5. Pilgrimage:
Mecca (incumbent)
Medina (meritorious but voluntary)
Kerbela, Meshed Ali, etc., (Shiahs)

I. By the KORAN
(Wahi El Matu)

Revelation, verbal, and which teaches the twofold demands of Islam:—

[The Book]

II. By TRADITION
(Wahi gheir Matlu)

Revelation by example of the perfect prophet

[The Man]

1. Records of what Mohammed did (Sunnat-el-fa'il) (example)
2. Records of what Mohammed enjoined (Sunnat-el-kaul) (precept)
3. Records of what Mohammed allowed (Sunnat-el-takrir) (license)

A. The Sunnite Traditons: (collected and recorded by the six authorities) following:

		A. H.
1.	Buchari	256*
2.	Muslim	261*
3.	Tirmizi	279*
4.	Abu Daood	275*
5.	An-Nasaee	303*
6.	Ibn Majah	273*

B. The Shiah Traditions: (five authorities)

		A. H.
1.	Kafi	329
2.	Sheikh Ali	381
3.	"Tahzib"	466†
4.	"Istibsar"	466†
5.	Ar-Razi	406

III. Other Authority *

a. Among the Sunnites: IJMA'A or unanimous consent of the leading companions of Mohammed concerning I.
KIYAS or the deductions of orthodox teachers from sources I. and II.

b. Among the Shiahs: The doctrine of the twelve IMAMS—beginning with Ali who interpret I. and II.

* (Not one of them flourished until three centuries after Mohammed.)

† By Abu Jaafer.

ANALYSIS OF THE BORROWED ELEMENTS OF ISLAM.

I. From HEATHENISM
(As existing in Mecca or prevalent in other parts of Arabia.)

a. Sabeanism:
- Astrological superstitions, e.g., that meteorites are cast at the devil.
- Oaths by the stars and planets. (Surahs 56, 53, etc.)

b. Arabian Idolatry:
- Circumambulation of Kaaba—and, perhaps, the *lunar* calendar.
- Allah (as *name* of supreme deity), used in old poets and worshipped by Hanifs.
- Mecca—centre of religious pilgrimage—The black-stone, etc. [running.
- Pilgrimage—*in every detail*: dress, hair offerings, casting stones, sacrifice,
- Polygamy, slavery, easy divorce, and social laws generally.
- Ceremonial cleanliness, forbidden foods, *circumcision*.
- Cosmogony—The different stores of the earth. Bridge over hell.
- Paradise—Its character—the *houris*=pairikas of Avesta.

c. Zoroastrianism.

d. Buddhism:
The use of the rosary.

(See Hughes' Dict. of Islam.)

II. From JUDAISM
(The Old Testament but more especially the *Talmud* as the source of Jewish ideas prevalent in Arabia just before Mohammed.)

A. Ideas and Doctrines:
(According to the divisions of Rabbi Geiger.)

1. Words that represent Jewish ideas (and are *not* Arabic but Hebrew), e.g.: *Eden*; *Gehinnom*; *Rabbi, Abba*=teacher; *Sakinat*= error; *Furkan*, etc., etc., etc. Shekinah; *Taghoot* (ark); *Torah* law; *Taboot* (used hundreds of times in Koran) =
   - Doctrine of *jinn* and their various kinds. Exorcism of jinn (Surah 113, 114).

2. Doctrinal views.
   - Unity of God.
   - Resurrection.
   - Seven hells and seven heavens.
   - Final judgment. Signs of last day.
   - Gog and Magog.

3. Moral and Ceremonial laws.
   - Prayer. Its time, posture, direction, etc.
   - Laws regarding impurity of body. Washing with water or with sand.
   - " " purification of women, etc.

4. Views of life: Use of "inshallah"; age of discretion corresponds to Talmud.

B. Stories and Legends:
(According to Rabbi Geiger.)

- Adam, Cain, Enoch; the fabulous things in the Koran are *identical* with Talmud.
- Noah—the flood—Eber (Hud)—Isaac,—Ishmael—Joseph. Cf. Koran with Talmud.
- Abraham—His idolatry—Nimrod's oven—Pharao—the calf—(taken from Talmud.)
- Moses.—The fables related of him and Aaron are old Jewish tales.
- Jethro (Shuaib); Saul (Taloot); Goliath (Jiloot), and Solomon especially. Cf. Talmud.

III. From CHRISTIANITY
(Corrupt form, as found in the apocryphal gospels), "Gospel of Barnabas."

1. Reverence for New Testament—Injil—(Zacharias, John, Gabriel).
2. Respect for religious teachers; the Koran references to priests and monks.
3. Jesus Christ—His names—Word of God, Spirit of God, etc.—Puerile miracles. (Basilidians, etc.) —*Denial of crucifixion.*
4. The Virgin—Her sinlessness—and the apostles—"hawari" an *Abyssinian* word [meaning "pure ones."]
5. Wrong ideas of the Trinity. As held by Arabian heretical sects.
6. Christian legends as of "Seven Sleepers," "Alexander of the horns," "Lok-it,"(=Æsop).
7. A fast month. Ramadhan to imitate lent.
8. Alms-giving as an essential part of true worship.

> "The Koran could not have been composed by any except God
> Will they say he forged it? Answer bring there-fore a chapter like unto it,"—THE KORAN.
> (Surah Yunas.)

XVIII

THE PROPHET AND HIS BOOK

IN 570 A. D. Abdullah the son of Abd el Muttalib a Mecca merchant went on a trading trip from Mecca to Medina and died there; the same year his wife, Amina, gave birth to a boy, named *Mohammed*, at Mecca. One hundred years later the name of this Arab lad, joined to that of the Almighty, was called out from ten thousand mosques five times daily, from Muscat to Morocco, and his new religion was sweeping everything before it in three continents.

What is the explanation of this marvel of history? Many theories have been laid down and the true explanation is probably the sum of all of them. The weakness of Oriental Christianity and the corrupt state of the church; the condition of the Roman and Persian empires; the character of the new religion; the power of the sword and fanaticism; the genius of Mohammed; the partial truth of his teaching; the genius of Mohammed's successors; the hope of plunder and love of conquest;—such are some of the causes given for the early and rapid success of Islam.

Mohammed was a prophet without miracles but not without genius. Whatever we may deny him we can never deny that he was a great man with great talents. But he was not a self-made man. His environment accounts in a large measure for his might and for his method in becoming a religious leader. There was first of all the political factor. "The year of the elephant" had seen the defeat of the Christian hosts of Yemen who came to attack the Kaaba. This victory was to the young and ardent mind of Mohammed prophetic of the political future of Mecca and no doubt his ambition assigned himself

179

the chief place in the coming conflict of Arabia against the Roman and Persian oppressors.

Next came the religious factor. The times were ripe for religious leadership and Mecca was already the centre of a new movement. The Hanifs had rejected the old idolatry and entertained the hope that a prophet would arise from among them.[1] There was material of all sorts at hand to furnish the platform of a new faith; it only required the builder's eye to call cosmos out of chaos. To succeed in doing this it would be necessary to reject material also; a comprehensive religion and a compromising religion, so as to suit Jew and Christian and idolater alike.

Then there was the family factor, or, in other words, the aristocratic standing of Mohammed. He was not a mere "camel-driver." The Koreish were the ruling clan of Mecca; Mecca was even then the centre for all Arabia; and Mohammed's grandfather, Abd el Muttalib, was the most influential and powerful man of that aristocratic city. The pet-child of Abd el Muttalib was the orphan boy Mohammed. Until his eighth year he was under the shelter and favor of this chief man of the Koreish. He learned what it was to be lordly and to exercise power, and never forgot it. The man, his wife and his training were the determinative factors in the character of Mohammed. The ruling factor was the mind and genius of the man himself. Of attractive personal qualities, beautiful countenance, and accomplished in business, he first won the attention and then the heart of a very wealthy widow, Khadijah. Koelle tells us that she was "evidently an Arab lady of a strong mind and mature experience who maintained a decided ascendency over her husband, and managed him with great wisdom and firmness. This appears from nothing more strikingly, than from the very remarkable fact that she succeeded in keeping him from marrying any other wife as long as she lived, though at her death, when he had long ceased to

[1] Koelle's Mohammed, p. 27.

be a young man he indulged without restraint in the multipli-
cation of wives. But as Khadijah herself was favorably disposed toward Hanifism, it is highly probable that she exercised
her commanding influence over her husband in such a manner
as to promote and strengthen his own attachment to the re-
formatory sect of monotheists.''

Mohammed married this woman when he had reached his
twenty-fifth year. At the age of forty he began to have his
revelations and to preach his new religion. His first convert,
naturally perhaps, was his wife ; then Ali and Zeid his two
adopted children ; then his friend, the prosperous merchant,
Abu-Bekr. Such was the nucleus for the new faith.

Mohammed is described in tradition as a man above middle
height, of spare figure, commanding presence, massive head,
noble brow, and jet-black hair. His eyes were piercing. He
had a long bushy beard. Decision marked his every movement and he always walked rapidly. Writers seem to agree
that he had the genius to command and expected obedience
from equals as well as inferiors. James Freeman Clarke says
that to him more than to any other of whom history makes
mention was given

> " The monarch mind, the mystery of commanding,
> The birth-hour gift, the art Napoleon
> Of wielding, moulding, gathering, welding, banding
> The hearts of thousands till they moved as one."

As to the moral character of Mohammed there is great diversity of opinion and the conclusions of different scholars cannot be easily reconciled. Muir, Dods, Badger, and others
claim that he was at first sincere and upright, himself believing
in his so-called revelations, but that afterward, intoxicated by
success, he used the dignity of his prophetship for personal
ends and was conscious of deceiving the people in some of his
later revelations. Bosworth Smith and his like, maintain that
he was " a very Prophet of God " all through his life and that

the sins and faults of his later years are only specks on the sun of his glory. Older writers, with whom I agree, saw in Mohammed only the skill of a clever impostor from the day of his first message to the day of his death. Koelle, whose book is a mine of accurate scholarship and whose experience of many years mission-work in Moslem lands qualifies him for a sober judgment, sees no striking contrast between the earlier and later part of Mohammed's life that cannot be easily explained by the influence of Khadijah. He was *semper idem*, an ambitious enthusiast choosing different means for the same end and never very particular as to the character of the means used.

Aside from the question of Mohammed's sincerity no one can apologize for his moral character if judged according to the law of his time, the law he himself professed to reveal or the law of the New Testament. By the New Testament law of Jesus Christ, who was the last prophet before Mohammed and whom Mohammed acknowledged as the Word of God, the Arabian prophet stands self-condemned. The most cursory examination of his biography proves that he broke repeatedly every sacred precept of the Sermon on the Mount. And the Koran itself proves that the Spirit of Jesus was entirely absent from the mind of Mohammed. The Arabs among whom Mohammed was born and grew to manhood also had a law, although they were idolaters, slave-holders and polygamists. Even the robbers of the desert who, like Mohammed, laid in wait for caravans, had a code of honor. Three flagrant breaches of this code stain the character of Mohammed.[1] It was quite lawful to marry a captive woman whose relatives had been slain in battle, but not until *three months after their death*. Mohammed only waited three days in the case of the Jewess Safia. It was lawful to rob merchants but not pilgrims on their way to Mecca. Mohammed broke this old law and "revealed a verse" to justify his conduct. Even in the "Time of Ig-

[1] See an article on "Mohammedanism and Christianity."—Dr. Robert Bruce, *The Christian Intelligencer* (New York) April, 1894.

norance" it was incest to marry the wife of an adopted son even after his decease. The prophet Mohammed fell in love with the lawful wife of his adopted son Zeid, prevailed on him to divorce her and then married her immediately; for this also he had a "special revelation." But Mohammed was not only guilty of breaking the old Arab laws and coming infinitely short of the law of Christ, he never even kept the laws of which he claimed to be the divinely appointed medium and custodian. When Khadijah died he found his own law, lax as it was, insufficient to restrain his lusts. His followers were to be content with four lawful wives; he indulged in ten and entered into negotiations for matrimony with thirty others.

It is impossible to form a just estimate of the character of Mohammed unless we know somewhat of his relations with women. This subject however is of necessity shrouded from decent contemplation by the superabounding brutality and filthiness of its character. A recent writer in a missionary magazine touching on this subject says, " We must pass the matter over, simply noting that there are depths of filth in the Prophet's character which may assort well enough with the depraved sensuality of the bulk of his followers . . . but which are simply loathsome in the eyes of all over whom Christianity in any measure or degree has influence." We have no inclination to lift the veil that in most English biographies covers the family-life of the prophet of Arabia. But it is only fair to remark that these love-adventures and the disgusting details of his married life form a large part of the "lives of the prophet of God" which are the fireside literature of educated Moslems.

Concerning the career of Mohammed after the Hegira, or flight from Mecca (622 A. D.), a brief summary suffices to show of what spirit he was. Under his orders and direction the Moslems lay in wait for caravans and plundered them; the first victories of Islam were the victories of highwaymen and robbers. Asma, the poetess who assailed the character of Mohammed, was foully murdered in her sleep by Omeir, and Mohammed praised him for the deed.   Similarly Abu Afik, the Jew, was killed at the request of Mohammed.   The story of the massacre of the Jewish captives is a dark stain also on the character of the prophet whose mouth ever spoke of "the Merciful and Compassionate."   After the victory, trenches were dug across the market-place and one by one the male-captives were beheaded on the brink of the trench and cast in it.   The butchery lasted all day and it needed torch-light to finish it. After dark Mohammed solaced himself with Rihana a Jewish captive girl, who refused marriage and Islam, but became his bond-slave.   It is no wonder that shortly after, Zeinab, who had lost her father and brother in battle, tried to avenge her race by attempting to poison Mohammed.

In the seventh year of the Hegira Mohammed went to Mecca and instituted for all time the Moslem pilgrimage.   The following year he again set out for Mecca at the head of an army of 10,000 men and took the city without a battle. Other expeditions followed and up to the day, almost the hour, of his death the prophet was planning conquests by the sword. It is a bloody story from the year of the Hegira until the close of the Caliphates.   He who reads it in Muir's volumes cannot but feel the sad contrast between the early days of Islam and the early days of Christianity.   The germ of all *sword-conquest* must be sought in the life and book of Mohammed. Both consecrate butchery in the service of Allah.   The successors of Mohammed were not less unmerciful than was the prophet himself.

Thus far we have considered Mohammed from a critical standpoint and have written facts.   But the Mohammed of history and the Mohammed of the present day Moslem biographers are two different persons.   Even in the Koran, Mohammed is human and liable to error.   Tradition has changed all that. He is now sinless and almost divine.   The two hundred and one names given him by pious believers proclaim his apotheosis.

He is called Light of God, Peace of the World, Glory of the
Ages, First of all Creatures and names yet more lofty and
blasphemous. He is at once the sealer and concealor of all
former prophets and revelations. They have not only been
succeeded but also supplanted by Mohammed. No Moslem
prays *to* him, but every Moslem daily prays for him in endless
repetition. He is the only powerful intercessor on the day of
judgment. Every detail of his early life is surrounded with
fantastical miracles and marvels to prove his divine commission.
Even the evil in his life is attributed to divine permission or
command and so the very faults of his character are his endless glory and his sign of superiority. God favored him
above all creatures. He dwells in the highest heaven and is
several degrees above Jesus in honor and station. His name
is never uttered or written without the addition of a prayer.
" Ya Mohammed " is the open sesame to every door of difficulty, temporal or spiritual. One hears that name in the bazaar
and in the street, in the mosque and from the minaret. Sailors
sing it while raising their sails; *hammals* groan it to raise a
burden ; the beggar howls it to obtain alms ; it is the Bedouin's
cry in attacking a caravan ; it hushes babies to sleep as a cradle song ; it is the pillow of the sick and the last word of the
dying ; it is written on the door-posts and in their hearts as
well as since eternity on the throne of God ; it is to the devout Moslem the name above every name ; grammarians can
tell you how its four letters are representative of all the sciences
and mysteries by their wonderful combination. The name of
Mohammed is the best to give a child and the best to swear by
for an end of all dispute in a close bargain. The exceeding
honor given to Mohammed's name by his followers is only *one*
indication of the place their prophet occupies in their system
and holds in their hearts. From the fullness of the heart the
mouth speaketh. Mohammed holds the keys of heaven and
hell. No Moslem, however bad his character, will perish
finally ; no unbeliever, however good his life, can be saved ex-

cept through Mohammed. One has only to question the Moslem masses or read a single volume of the traditions to prove these statements.

Islam denies a mediator and an incarnation but the " Story of the Jew " and similar tales put Mohammed in the place of a mediator without an incarnation, without an atonement, without holiness. Our Analysis of the Moslem creed shows how all the later teaching which so exalted Mohammed was present in the germ. " *La ilaha illa Allah* " is the theology, "*Mohammed er rasool Allah*," the complete Soteriology of Islam. The logical necessity of a perfect mediator was at the basis of the *doctrine of Tradition*. Islam has, it claims, a perfect revelation in the letter of the Koran ; and a perfect example in the life of Mohammed. The stream has not risen higher than its sources.

THE BOOK OF ISLAM. When Mohammed Webb the latest American champion of Islam spoke at the Chicago Parliament of religions in praise of the Koran and its teaching, Rev. George E. Post, M. D., of Beirut deemed it a sufficient reply to let the book speak for itself. He said : " I hold in my hand a book which is never touched by 200,000,000 of the human race with unwashen hands, a book which is never carried below the waist, a book which is never laid upon the floor, a book every word of which to these 200,000,000 of the human race is considered the direct word of God which came down from heaven. I propose without note or comment to read to you a few words from the sacred book and you may make your own comments upon them afterward." After quoting several verses to show that Mohammed preached a religion of the sword and of polygamy, he added : " There is one chapter which I dare not stand before you, my sisters, mothers and daughters, and read to you. I have not the face to read it ; nor would I like to read it even in a congregation of men. It is the sixty-fourth chapter of the Koran."

What sort of a book is this revelation of Mohammed of which

parts are unfit to read before a Christian audience and which yet is too holy to be touched by other than Moslem hands? A book which the orthodox Moslem believes to be uncreated and eternal, all-embracing and all-surpassing, miraculous in its origin and contents. A book concerning which Mohammed himself has said, "If the Koran were wrapped in a skin and thrown into the fire it would not burn." Goethe described it thus: "However often we turn to it, at first disgusting us each time afresh it soon attracts, astounds, and in the end enforces our reverence. Its style in accordance with its contents and aim is stern, grand, terrible—and ever and anon truly sublime. Thus this book will go on exercising through all ages a most potent influence." And Nöldeke writes, "if it were not for the exquisite flexibility and vigor of the Arabic language itself, which, however is to be attributed more to the age in which the author lived than to his individuality, it would scarcely be bearable to read the later portions of the Koran a second time." Goethe read only the translation; and Nöldeke was master of the original. It is as hopeless to arrive at a unanimous verdict regarding the Koran as it is to reach an agreement regarding Mohammed.

The book has fifty-five noble titles on the lips of its people but is generally called *the Koran* or "The Reading." It has one hundred and fourteen chapters, some of which are as long as the book of Genesis and others consisting of two or three sentences only. The whole book is smaller than the New Testament, has no chronological order whatever and is without logical sequence or climax. What strikes the reader first of all is its jumbled character; every sort of fact and fancy, law and legend is thrown together piecemeal. The four proposed chronological arrangements, by Jorlal-ud-Din, Muir, Rodwell and Nöldeke are in utter disagreement. Only two of Mohammed's contemporaries are mentioned in the entire book and his own name occurs only five times. The book is unintelligible to the average Moslem without a commentary, and I defy any one else to read it through, without the aid of notes, and understand a single chapter or even section.

We will not stop to consider the fabulous account which Moslems give of the origin of the Koran and how the various chapters were revealed. Although Moslems claim that the book was eternally perfect in form and preserved in heaven, they are compelled to admit that it was revealed piece-meal and at various times and places by Mohammed to his followers. It was recorded in writing, after the rude Arab fashion, "on palm-leaves and sheep-bones and white stones" to some extent; but for the most part was preserved orally by constant repetition. Omar suggested to Abu-Bekr after the battle of Yemama that since many of the Koran reciters were slain, it would be the part of wisdom to put the book of God in permanent form. The task was committed to Zaid, the chief amanuensis of Mohammed and the resulting volume was entrusted to the care of Hafsa, one of the widows of the prophet. Ten years later a recension of the Koran was ordered by the Caliph Othman and all previous copies were called in and burned. This recension of Othman, sent to all the chief cities of the Moslem world, has been faithfully handed down to the present. "No other book in the world has remained twelve centuries with so pure a text." (Hughes.) The present variations in editions of the Arabic Koran are numerous but none of them are, in any sense important. The present Koran is the same book that Mohammed professed to have received from God. Out of its own mouth will we judge the book; and we cannot judge the book without judging the prophet.

We will speak later of the poetical beauties of the Koran and of its literary character. We do not deny also that there are in the Koran certain moral beauties, such as its deep and fervent trust in the one God, its lofty descriptions of His Almighty power and omnipresence, and its sententious wisdom. The first chapter and the verse of the throne are examples.

" In the name of God, the Compassionate, the Merciful.
Praise be to God, Lord of all the worlds !
The Compassionate, the Merciful !
King on the Day of Judgment !
Thee do we worship, and to Thee do we cry for help !
Guide Thou us on the right path !
The path of those to whom Thou art gracious !
Not of those with whom Thou art angered, nor of those who go astray."

> "God ! there is no God but He ; the living, the Eternal
> Slumber doth not overtake Him, neither sleep.
> To Him belongeth whatsoever is in heaven and on the earth.
> The preservation of both is no weariness unto Him.
> He is the high, the mighty."

The great bulk of the Koran is either legislative or legendary; the book consists of laws and stories. The former relate entirely to subjects which engrossed the Arabs of Mohammed's day—the laws of inheritance, the relation of the sexes, the law of retaliation, etc.—and this part of the book has a local character. The stories on the other hand go back to Adam and the patriarchs, take in several unknown Arabian prophets or leaders, centre around Jesus Christ, Moses and Solomon and do not venture beyond Jewish territory except to mention Alexander the Great and Lukman (Æsop.).

From the analytical tables it is not very difficult to see whence the material for the Koran was selected. Rabbi Geiger's book, recently translated into English, will satisfy any reader that Hughes is nearly right when he says, "Mohammedanism is simply Talmudic Judaism adapted to Arabia plus the apostleship of Jesus and Mohammed." But it is *Talmudic* Judaism and not the Judaism of the Old Testament. For the Koran is remarkable most of all not because of its contents but because of its omissions. Not because of what it reveals but for what it *conceals* of " former revelations." The defects of its teaching are many. It is full of historical errors and blunders. It has monstrous fables. It teaches a false cosmogony. It is full of superstitions. It perpetuates slavery, polygamy, religious intolerance, the seclusion and degradation of woman and petrifies social life. But all this is of minor importance compared with the fact that the Koran professing to be a *revelation* from God does not teach the way to reconciliation with God and seems to ignore the first and great barrier to such reconciliation, viz : SIN. Of this the Old and New Testaments are always speaking. Sin and salvation are the subject of which the *Torah* and the *Zaboor* and the *Injil* (Law Prophets and Psalms) are full. The Koran is silent or if not absolutely silent, keeps this great question ever in the background.[1]

It is a commonplace of theology that " to form erroneous conceptions of sin is to fall into still graver errors regarding the way of salvation." Mohammed, as is evident from his whole life, had no deep conviction of sin in himself; he was full of self-righteousness. His ideas, too, of God, were *physical*, not *moral;* he saw God's power, but never had a glimpse of His holiness. And so we find that there is an inward unity binding together the prophet and his book as to their real character in the light of the gospel. With *such* ideas of God, *such* a prophet and *such* a book, it is easy to understand why the Mohammedan world became what it is to-day. These bare outlines of the system of Islam are all that are necessary to indicate its nature and genus. Allah's character as the revealer, Mohammed's character as the channel of the revelation, and the revelation itself, show us Islam in its cradle.

[1] Even the sacred books of India and China and Ancient Egypt compare more favorably with the Bible in this respect than does the Koran. They teach the heinous character of sin, as sin, and do not deny the need of a mediator or of propitiatory sacrifice but are full of both ideas.

XIX

THE WAHABI RULERS AND REFORMERS

*"*Nothing is so easy to appreciate as true Christian commerce. It is a
speaking argument, even to the lowest savage, for a gospel of truth and
love, and yet more to the races sophisticated by a false civilization."—
Principal Cairns.

THE history of the Arabian Peninsula has never yet been
written. Many books describe certain periods of its
history from the time of the earlier Arabian rulers, but there
is no volume that tells the story from the beginning in a way
worthy of the subject. It would be interesting to search out
the earliest records and trace the Himyarite dynasties to their
origin ; to learn the story of the Jewish immigrants who settled
in Medina, Mecca and Yemen even before the Christian Era ;
to follow the Arabs in their conquests under the banner of the
prophet ; to watch the sudden rise of the Carmathians and follow them in their career of destruction ; to search the old libraries and rediscover the romantic story of the Portuguese,
the Dutch and the English in Arabian waters ;—but our space
limits us to the story of the past century.[1]

To understand the present political conditions and recent
history of Arabia, we must go back to the year 1765, which
marks the rise of the remarkable Wahabi movement, which was
at the bottom of all the political changes that the Peninsula has
seen since ·that time. This movement was the renaissance of
Islam, even though it ended in apparent disaster, and was politically a splendid fiasco. The Wahabi reform attracted the attention of Turkey to Arabia ; its influence was felt in India to

[1] For a Chronological table of Arabian history, from the earliest times
to the present, *see Appendix.*

the extent of declaring a *jihad* or religious war against the government, and compelled England to study the situation and send representatives to the very heart of Arabia.

Beginning with the Wahabi dynasty, the history of the past century in Arabia centres in the rulers of Nejd and Oman, the Turkish conquests and the English influence and occupation. The strong independent government of Nejd under Ibn Rashid and his successor, Abd-ul-Aziz, would have been an impossibility except for the result of the Wahabi movement, in demonstrating the weakness of Turkish rule. And it was for fear of the Wahabi aggressions that Turkey strengthened her Arabian possessions and invaded Hassa.

Mohammed bin Abd-ul-Wahab was born at Ayinah in Nejd, in 1691. Carefully instructed by his father in the tenets of Islam according to the school of Hambali, the strictest of the four great sects.[1] Abd-ul-Wahab visited the schools of Mecca, Busrah and Bagdad, to increase his learning. At Medina, too, he absorbed the deepest learning of the Moslem divines and soaked himself in the "six correct books" of traditions. In his travels he had observed the laxity of faith and practice which had crept in, especially among the Turks and the Arabs of the large cities. He tried to distinguish between the essential elements of Islam and its later additions, some of which seemed to him to savor of gross idolatry and worldliness. What most offended the rigid monotheism of his philosophy was the almost universal visitation of shrines, invocation of saints and honor paid to the tomb of Mohammed. The use of the rosary, of jewels, silk, gold, silver, wine and tobacco, were all abominations to be eschewed. These were indications of the great need for reform. The earlier teaching of the companions of the prophet had been set aside or overlaid by later teaching. Even the four orthodox schools had departed from

[1] The four orthodox sects are called: Hanafis, Shafis, Malakis, and Hambalis. The last was founded by Ibn Hambal at Bagdad, 780 A. D. it is the least popular sect.

the pure faith by allowing pilgrimage to Medina, by multiply-
ing festivals and philosophizing about the nature of Allah.
Therefore it was that Abd-ul-Wahab preached reform not only,
but proclaimed himself the leader of a new sect. His teaching was based on the Koran and the early traditions.

This movement is chiefly distinguished from the orthodox
system in the following particulars :

1. The Wahabis reject *Ijma* or the agreement of later interpreters.

2. They offer no prayers to prophet, wali, or saint, nor visit their
tombs for that purpose.

3. They say Mohammed is *not yet* an intercessor; although at the last
day he will be.

4. They forbid women to visit the graves of the dead.

5. They allow only four festivals; *Fitr, Azha, 'Ashura* and *Lailat El
Mobarek.*

6. They do not celebrate Mohammed's birth.

7. They use their knuckles for prayer-counting, and not rosaries.

8. They strictly forbid the use of silk, gold, silver ornaments, tobacco,
music, opium, and every luxury of the Orient, except perfume and
women.

9. They have anthropomorphic ideas of God by strictly literal interpretation of the Koran texts about " His hand," " sitting," etc.

10. They believe *jihad* or religious war, is not out of date, but in-
umbent on the believer.

11. They condemn minarets, tombstones, and everything that was not
in use during the first years of Islam.

There is no doubt that Abd-ul-Wahab honestly tried to bring
about a reform and that in many of the points enumerated his
reform was strictly a return to primitive Islam.   But it was too
radical to last.   It took no count of modern civilization and
the ten centuries that had modified the very character of the
Arabs of the towns not to speak of those outside of Arabia.
Yet the preaching of the Reformer found willing ears in the
isolation of the desert.   As in the days of Omar, the promise
of reform in religion was made attractive by the promise of
rich booty to those who fought in the path of God and de-

stroyed creature-worshippers.   Mohammed Abd-ul-Wahab was
the preacher, but to propagate his doctrine he needed a sword.
Mohammed bin Saud, of Deraiyah, supplied the latter factor
and the two Mohammeds, allied by marriage and a common
ambition, began to make converts and conquests.   The son
of Bin Saud, Abd-ul-Aziz, was the Omar of the new movement,
and his son Saud even surpassed the father in military prowess
and successful conquest.   Abd-ul-Aziz was murdered by a
Persian fanatic while prostrate in prayer in the mosque at
Deraiyah, in 1803.   Saud at this very time was pushing the
Wahabi conquest to the very gates of Mecca.   On the 27th
of April, 1803, he carried his banner into the court of the
Kaaba and began to cleanse the holy place.   Piles of pipes,
tobacco, silks, rosaries and amulets were collected into one
great heap and set on fire by the infuriated enthusiasts.   No
excesses were committed against the people except that religion was forced upon them.   The mosques were filled by
public "whips" who used their leather thongs without mercy
on all the lazy or negligent.   Everybody, for a marvel, prayed
five times a day.   The result of his victory at Mecca was
communicated by the dauntless Saud in the following naïve
letter addressed to the Sultan of Turkey :

"Saud to Salim.—I entered Mecca on the fourth day of Moharram
in the 1218th year of the Hegira.   I kept peace toward the inhabitants.
I destroyed all things that were idolatrously worshipped.   I abolished all
taxes except those that were required by the law.   I confirmed the Kadhi
whom you had appointed agreeably to the commands of the prophet of
God.   I desire that you will give orders to the rulers of Damascus and
Cairo not to come up to the sacred city with the *Mahmal*[1] and with
trumpets and drums.   Religion is not profited by these things.   May the
peace and blessing of God be with you."

The absence of long salutations and the usual phrases of
honor is characteristic of all Wahabi correspondence.   In this

[1] The Mahmal is a covered litter, an emblem of royalty and of superstitious honor sent from Cairo and Damascus to Mecca, to this day.

respect it is a great improvement on the excessive lavishment of titles and honors so usual among Moslems, especially among the Persians and the Turks.

Before the close of the year Saud avenged his father's death by attacking Medina and destroying the gilded dome that covered the prophet's tomb. As early as 1801 parties of plundering Wahabis had sacked the tomb of Hussein and carried off rich booty from the sacred city of Kerbela. According to the official inventory this booty consisted of vases, carpets, jewels, weapons innumerable; also, 500 gilded copper-plates from the dome, 4,000 cashmire shawls, 6,000 Spanish doubloons, 350,000 Venetian coins of silver, 400,000 Dutch ducats, 250,000 Spanish dollars and a large number of Abyssinian slaves belonging to the mosque.[1] Their raids and conquests extended in every direction so that in a few years the Wahabi power was supreme in the greater part of Arabia.

A single illustration will show the great Saud's[2] prudence and celerity in action. When he invaded the Hauran plains, in 1810, although it was thirty-five days' journey from his capital, yet the news of his approach only preceded his arrival by two days, nor was it known what part of Syria he planned to attack, and thirty-five villages of Hauran were sacked before the Pasha of Damascus could make any demonstrations for defence!

Meanwhile the Sublime Porte remained inactive and nothing was done to regain the sacred territories. It was deemed impossible to reach Mecca from Damascus with any large body of soldiers through hostile territory where supplies were scarce. Salvation was expected from Egypt; and it was hoped that an

[1] Zehm's Arabie, p. 332.

[2] Saud died at the age of forty-five, in April, 1814, from fever, at Deraiyah. He was a strong-willed ruler but administered justice with rigor; he was wise in council and skillful in settling disputes and healing factions. Of his eight children, Abdullah, the eldest, succeeded him as ruler.

expedition by sea might succeed in taking Jiddah and thence advance upon Mecca. Mohammed Ali began preparations in 1810, and in the summer of 1811 an expedition under his son Touson Pasha was sent out from Suez. In October the fleet arrived at Yenbo and the troops took the town. Ghaleb the Sherif of Mecca proved false to the Wahabis and made negotiations with the Turkish commander to hand over the town. In January the army occupied Medina but at Bedr the troops were attacked by Wahabis and utterly routed.

All through this first campaign the cruelty and treachery of the Turks was shocking even to the mind of their Bedouin allies. None of their promises were kept; the skulls of the enemy slain were constructed into a sort of tower near Medina ; Ghalib, the Sherif, was betrayed and in violation of the most sacred promises he was taken prisoner and deported ; wholesale butchery of the wounded and mutilation of the slain were common.

A second army under Mustafa Bey advanced toward Mecca and also took possession of Taif. Although the five cities of the Hejaz were now in the hands of the Turks the Wahabi power was not yet broken. Mohammed Ali Pasha himself proceeded from Egypt with another army ; he had great difficulty in securing transportation and provisions. Finally he landed his troops at Jiddah and went on to Mecca, planning to attack Taraba the great Wahabi centre of the south, as Deraiyah was the capital of the north. Here the enemy had gathered in great numbers under an Amazon leader, a widow named Ghalye who ruled the Begoum Arabs. She was reported to be a sorceress among the Turks and stories of her skill and courage inspired them with fear. When the attack was made the Wahabis came off victorious and so harassed the army of occupation that during 1813 and the beginning of 1814 they remained perfectly inactive. Later the Turks made a sea attack on Gunfida, the port south of Jiddah, and captured it. The Wahabis however captured the wells that supplied the town, made a sortie and the Turkish troops fled panic-stricken, to their ships. Discontentment arose among the Turkish troops. Supplies failed and wages were in arrears. Mohammed Ali changed now his tactics and tried to bribe the Bedouin chiefs to desert the Wahabi leaders. At this time the Turkish army consisted of nearly 20,000 men and yet the campaign dragged on without a definite victory.[1]

The greatest battle was fought at Bissel near Taif where Mohammed Ali defeated the Wahabis with great slaughter. Six dollars were offered for every Wahabi head and before the day ended 5,000 bloody heads were piled up before the Pasha. About 300 prisoners were taken and offered quarter. But on reaching Mecca the cruel commander impaled fifty of them before the gates of the city; twelve suffered a like horrible death at every one of the ten coffee-houses, halting places between Mecca and Jiddah ; the remainder were killed at Jiddah and their carcasses left to dogs and vultures.

But the battle went against the Turks when they met the desert and its terrors. Hunger, thirst, fevers and the Bedouin robbers attacked the camp. In one day a hundred horses died ; the soldiers were dissatisfied and deserted. At length Mohammed Ali made proposals of peace to Abdullah bin Saud the Wahabi chief ; and when Saud entered Kasim with an army the negotiations were concluded and peace was declared. But peace was not kept, and Ibrahim Pasha, the son of Mohammed Pasha was despatched with a large expedition against the Wahabis in August, 1816.

While Egypt was attacking the Wahabi strongholds from the west, with infinite trouble and dubious results, the greatest loss the Wahabi government had yet suffered, was from a blow dealt by the British. In 1809 an English expedition went from Bombay against the piratical inhabitants of their chief

---

[1] The history of its tedious prosecution and all its cruelty on the side of the Turks is told by Burckhardt, the traveller, who was himself living in Mecca at this time.

castle and harbor, Ras-el-Kheimah.   The place was bombarded and laid in ashes.

Ibrahim Pasha accomplished by intrigue and bribery what his father failed to do by force of arms.   After a series of advances one tribe after another was detached from the Wahabi government.   At last without a battle the capital Deraiyah was taken, Abdullah captured, sent to Constantinople and there publicly executed on December 18th, 1818.

The Turks were naturally jubilant over their success and thought they had made an end of the hated Wahabis.   They soon learned their mistake.   No sooner was the army of Ibrahim Pasha withdrawn than the old spirit rehabilitated the fallen empire with the old time strength of fanaticism.   The army of the Pashas could not govern or even occupy the vast territories they had overrun.   Within a few years Turki the son of the late Amir was proclaimed Sultan of Nejd, recovered all and more than his father's territories, and by the judicious payment of a small tribute and yet smaller honor to the Egyptian Khedive retained the throne until he was murdered in 1831.   His son and successor, Feysul, took the reins of government and was rash enough to repudiate the Egyptian Suzerainty.   Nejd was again invaded. Hofhoof and Katif were temporarily occupied by Egyptian and Turkish troops and Feysul was banished to Egypt.[1]

Feysul died in 1865, having returned from his banishment in 1843 and ruling alone and supreme for all those years.   His son Abdullah, who had acted as regent during the later years

---

[1] Palgrave visited the Wahabi capital during the reign of Feysul and gives his usual picturesque descriptions of the court and family life of the genial tyrant.   But it is necessary to take his accounts of Riad *cum grano salis;* a Jesuit Roman Catholic would not describe the strict Puritanism of the Wahabis with any degree of admiration.   Palgrave's statistics of the strength of Feysul's army and of the population of his dominions are utterly unreliable and greatly exaggerated.   However one must read Palgrave to know what was the condition of the Wahabi empire in 1860–63, for he is our only authority for that period.

of Feysul, succeeded to the throne. But there was a rival in his brother Saud. Intrigues, treasons and violence were hatching in the palace courts even before the death of Feysul. The dagger and the coffee-cup of poisoned beverage have always been favorite weapons in seating and unseating the rulers of Arabia. A prolonged fight ensued between the two brothers. Saud was at first successful but Abdullah flying to Turkey invited the aid of that power with the result that an expedition from Bagdad ended in formally and permanently occupying El Hassa as a Turkish province.

At the time of Saud's death, in 1874, the conflict was renewed, but Abdullah ultimately regained the supremacy and was ruler at Riad until 1886, when events occurred that heralded the rise of another power in Nejd, based on political intrigue and the sword rather than on religion and fanaticism.

When Turki the Amir was murdered by his own cousin, Meshari, and Feysul succeeded to the throne, there was present at Riad in the army an obscure youth from Hail, Abdullah bin Rashid. He it was who entered the palace by stealth, stabbed Meshari, and helped to restore Feysul to his father's seat as ruler. His valor and loyalty were rewarded by bestowing upon him the governorship of his own native province Shammar; he was also granted a small army to strengthen the Wahabi rule in that region. He soon became almost as strong as his master and showed himself an expert in all the intrigue and skill possible to the Arabs. He extended his personal influence on all sides, built a massive palace at Hail and defeated all who plotted his destruction. Hired assassins dogged him on the streets, but Abdullah escaped every danger and his star remained in the ascendant. In 1844 he died suddenly, leaving unaccomplished ambitions and three sons, Telal, Mitaab, and Mohammed. Telal, the eldest son, was proclaimed ruler and was ever more popular than his father had been, and no less successful as a ruler. He strengthened his capital, invited merchants from Busrah and Bagdad to reside there, and gradually but surely established his entire independence of the Wahabi ruler at Riad. Tormented, however, by an internal malady he shot himself in 1867. His younger brother, Mitaab, who succeeded, ruled very briefly and was murdered by his nephews, the sons of Telal, within a year. Meanwhile, the third son of Abdullah bin Rashid, Mohammed, had been a refugee at the Riad capital. But his ambitions now found their opportunity and his true character was revealed. By permission of the Amir Abdullah bin Feysul he went back to Hail. He commenced by stabbing his nephew Bander who had usurped the throne; he then killed the five remaining children of his brother Telal and became undisputed Amir at Hail in 1868. During the next eighteen years he consolidated his authority. His rule was after the Arab heart—with a rod of iron and lavish hospitality; continual executions and continual feasting.

The Arabs at Bahrein tell many almost incredible tales of Mohammed bin Rashid's stern justice and speedy method of executing it, as well of his cruelty to those who resisted his will. In those days the public executioner's sword was always wet with blood; men were tied to camels and torn asunder; but the desert-roads were everywhere safe and robbers met with no mercy. As an indication of his wealth and hospitality it is related that he constructed in the courtyard of his palace a stone-cistern of great size always kept filled with that best of Bedouin dainties, clarified butter (*dihn*). A bucket and rope were at hand and oil was dealt out as freely as water to the honored guests of the great ruler.

In the year 1886 the long-looked for opportunity came for Mohammed bin Rashid to complete the work of Telal. He not only aspired to be independent of the Riad rulers but to make Riad, the Saud dynasty and all the Wahabi state a dependency of his Nejd kingdom. In that year Amir Abdullah bin Feysul was seized and imprisoned by two of his nephews, one of whom usurped the throne. Mohammed, as a loyal subject, marched to the rescue, deposed the pretender, but carried the Amir himself to Hail, leaving a younger brother as his deputy governor. The great empire of the Sauds was virtually ended; henceforth it was the green and purple banner of Rashid and not the red and white standard of the Wahabis that ruled all central Arabia.

Mohammed bin Rashid had shown supreme diplomatic ability in all his dealings with the Turks from the day of his power until his death. He humored their vanity by professing himself an ally of the Porte; he paid a small annual tribute to the Sherif of Mecca in recognition of the Sultan. But for the rest he never loved the Turk except at a good distance. None of the Arabs of the interior have forgotten the perfidy, treachery and more than Arab cruelty of the Egyptian Pashas in their campaigns.

In 1890 a final attempt was made by the partisans of the old dynasty to rebel against the Amir and secure the independence of Riad. It was fruitless; and the severe defeat of the rebels proved it final. In the year 1897 Mohammed bin Rashid died and his successor Abd-el-Aziz bin Mitaab now rules his vast dominions. He is less stern but not less able than his illustrious predecessor.

XX

THE RULERS OF OMAN

BEFORE we turn to the history of the Turks in Arabia a word is necessary regarding the rulers of Oman—that province unique in Arabia for its isolation from all the other provinces in the matter of politics. Prior to the appearance of the Portuguese in the Persian Gulf (1506) Oman had been governed for nine hundred successive years by independent rulers called Imams; elected by popular choice and not according to family descent. From that time until 1650 the Portuguese remained in power at Muscat. In 1741 Ahmed bin Said, a man of humble origin, a camel-driver, rose by his bravery to be governor of Sohar, drove the Persians who had succeeded the Portuguese, out of Muscat and founded the dynasty that has ever since ruled Oman. As early as 1798 the East India Company made a treaty with the Sultan of Muscat to exclude the French from Oman. This fact is important to show the character of the recent incident at Muscat.

Seyid Said, who ruled from 1804 to 1856, had constant struggles against the Wahabi power who threatened his territory. With England he joined the war against the Wahabi pirates; and made treaties in 1822, 1840 and 1845 to suppress the slave-trade. On the death of Said the Sultanate of Oman and Zanzibar was divided. Seyid Thowani reigned at Muscat while a younger brother reigned at Zanzibar. Thowani was assassinated at Sohar in 1866. Salim, his son, succeeded him, although he was suspected of patricide. Then there was an interregnum under a usurper until Seyid Turki another son of Said took the throne in 1871. Continual rebellion marked his period of rule. But he was friendly to the English and in re-

turn for the abolition of free traffic of slaves between Africa and
Zanzibar the English government allowed him an annual subsidy of a little over £6,000 a year. In 1888 the Sultan died
and his son, Feysul bin Turki, succeeded him. His rule was
mild ; from the palace at Muscat his influence was not far-
reaching ; rebellions, inter-tribal wars and plots of one moun-
tain-chief against another mark all the years of his reign up to
date. In February, 1895, there was a serious Bedouin uprising
in which the Arabs took the town and looted it. The Sultan
himself barely escaped and was for a time a prisoner in his fort
while the town was in the hands of the enemy. The cause of
the trouble was a difference as to the amount of yearly tribute
a certain Sheikh Saleh of Samed should pay the Muscat ruler.
From November, 1894, the rebels collected arms and strengthened their numbers until on February 12th of the following
year they were ready to strike the desired blow. As this
episode was characteristic of all Arab warfare we quote a brief
account of it sent at the time by a resident at Muscat to the
Bombay press :

"On February 12th Abdullah, the leader of his father's
(Sheikh Saleh's) troops, with a retinue of perhaps 200 armed
Bedouins arrived at Muscat in a scattered and peaceable manner, and obtained an audience with the Sultan. A musket
salute was fired, and no attack was thought of. The Sultan
presented the leader with a purse of $400 and a liberal allow-
ance of rice, dates, coffee, and the famous Muscat "halwa"
for the men. The Bedouins although armed were allowed to
go and come as they choose and no attack was feared. Sheikh
Abdullah himself sat for a time in the bazaar and received the
salaams of the people who kissed his hand in respect. When
evening came the Sultan requested the men to encamp outside
of the gates, the only means of entrance and exit through the
old Portuguese walls. Although failing to comply with the request the Bedouins claimed none but peaceful intentions. At
8 P. M. when according to custom the gates were closed, per-

haps one-half of the Bedouins were within the walls. This was
their Trojan horse. Shortly after midnight the gates were attacked, the few customary guards being easily overcome, and
thrown open to the large numbers of Bedouins who up to this
time had been hiding in a neighboring mosque. Both the
small gate leading to the bazaar and the larger one to the west
of the town were easily taken, and the Bedouins then advanced to the Sultan's palace, effected an entrance and rudely
awoke the Sultan and his family from their sleep. Seyyidi
Esel after a courageous struggle of a few minutes, (in which he
shot two of the attacking party,) escaped by a small door opening to the sea and fled to one of the two forts which command
the city as well as the harbor. His brother escaped to the
other. Each of these forts is manned by a force of perhaps
fifty men and has several old twelve pounder Portuguese guns.

"The forts opened fire at once upon the palace which the
Bedouins now occupied. The Bedouins took possession of the
town closing the gates and stationing armed men through the
bazaar and streets in the early hours of the 13th of February.

"A few shops containing muskets and ammunition were
opened, and the contents robbed. The Sultan's palace was
completely looted and all his personal property either destroyed
or sold at any price. On account of the suddenness of the
attack there was but a small number of the Sultan's soldiers in
readiness. These repaired to the forts and opened fire upon
the Bedouin invaders with both the guns of the foils and muskets. For three days we were the witnesses of the extraordinary spectacle of a Sultan bombarding his own palace; no attempt was made to meet the rebels on the streets. By order
of the invading captain the portion of the town inhabited by
British subjects was not entered. Until Sunday evening things
remained about the same. The attack from the forts was continued day and night. The Bedouins did not answer the fire
but remained in the palace and streets holding possessions but
making no attack on the forts. Within the town, although it is

in possession of the enemy, all was orderly and quiet. Un-
armed people were allowed to pass to and fro and guards were
stationed in the bazaar to prevent plunder. Reinforcements
were expected by both parties. On Monday morning a body
of about 1,000 arrived from the coast towns in aid of the Sultan. They encamped beneath the fort in command of the Sultan, and at about 8 A. M. made an attack on the invaders,
which became so serious a danger to the British subjects that
the Political Agent Major J. H. Sadler ordered a cessation of
hostilities at 1 P. M. until 8 P. M. giving the British subjects an
opportunity to sojourn to the sheltered village of Makalla.
More reinforcements to the Sultan's troops arrived at 6 P. M.
and encamped beneath the fort throwing temporary barricades
across the streets at several advantageous points. The main
body of the Bedouins were waiting to reinforce just outside
Matral which village was however still in the hands of the Sultan. At 8 A. M. on Monday H. M. S. Sphina arrived from
Bushire and at 2 P. M. the R. I. M. S. Lawrence."

The British gunboats, contrary to the expectations and fond
hopes of the population of Muscat, did not interfere in the
matter. For reasons of diplomacy they left the Sultan to fight
his own battles and when the rebels were finally persuaded to
leave saddled the poor Sultan with a large bill for the damage
incurred by British subjects during the attack.

In 1894 a French consulate was established at Muscat; as
the French have no commerce to speak of in this part of the
world the object of the consulate was evidently political. Of
the intrigues that resulted, the alleged sale of a coaling-station
to France and the British attitude toward the matter we will
speak later.

XXI

THE STORY OF THE TURKS IN ARABIA

"No one travels in Turkey with his eyes open without seeing that her government is a curse on mankind. Fears, feuds and fightings make miserable the councils of her rulers. They are bloodsuckers fastened on the people throughout her dominions drawing from each and all the last drop of blood that can be extracted. Turkey skillfully and systematically represses what Christian nations make it their business to nurture in all mankind as manhood. In her cities there are magnificent palaces for her sultans and her favorites. But one looks in vain through her realm for statues of public benefactors. There are no halls where her citizens could gather to discuss policies of government or mutual obligations. Their few newspapers are emasculated by government censors. Not a book in any language can cross her borders without permission of public officers, most of whom are incapable of any intelligent judgment of its contents. Art is scorned. Education is bound. Freedom is a crime. The tax gatherer is omnipotent. Law is a farce. Turkey has prisons instead of public halls for the education of her people. Instruments of torture are the stimulus to their industries."—*The Congregationalist*, April 8, 1897.

IN reviewing the story of the Turks in Arabia, we will begin with Hejaz, the most important province of Turkey in Arabia, continue with Yemen, the most populous, and end with the Mesopotamian vilayets which were her richest possessions.

It is not generally understood how highly the Sultan values his Arabian provinces. It is on them and on them alone that he can base his claim to the title of caliph. The possession of the Holy Cities in the hands of the Sultan makes him the chief Mohammedan ruler; there his name is blessed daily in the great mosques; in the eyes of all the pilgrims from every part of the Moslem world Turkey is the guardian of the Kaaba. How many thousands of Mohammedans daily in the mosques of India and Java call for blessings on the head of Abd-ul-Hamid the Caliph who would never pray for Abd-ul-Hamid the Sultan.

Mecca, and Hejaz generally, was governed by the early Caliphs until 980 A. D., when it passed under the rule of the first Sherif, Jaafar.[1] Under Suleiman the magnificent (1520–1566) the Ottoman Empire reached the zenith of its power and greatness ; at that time Arabia too was reckoned a Turkish possession, and the entire peninsula was included on the maps of Turkish Asia. But, as we have seen, at the beginning of the present century the Wahabis and not the Turks were the real rulers of Arabia. The Arabs have never taken kindly to the rule of the Turk, but the province of Hejaz, once snatched from the hand of the Wahabis, has ever since been held by the Sublime Porte.   Plots of rebellion have been thick and Sherifs have succeeded Sherifs but the fort that frowns over Mecca has always a strong Turkish garrison and the Pashas eat the fat of the land at the expense of the people.

Actual Turkish rule was declared over the whole of Hejaz in 1840.   At that time Abd-el-Mutalib was made Great Sherif of Mecca, but there was continual trouble between the Sherif and the Pasha.   The religious head of the holy city would not bow to the political head ; the anti-slave trade regulations although only very slightly enforced caused riots.   The Sherif was deposed and Mohammed bin 'Aun declared ruler in his place.   On June 15th, 1858, the murder of certain Christians at Jiddah brought England into collision with the rulers of Hejaz.   Jiddah was bombarded and the gate to the holy city was held by the Christian powers until the required indemnity was paid and the murderers punished.   The next Sherif appointed was Abdullah.   During his time the

[1] The history of Mecca under these Sherifs is given by Snouck Hurgronje at length in his " Mekka."

opening of the Suez Canal brought Turkey much nearer to Mecca and inspired the religious zealots with the fear that now the Christian fleets would attack the whole coast of Hejaz! For had not the vizier of Haroun el Rashid dissuaded that monarch from his plan to dig the canal lest the gateway to the Holy Cities would then be too accessible to the infidels?

The Ottoman government introduced other horrors into the quiet seclusion of the ancient city of Mecca; Jiddah was connected with the Red Sea cable; a wire carried the world to Mecca and put the Pasha in daily touch with the Sublime Porte; afterward it was extended to Taif, and the Turks were masters of their own army corps, so that the Sherifs could not act in secret. It was even attempted to raise a Meccan regiment for the Russian war.

In 1869 the whole complicated bureaucratic system was introduced at Medina, Jiddah, Mecca and Taif. Abdullah was a great favorite as Sherif, both to the Arabs and the Turks; he was mild and given to all sorts of compromise so that he managed to please both parties which are always at war in Mecca. His brother Husein succeeded as Sherif but was murdered in 1880. In the same year the aged Abd-el-Mutalib for the third time became Sherif and although at first very popular he soon won the hatred of the conservative Meccans by his cruelty and of the Turks by his double-dealing. On request of the people of Mecca for his deposition, Othman Pasha came to Hejaz and although he did not depose the aged Sherif, managed to outwit him in governing the city. In 1882 Aun-er-Rafik, a brother of Husein, became Sherif. Troubles between the dual powers of government became thick and the Bedouin tribes took the occasion for a general uprising. Rafik fled to Medina and could not return until Othman Pasha was deposed. Since then the old struggle continues.

The Arabs in Hejaz have no love for the Turks or for any Turkish ruler; the Bedouin tribes hate the very sight of a red fez and the town-dweller is ground down with taxation. Aside from militarism there have been no public improvements in either of the Holy Cities since the Star and Crescent waved from their forts. The "pantaloon-wearing" Turks are considered little better than "Christian dogs" by the pious folk of Mecca. Have they not introduced the abomination of quarantine instead of the old time simple trust in Allah? Have they not acquiesced to the residence of Christian consuls at Jiddah? And what is worse, have they not interfered with the free importation of slaves and the manufacture of eunuchs for the residents of Mecca?

The following literal translation of a placard posted everywhere in Mecca, at the end of the year 1885, may give the best insight into the relations that exist between the Turk and the Arab in the cradle of Islam:

" ' And who does not rule according to the revelation of Allah he is an infidel.'—*Koran* v. 48.

" Be it known to you, ye people of Mecca, that this accursed Wali intends to introduce Turkish laws into the holy city of Allah, therefore beware of sloth and awake from sleep. Do not suffer the laws to be executed for they are only the opening of the door to further legislation. Our proof is that the Wali Othman Pasha proposed his plan to divide Mecca into four quarters and to appoint three officers for each quarter. This plan he laid before the city council and when they declared it was impossible to do this in Mecca the accursed replied, Is Mecca better than Constantinople? We will carry the plan through by force. For this reason, O Meccans, an association has been formed called the Moslem Club and whoever desires to enter it let him make inquiries. The object of the association is to assassinate this cursed Wali and his chief of police. He who cannot join us let him utter his complaint before Allah in the holy house that the public safety is endangered while the present ruler lives. And this cursed Wali also attempts to secure the administration of the annual corn-shipment from Egypt. And remember also how the accursed butchered the sons of the Sherif and his slaves and exposed their heads at Mecca. What sort of deeds are these? More atrocious than those at Zeer. So that whoever kills this man will enter paradise without rendering an account. The purpose of dividing the city appointing Sheikhs for each quarter is nothing else than a pretext for new taxations as the Cursed himself let out before the council.

" In the name of the

" JEMIAT-EL-ISLAMIYEH."

The same people who promised paradise to the murderer of Othman Pasha rebelled against his successor Safwet Pasha and will rebel as long as the character of the Meccan remains what it is. Those who dream that the Turk will make Mecca the centre of their power when Constantinople falls, know not the condition of affairs among the proud fanatics of Hejaz who will never allow Mecca to become anything but the city of the Sherifs. And as for the Bedouin tribes, they blackmail every pilgrim caravan and draw heavy subsidies from Constantinople to keep the peace. Jiddah is in decay and the pilgrim-traffic is not as flourishing as it was a decade ago. Even in Hejaz the days of Ottoman rule are numbered.

Between Hejaz and Yemen is the region of Asir. Its population has been celebrated from the earliest times for personal bravery and courage. Mountain-dwellers they love freedom ; belonging to the Zaidee sect they hate the Sunnites. And these two reasons united made them abominate the Turks. In order to extend Ottoman power southward and reconquer Yemen for the Sublime Porte it was necessary to pass through the territory of the Asir Arabs. From 1824 to 1827 the Turkish troops carried six successive campaigns against the brave highlanders but were in every case repulsed with great loss. In 1833 and 1834 the attempt was again made ; a desperate battle was fought on August 21st of the latter year, the Turkish troops were victorious. But the Arabs rallied, made sorties on the garrisons, famine reigned, fever killed off many and in September the Turks again withdrew, defeated. In 1836 a final attempt was made to conquer Asir ; this was with greater loss than ever before. To this day the entire region between Taiz and Roda (a few miles north of Sana) is really independent, although marked as Turkish on the maps. The Ottoman troops are bold

to fight the Yemen Arabs to the very gate of Sana but they grow
pale when they hear of an expedition against the dare-devil
Bedouins of Asir who fight with the ferocity of the American
Indian and the boldness of a Scotch Highlander.

The story of the Turks in Yemen is very modern. In 1630
they were compelled to evacuate Yemen by the Arabs and they
did not set foot in the capital again until 1873. In 1871 the
Imam of Yemen lived his life in peace, secluded and sensual
like an oriental despot in the palace at Sana. Looked upon by
the Arabs as a spiritual Sultan he was great, but also powerless
to hold in check the depredations and robberies of the many
tribes under his nominal sway. Things went from bad to worse.
Trade almost ceased on account of the attacks on the caravans
that left for the coast. The Sana merchants, quiet and respectable Arabs, saw nothing but ruin before them, and considering
solely the benefits that would accrue to themselves by such a
step invited the Turks to take the place. They did not consult
the large agricultural population or the effect of Turkish rule on
the peasantry, otherwise there would have been an equally cor-
dial invitation to the Turks to stay out of Yemen.

The Turks needed no urging at this time, when they were
strengthening their hold on Mesopotamia, extending their conquests in Hassa and trying to obtain the mastery of the Hejaz
Bedouins. It fell in most admirably with their plans, and an
expedition set out at once. In March, 1872, an army under
command of Ahmed Mukhtar Pasha reached Hodeidah. On
April 25th the army entered Sana twenty thousand strong and
the city opened its gates without a battle. The conquest of the
country now proceeded; a force was sent to the region of
Kaukeban, north of Sana, another to the southern district of
Anes and still another to Taiz and Mocha. The conquest toward the south was limited by the presence of England at Aden.
For when the Turkish army advanced to the domain of the
independent Sultan of Lahaj who had a treaty with England,
the British Resident at Aden sent a small force of artillery and

cavalry to occupy the Lahaj territory.   In consequence of representations made at the same time by the English government to the Sublime Porte, the Turkish army withdrew in December, 1873.   In 1875 the tribes bordering the southern boundary of Yemen rebelled against Turkey but the rebellion was crushed.

When the army took Sana the Imam was deposed, but on account of his religious influence over the Arabs was permitted to reside in the city, receiving a pension on condition that he would exert himself in behalf of Ottoman rule.   This he fulfilled until his death when the birthright as Imam passed to his relative Ahmed-ed-Din who also was nothing loth to receive the honor of the Arabs and the money of the Turks.

Sana received a certain amount of civilization, more prestige and still more commercial prosperity than in the older days. As for the country in general it was divided and subdivided into provincial districts and sub-districts ; the peasantry were taxed and taxed again ; military roads were constructed by forced labor.   The hill-tribes, who in the times of the Imam had been left undisturbed in their agriculture and who boasted an independence of centuries, were now little better than slaves.   Extortion ruined them ; they hated the personality of the Turks whose religion was not as their own ; discontent smouldered everywhere and was ready to burst into a flame.   And this discontent was increased from year to year as the caravan-drivers returned from their long journeys to Aden and told of the greatest marvel ever heard of—a righteous government and a place where justice could not be *bought*, but belonged to every one— even the black skinned ignorant Somali.   When we remember that over 300,000 camels with their drivers enter Aden from the north every year we can realize how widespread was this news. I can testify to the worldwide difference between the municipal government of Aden cantonment and that of the capital of Yemen under the Turks as I saw it in 1891.   When the Turks accused England of fomenting the recent rebellions in Yemen

they were right to the extent that if the Yemen peasantry had
not seen the blessed union of liberty and law at Aden they would
not seek to rise against the Turks.

In the summer of 1892 a body of 400 Turkish troops were
sent to collect by force the taxes due from the Bni Meruan who
inhabit the coast north of Hodeidah.   The Turks were surprised by a large body of Arabs and nearly annihilated.
Wherever the news travelled the people rose in arms.   Tribal
banners long laid away were unfurled and the cry " long live
the Imam " rang through mountain and valley.   A new Jehad
was proclaimed and Ahmed-ed-Din was unwillingly forced to
take the leadership against the Turks.   When the rebellion
broke out the Turks had only about 15,000 men in the whole
of Yemen ; and cholera had wrought havoc among these.   Ill-
fed, ill-clothed, and unpaid; badly housed in the rainy and
cold mountain villages, they could nevertheless fight like devils
when led by their commanders.   The Imam escaped from Sana,
and a few days later the capital was besieged by an enormous
force of Arabs.   All the unwalled cities fell an easy prey to
the rebels ; Menakha was taken after a short struggle ; Ibb,
Jibleh, Taiz, and Yerim all declared themselves for the Imam.
The Arabs treated their foes with respect after their victory ; [1]
they were feeding Turkish prisoners at the Imam's expense and
in many cases money was given the soldiers to enable them to
escape to Aden.

Meanwhile telegrams were sent to Constantinople from Sana
and Hodeidah beseeching assistance.   The whole of Yemen,
with the exception of the capital and two smaller towns in the
north with Hodeidah on the coast, was in the hands of the
rebels.   An expedition reached Hodeidah, under command of
Ahmed Feizi Pasha, formerly governor of Mecca, which after
bombarding the villages on the coast north of Hodeidah,
marched to the relief of Sana.   Without opposition the army

[1] This is according to the testimony of Walter B. Harris who was in
Yemen shortly after the rebellion.

reached Menakha and took the town by storm; match-locks and fuse-guns could not hold out against field-guns and trained troops. About thirty miles beyond a desperate attempt was made to stop the army of relief; in a narrow defile the rebels under Seyid es-Sherai took up their position and for twelve days withstood cavalry, infantry and artillery assaults; then they were driven back and retired into the mountains. By hurried marches the troops reached Sana and took the city. Military law was proclaimed and a universal massacre of prisoners took place. A reward was offered for the head of every rebel. Camel-loads of heads were brought into Sana every day. The troops were turned loose to plunder the villages. There is no nation in the world that can put down a rebellion as rapidly as the Turks when they have a good-sized army, but they have great objection to any one seeing the process.

By the end of January, 1893, all the cities of Yemen were reconquered and the main roads were again open. But the spirit of rebellion lived on and the brave mountaineers withdrew to the inaccessible defiles and peaks only to plot further mischief. Telegraph-wires were cut; soldiers were shot on the road; and once and again bold attempts were made to blow up the Pasha's house in Sana with gunpowder. In 1895 there was rebellion in the north. In 1897–98 all Yemen was again in arms and the uncertain and conflicting reports that reach the coast only emphasize the serious character of the uprising.

On the map and in Turkish official reports the boundaries of Yemen join those of Hejaz and extend many miles *east* of Sana. This has never been and is not now correct. Twenty-five miles north and east of Sana there is no one who cares for a Turkish passport or dares to collect Turkish taxes.

As to the future of Turkey in Yemen it is difficult to surmise. Rather than risk further rebellions the Sultan may adopt a conciliatory policy. But Yemen is too far from Con-

stantinople to be governed from there. Extortion is the only
way open to a Pasha to enrich himself and for soldiers to get
daily bread where wages are not paid on time. When the
Pasha has filled his pocket his successor will try it a second
time and come to grief. Rebellion will be the chronic state
of Yemen as long as Turkey rules at Sana. The leopard cannot change his spots.

We now turn to notice the rule of the Turks in Northeastern
Arabia, and in their newly-acquired province of Hassa.
Bagdad was taken by the Turks in 1638 and that city
has ever since been the capital of a Turkish Province. It
is unnecessary to enter here into the succession of Pashas
and rulers and the attempts to subjugate the Bedouin Arabs.
In 1830 the great plague visited all Mesopotamia and when
epidemic was at its height the river burst its banks and in one
night 15,000 people perished. In 1884 the vilayet of Busrah
was separated from that of Bagdad and has since remained
under its own governor. The two provinces have all the
machinery of Ottoman rule in working order. Except for an
occasional outbreak among the Montefik Arabs, Turkey has
no trouble to hold Mesopotamia in her grasp. Nor is she at
all willing that this rich province should even dream of passing under other rulers. In the year 1891 the Turkish Official
Bulletin gave the total revenue from taxation in the Bagdad
vilayet alone at 246,304 Turkish pounds.

It may be interesting to note in passing the various sources
of taxation-money. They are in brief: tax on Arab tents, exemption from military service, tax on sheep, buffaloes, camels,
tax on mines (salt), tax on special privileges, tax on forests and
timber, tax on fishing, custom dues, tax on shipping, on irrigation, on farming improvements; "receipts from tribunals"
(£3,000 tax on justice!) and beside all this "taxes diverses"
and "revenues diverses" to make up the budget. All this is
legal, ordinary taxation. But the actual conditions of Turkish
misrule made it impossible to exercise the inalienable rights of

" life, liberty and the pursuit of happiness " without continual backsheesh to every official.

The population of Mesopotamia, Moslem and Jew and Christian are thoroughly weary of Turkish misrule, but no one dares to lift up a voice in protest. They have become accustomed to it; and there is nothing else but to bear it patiently. As for the nomads they have either, like the Montefik, settled down along the rivers to cultivate the soil and eke out a miserable existence; or, like the Aneyza and Shammar tribes, they are as thoroughly independent of the Sultan as when they first appeared in his borders.

Turkish Arabia on the north is represented on most maps by a regular curved line starting from the Persian Gulf and ending at the Gulf of Akaba; but the line is purely imaginary. Turkish rule does not extend far south of the banks of the Euphrates, and the whole desert region from Kerbela to the Dead Sea and the Hauran is practically independent.[1] Outside of Bagdad and Busrah even the river towns are frequently threatened by the nomads, and Turkish soldiers have often to guard the river steamers against pirates. Military rule is in vogue two hundred years after the occupation of the country, and the nomads are nomads still. The commander-in-chief of the Sixth Ottoman army corps resides at Bagdad, and a good number of soldiers occupy the barracks in the city of the old caliphs.

In Turkey all Moslems over twenty years of age are liable to military conscription, and this liability continues for over twenty years. Non-Moslems pay an annual exemption tax of about six shillings per head. The army consists of *Nizam* or regulars, *Redif* or reserves, and *Mustahfuz* or national guard. The infantry are supposed to be all armed with Martini-Peabody rifles, but in Mesopotamia older patterns are still in use. The life of a Turkish soldier is not enviable; and none of them would be volunteers for government service. The Turkish

[1] See Lady Ann Blunt's " Bedouins of the Euphrates."

navy is represented in the Persian Gulf and on the rivers by one or two third-rate cruisers and a small river gunboat.

The result of the calling of Turkey into the Wahabi quarrel between the two sons of Feysul, was the occupation of Katif and Hassa by the Ottoman government. Since that time (1872) Hassa has been a part of the Busrah vilayet, and the Pasha, who resides at Hofhoof, has the title Mutaserif Pasha of Nejd. Continual troubles with the Arabs mark the history of the occupation of Hassa; the caravan routes are not as safe as in the dominions of the Amir of Nejd; the whole country shows decay and lack of government; taxation of the pearl fishers has driven many of them to Bahrein; the peninsula of Katar is occupied by a garrison, but that does not prevent continual blood feuds and battles between the Arab tribes. The Ottoman government has established an overland post-service between Hofhoof and Busrah has between Bagdad and Damascus, but both routes are unsafe and slow. Most of the Hofhoof merchants use the British Post Office at Bahrein; and so do the government officials.

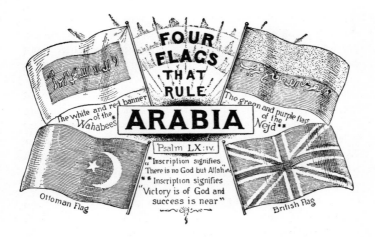

FOUR FLAGS THAT RULE ARABIA

The white and red banner of the Wahabees

The green and purple flag of the Nejd

Psalm LX:IV

Inscription signifies "There is no God but Allah"
Inscription signifies "Victory is of God and success is near"

Ottoman Flag

British Flag

XXII

BRITISH INFLUENCE IN ARABIA

"The English, said the old Arab Sheikh in reply, are like ants; if one finds a bit of meat, a hundred follow."—*Ainsworth.*

"Oman may, indeed, be justifiably regarded as a British dependency. We subsidize its ruler; we dictate its policy; we should tolerate no alien interference. I have little doubt myself that the time will come . . . when the Union Jack will be seen flying from the castles of Muscat."

"I should regard the concession of a port upon the Persian Gulf to Russia by any power as a deliberate insult to Great Britain, as a wanton rupture of the *status quo* and as an international provocation to war; and I should impeach the British minister, who was guilty of acquiescing in such surrender, as a traitor to his country."

—*Lord Curzon*, Viceroy of India.

IN sketching the relations of England to the peninsula, we will consider: Her Arabian possessions and protectorates; her supremacy in Arabian waters; her commerce with Arabia; her treaties with Arab tribes; and her consulates and agencies in Arabia.

Of all British possessions in Arabia, Aden is by far the most important, on account of its strategic position as the key not only of all Yemen, but of the Red Sea and all Western Arabia. Aden was visited as early as 1609 by Captain Sharkey of the East India Company's ship "Ascension." He was at first well received, but afterward imprisoned until the inhabitants had secured a large ransom. Two of the Englishmen on board refusing to pay were sent to the Pasha at Sana. In 1610 an English ship again visited Aden and the crew were treacherously treated. In 1820, Captain Haines of the Indian navy

visited Aden, and in 1829 the Court of Directors entertained
the idea of making Aden a coaling-station, but the idea was
abandoned. In consequence of an outrage committed on the
passengers and crew of a buggalow wrecked near Aden, an expedition was despatched against the place by the Bombay government in 1838. It was arranged that the peninsula of Aden
should be ceded to the British. But the negotiations were anything but friendly, and in January, 1839, a force of 300 Europeans and 400 native troops in the "Volage" and "Cruizer"
bombarded and took the place by storm.

This was the first new accession of territory in the reign of
Queen Victoria. Immense sums of money have been spent in
fortifying this natural Gibraltar and in improving its harbor.
Four times the Arabs have attempted to take Aden by land,
each time with fearful loss and without success. By sea Aden
is impregnable ; only the initiated know the strength of its mole-
batteries, mines, forts and other defences ; and every year new
defences are constructed and old ones strengthened. Aden has
become a great centre for trade, and is one of the chief coaling
depots in the world. It bars the further advance of Turkey
into South Arabia, guarantees independence and good government to all the neighboring petty states, and is an example of
good government to all Arabia and the African coast. The settlement is politically subject to the Bombay Presidency and is
administered by a Resident with two assistants. Since the
opening of the Suez canal, trade has steadily increased and
Turkish custom extortions at Hodeidah direct the caravan trade
more and more to Aden from every part of Yemen.

The island of Socotra and the Kuria Muria islands are also
attached to Aden, together with the Somali Coast in Africa.
Socotra has an area of 1,382 square miles and about 10,000
inhabitants. It came under British protection in 1886 by treaty
with its Sultan. The Kuria Muria group was ceded to the
British by the Sultan of Muscat, for the purpose of landing the
Red Sea cable ; the islands are five in number and have rich

guano deposits. The island of Kamaran is also classed as belonging to the British Empire.[1] It is a small island in the Red
Sea, some miles north of Hodeidah ; it is only fifteen miles
long and five wide, and has seven small fishing-villages. But
it has a good sheltered anchorage and is the quarantine Station
for all Moslem pilgrims from the south to Mecca.

The Bahrein Islands are also included in the British Empire,
although Turkey still claims them as her own and the native
ruler imagines that he is independent. " The present chief
Sheikh Isa owes the possession of his throne entirely to British
protection which was instituted in 1867. Sheikh Isa was again
formerly placed under British protection in 1870 when his rivals
were deported to India." The Political Resident at Bushire
superintends the government of the islands to as great an extent as is deemed diplomatic.

Perim at the southern end of the Red Sea was taken possession of in 1799 by the East India Company and a force was
sent from Bombay to garrison the island. But it was found
untenable at that time as a military position and the troops
were withdrawn. Perim was reoccupied in the beginning of
1857. The lighthouse was completed in 1861, and quarters
were built for a permanent garrison.[2]

We may also consider the possessions of Egypt in Arabia as
practically under English protection. Since the British occupation, the peninsula of Sinai and the Red Sea litoral on the
Arabian side, nearly as far as Yembo is under the Governor-
General of the Suez canal.

England not only possesses the key positions on the coasts of
Arabia, but has for many years held the naval supremacy in all
Arabian waters. As the Dutch succeeded the Portuguese and
established trading-stations in the Persian Gulf and in the Red
Sea, so England followed the Dutch. The East India Com-

[1] Statesman's Year Book.

[2] For a complete account of Perim, see " The Description and History
of Perim," by J. S. King, Bombay, 1877.

pany was at Aden and Mocha in the beginning of the seventeenth century, and in 1754 the English East India Company
established itself at Bunder Rig, north of Bushire, and later at
Bushire itself, supplanting the Dutch. The island of Karak
in the north of the Gulf was twice occupied by the British, in
1838 and in 1853. After the bombardment of Bushire in 1857
and of Mohammerah in the same year, hostilities ceased and
Karak was again evacuated. The island of Kishm, in the
southern part of the Gulf, was during the greater part of the
present century, a British military or naval station. The Indian
naval squadron had its headquarters first at El Kishm, then at
Deristan and finally for many years at Bassadore. In 1879
because of the insalubrity of the climate the last company of
Sepoys was withdrawn to India. But the island is still in a
sense considered British. As early as 1622 the Persians and
the British expelled the Portuguese from Ormuz and shortly
after, in common with the Dutch and French set up trading
factories at Gombrun, (now Bunder Abbas). In 1738 the English Company established an agency at Busrah and much of
their Gulf business was shifted to that port. Since 1869 there
has been a telegraph station at Jask with a staff of six English
officials; here the land and marine wires of the Indo-European
telegraph meet and join India to the Gulf.

The Sultanate of Oman, since 1822, has been in the closest
relations possible with British naval power. At several critical
periods in Oman history, it was Great Britain that helped to
settle the affairs of state. In 1861 a British commissioner arbitrated between two claimants for the rule of Muscat and
Zanzibar, then one kingdom, and divided the Sultanate. Since
1873 the Sultan of Muscat has received an annual subsidy
from the British government. Near Cape Musendum, on the
Arabian side of the Gulf, the British once occupied a place
called Malcolm's Inlet when they were laying the telegraph
cable from Kerachi to the Gulf in 1864. Five years later it
was transferred to Jask. From 1805 to 1821 there were British

naval encounters with the pirates of the Gulf, and since that date all piracy in these waters has ceased.[1] British naval supremacy established peace at Bahrein and has protected its native government since 1847. When in 1867 the native ruler, "a crafty old fox" as Curzon calls him, broke the treaty, the bombardment of Menamah brought further proof of British naval supremacy. Kuweit was for a time (1821–22) the headquarters of the British Resident at Busrah; and, semi-independent of Turkey, is now becoming wholly dependent on England—another indication of British naval supremacy. Even at Fao, Busrah and Bagdad British gunboats often keep the peace or at least emphasize authority. In a word Great Britain holds the scales of justice for all the Persian Gulf litoral. She guarantees a *pax Brittanica* for commerce; she taught the Arab tribes that rapine and robbery are not a safe religion; where they once swept the sea with slave-dhows and pirate-craft they have now settled down to drying fish and diving for pearls. For the accomplishment of this subject England has spent much both in treasure and in lifeblood. Witness the graves of British soldiers and marines in so many Gulf ports. The testimony of an outsider, is given in a recent article in the *Cologne Gazette*, which thus describes the political and naval supremacy of England in Eastern Arabia and the Persian Gulf:

"A disguised protectorate over Oman and control over the actions of the Sultan of Muscat; actual protectorate over Bahrein; coaling station on the island of Kishm, in the Straits of Ormuz; presence of a political Resident at Bushire who, with the help of an association called the Trucial League, decides all disputes between Turkish, Arab, and Persian chiefs in the Persian Gulf. . . . This league gives the English a constant pretext for intervention; the object of keeping peace and policing the gulf is only a pretence. . . . All events on the Persian Gulf, however disconnected apparently, are really

[1] Treaties were made with the Arabs of the pirate coast in 1835, 1838, 1839, 1847, 1853, and 1856; of these we shall speak later.

dependent on each other through the Trucial League. It is a confused tangle of hatreds and jealousies whose threads are united in the hands of the Resident at Bushire. . . . Russia shows an indifference which is quite incomprehensible considering the interest she has and must have in these affairs. One could recount numerous instances where English agents have injured Russian interests without meeting with any opposition. The Russian Consul in Bagdad is thrust into the background by the activity of his British colleague. Southern Persia, the gulf, Eastern Arabia, and the Land of Oman have fallen completely within the English sphere of influence. This state of affairs has not been officially ratified, but exists as a fact. That will last till some movement comes about to restore the proper balance. Meanwhile, the English are the masters. They are so accustomed to manage the whole Persian Gulf that if the least thing occurs that they have not foreseen or themselves arranged they completely lose all self-control.''

But the supremacy of England in the Gulf and on the other coasts of Arabia is hers not only because of gunboats and gunpowder. It is most of all by the arts of peace that she has established and glorified her power on the Arabian litoral. It must never be forgotten, for example, that the magnificent surveys of the entire 4,000 miles of Arabian coast were the work of British and Indian naval officers ; by means of this survey, completed at great cost, commerce has been aided and navigation of the dangerous waters east and west of Arabia has been made safe. England too is the only power that has established lighthouses ; *e. g.*, at Aden, Perim, in the Red Sea and lately on Socotra. England laid the cables that circle Arabia ; from India to Bushire and Fao connecting with the Turkish overland telegraph system ; from Aden to Bombay and from Aden to Suez through the Red Sea. These cables were not the work of a day but were laid with great expense and opposed by the very governments they were intended to benefit.

Again, Arabia has two postal systems and two only. In the Turkish province of Yemen there is a weekly post between the capital and the chief towns to the coast; in Hejaz there is a post to Mecca; and in Mesopotamia and Hasa there is another Turkish postal system notorious for its slowness and insecurity. For the rest all of Eastern and Southern Arabia are dependent on the Indian Postal system; the whole interior is ignorant of a post office or of a postman. The government of India has post offices at Muscat, Bahrein, Fao, Busrah and Bagdad with regular mail service, and the best administration in the world. The English post carries the bulk of the mail between Busrah and Bagdad while Bahrein is really the post office for all Eastern Arabia; pearl-merchants at Katar and in Hasa mail their letters at Bahrein and even the Turkish government needs the English post to communicate with Busrah from Hasa.

England has also earned her supremacy in Arabian waters by honest attempts to put a stop to the slave-trade, in accord with the Anti-slave Trade treaties between the powers. She is the only power whose navy has acted in seizing slave-dhows, liberating slaves and patrolling the coast. The work has not always been done thoroughly or vigorously, but that it has been done at all, places England first among the powers that sail in Arabian waters.

Where the Union Jack proclaims naval supremacy, there the red mercantile flag of England follows the blue and carries commerce; the two go together, and although of different color are the same flag to Englishmen. The world-wide commercial activity of Great Britain has touched every part of the Arabian coast and British wares from Manchester and Birmingham have penetrated to every secluded village of Nejd, and are found in every valley of Yemen.

The mercantile navigation of the Gulf as it now exists is the creation of the last thirty years, and is largely to be attributed to the statesmanship of Sir Bartle Frere. It was he who,

when at Calcutta as a member of Lord Canning's Supreme
Council, befriended the young Scotchman, William Mackinnon, who was planning a new shipping business beyond his
slender means; and a subsidy was granted to Mackinnon's
new line of Steamers. Thus it was that the British India Steam
Navigation Company was launched which first opened trade
not only with Zanzibar but in the Persian Gulf. In 1862 not
a single mercantile steamer ploughed the Persian Gulf. A
six-weekly service was then started, followed by a monthly, a
fortnightly and finally by a weekly steamer. From Busrah
there are two lines of English steamers direct for London. The
British India was the pioneer line and still holds the first position, although there are other lines that do coasting trade with
India.

Thus English commerce controls not only the markets of both
sides of the Gulf, but of all Northwestern Arabia and as far beyond Bagdad as piece-goods and iron-ware can be carried on
camels. There is not a spool of thread in Nejd or a jack-knife
in Jebel-Shammar that did not come up the Persian Gulf in an
English ship. All of Hassa eats rice from Rangoon and thousands of bags are carried in British ships to Bahrein to be trans-
ported inland by caravan. Not only is the steamshipping mostly
in English hands, but many of the native buggalows fly the
British flag and the chief merchants are Englishmen or British
subjects from India. The Rupee is the standard of value along
the whole Arabian coast from Aden to Busrah. In the interior
the Maria Theresa dollar has long held sway, but even that is
becoming scarce among the Bedouins and they have little pref-
erence between the "*abu bint*" (the Rupee with a girl's head)
and the "*abu tair*" ("the father of a bird"—the eagle on
the Austrian dollar). For a time a French line of steamers ran
in the Gulf but the project was abandoned, though there is now
a rumour of its revival.[1]

[1] The British India steamer, carry the mails and leave Bombay and
Busrah once a week, touching at the intermediate ports in the Gulf, after

Aden is the commercial centre for all Southern Arabia and the enormous increase of its trade since 1839 is proof of what English commerce has done for Yemen. Mocha is dead, and Hodeidah is long since bed-ridden, but Aden is alive and only requires a railroad to Sana to become the commercial capital of all Western and Southern Arabia. That railroad will be built as soon as the Turk leaves Yemen's capital; God hasten the day. After the occupation of Aden in 1839 until the year 1850 customs dues were levied as in India but at that time it was declared a free port. During the first seven years the total value of imports and exports averaged per year about 1,900,000 Rupees; in the next seven years the annual average rose to 6,000,000 Rupees, and it has been on the increase ever since, until it now is over 30,000,000 Rupees; nor did this annual average include the trade by land which is also large.

The Suez canal is another indication of the prestige which English commerce has in the Red Sea and along the routes of traffic that circle Arabia. In 1893 the gross tonnage that passed through the canal was 10,753,798 ; of this 7,977,728 tons passed under the English flag which means that nearly four-fifths of the trade is English. In the same year the number of vessels passing through the canal was 3,341 of which 2,405 belonged to Great Britain.

The proposed Anglo-Egyptian railway across the north of Arabia will join the Persian Gulf to the Mediterannean. To shorten the time of communication between England and her Eastern Empire is evidently a matter of the highest importance, not only for commerce and post, but in the event of war, mutiny or other great energency. The first surveys for this overland railway were made as early as 1850, by the Euphrates Expedition under General Chesney. The scheme was warmly advocated

Kerachi, as follows : Gwadur, Muscat, Jask, Bunder Abbas, Lingah, Bahrein, Bushire, Fao and Mohammerah ; the journey lasts a fortnight and the distance, zigzag, is about one thousand nine hundred miles.

in England by Sir W. P. Andrew, the Duke of Sutherland and others, but although it still awaits execution the plan comes up again every few years with new advocates and new improvements.   Once it was to be the Euphrates Valley railway coming down to Bagdad and Busrah or to Kuweit (Grane) by way of Mosul.   Now the plan proposed is to open a railway from Port Said due eastward across the Peninsula along the thirtieth parallel of latitude to Busrah.   A branch would deviate a little to the south to the port of Kuweit which was also the proposed terminus of the Euphrates Valley line on which a select committee of the House of Commons sat twenty-five years ago.   From Busrah the main line would cross the Shatt-el-Arab and the Karun by swing-bridges and follow the coast-line of the Persian Gulf and Makran to Kerachi.   Such a line would reduce the time occupied in transit between London and Kerachi to eight days.[1]   Whether this route or any other is followed is a matter of minor importance.   The fact that since 1874 England has been to the front in the matter of the overland railroad puts it beyond a doubt, that when the railway is built its terminus at least will be under English control and most probably the whole road will represent English capital and enterprise.

Meanwhile there is intelligence that Turkey has made a concession to German capitalists for the extension of the Anatolian railways to Bagdad.   The line which runs from the Asiatic shores of the Bosphorus to Angora is in the hands of a German syndicate and the terms of the concession contain compulsory clauses under which, in certain eventualities, the Turkish government can compel the syndicate to extend the road to Sivas and ultimately to Bagdad.[2]   But politically Great Britain

[1] In a recent paper read before the Society of Arts in London Mr. C. E. D. Black of the Geographical Department of the India office urges other reasons for the practicability of this route.—(London *Times*, May 7th, 1898.)

[2] *Times* of India, June 17, 1899.

has little to fear from the spread of German influence in the Levant and Mesopotamia.   The editor of an influential English paper says, "Every mark expended by the Germans upon public works in the Asiatic dominions of the Sultan helps to build up the bulwark against the menace of Russia.   And the creation of a German railway in Asia Minor will, in a limited degree tend to identify the interests of Germany and Great Britain."   Nevertheless England would never grant a terminus or harbor to a German railroad syndicate on the Persian Gulf.

Great Britain has treaties or agreements of some sort with every tribe and settlement of Arabs from Aden to Muscat and thence to Bahrein.   England has two kings for Arabia; the first lives at Bushire and is called the British Resident and Consul General, the other with a similar title lives at Aden.   Of the Bushire Resident Lord Curzon wrote, "One or more gunboats are at the disposal of the British Resident at Bushire who has also a despatch boat for his own immediate use in the event of any emergency.   Not a week passes but, by Persians and Arabs alike, disputes are referred to his arbitration, and he may with greater truth than the phrase sometimes conveys be entitled the Uncrowned King of the Persian Gulf."   To the energy and political capacity of Colonel Ross and his capable predecessor, Sir Lewis Pelly, this royal throne owes its foundation.   All the treaties made by England with the Arab tribes on the Eastern coast of Arabia are here interpreted and enforced.

The treaties made with the chiefs of Bahrein and with the tribes on the so-called Pirate coast embraces clauses to enforce the maratime peace of the Gulf, to exclude foreign powers from the possession of territory, to regulate or abolish the slave-traffic and to put down piracy.   Since 1820 various treaties of truce have been concluded with the warlike Arabs on the coast south of Katar and have been frequently renewed or strengthened.   In 1853 a Treaty of Perpetual Peace was made with other tribes [1] which provided that there should be a complete cessation of hostilities at sea and that all disputes should be referred to the British Resident. The contracting parties were called Trucial Chiefs and the treaty is known as the Trucial Arrangement or League. Beside these treaties the English have an exclusive treaty with the Sheikh of Bahrein to such a degree, that the islands are practically a British protectorate.

Although there are no formal treaties with the tribes along the Hassa coast and Katar, these being under Turkish rule, that region is not disregarded by Great Britain, nay Nejd itself finds a place in the administration reports of the Persian Gulf. Political agency whenever the horizon in that part of the peninsula shows a storm cloud though it be no bigger than a man's hand. The claims of the Porte to sovereignty over El Katar are not admitted by the British government [2] and are the cause not only of diplomatic controversy but of actual interference on the part of the British when necessary.

The great benefits that have followed the treaties of peace with the Arab tribes are manifest most of all by a comparison of that part of the Arabian coast under English supervision and the long stretch from Katif to Busrah which is Turkish. The former enjoys peace and the tribes have settled down to commerce and fishing, there is safety for the traveller and the stranger everywhere; the latter is in continual state of warfare, there is neither commerce nor agriculture and the entire coast is utterly unsafe because of the *laissez faire* policy of Turkey.

[1] 1. Ras el Kheima—Jowasim tribe.
2. Um-el-Kawain—Al-bu-Ali tribe.
3. Ajman—Al-bu-Ali tribe.
4. Sharka—Jowasim tribe.
5. Debai—Al-bu-falasal tribe.
6. Abn Dhabi—Bni Yas tribe.
All of these tribes reside between Katar and Ras el Had on the Arabian coast. (See Aitchison, Vol. VII., No. xxvi.)

[2] Curzon's " Persia," Vol. II., p. 453.

Turning to Oman we find, in the words of Lord Curzon, that, treaty succeeding treaty, "it may be justifiably regarded as a British dependency." The recent history of Muscat has only hastened the day when "the Union Jack will be seen flying from the castles of Muscat." The Bedouin revolt and their occupation of the town resulted in saddling the unhappy Sultan with a large bill for damages sustained by British subjects. The episode of the French coaling-station cost the Sultan his annual subsidy. Thus from the side of finance he is doubly dependent on English clemency.

The second British king of Arabia resides at Aden. There he is at once Political Resident and commander of the troops. His authority extends not only to the settlement of Aden proper but includes supervision of a territory 200 miles long by forty broad with a population of 130,000. Many of the neighboring tribes are subsidized and all of them are bound by treaty to Great Britain. What the Bushire Resident is for the Gulf that the Aden Resident is for the Southern litoral of the Peninsula. Moreover the Island of Socotra is also under the Resident at Aden and the Island of Perim. The ruler of Makalla in Hadramaut is under special treaty with England; although the newspaper report, that Great Britain had declared a protectorate over all Southern Arabia, has no foundation. [1]

[1] The following tribes in the vicinity of Aden receive (or received) annual subsidies from the British Government:

Tribe.	Estimated Population.	Tribe.	Estimated Population.
Abdali	15,000	Haushabi	6,000
Fadhli	25,000	Alawi	1,500
Akrabi	800	Amir	30,000
Subaihi	20,000	Yaffai	35,000

Thus the total estimated population of these tribes is 133,300 and the total amount of the annual stipend paid them in 1877, was 12,000 German crowns. (Hunter's "Aden," p. 155.)

In the tribes which are bound by treaty with Britain a patriarchal system of supervision seems to prevail.   Good children
are rewarded and bad ones are punished.   Nothing escapes the
eye of the political parent; one has only to read the yearly
Administration reports to find many striking and sometimes
amusing examples.   We quote from the Residency Report of
Muscat for 1893–94 verbatim :   " One case of breach of the
maritime peace of the Gulf occurred in which the Sultan was
advised to inflict a fine of Rs. 50 (about sixteen dollars) on Meh-
dibin-Ali, the Sheikh of the Kamazarah tribe of Khassab, for
proceeding with a party of armed men by sea to Shaam with
the object of prosecuting a certain claim his wife had against
the estate of her deceased father.   After some months' delay
the attendance of the Sheikh was enforced at Muscat and the
fine was recovered."   The same report tells how the government of India acknowledged the kindness shown to the shipwrecked crew of the S. S. Khiva in April, 1893, by the Sultan
of Muscat, "by presentation to His Highness of a handsome
telescope and watch."   Every year all the tribal chiefs who
have proved "good boys " receive some yards of bright flan-
nel, a new rifle or a pair of army pistols.   But the patriarchal
system works well ; and there are few Arabs who would like
English power in the Gulf or near Aden to grow less ; all express admiration for English *rule*, if not for English politics.
In Arabia too the old promise of Noah is finding its fulfillment
to-day.   "God shall enlarge Japhet and he shall dwell in the
tents of Shem."   Shem never took a better guest into his tent
than when he signed a treaty of perpetual peace with England
on his coasts.

England has consulates and consular agents at more places
in Arabia than has any other power and her consuls exercise
more authority and have greater prestige.   In nearly every
case they were first appointed and have therefore had longer
time to extend their influence.   At Jiddah, Hodeidah, and on
the island of Kamaran there are British consulates or vice-con

sulates ; and there are reports of a consulate at Sana. At Makalla there is a British agent. Muscat, Bagdad, Busrah, Bushire and Mohammerah all have consulates, with different degrees of authority and position, all exercising power of some sort in Arabia. Bahrein, Lingah, Sharka, Bunder Abbas, and other points in the Gulf have British agents. At Jiddah, Hodeidah and Aden there are several consulates beside the English. Muscat has for some years had an American consul and in 1894 the French established a consulate there. Russia has no representative in the Gulf save at Bagdad ; nor has Germany. None of the European powers, save England, have agents at any of the Arabian ports in the Gulf nor do the ships of their navies often visit this part of the world. In fact so little do the Arabs know of other consuls than English, that their words for agent, *wakil*, and for consul, *baljoz*, always signify to them British officers or appointees.

XXIII

PRESENT POLITICS IN ARABIA

"The signs of the times show plainly enough what is going to happen. All the savage lands in the world are going to be brought under subjection to the Christian Governments of Europe. The sooner the seizure is consummated, the better for the savages."—*Mark Twain.*

WHILE Turkey continues in power the western coast of Arabia will see no change and everything will be quiet in Hejaz. If however the trouble between the Sherifs of Mecca and the Sublime Porte should reach a crisis or Moslem fanaticism at Jiddah should endanger the lives of Christians, we may expect England, and perhaps France and Holland to interfere as did England in 1858.[1] Regarding Yemen there is

[1] In a remarkable article, the *Novoe Vremya* makes known the Russian discovery of "a new British intrigue." It appears that Great Britain, not content with the virtual annexation of Egypt and the Sudan, is even, while carrying out her plans for the absorption of the Transvaal and the advancement of her interests in Persia, busily engaged in setting up a Mohammedan Power which is to rival that of the Sultan, and is ultimately to be used as a means of menacing, if not destroying, Russian authority in Central Asia. The puppet Prince selected for this purpose is the Sherif of Mecca. According to the *Novoe Vremya*, the Sherif has recently received from England a letter stating that the British government, having decided to invest a certain worthy but impecunious Mohammedan Sheikh with the Caliphate of Zeila, on the borders of Somaliland, and recognizing the Sherif as a descendant of the Prophet and great protector of Islam, considers it desirable for the Sherif on the day of the appointment of the new Caliph to issue a manifesto expressing his approval. In return for this service, Great Britain will proclaim Mecca and Medina the private property of the Sherif, will assure to him the greater part of the revenues of the new Caliphate, and will defend him by diplomatic means, or even

more probability of a great political change in the near future. Aden is a cinder-heap, but Sana has a fine, cold climate and is the capital of a rich mountain region capable of extraordinary development.   There are those who desire to see England assume a protectorate over all Yemen, and if ever the Arabs should turn out the Turks, England would be almost compelled to step in and preserve peace for her allied tribes near Aden. Long since the army at Aden has felt the need of a hill-station and only the Crescent keeps the English troops penned up in an extinct crater where life at best is misery.

The southern part of Arabia is of such a character geographically and the coast so barren that it offers no attractions to the most ambitious land-grabber.   Oman, like Yemen, is fertile and has in addition certain mining possibilities.   Until recent years England was the only foreign power that claimed an interest in the heritage of the Sultan of Muscat.   Now France is on the scene and is apparently unwilling that British power should increase in Oman or the Gulf.   The alleged lease of a coaling-station to France by the Sultan of Muscat in February, 1899, was only the beginning of French opposition made manifest.   Her establishment of a consulate at Muscat, her relations to the slave-trade, her attempt to subsidize a line of French steamers in the Gulf, her secret agents recently travelling in the Gulf—all these were only ripples that show which way the current flows.   So far England has had free play in Oman ; now another power has appeared.   The coaling-station incident was soon settled to the satisfaction of all Englishmen, and in a thoroughly English way.   Under threat of bombardment the Sultan repudiated his agreement with the French and by way

by force of arms, against the interference of the Sultan or any other Foreign Power.   It is perhaps needless to say that the author of this intrigue is said to be Mr. Chamberlain, who is described as a man " without faith, without truth, capable of trampling under foot every commandment, whether of God or man, in order to accomplish his purpose of placing Great Britain at the head of the Powers of the world."—*Times* of India, 1899.

of punishment for his misconduct his annual stipend was stopped. Whether France will continue to seek to increase her influence in the Gulf remains to be seen. It is certain that English policy is strenuously opposed to allowing one square foot of Oman territory to pass into the hands of France or any other foreign power.

In April, 1899, it was announced that Russia had entered the Persian Gulf as a political power and acquired the harbor of Bunder Abbas in Persia as a terminus for her proposed railway. Since that time this has been officially denied both at Teheran and St. Petersburg and also stoutly reasserted with new proofs by the English press and the press of India. It is undoubtedly news of a sensational character if it be true. The presence of Russia in the Persian Gulf would probably change the future history of all its litoral and help to decide the future partition of Arabia and Mesopotamia. All things seem to be moving toward a crisis in this region of the east. And if the battle for empire and for possession of the keys to the gateway of India should be fought in the Persian Gulf the possible consequences are too vast to be surmised. What England's policy would be in case there is truth in the alleged Russian aggression, is summarized in a recent article in the *Times* of India:

" It remains to consider what steps should be taken by Great Britain in view of the new development in Gulf politics. It may be taken for granted that Russia will not attempt to take possession of Bunder Abbas for a considerable time to come. She will make every effort to deny the existence of the advantage she has gained until a convenient opportunity arises for putting her plan into execution. In the meantime, Great Britain can be well content to remain quiet, and to imitate her adversary by playing a waiting game. It will possibly be suggested that by again occupying Kishm, and by seizing Ormuz, the value of Bunder Abbas to Russia could at once be neutralized to a large extent. That is doubtless true ; but it is material to point out that little is to be gained by precipitate action, that these points of vantage can be occupied with facility at any time, and that the true policy of Great Britain is to endeavor to preserve the *status quo* for as long a period as possible.

" Meanwhile, there are many methods by which British power and influence in the Gulf can be safeguarded. We understand that the Admiralty has already decided to strengthen the naval force maintained in Persian waters, and that the Admiral commanding the East Indies squadron will in future give the Gulf a larger share of his personal supervision. But this is not enough. The staff of political officers in the Gulf needs to be enlarged. . . . Then, too, more telegraph cables are needed. Muscat is now shut off from communication with the rest of the world, although the port was once linked up with Aden by cable. A line should be laid from Muscat to Jask forthwith, and another branch should connect Jask with Bunder Abbas and Lingah. More political agents should be stationed in the hinterland between Bunder Abbas and Seistan, with roving commissions, if necessary. One other matter needs urgent attention. Russia now possesses the sole right to construct railways in Persia, under an agreement which, after being in existence ten years, expires this year. Is anything being done to prevent the renewal of this objectionable concession, which is deeply opposed to British interests in the Shah's dominions? It is in the highest degree important that Great Britain should secure a share in the concessions for roads and railways which will certainly be granted by the Persian government in the near future. Unfortunately, the gaze of the British public is so steadily concentrated upon China that it is unable to perceive dangers which threaten the empire in a far more vital place. There must soon be a rude awakening. It is not in China, but in Persia and the Persian Gulf, that the centre of political strife and international rivalry in Asia will soon be fixed."

With the event of Russia in the Gulf and her Persian policy, with France envious of England's growing prestige in this Orient, with Germany at work building railways and Turkey's days numbered, what is to be the future of the fertile provinces of Busrah and Bagdad ? Will England continue to hold the upper hand in every part of Arabia and will some future Lord Cromer develop the Euphrates-Tigris valley into a second Egypt? The battle of diplomacy is on. European cabinets, backed by immense armies and navies are playing a game involving tremendous issues—issues not only tremendous to themselves and to the populations of Arabia and Persia, but involving the interest of another King and the greatest Kingdom. The event toward which history and recent politics in Arabia have so far been moving is " the one far off Divine event " of the Son of God. Not only to the missionary but to every Christian the study of the politics of Arabia makes evident the great Providential hand of God in the history of the Peninsula during the past century. Jesus Christ holds the key to the situation. All the kings of the earth are in His hand and to whomsoever He gives power or privilege, the end will be the glory of His own name and the coming of His own kingdom ; also in Arabia.

XXIV

THE ARABIC LANGUAGE

"Arabic grammars should be strongly bound, because learners are so often found to dash them frantically on the ground."—*Keith Falconer.*

" It is a language more extended over the face of the earth and which has had more to do with the destiny of mankind than any other, except English."—*Rev. Geo. E. Post, M. D.,* Beirut.

"Wisdom hath alighted upon three things—the brain of the Franks, the hands of the Chinese and the tongue of the Arabs."—*Mohammed ed-Damiri.*

TWO religions contend for the mastery of the world; Christianity and Islam. Two races strive for the possession of the dark continent; the Anglo-Saxon and the Arab. Two languages have for ages past contested for world-wide extension on the basis of colonization and propagandism—the English and the Arabic. To-day about seventy millions of people speak some form of the Arabic language, as their vernacular; and nearly as many more know something of its literature in the Koran because they are Mohammedans. In the Philippine islands the first chapter of the Koran is repeated before dawn paints the sky red. The refrain is taken up in Moslem prayers at Pekin and is repeated across the whole of China. It is heard in the valleys of the Himalayas and on "the roof of the world." A few hours later the Persians pronounce these Arabic words and then across the Peninsula the muezzins call the " faithful " to prayer. At the waters of the Nile, the cry *" Allahu akbar "* is again sounded forth ever carrying the Arab speech westward across the Sudan, the Sahara and the Barbary States until it is last heard in the mosques of Morocco.

The Arabic Koran is a text-book in the day-schools of
Turkey, Afghanistan, Java, Sumatra, New Guinea, and
Southern Russia. Arabic is the spoken language not only of
Arabia proper but forces the linguistic boundary of that peninsula 300 miles north of Bagdad to Diarbekr and Mardin, and
is used all over Syria and Palestine and the whole of northern
Africa. Even at Cape Colony there are daily readers of the
language of Mohammed. As early as 1315 Arabic began to
be taught at the universities of Europe through the missionary influence of Raymund Lull and to-day the language is
more accurately known and its literature more critically in-
vestigated at Leiden than at Cairo and at Cambridge than in
Damascus.

A missionary in Syria who is a master of the Arab tongue
thus characterizes it, "A pure and original speech of the greatest flexibility, with an enormous vocabulary, with great grammatical possibility, fitted to convey theological and philosoph-
ical and scientific thought in a manner not to be excelled by
any language except the English, and the little group of languages which have been cultivated so happily by Christianity
in Central Europe." Ernest Renan, the French Semitic
scholar, after expressing his surprise that such a language as
Arabic should spring from the desert-regions of Arabia and
reach perfection in nomadic camps, says that the Arabic surpasses all its sister Semitic languages in its rich vocabulary,
delicacy of expression, and the logic of its grammatical construction.[1]

[1] He speaks of it as follows in his Histoire des Langues Semitques, p.
342: "Cette langue, auparavant inconnue, se montre à nous soudainement
dans toute sa perfection, avec sa flexibilite, sa richesse infinie, tellemen-
complete, en un mot, que depnis ce temps jusqu'a nos jours elle n'a subi
ancune modification importante. Il n'y a pour elle ni enfance, ni
vieillesse ; une fois qu'on a signalé son apparition et ses prodijieuses cont
quêtes, tout est dit sur son compte. Je ne sais si l'on trouverait un autre
exemple d'un idiome entrant dans le monde comme celui-ci, sans état
archaïque, sans degrés intermediaires ni tatonnements."

The Semitic family of languages is large and ancient, although not as extensive geographically nor so diverse as those of Indo-European family. Some maintain [1] that the Semites were ancient immigrants from the region northeast of Arabia. They hold that before the formation of the different Semitic dialects the Semites everywhere used a name for the camel (*jemel*) which still appears in all of the dialects. They have however no names in common for the date-palm, the fruit of the the palm nor for the ostrich, therefore, in their first home, the Semites knew the camel but did not know the palm. Now the region where there is neither date-palm nor ostrich and yet where the camel has lived from the remotest antiquity is the central table-land of Asia near the Oxus. Von Kremer holds that from this region the Semites migrated to Babylon even before the Aryan emigration; the Mesopotamian valley is the oldest seat of Semitic culture.

Others [2] hold that the original home of the Semites was in the south of Arabia whence they gradually overspread the peninsula, so that, as Sprenger expresses it, "All Semite are successive layers of Arabs." The arguments for this theory are briefly given by Sayce: [3] "The Semitic traditions all point to Arabia as the original home of the race. It is the only part of the world which has remained exclusively Semites. The racial characteristics—intensity of faith, ferocity, exclusiveness, imagination—can best be explained by a desert origin." De Goeje lays stress on the fine climate of Central Arabia and the splendid physical development of the Arab as additional proof together with the indisputable fact that "of all Semitic languages the Arabic approaches nearest to the original mother-tongue as was conclusively demonstrated by Professor Schrader of Berlin."

The following table will show at a glance the position of

[1] Von Kremer, Guidi, Hommel.

[2] Sayce, Sprenger, Schrader, De Goeje, Wright.

[3] Assyrian Grammar, p. 13.

Arabic in the Semitic family group, *dead languages being put in italics*. Arabic, ancient and modern belongs to the South Semitic group and at an early period supplanted the Himyaritic in Yemen, although the Mahri and Ehkeli dialects are still used in the mountains of Hadramaut.[1] It was practically the only conquering language on the list and is the only one that is growing in use.

TABLE OF SEMITIC LANGUAGES.

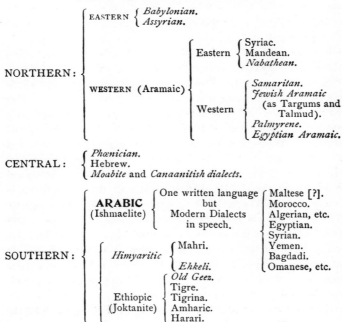

NORTHERN:

EASTERN { *Babylonian.* / *Assyrian.*

WESTERN (Aramaic)

Eastern { Syriac. / Mandean. / *Nabathean.*

Western { *Samaritan.* / *Jewish Aramaic* (as Targums and Talmud). / *Palmyrene.* / *Egyptian Aramaic.*

CENTRAL: { *Phœnician.* / Hebrew. / *Moabite* and *Canaanitish dialects.*

SOUTHERN:

ARABIC (Ishmaelite) { One written language but Modern Dialects in speech. { Maltese [?]. / Morocco. / Algerian, etc. / Egyptian. / Syrian. / Yemen. / Bagdadi. / Omanese, etc.

Himyaritic { Mahri. / *Ehkeli.*

Ethiopic (Joktanite) { *Old Geez.* / Tigre. / Tigrina. / Amharic. / Harari.

There are to-day over one hundred Arabic newspapers and magazines regularly published and which together have an immense circulation in all parts of the Arabic-speaking world.

[1] An account of this language or dialect was given by Surgeon H. J. Carter in Journal Roy. Asiat. Soc., July, 1847.

While the Arabic language has now acknowledged supremacy above all its sisters, in its historical and literary development
it was last of them all.   Not until the seventh century of our era
did Arabic become, in any sense, important.   The language received its literary birthright and its inspiration through the
illiterate prophet who could not read but who set all the Eastern world to studying his book.   The Arabic literature of the
days before Mohammed has a high literary character, but with
all its beauty it was only the morning star that ushered in the
sunrise.   When once the Koran was promulgated, literature
and grammar and the sciences all spoke Arabic.   It was the
renaissance of the dead and dying East.   Whatever effect
the Koran may have had on the social life and morals of a people, no one denies that it was the Koran and that alone which
rescued Arabic from becoming a local idiom.   Again this
Koran was the unifying factor of the new religion, sweeping
everything down before it; not only did it unify the hostile
tribes of Arabia but melted all their dialects into one and
established an ever-abiding classical standard for the remotest
student of the language of revelation.   We do not of course
hold, as do the Arabs, that the Arabic of the Koran is absolutely without a parallel in grammatical purity and diction.
The contrary has been proved by Nöldeke and Dozy.   The
latter states that the Koran is "full of bastard-Arabic and has
many grammatical blunders, which are at present unnoticed,
since the grammarians have kindly constructed rules or exceptions to include even these in the list of unapproachable style
and perfection."

The origin and history of the Arabic alphabet is exceedingly
interesting.   All writing was originally pictorial, the next stage
being that of the ideogram.   Perhaps a trace of this earliest
writing still remains in the *wasms* or tribal marks of the Bedouin.   Scholars maintain that the earliest Semitic writing we
possess of certain date is that on the Moabite Stone, discovered
by the missionary Klein in 1868.   Almost of equal age is the

Cyprus and Sidon alphabet, and that of the Phœnicians, found
on ancient coins and monuments.   The date of this writing is
put at 890 B. C.   On these monuments and coins the system of
orthography is already so carefully developed as to prove that
the Semites understood the art centuries before that date.   The
oldest forms of these Semitic alphabets are in turn derived
(Halévy, Nöldeke) from the Egyptian hieratic characters.
The oldest inscriptions found in North Arabia by Doughty and
Enting, in the Nabatean character, and in South Arabia by
Halévy and others in Himyaritic character, are both written,
like modern Arabic, from right to left.   Although the characters do not resemble each other, this would seem to indicate a
common origin.   The intimate connection of the present Arabic
alphabet with the Hebrew or Phœnician, is shown not only by
the forms of the letters, but, by their more ancient numerical
arrangement called by the Arabs *Abjad,* and which corresponds
with the Hebrew order.

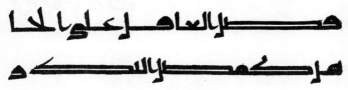

CUFIC CHARACTERS.

Accounts differ even among the Arabs as to who adapted or
invented the present Arabic alphabet from the older Cufic
forms.   Some even hold that they both developed simultaneously
out of the Himyaritic.   The Cufic, it is true, is found on old
monuments and coins from the Persian Gulf to Spain, and is a
square, apparently more crude kind of writing.   But the cur-
sive script (now called *Naskhi*) seems to have been in use also
long before Mohammed's time, the Arab historians to the contrary notwithstanding, for the exigencies of daily life.   That
writing was known at Mecca before the era of Mohammed is
acknowledged by Moslem tradition and the close intercourse

with Yemen long before that time would certainly indicate some knowledge of Himyaritic. Syriac and Hebrew were also known in Mecca and Medina because of the Jewish population, and it is not improbable that this may have had influence on the present form of the Arabic alphabet.

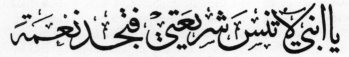

MODERN COPYBOOK STYLE OF ARABIC (VOWELED.)

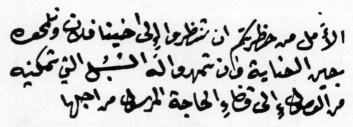

ORDINARY ARABIC HANDWRITING (UNVOWELED.)

It is not without reason that Mohammed's cognomen for Jew and Christian alike was, "the people of the *Book*." At first, like the Hebrew, Arabic had no vowel-points or diacritical marks. In the earliest Cufic Koran manuscripts these have the form of accents, horizontal lines or even triangles. The Arabs tell many interesting stories about the cause and occasion of their invention by Abu Aswad ad Duili or by Nasr bin 'Asim. In each case the awful sin of mispronouncing a word in the Koran leads to the device of vowel-points as a future preventative. According to another tradition it was Hasan-el-Basri (who died A. H. 110) that first pointed the Koran text with the assistance of Yahya bin Yámar. The vowel-points, so called, were in reality the abbreviated weak-consonants and were placed, in accordance with the sound of these letters, when so pronounced. The vowel-points and diacritical marks are al-

ways found in copies of the Koran, but seldom in other books
and never in epistolary writing. They are considered by the
Arabs themselves as at best a necessary evil, except for grammarians and purists. The story is told that an elaborate piece
of Arabic penmanship was once presented to the governor of
Khorasan under the Caliph al Mamun, and that he exclaimed,
" How beautiful this would be if there were not so much cori-
ander seed scattered over it ! "

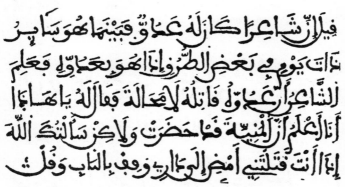

MOGREBI ARABIC OF NORTH AFRICA (UNVOWELED.)

The demand for perfect accuracy in copying the Koran in
every detail of point and accent, led the Arabs to glorify the
art of caligraphy, and, as they followed neither painting nor
sculpture because of their creed, they naturally put all their
artistic taste into their manuscripts. Brilliantly colored and
adorned with gold on delicately tinted parchment, or paper, the
fanciful chapter-headings and the elegant tracery of each letter
in the book make such an old manuscript Koran a real work
of art. Three names are recorded of those who in the early
days of Islam were the Raphaels and Michael Angelos of the
reed-pen ; Wazir Muhammed bin Ali, Ali bin Hilal al Bauwab,
and Abu-'d-Dur bin Yakut al Musta'sami. As time went by
there arose various schools of this art ; chiefly distinguished as

the Magrib-Berber or Western, and the Turko-Arab or Eastern style.   In the decorations of the Alhambra the western school shows some of its most finished art, while Damascus and Cairo mosques show the delicate "Arabesque" traceries of the lighter oriental school.   It is in manuscripts, however, that the best work is found; some of these are of priceless value and exceeding beauty.   Even to-day there are Arab penmen whose work commands a good price as *art* and gives them a position in society as it did the monkey, described in the Arabian Nights, who improvised poetry in five styles of caligraphy for the astonished king.

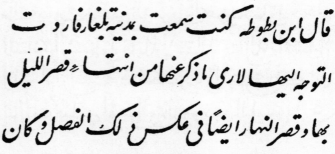

PERSIAN STYLE EXTENSIVELY USED IN EASTERN ARABIA.

The Arabic language is distinguished among those that know it for its *beauty*, and among those who are learning it for its *difficulty*.   To the Arabs their language is not only the language of revelation, but of the Revealer himself.   Allah speaks Arabic in heaven, and on the day of judgment will judge the world in this "language of the angels."   All other tongues are vastly inferior in grammatical construction, and what else could they be since the Koran with its classical perfection has existed before all words, uncreated, written on the preserved tablet in heaven, the daily delight of the innumerable company of angels! As Renan says, "among a people so preoccupied with language as the Arabs, the *language* of the Koran became as it were a

second religion, a sort of dogma inseparable from Islam." But
the innate beauty of the language is acknowledged by all who
have made it a study, whether born on the soil of Arabia or
educated in the universities of Europe. From the days of the
Dutch scholars, De Dieu, Schultens, Schroeder and Scheid,
and the Swiss Hottinger to the times of Nöldeke, Gesenius and
Renan, the praises of Arabic have been proclaimed in Europe,
and its study pursued with a devotion that almost amounted to
a passion.

The elements of beauty in this language are many. There
is first its logical structure, which, we are told, surpasses that of
any other language. Even the order of the alphabet is more
logical as regards form than the Hebrew; its grammar is altogether logical; the exceptions to its rules can be formed, so to
say, into a syllogism. Palmer's and Lansing's grammars show
how this logical structure can be discovered in the minutest detail, so that, *e. g.*, the three short vowels control the forms not
only, but the significance of roots, and are the key to the interpretation of all grammatical mysteries.

A second element of beauty is found in the lexical richness
of the Arabic. Its boundless vocabulary and wealth of synonyms are universally acknowledged and admired. A dictionary is called a *Kamoos* or " Deep Ocean " where "full many
a gem of purest ray serene, the dark unfathomed caves " conceal for the diligent student. Renan tells of an Arab linguist
who wrote a book on the 500 names given to the lion in literature; another gives 200 words for serpent. Firozabadi, the
Arabian Webster, is said to have written a sort of supplement
on the words for honey and to have left it incomplete at the
eightieth word; the same authority asserts that there are over
1,000 different terms in Arabic for sword and, judging from
its use by the Arabs, this appears credible. De Hammer
Purgstall, a German scholar, wrote a book on the words re-
lating to the *camel* and finds them, in Arabic literature, to the
number of 5,744. But this remarkable exhibition loses some

of its grandeur when truth compels us to state that many of the so-called synonyms are epithets changed into substantives or tropes accidentally employed by some poet to conform to his rhyme. It is also true that the wealth of synonym is limited in Arabic to a certain class of words; in other departments of thought, ethics for example, the language is wofully poor, not even having a distinctive word for conscience.

A third point of beauty in the Arabic language is its purity as compared with other Semitic languages or even all other languages. This was partly due to the geographical location of the Arabs and is still due to their early literature together with the Koran which has put a classical standard into the hands of every schoolboy and has prevented, by the law of religion, both development and deterioration. " While other languages of the same family became dead and while many of their forms and meanings changed or disappeared, the Arabic remained comparatively pure and intact excepting perhaps the temporary corruption which necessarily occurred during the Moslem conquests and foreign applications of the first four Caliphs." [1]

The Arabic race occupied at first a circumscribed territory and came little into contact with the surrounding nations so that the forces which produce linguistic decay were absent. The only thing that will preserve a language pure next to isolation is a classical literature. English has changed less since Shakespeare's time than it did in the interval between him and Chaucer. So too with Arabic. Had it not been for the Koran and its cognate literature, by this time the people of Syria, Egypt, Morocco and Oman would perhaps scarcely understand each other, and their written language would differ vastly; but the existence of this literature has kept the written language a unit and put a constant check on the vagaries of dialect.

The last, and chief element of beauty in the Arabic tongue

[1] Lansing.

is undoubtedly its wonderful literature. In poetry alone, the Arabians can challenge the world; in grammar, logic and rhetoric the number of their works is legion; while both at Bagdad and Cordova Arab historians and biographers filled whole libraries with their learning; in Cordova the royal library contained 400,000 volumes. Algebra and Astronomy are specially indebted to the Arabs; all the sciences received attention and some of them addition from the Arabian mind.

The Arabic tongue is not only beautiful but it is difficult, exceedingly difficult, to every one who attempts to really master it. One of the veteran missionaries of Egypt wrote, in 1864, "I would rather traverse Africa from Alexandria to the Cape of Good Hope, than undertake a second time to master the Arabic language." The first difficulty is its correct pronunciation. Some Arabic letters cannot be transliterated into English, although certain grammars take infinite pains to accomplish the impossible. The gutturals belong to the desert and were doubtless borrowed from the camel when she complained of overloading. There are also one or two other letters which sorely try the patience of the beginner and in some cases remain obstinate to the end. Then the student soon learns, and the sooner the better, that Arabic is totally different in construction from European tongues and that "as far as the East is from the West" so far he must modify his ideas as to the correct way of expressing thought; and this means to disregard all notions of Indo-European grammar when in touch with the sons of Shem. Every word in the Arabic language is referred to a root of three letters. These roots are modified by prefixes, infixes and suffixes, according to definite models, so that from one root a host of words can be constructed and vice versa, from a compounded word all the servile letters and syllables must be eliminated to find the original root. This digging for roots and building up of roots is not a pastime at the outset because of the extent of the root-garden. Dozy's *supplement* to Lane's Monumental Arabic Lexicon has 1,714 pages. So large in fact is the vocabulary of Arabic writers that the classics require copious explanatory notes for the Arabs themselves and some of them have written notes on the notes, to explain the difficult words used in explaining others more difficult. Moreover Arabic literature is so vast in its extent that acquaintance with the vocabulary of a dozen authors in one line of literature does not yet enable the student to appreciate the language of other works. You may be able to read the Koran tolerably well and understand its diction and yet when you turn to the Arabian Shakespeare or Milton find yourself literally at sea, in the *Kamoos*, and unable to understand a single line.

The regular verb in Arabic has fifteen conjugations, two voices, two tenses, and several moods; the irregular verbs are many and mysterious to the beginner although grammarians try to make them appear easier by demonstrating that all their irregularities are strictly logical, not the result of linguistic perversity but foreseen calculation and providential wisdom. Is it not "the language of the angels"?—even the broken-plurals?

As a final testimony to the difficulties of the Arabic language listen to Ion Keith Falconer. After passing the Semitic Languages Tripos at Cambridge under Dr. Wright, and taking a special course in Arabic at Leipzig, he writes from Assiut in Egypt: "I am getting on in Arabic, but it is most appallingly hard. . . . I have learned a good deal and can make myself intelligible to servants and porters. I have a teacher every day for two hours and translate from a child's reading book." After *five years* of further study he writes once more from Aden (Jan. 17, 1886), "I am learning to speak Arabic quite nicely but it will be long before I can deliver real discourses." And this man was an all-around scholar with a passion for languages. Without any doubt Arabic *is* one of the most difficult languages in the world to acquire with any degree of fluency, and progress in its attainment means ceaseless plodding and endless diligence.

XXV

THE LITERATURE OF THE ARABS

THE literature of the Arabs is either pre-Islamic or post-Islamic; the former has as its chief classics the Muallakāt or seven suspended poems, the latter finds its centre and apex as well as its origin and inspiration in the Koran. The seven ancient poems, still extant, are also called *Muthahabat* or the "golden poems," and it is generally admitted by Arabic scholars that this was indeed the golden age of Arab literature. Zuhair, Zarafah, Imru-l-Kais, Amru-ibn-Kulsum, Al Harith, 'Antar and Labid were the authors of these poems and all but the last were idolaters, and belong to what the conceit of Islam calls "the Time of Ignorance." These poems furnished the model ever afterward for later writers and, according to Baron de Slane, are remarkable for their perfection of form and exhibit a high degree of linguistic culture.

But the Koran has eclipsed all that ever went before it or came after it in the eyes of the Arabs. It is the paragon of literary perfection as well as of moral beauty. Its style is inimitable because it is Divine in the highest sense of the word. To criticise its diction is to be guilty of blasphemy and to compare it with other literature is to commit sacrilege. There is no doubt that the chief charm of the Koran from a literary standpoint is its musical jingle and cadence. It is such as the Arabs, the earliest masters of rhyme, love, and servilely imitate in all their later prose works. Our English translations of the Koran, although accurate, (and even idiomatic, as Palmer's) cannot reproduce this; in consequence the book appears vapid, monotonous and to the last degree wearisome and uninteresting. Attempts have been made by Burton and others to acquaint English readers with this element of beauty in Mohammed's revelation. The following [1] is almost equal to the Arabic itself, and, to say the least, sounds more interesting than Sale's prose version of the same passage :

> " I swear by the splendor of light
> And by the silence of night
> That the Lord shall never forsake thee
> Nor in His hatred take thee ;
> Truly for thee shall be winning
> Better than all beginning.
> Soon shall the Lord console thee, grief no longer control thee,
> And fear no longer cajole thee.
> Thou wert an orphan-boy, yet the Lord found room for thy head.
> When thy feet went astray, were they not to the right path led ?
> Did He not find thee poor, yet riches around thee spread ?
> Then on the orphan-boy, let thy proud foot never tread,
> And never turn away the beggar who asks for bread,
> But of the Lord's bounty ever let praise be sung and said."

It is not to be expected that all the transcendant excellencies and miraculous beauties which Moslem commentators find in the Koran should unveil themselves to cold, unsympathizing western gaze, but that the book has a certain literary beauty no one can deny who has read it in the original.   As Penrice says in his preface to his Dictionary of the Koran, " Beauties there are many and great ; ideas highly poetical are clothed in rich and appropriate language, which not unfrequently rises to a sublimity far beyond the reach of any translation ; but it is unfortunately the case that many of those graces which present themselves to the admiration of the finished scholar are but so many stumbling-blocks in the way of the beginner ; the marvellous conciseness which adds so greatly to the force and energy of its expressions cannot fail to perplex him while the frequent use of the ellipse leaves in his mind a feeling of vagueness not altogether out of character in a work of its oracular and *soidisant* prophetic nature."

[1] Found in the *Edinburgh Review* for July, 1866, article " Mohammed."

The greatest literary treasure of the Arabs next to the Koran is the *Makāmat* of Al Hariri. No one of polite scholarship would dare profess ignorance of this great classic, and the reader of these " Assemblies " is introduced to every branch of Mohammedan learning—poetry, history, antiquities, theology and law. Recently Hariri has been translated into English by Chenery and an earlier translation by Preston has also been printed. Stanley Lane-Poole reviewing these translations thus characterizes this Shakespeare of the Arabic world :

" It is difficult, no doubt, for most Westerns to appreciate the beauties of this celebrated classic. There is no cohesion, no connecting idea, between the fifty separate ' Assemblies, ' beyond the regular reappearance of an egregious Tartufe, called Abu-Zeyd, a Bohemian of brilliant parts and absolutely no conscience, who consistently extracts alms from assemblies of people in various cities, by preaching eloquent discourses of the highest piety and morality, and then goes off with his spoils to indulge secretly in triumphant and unhallowed revels. Even in this framework there is no attempt at originality ; it is borrowed from Hamadâni, the ' Wonder of the Age.' The excellence lies in the perfect finish : the matter is nothing ; the charm consists in the form alone. Yet this form is, to English readers, exotic and artificial. Among its special merits, in the eyes of Easterns, is the perpetual employment of rimed prose. To us this is apt to seem at once monotonous and strained, with its antithetic balance in sense, and jingle of sound ; but to the Arabs, as to many primitive peoples, either riming or assonant prose was from early times a natural mode of impassioned and impressive speech. It is the mode adopted constantly and without strain in the Koran, and it is the mode into which an historian, such as Ibn-el-Athîr, falls naturally when he waxes eloquent over a great victory or a famous deed. . . .

" But if we do not care for rimed prose, there is plenty besides in Hariri to minister to varied tastes. In these wonderful ' Assemblies,' we shall find every kind of literary form, except

the shambling and the vulgar.   Pagan rhetoric, Moslem ex-
hortation, simple verse, elaborate ode, everything that the im-
measurable flexibility of the Arabic tongue and the curious art
of a fastidious scholar could achieve—all is here, and we may
take our choice.''

What is said by this scholarly critic of Hariri holds true of
most Arabic poetry, it lacks unity of idea and sobriety of expression.   All is intense.   Every beautiful eye is a narcissus ; tears
are pearls ; teeth are pearls or hail-stones ; lips are rubies ; the
gums, pomegranate blossoms ; piercing eyes are swords, and
the eyelids, scabbards ; a mole is an ant creeping to suck the
honey from the lips ; a handsome face is a full-moon ; an erect
form is the letter alif as penned by Wazir Muhammed ; black
hair is night ; the waist is a willow-branch or a lance, and love
is always passion.   Far-fetched allusions abound and the *sense*
at every turn must do homage to the *sound*.   In the judgment
of Baron de Slane the two notable exceptions to the rule are Al
Mutanabbi and Ibn El Farid who exhibit a daring and surprising originality often approaching the sublime and, in the case
of the latter, mystic reveries and spiritual beauties of no mean
order.

The influence of the Arabic language on other tongues and
peoples has also been great, ever since the rise of Islam.   The
Persian language adopted the Arabic alphabet and a large
number of Arabic words and phrases ; so that, as Renan remarks, in some Persian books all the words are Arabic and
only the grammar remains in the vernacular.   As for Hindustani, three-fourths of its vocabulary consists of Arabic words
or Arabic words derived through the Persian.   The Turkish
language also is indebted for many words taken from the
Arabic and uses the Arabic alphabet.   The Malay language,
with the Moslem conquest, was also touched by Arabic influence and likewise adopted its alphabet.   In Africa its influence
was yet more strongly felt.   The language extended over all
the northern half of the continent and is still growing in use

to-day. The geographical nomenclature of the interior is Arabic and Arabs preceded Livingstone, Stanley and Speke in all their journeys. The languages of the southern Sudan, the Hausa, and even those of Guinea borrowed largely from the Arabic. Europe itself did not escape the influence of the conquering Semitic tongue. Spanish and Portuguese betray a vast number of Arabic words and idioms. French and English are also indebted to Arabic in no small degree for many scientific and technical words introduced at the time of the crusades and even earlier. Here is a partial list of those which we received directly or indirectly from the Arab tongue, as given in Skeat's Etymological Dictionary and arranged into sentences; every word in italics is of Arabic origin.

"The *Nabob Mohammedan Magazine* relates, that years after the *Hegira*, a *saracen caliph* or *Mameluke sultan*, sat with his *mussulman emir*, *admiral*, *vizier*, *moslem mufti* and *Koran-munshee*, (who knew *alchemy* and *algebra* and could *cipher* the *azimuth* and *nadir* to *zero*), *sheikh* of the *hareem*, *muezzin* and *tariff-dragoman* of the *arsenal*, under a *carob-* tree, on *sofas* of *mohair-mattress* covered with *jerboa-* and *gazelle-skins*, drinking *coffee*, *saffron-elixer*, *arrack*, *alcohol* and *syrup* of *senna carraway* and *sumach*. For tonic they also had *rose-attar*, *artichokes*, *alkaline-nitre* in *myrrh*, *taraxacum*, *otto-sherbet*, and *naphtha* in *amber* cups. The *Sultan's* infant daughter wore a *carmine cotton*-and-*muslin chemise* or *diaper* with a *civet talisman* and *jasper amulet;* she played a *Tartar lute*. Suddenly a *giaour Bedouin assassin* with an *assagai* and *hookah-masque* came down on them from behind an *alcove* of the neighboring *arabesque mosque minaret* like a *sirocco-simoon* or *monsoon* and killed them all."

Most of these words came from the Arabic through other languages such as French and Spanish; others were directly transferred from the Arabic to English; and still others have passed the long journey from Arabic to Greek, to Latin, to

Italian, to French and thence to English.   The word *magazine* is perhaps the best example of how an Arabic-root found shelter in the soil of all the European languages and grew into manifold significations from its original meaning with the Arabs, *ghazana*=to collect or store.

In modern days, especially since the opening of the Suez canal, the English language is beginning to exert its influence on Arabic.   In Egypt, Syria and the Persian Gulf many English commercial terms are being adopted into the language and the newspapers spread their use everywhere.

Last, but not least, there is the immense, incalculable influence on the Arabic-tongue for all time exerted by the toil and sacrifice of the early missionaries to Syria through their college and press in giving to the world a modern Christian and scientific literature and that crowning work of Drs. Eli Smith and C. V. A. Van Dyck—the Arabic Bible.   The mission press at Beirut has four hundred and eighty three volumes on its catalogue and prints about twenty-five million pages annually.[1]   The Arabic Bible "one of the noblest literally monuments of the age " will yet prove a mighty influence in purifying and ennobling the language and preserving its classical dic-

---

[1] "It would take a long list to exhaust the religious, literary and scentific contributions to the Arabic language from the missionaries in Syria. They include the translation of the Scriptures and the stereotyping of the same in numerous styles; the preparation of a Scripture guide, commentaries, a concordance, and a complete hymn and tune book; text-books in history, algebra, geometry, trigonometry, logarithms, astronomy, meteorology, botany, zoölogy, physics, chemistry, anatomy, physiology, hygiene, materia medica, practice of physic, surgery, and a periodical literature which has proved the stimulus to a very extensive native journalism. The Protestant converts of the mission, educated by the missionaries, have written elaborate works on history, poetry, grammar, arithmetic, natural science, and the standard dictionary of the language, and a cyclopædia which will make a library by itself, consisting of about twenty volumes of from six hundred to eight hundred pages each."
—*Dr. G. E. Post, in New York Evangelist.*

tion to the utmost bounds of the Arab-world. There was only one Koran and there will be only one Arabic Bible—the finished product of American scholarship and her best gift to the Mohammedan world.

TITLE PAGE OF A CHRISTIAN PAPER PRINTED IN ARABIC.

XXVI

THE ARAB

"Children of Shem!   Firstborn of Noah's race
And still forever children ; at the door
Of Eden found, unconscious of disgrace,
    And loitering on while all are gone before;
Too proud to dig, too careless to be poor
    Taking the gifts of God in thanklessness,
Not rendering aught, nor supplicating more,
    Nor arguing with Him if He hide His face.
Yours is the rain and sunshine, and the way
    Of an old wisdom, by our world forgot,
The courage of a day which knew not death ;
    Well may we sons of Japhet, in dismay,
Pause in our vain mad fight for life and breath,
    Beholding you.—I bow and reason not."—*Anon.*

CONCERNING the origin of the tribes and people that
now inhabit the Arabian peninsula there is disagreement
among the learned.   It is generally held that the original
tribes of Northern Arabia are descendants of Ishmael.   This
is also the tradition of all Arab historians.   As to the South
Arabians, who occupied their highlands with the Hadramaut
coast for centuries before the Ishmaelites appeared on the scene
there are two opinions.   Some believe them to be descendants
of Joktan (Arabic *Kahtan*) the son of Heber and therefore,
like the Northern Arabs, true Semites.   Others think that the
earliest inhabitants of South Arabia were Cushites or Hamitic ;
while some German scholars hold that in the earlier Arabs the
children of Joktan and of Cush were blended into one race.

Among the Ishmaelites are included not only Ishmael's direct
descendants through the twelve princes,[1] but the Edomites, Moa-

[1] Gen. xxv. 16.

bites, Ammonites, Midianites and probably other cognate tribes. The names of the sons of Ishmael in relation to their settlements and the traces of these names in modern Arabia is a subject which has been taken up by Bible dictionaries but which still offers an interesting field for further study. The Arabs themselves have always claimed Abrahamic descent for the tribes of the north. The age-long, racial animosity between the Yemenites and Māadites seems to confirm the theory of two distinct races inhabiting the peninsula from very early times ; and they remain distinct until to-day in spite of a common language and a common religion. " The animosity of these two races to each other is unaccountable but invincible. Like two chemical products which instantly explode when placed in contact, so has it always been found impossible for Yemenite and Māadite to live quietly together. At the present day the Yemenite in the vicinity of Jerusalem detests the Māadite of Hebron, and when questioned as to the reason of their eternal enmity has no other reply but that it has been so from time immemorial. In the time of the Caliphs the territory of Damascus was desolated by a murderous war for two years, because a Māadite had taken alemon from the garden of a Yemenite. The province of Murcia in Spain was deluged with blood for seven years because a Māadite inadvertently plucked a Yemenite vine-leaf. It was a passion which surmounted every tie of affection or interest. ' You have prayed for your father : why do you not pray for your mother ? ' a Yemenite was asked near the Kaaba. ' For my mother ! ' said the Yemenite, ' How could I ? She was of the race of Māad.' "[1]

The Yemenites at a very early period founded the strong and opulent Himyarite Kingdom. The Himyarites were the navigators of the East and they were celebrated for their skill in manufacture as well as for enterprise in commerce ; they had a written language, inscriptions in which were discovered all over south Arabia during the present century. The Māadite or

[1] In the *Edinburgh Review*, July, 1866.

Ishmaelite Arabs on the contrary were more nomad in their habits and were masters of the caravans which carried the enormous overland trade by the two great trunk-lines of antiquity, from the East to the West. One of these lines extended from Aden, (Arabia Emporium of Ptolemy) along the western part of the peninsula and through Yemen to Egypt; the other extended from Babylon to Tadmor and Damascus. A third route, nearly as important, was also in the hands of the Ishmaelite Arabs, by Wady Rumma and Nejd to the old capital of the Himyarites, Mareb.[1] These caravans unified the Arabian peninsula and fused into one its two peoples; the northern Arabs receiving somewhat of the southern civilization and the southern Arabs adopting the language of the north. But the decline in the caravan trade brought disaster to Arabia; the ship of the desert found a competitor in the ships of the sea. Old settlements were broken up, great cities, which flourished because of overland trade, were abandoned and whole tribes were reduced from opulence to poverty. In this time of transition, long before the birth of Mohammed, the Arabic nation as it is known to modern history seems to have been formed.

The modern Arabs classify themselves into Bedouins and town-dwellers; or, in their own poetic way, *ahl el beit* and *ahl el h'eit*, "the people of the tent," and "the people of the wall." But this classification is hardly sufficient, although it has been generally adopted by writers on Arabia. Edson L. Clark, in his book, The Arabs and the Turks, gives five classes: "Beginning at the lowest round of the ladder we have first the sedentary or settled Arabs . . . who though still many of them dwelling in tents have become cultivators of the soil. By their nomadic brethren these settled Arabs are thoroughly despised as degraded and denationalized by the change in their mode of life. Secondly, the wandering tribes in the neighborhood of the settled districts, and in constant intercourse with

[1] International Routes of Asia, by Elisée Reclus, in New York *Independent*, May 4, 1899.

their inhabitants. Both these classes, but more especially the latter, are thoroughly demoralized. . . . The third class consists
of the Arabs of the Turkish towns and villages; but they too
are a degenerate class both in language and character. . . .
The fourth class consists of the inhabitants of the towns and
villages of Arabia proper, who by their peculiar situation have
remained more secluded from the rest of the world than even
the wandering tribes. . . . Finally the great nomadic
tribes of the interior, still preserving unchanged the primitive
character, habits and customs of their race." This last class
and this alone are the real Bedouins.

In addition to this classification according to civilization
there is the universal genealogical classification ; and no people
in the world are fonder of genealogies than the Arabs. The
names of tribes and families go back, in many cases to pre-
islamic days. The earliest tribal-names, therefore, are either
taken from animals or totem-names, like Panthers, Dogs, Lizards, *e. g.*, *Anmar Kilab*, *Dibab*, etc; place-names transformed afterward by the genealogists into ancestors, *e. g.*,
Hadramaut, *Hauab*; or from idols and idol-worship, *e. g.*,
Abd el Kais, *Abd al Lat*, etc. But the later system of genealogies as given by the Arabs are utterly unreliable because they
are so evidently artificial. The backbone of the system was
the pedigree of Mohammed and this is notoriously untrust-
worthy. "Dummy ancestors" were inserted in order to connect a particular but unimportant tribe with a distinguished one,
and Hamdani himself tells us that he found it a common practice of obscure desert groups to call themselves by the name of
some more famous tribe.[1]

Character is difficult to define. To depict the moral phys-
iognomy of a nation and their physical traits in such a way
that nothing important is omitted and no single characteristic
exaggerated at the cost of others. This difficulty is increased
in the case of the Arabs, by their twofold origin and their

[1] Smith's Kinship and Marriage in Early Arabia, pp. 9, 17, 131.

present twofold civilization. That which is true of the town-
dweller, is not always true of the Bedouin and vice versa.
Moreover the influence of the neighboring countries must be
taken into account. Eastern Arabia has taken color by long contact with Persia; this is seen in speech, architecture, food and
dress. Southern Arabia, especially Hadramaut, has absorbed
East Indian ideas. While Western Arabia, especially Hejaz,
shows in many ways its proximity to Egypt. Not losing sight
of these distinctions, which will account for many exceptions
to the general statements made, what is the character of the
Arabs?

Physically, they are undoubtedly one of the strongest and
noblest races of the world. Baron de Larrey, surgeon-general
of the first Napoleon, in his expeditions to Egypt and Syria,
says: "Their physical structure is in all respects more perfect
than that of Europeans; their organs of sense exquisitely acute,
their size above the average of men in general, their figure ro-
bust and elegant, the color brown; their intelligence propor-
tionate to their physical perfection, and without doubt superior,
other things being equal, to that of other nations."

The typical Arab face is round-oval, but the general leanness
of the features detracts from its regularity; the bones are
prominent; the eyebrows long and bushy; the eye small, deep-
set, fiery black or a dark, deep brown. The face expresses
half dignity, half cunning, and is not unkindly, although never
smiling or benignant. The teeth are white, even, short and
broad. The Arabs have very scanty beards as a rule, but those
of the towns often cultivate a patriarchal beard like the traditional beard of the prophet. The figure is well-knit, muscular, long-limbed, never fat. The arms and legs are thin, almost shrunken, but with muscles like whip-cords. As young
men the Bedouins are often good-looking, with bright eyes and
dark hair, but the constant habit of frowning to protect the eyes
from the glare of the sun, soon gives the face a fierce aspect; at
forty their beards turn grey and at fifty they appear old men.

It is a common mistake to consider the Arabs democratic in their ideas of society. The genuine Arab was and is always an aristocrat. Feuds originate about the precedence of one family or tribe over another; marriage is only allowed between tribes or clans of equal standing; the whole system of sheikh-government is an aristocratic idea; and as final proof there still exists a species of caste in South Arabia, while in North Arabia the Ma'adan Arabs of Mesopotamia and the *Suleyb* of the desert are little better than Pariahs as regards their neighbors. It is with a heavy heart that any Arab sees set over him a man of less noble extraction than himself. The religion of Arabia has made its people fanatics, although according to Nöldeke, "fanaticism is characteristic of all Semitic religions." But he forgets the real distinction between intolerance of another religion on ethical grounds as in the case of Judaism, and the infinitely hard, one-sided, crude exclusiveness of Islam.

The Arabs rarely have the power of taking in complex unities at a glance; the talent for arrangement is absent. An Arab carpenter cannot draw a right angle, nor can an Arab servant lay a tablecloth square on the table. The old Arab temple called a cube (Kaaba) has *none* of its sides or angles equal; their houses show the same lack of the "carpenter's eye" to-day. Streets are seldom parallel; even the street, so-called, was not *straight* in Damascus. The Arab mind loves units, not unity; they are good soldiers, but poor generals; there is no partnership in business; and no public spirit; each man lives for himself. That is the reason why Yemen cannot shake off the yoke of the Turk, and this explains why the smallest towns in Arabia have a great many little mosques. The Arab has a keen eye for particulars, great subjectivity, nervous restlessness, deep passion and inward feeling, and yet joined with strong conservatism and love of the past. In everything he follows old models and traditions; witness their poetry and their tent-life—in Arab phrase, termed their "houses of hair" and their "houses of poetry." As a result of their language-structure, the Arabs have naturally a strong tendency to a pointed, sharp speech of epigrammatic brevity, but also go to the other extreme of ornate tautology.   The former is characteristic of the desert; the latter of the towns.   Eloquence and poetry are still worshipped.   The only fine art which Arabs admire is that of caligraphy; and those who have seen finished specimens of an Arab master-penman, must acknowledge that in them are all the elements of painting and sculpture.

The Arabs are polite, good-natured, lively, manly, patient, courageous and hospitable to a fault.   They are also contentious, untruthful, sensuous, distrustful, covetous, proud and superstitious.   One must always keep in mind this paradox in dealing with an Arab.   As Clark expresses it, "an Arab will lie and cheat, and swear any number of false oaths, in a pecuniary transaction; but when once his faith is pledged he can be implicitly trusted, even to the last extremity."   There are Arab oaths such as *wallah*, which are intended to confirm falsehoods and signify nothing.   There are others, such as the threefold oath, with *wa*, *bi* and *ti* as particles of swearing, which not even the vilest robber among them dare break. Grammatically, the two oaths are nearly the same.

Robbery is a fine art among the nomads; but the high-minded Arab robs lawfully, honestly and honorably.   He will not attack his victims in the night; he tries to avoid all bloodshed by coming with overwhelming force; and if his enterprise miscarries, he boldly enters the first tent possible, proclaims his true character and asks protection.   The *Dakheil*, or privilege of sanctuary, the salt covenant, the blood covenant and the sacredness of the guest, all prove that the Arabs are trustworthy.   And yet, in the ordinary affairs of life, lying and deception are the rule and seldom the exception.   The true Arab is niggardly when he buys, and will haggle for hours to reduce a price; and yet he is prodigal and lavish in giving away his goods to prove his hospitality.

According to Burckhardt, the Arab is the only real lover of

the Orient; if he limits this to the Bedouin-Arab he is correct.
In matters of love and marriage the Arab of the towns is what
Mohammed, the Meccan merchant was, after the death of the
old lady Khadijah. But Arabic poetry of the times of ignorance does occasionally breathe the true tale of love and chiv-
alry; and the desert Arabs as a rule are not polygamists nor
given to divorce.

It was a law among the ancient Arabs that whoever sheds the
blood of a man owes blood on that account to the family of the
slain. This law of blood-revenge was confirmed by the Koran
and is a sacred right everywhere in Arabia. An Arab is considered degenerate who accepts a fine or any consideration save
blood for blood. This law is both the cause of continual
feuds, and tends to terminate them without much bloodshed.
Arabs of the town and of the desert will quarrel for hours
without coming to blows; it is not cowardice that prevents an
open encounter, but the fear of shedding blood and blood-revenge.

Family life among the Arabs is best studied by looking at
child-life in the desert and at the position of women among the
Bedouin and the town-dwellers. In no part of the world does
the newborn child meet less preparation for its reception than
among the Bedouin. A land bare of many blessings, general
poverty and the law of the survival of the fittest, has made the
Arab mother stern of heart. In the open desert under the
shade of an acacia bush or behind a camel, the Arab baby first
sees the daylight. As soon as it is born the mother herself rubs
and cleans the child with sand, places it in her handkerchief
and carries it home. She suckles the child for a short period,
and at the age of four months it already drinks profusely of
camels' milk. A name is given to the infant immediately;
generally from some trifling incident connected with its birth,
or from some object which attracts the mother's fancy. Moslem names such as Hassan Ali or Fatimah, are extremely uncommon among the true Bedouins; although Mohammed is

sometimes given.   Beside his own peculiar name every Bedouin
boy is called by the name of his father and tribe.   And what
is more remarkable, boys are often called after their sisters,
e. g., *Akhoo Noorah*, the brother of Noorah.   Girls' names
are taken from the constellations, birds, or desert animals like
Gazelle.

In education the Arab is a true child of nature.   His parents
leave him to his own sweet will; they seldom chastise and
seldom praise.   Trained from birth in the hard school of
nomad life, fatigue and danger do contribute much to his education.   Burckhardt says, "I have seen parties of naked boys
playing at noonday upon the burning sand in the middle of
summer, running until they had fatigued themselves, and when
they returned to their fathers' tents they were scolded for not
continuing the exercise.   Instead of teaching the boy civil
manners, the father desires him to beat and pelt the strangers
who come to the tent; to steal or secrete some trifling article
belonging to them.   The more saucy and impudent children
are the more they are praised since this is taken as an indication of future enterprise and warlike disposition.   Bedouin
children, male and female, go unclad and play together until
their sixth year.   The first child's festival is that of circumcision.   At the age of seven years the day is fixed, sheep are
killed and a large dish of food is cooked.   Women accompany
the operation with a loud song and afterward there is dancing
and horseback riding and encounters with lances.   The girls
adorn themselves with cheap jewelry and tent-poles are decorated with ostrich feathers.   Altogether it is a gala-day.

The Bedouin children have few toys but they manage to
amuse themselves with many games.   I have seen a group of
happy children, each with a pet locust on a bit of string,
watching whose steed should win the race.   The boys make
music out of desert-grass winding it in curious fashion to resemble a horn, and calling it *Masoor*.   In Yemen and Nejd a
sling, like David's, with pebbles from the brook is a lad's first

CHURNING BUTTER IN A BEDOUIN CAMP

weapon. Afterward he acquires a lance and perhaps an old discarded bowie-knife. The children of the desert have no books. [1] But, of paper, they have the Book of Nature. This magnificent picture book is never more diligently studied than by those little dark eyes which watch the sheep at pasture or count the stars in the blue abyss from their perch on a lofty camel's saddle in the midnight journeyings.

When the Bedouin lad grows up, and begins to swear by the few straggling hairs on his chin, he cannot read a letter, but he knows men and he knows the desert. The talk heard at night around the Sheikh's tent or the acacia-brush fireside is much like the wisdom of the book of Job. A philosophy of submission to the world as it is; a deification of stoicism or patience; a profound trust that all will end well at last. Sad to say even the little nomads, with their ignorance of all religion, share in the fanatical antagonism of their elders toward the Christian religion and Christians. One of their games, in Nejd, is to draw a cross on the desert sand and then defile it ; they learn that all outside the pale of Mohammed's creed are *kafirs* and to please Allah are glad to throw stones at any way-faring Nasrani. Little do the Bedouins and still less do their children, however, know of the religion of Islam. The Koran is not a book for children's minds and of such is not the kingdom of Mohammed.

The Bedouin child early puts away childish things. To western eyes the children of Arabia appear like little old men and women ; and the grown-up people have minds like children. This is another paradox of the Arab-character. At ten years the boy is sent to drive camels and the girl to herd sheep; at fifteen they are both on the way to matrimony. He wears the garb of a man and boasts a matchlock ; she takes to spinning camel hair and sings the songs of the past. Their brief childhood is over. In the towns marriage takes place

[1] What the boys and girls of the towns can study we have described in our chapter on Mecca.

even earlier ; and there are boys of eighteen who have already divorced two wives.

Among the Bedouins polygamy is not common nor is it among the poorer Arabs of the towns.   The marriage cere- mony among the Bedouins is as simple as it is long and com- plex among the townsmen.   After the negotiations which pre- cede the marriage contract, the bridegroom comes with a lamb in his arms to the tent of the girl's father and there cuts the lamb's throat before witnesses.   As soon as the blood falls on the ground the contract is sealed ; feasting and dancing follow, and at night the bride is conducted to the bridegroom's tent where he is awaiting her arrival.   Dowrys are paid more gen- erally and more largely in the towns than in the desert. Among certain Arab tribes a demand of money for the hand of a bride would be deemed scandalous.   From a western standpoint the women of the Bedouin stand on a higher plat- form of liberty and justice than those of the towns where the Koran has done its work on one half of society to repress in- tellect and degrade affection, and sensualize the sexual relation to the last degree.   On the other hand divorce is perhaps more common among the Bedouins,[1] than among the city Arabs. Burckhardt met Arabs not yet forty-five years of age who were known to have had above fifty wives.   Concerning the mar- riage-contract in the towns, the ceremony, the divorce proceed- ings, and the methods by which that is made legal which even the lax law of Islam condemns, the less said the better.

On the position of women in Arabia we quote four unim- peachable witnesses who have nothing in common save their knowledge of the subject ; there is truth on both sides where they differ ; where they agree there is no question of certainty as to the fact.

DOUGHTY, the Christian explorer, whose volumes are a mine of information says :[2]   " The female is of all animals the better,

[1] This is the testimony of Burckhardt and Doughty.

[2] Arabia Deserta, Vol. I., p. 238.

say the Arabians, save only in mankind. Upon the human
female the Semites cast all their blame. Hers is, they think, a
maleficent nature, and the Arabs complain that 'she has seven
lives.' The Arabs are contrary to womankind, upon whom
they would have God's curse; some, they say, are poisoners
of husbands and there are many adulteresses. . . . The
horma [*i. e.*, woman] they would have under subjection; admitted to an equality, the ineptitude of her evil nature will
break forth. They check her all day at home and let her
never be enfranchised from servitude. The veil and the jealous lattice are rather of the obscene Mohammedan austerity in
the towns; among the mild tent-dwellers in the open wilderness the housewives have a liberty as where all are kindred;
yet their hareem are now seen in the most Arabian tribes half-
veiled."

BURCKHARDT, the time-honored authority on things Arabian,
writes: "The Bedouins are jealous of their women, but do not
prevent them from laughing and talking with strangers. It
seldom happens that a Bedouin strikes his wife; if he does so
she calls loudly on her *wasy* or protector who pacifies the husband and makes him listen to reason. . . . The wife and
daughters perform all the domestic business. They grind the
wheat in the handmill or pound it in the mortar; they prepare
the breakfast and dinner; knead and bake the bread; make
butter, fetch water, work at the loom, mend the tent-covering
and are, it must be owned, indefatigable. While the husband
or brother sits before the tent smoking his pipe."

LADY ANN BLUNT, who travelled among the tribes of the
Euphrates valley with her husband, speaks thus from a
woman's standpoint: "Of the Bedouin women a shorter description will be enough. As girls they are pretty in a wild
picturesque way and almost always have cheerful, good-natured
faces. They are hard-working and hard-worked, doing all the
labor of the camp. . . . They live apart from the men
but are in no way shut up or put under restraint. In the

morning they all go out to gather wood for the day, and
whenever we have met them so employed they have seemed
in the highest possible spirits.   .   .   .   In mental qualities
the women of the desert are far below the men, their range
of ideas being extremely limited.   Some few of them, however, get real influence over their husbands and even, through
them, over their tribes.   In more than one Sheikh's tent it
is in the woman's half of it that the politics of the tribe are
settled."

SNOUCK HURGRONJE, the Dutch traveller who spent an entire year (1884–85) in Mecca thus characterizes the position
of women in Arabian towns : [1]

" What avail to the young maiden the songs of eulogy which
once in her life resound for her from the mouth of the sing-
ing-woman, but which introduce her into a companionship by
which she, with her whole sex, is despised ?   Moslem literature,
it is true, exhibits isolated glimpses of a worthier estimation of
woman, but the later view, which comes more and more into
prevalence, is the only one which finds its expression in the
sacred traditions, which represent hell as full of women, and
refuse to acknowledge in the woman, apart from rare exceptions, either reason or religion, in poems, which refer all the
evil in the world to the woman as its root ; in proverbs, which
represent a careful education of girls as mere wastefulness.
Ultimately, therefore, there is only conceded to the woman the
fascinating charm with which Allah has endowed her, in order
to afford the man, now and then in his earthly existence, the
prelibation of the pleasures of Paradise, and to bear him children."

The poems which revile womankind, and of which the
Dutch traveller speaks, are legion.   Here are two examples in
English translation from Burton :

[1] Translation from Mekka, Vol. II., p. 187.

" They said, marry !—I replied,—
Far be it from me
To take to my bosom a sackful of snakes.
I am free why then become a slave ?
May Allah never bless womankind."

" They declare woman to be heaven to man ;
I say, Allah, give me Jehannum, not this heaven."

Three kinds of dwellings are found in Arabia. There is the *tent*, the date-palm hut, and the house built with mortar of stone or mud-brick. The tent is distinctive, in a general sense, of the interior and of Northern Arabia ; the palm-hut of the coast and of South Arabia ; while houses of brick and mortar exist in all the towns and cities. The evolution of the house is from goats'-hair to matting, and from matting to mud-roof. Each of these dwellings is called *beit*, " the place where one spends the night."

The Bedouin tent[1] consists of nine poles, arranged in sets of three and a wide, black goats'-hair covering so as to form two parts ; the men's apartment being to the left of the entrance and the women's to the right, separated by a white woollen carpet hanging from the ridge-pole. The posts are about five to seven feet in height ; the length of the tent is between twenty and thirty feet, its depth at the most is ten feet. The only furniture consists of cooking utensils, pack-saddles, carpets, water-skins, wheat-bags and millstones.

The date-palm hut is of different shapes. In Hejaz and Yemen it is built like a huge beehive, circular and with a pointed roof. In Eastern Arabia it consists of a square enclosure with hip-roof generally steep and covered with matting or thatch-work. At Bahrein the Arabs are very skillful in so weaving the date-fronds together and tightening every crevice that the huts keep out wind and rain-storms most successfully. The average size date-hut can be built for twenty or thirty Rupees (seven to ten dollars) and will last for several years.

[1] See Burckhardt's book for further particulars.

The stone-dwellings of Arabia are as different in architecture and material as circumstance and taste can make them. In Yemen large castle-like dwellings crown every mountain and frown on every valley; stone is plentiful and the plan of architecture inherits grace and strength from the older civilization of the Himyarites. In Bagdad, Busrah and East Arabia Persian architecture prevails, with arches, wind-towers, tracery and the veranda-windows. While the architecture of Mecca and Medina takes on its own peculiar type from the needs of the pilgrimage. Generally speaking the Arabs build their houses without windows to the street, and with an open court; the harem-system dictates to the builder, even putting a high parapet on the flat-roof against jealous eyes. Bleak walls without ornament or pictures are also demanded by their surly religion. All furniture is simple and commonplace; except where the touch of western civilization has awakened a taste for mirrors, marble-top tables and music-boxes.

In dress there is also much variety in Arabia. Turkish influence is seen in the Ottoman provinces and Indian-Persian in Oman, Hassa and Bahrein. The Turkish *fez* and the *turban* (which are not Arabian) are examples. The common dress of the Bedouin is the type that underlies all varieties. It consists of a coarse cotton shirt over which is worn the abba or wide square mantle. The headdress is made with a square cloth, folded across and fastened on the crown of the head by a circlet of woollen-rope called an *'akal*. The color of the garment and its ornamentation depends on the locality; likewise the belt and the weapons of the wearer. Sandals of all shapes are used; shoes and boots on the coast indicate foreign influence. The dress of the Bedouin woman is a wide cotton gown, with open sides, generally of a dark blue color, and a cloth for the head. The veil is of various shapes; in Oman it has the typical Egyptian nose-piece with only the middle part of the face concealed; in the Turkish provinces of East Arabia, thin black cloth conceals all the features. Nose and earrings are

common. All Arab women also tattoo their hands and faces
as well as other parts of their bodies, dye with henna and use
antimony on their eyelashes for ornament.

The staple foods of Arabia are bread, rice, ghee (or clarified
butter, which the Arabs call *semu*) milk, mutton and dates.
These are found everywhere and coffee is the universal beverage. Other foods and fruits we have considered in our study
of the provinces. Tea is now widely used but was known
scarcely anywhere less than twenty years ago. Tobacco is
smoked in every village and the Bedouins also are passionately
fond of the weed; even the Wahabi religious prohibition did
not drive out desire for the universal narcotic. There is one
article of food we have left unmentioned, *locusts*. These are
quite a staple in the grocers' shops of all the interior towns of
Arabia. They are prepared for eating by boiling in salt and
water, after which they are dried in the sun. They taste like
stale shrimps or dried herring. The coast-dwellers still live
largely on fish and in the days of Ptolemy they were called
Ichthiophagoi.

XXVII

EVEN Islam could not suppress the Arab's love for music nor diminish his regard for the great poets of "the days of ignorance." For be it known that, although one can buy Austrian mouth-organs in the bazaar at Jiddah, and harmonicas from Germany in the toy-shop at Hofhoof, music is generally held by Moslems, even to-day, to be contrary to the teaching of the prophet. Mafia relates that when he was walking with Ibn Omar, and they heard the music of a pipe the latter put his fingers into his ears and went another road. Asked why, he said: "I was with the prophet, and when he heard the noise of a musical pipe, he put his fingers into his ears; and this happened when I was a child." Thus it comes to pass that by the iron law of tradition, more binding to the pious Moslem ofttimes than the Koran itself, the Mohammedan world considers music at least among the doubtful amusements for true believers. And yet both before and after the advent of the morose legislator, Arabia has had its music and song. But music in Mohammedan lands is ever in spite of their religion, and is never, as is the case with Christianity, fostered by it.

Among the ancient Arabs poetry and song were closely related. The poet recited or chanted his own compositions in the evening mejlis, or more frequently at the public fairs and festivals, especially the national one held annually at Okatz. Here it was that the seven noble fragments still extant of their earliest literature were first read and applauded, and accounted worthy (if this part of the story be not fabulous) to be suspended, written in gold, in the Kaaba.

It is unfortunate that the Arabs, with all their wealth of lan-

guage and literature, have no musical notation, so that we can
only surmise what their ancient tunes may have been.   Were
the early war songs of Omar and Khalid sung in the same key
as this modern war chant of the Gomussa tribe, as interpreted
by Lady Ann Blunt?

And did Sinbad the sailor sing the same tune on his voyages
down the Persian Gulf to India which now the Lingah boatmen lustily chant as they land the cargo from a British India
steamer?   Or was it like this sailors' song on the Red Sea?

To both of these questions the only answer is the unchange-
ableness of the Orient; and this puts the probability, at least,
so far that the sailors of to-day could easily join in Sinbad's
chorus.

The people of Jauf, in Northern Arabia, are most famous
for music at the present day, according to Burckhardt.   They
are especially adept at playing the *Rebaba*.   This may well be
considered the national instrument of music.   It is all but
universal in every part of the peninsula, and as well-known to
all Arabs as the bag pipe is to the Scotch.   I have heard the
highland shepherd boys of Yemen play on a set of reed-pipes
rudely fastened together with bits of leather thong.   The drum
tabl, is common among the town Arabs, and is used at their
marriage and circumcision feasts; but all over the desert one
only hears the rebaba.   It is simplicity itself in its construction, when made by the Bedouins; the finer ornamental ones
are from the cities.   A box frame is made ready, a stick is

thrust through, and in this they pierce an eye-hole for a single peg; a kidskin is then stretched upon the hollow box; the string is plucked from a mare's tail, and setting under it a bent twig for the bridge, their music is ready.

Time and measure are often very peculiar and hard to catch, but they are kept most accurately, and Ali Bey gives an example which he says, "exhibits the singularity of a bar divided into five equal portions, a thing which J. J. Rousseau conceived to be practicable, but was never able to accomplish." Here it is as he gives it; it strikingly resembles the boatmen's song at Bahrein:

The singing one commonly hears, however, is much more monotonous than this, and the tune nearly always depends on the whim of the performer or singer, sometimes, alas, on his inability to give more than a certain number of variations!

Antar, one of their own poets, has said that the song of the Arabs is like the hum of flies. A not inapt comparison to those who have seen the "fly bazaar" in Hodeidah or Menamah during the date season, and heard their myriad-mouthed buzzing. Antar, however, lived in the "times of ignorance," and most probably referred to the chanting of the camel drivers, which is bad enough. Imagine the following sung in a high monotonous key with endless repetition:

> "Ya Rub sallimhum min el tahdeed
> Wa ija'ad kawaihum 'amd hadeed."

That is to say, being freely interpreted:

> "Oh Lord, keep them from all dangers that pass
> And make their long legs pillars of brass.

To a stranger that which seems most peculiar in Arab song is their long drawn-out tones at the close of a bar or refrain, sometimes equivalent to three whole notes or any number of beats. Doughty did not appreciate it, apparently, for he writes: "Some, to make the stranger cheer, chanted to the hoarse chord of the Arab viol, making to themselves music like David, and drawing out the voice in the nose to a demensurate length, which must move our yawning or laughter." There are, however, singers and singers. I remember a ruddy Yemen lad who sang us *kasidahs* during a heavy rain-storm in an old Arab café near Ibb. The singer was master of his well-worn rebaba, and its music seemed to overmaster him. Now his hand touched the strings gently, and then again swept over them with a strong nervous motion, awakening music indeed. His voice, too, was clear and sweet, although I was not enough versed in Arabic poetry to catch the full meaning of his words. It may have been the surroundings or the jovial companionship of friendly Arabs after my Taiz seclusion and a weary journey up the mountain passes, but I have never heard sweeter music in Arabia, and have often heard worse elsewhere. God bless that travelling troubadour of Yemen!

Here is a Mecca song for female voices, as given by Ali Bey in his travels (1815), and a second sung by the women of Hejaz in a more monotonous strain:

Such songs are called *asamer;* love-songs are called *hodjeiny*, and the war song is known as *hadou*. Arabic prosody and the science of metres is exceedingly extensive and seemingly difficult. What we call rhyme is scarcely known, and yet every verse ends with the same syllable in a stanza of poetry.

In Mecca as well as in other "religious," centres there is a
sort of sacred-music of which Hurgronje gives several specimens.   They are chants in honor of the prophet or prayers for
him which are sung at the *Moleeds* or festivals in memory of
Mohammed.   Here are two of them:

Most generally, however, music is looked upon as decidedly
secular, especially all instrumental music.   The desert Arabs
know no religious song and only sing of love and war in their
old wild way.   It is only at a distance from the mosque and
away with the caravan, that Ghanim clears his throat and sings
in a voice that can be heard for a mile as we leave him behind:

The Arabs of the desert have a reading-book all their own
called *Athar* ; and a writing all their own called *wasm*.   No
Bedouin so ignorant but he can read *Athar* and none so dull
but he can write his *wasm*.

Athr or *ilm el athar* is the science of footsteps; and like the free Indians of America, the Arab is keen to study and quick to judge from sand tracks of both men and animals. The genuine Arab who has made *athar* a study can tell the

TRIBAL MARKS or WASMS of the ARABS.

)|	BNI DHONEHY	X	NAYM		JEHEYNA
	IBU ESMEYER	I X ~ †	IBU_RASHID		HOWEYTAT
	EL TEYAR	II))	EL_FEJIR		BNI SAKHR
	EL TEYAR		WELAD ALI		BNI_ATIYEH
T	EL HESSENE		WELAD ALI		SHERARAT
△	BESSHR		TOWWALA		M'FALAHA
	BESSHR		RUWALLA		M'FALAHA
	BNI SAKHR		MOAHIB		LAHAWWY
	BNI SAKHR		BISHR		HETEYM
OOO	NAYM		BILLI		KERAK (Christian Bedouins)

track of a friend from that of a foe, and can distinguish the tribe or even the clan; he knows from the depth of the foot-print whether the camel was loaded or lame; whether the man passed yesterday or a week before; from the regularity or irreg-

ularity he judges of fatigue or of pursuit.   If the camel's fore-
feet dig deeper than the hind he concludes the animal had a
weak breast ; from the offal he knows whence the camels came
and the character of their pasture.   Burckhardt writes of instances where camels were traced six days' journeys after being
stolen, and identified.

To identify property it must be marked, therefore, the kindred science of *wasm* has its place.   A *wasm* is a Bedouin
trade-mark or ideograph to label his property, real and personal.
Their origin is unknown, although Doughty says that they
ofttimes resemble Himyaritic letters and may therefore come
from Yemen.   Each family or tribe has its own cattle-brand or
token.   Not only is personal property such as cattle marked
with the *wasm* but the Bedouin put their mark on rocks near
favorite wells or pastures.   These signs are the only certain
records of former occupation of tribes.   Many of the tribes
have two or three different *wasms ;* these belong to family
groups.

The medical knowledge and medical treatment of the Arabs
deserve some notice.   The Arabs think themselves always ailing
and never fail to consult a *hakim* or doctor when there is opportunity.   The hakeem is supposed to know both their malady
and its cure by simple observation ; to tell the physician for
what cause they seek him would be an insult to his wisdom and
for him to ask them settles the matter that he is not a true
hakeem.   The common diseases of Arabia are the following,
according to Arab nomenclature, *El Kibd, i. e.,* the liver, or
all visceral infirmities ; *er rihh,* literally, "the wind," or
rheumatics and neuralgia ; *humma,* fevers ; *tahāl* or ague-cake ;
el-hasa or stone; ophthalmia ; "fascination" or hysterics, (as
when they say a man has a jinn or a child has been looked at
by the evil-eye) ; leprosy, phthisis, dropsy, stranguria, ulcers
and senile itch.   For any and all of these ailments, beside
others not so common, yet sometimes epidemic like smallpox
and cholera, the Arabs seek a hakeem.   All medicine, save

amulets, charms and exorcisms, is called *dawa*. Their pharma-
copia is not large but quite remarkable ; in addition to such
simple herbs of the desert as their hareem collect and dry they
use in grave emergencies that which is harām (forbidden) and
unclean. Patients have come to me for a small piece of swine's
flesh (which they suppose all Christians eat) to cure one in
desperate straits. Doughty tells how among the Bedouins they
give the sick to eat of the carrion-eagle and even seethe asses'
dung for a potion.

Kei or actual cautery is a favorite cure for all sorts of diseases ; so also is *khelal* or perforating the skin surface with a
red-hot iron and then passing a thread through the hole to
facilitate suppuration. Scarcely one Arab in a hundred who
has not some *kei*-marks on his body ; even infants are burned
most cruelly in this way to relieve diseases of childhood.
Where *kei* fails they have resource to words written on paper
either from the Koran or, by law of contraries, words of evil,
sinister import. These the patient "takes" either by swal-
lowing them, paper and all, or by drinking the ink-water in
which the writing is washed off. Blood-letting is also a sovereign remedy for many troubles. The Arab barber is at once
a phlebotomist, cauterizer, and dentist. His implements—
one can hardly call them instruments—are very crude and
he uses them with some skill but without any mercy. Going
to the proper place in any large Arab town you may always see
a row of men squatting down with bent back to be bled ;
cupping and scarifying are the two methods most in vogue,
although some are quite clever in opening a vein. The science
of medicine in the towns is not much in advance of that of the
desert—more book-talk but even less natural intelligence. A
disease to be at all respectable must be connected with one of
the four temperaments or " humors of Hippocrates."

Medicines are hot and cold, wet and dry; and the same
fourfold classification distinguishes all ailments. There are
four elements only, and the stars must be favorable to induce

a rapid cure. Whatever is prescribed must be solid and material; if it is bitter and painful so much the better. Rough measures act more strongly on the imagination and faith-cure is a reality in such cases. Burton gives this sample of a correct prescription :

" A." [1]

" In the name of Allah, the compassionate, the merciful, and blessings and peace be upon our Lord the apostle and his family and his companions one and all. But afterward let him take bees-honey and cinnamon and album græcum of each half a part and of ginger a whole part, which let him pound and mix with the honey and form boluses, each bolus the weight of a Mithkal, and of it let him use every day a Mithkal, on the saliva, (that is to say, fasting, the first thing in the morning). Verily its effects are wonderful. And let him abstain from flesh, fish, vegetables, sweetmeats, flatulent food, acids of all descriptions, as well as the major ablution and live in perfect quiet. So shall he be cured by the help of the King the healer, *i. e.*, the Almighty. And the peace."

Honey has always been a panacea in Arabia on authority of the Koran and tradition. The only reference to medicine in the revelation of Mohammed is this ignorant statement: " From the bee's belly comes forth a fluid of variant hue which yieldeth medicine to man." (Surah xvi. 71.) This being the only remedy prescribed by Allah, it is no wonder that tradition affirms its efficacy as follows : " A man once came to Mohammed and told him that his brother was afflicted with a violent pain in his belly; upon which the prophet bade him give him some honey. The fellow took his advice but soon came again and said that the medicine had done no good. Mohammed answered : ' Go and give him more honey, for God speaks truth and thy brother's belly lies,' and the dose being repeated the man was cured." [2]   Coriander-seeds, pepper-

[1] Signifying " Allah."   [2] Baidhawi's Commentary *in loco.*

mint, cinnamon, senna, iris-root, saffron, aloes, nitrates, ar-
senious-earth, pomegranate-rind, date-syrup and vinegar—such
are some of the common household remedies of Arabia. All
Arab women profess a knowledge of herbs and the art of healing so that the "hakeem" can scarcely make a living if he
clings solely to his profession. A Mecca " M. D.," says Hurgronje, was also watch-maker, gun-smith and distiller of perfume ; to fill up his idle hours he did a little silver-plating and
dealt in old coins ! Yet this man was at the head of the profession in Mecca and was able, so they said, to transmute the
base metals and write very powerful charms.

The following are used as amulets in Arabia : a small Koran
suspended from the shoulder ; a chapter written on paper and
folded in a leather case ; some names of God or their numerical
values ; the names of the prophet and his companions ; green-
stones without inscriptions ; beads, old coins, teeth, holy earth
in small bags. Amulets are not only worn by the Arabs themselves and to protect their children from the evil-eye but are
put on camels, donkeys, horses, fishing-boats and sometimes
over the doors of their dwellings. The Arabs are very superstitious in every way. In Hejaz if a child is very ill the mother
takes seven flat loaves of bread and puts them under its pillow ;
in the morning the loaves are given to the dogs—and the child
is not always cured. Rings are worn against the influence of
evil-spirits ; incense or even-smelling compounds are burned in
the sick-room to drive away the devil; mystic symbols are
written on the walls for a similar purpose. Love-philtres are
everywhere used and in demand ; and nameless absurdities are
committed to insure successful child-birth. The child-witch,
called *Um-el subyan*, is feared by all mothers ; narcotics are
used freely to quiet unruly infants and, naturally, mortality is
very large. Of surgery and midwifery the Arabs as a rule are
totally ignorant and if their medical-treatment is purely ridiculous their surgery is piteously cruel, although never intentionally
so. In all eastern Arabia *blind* women are preferred as mid-

wives, and rock-salt is used by them against puerpural hem-
morrhage. Gunshot-wounds are treated in Bahrein by a poultice
of dates, onions and tamarind; and the accident is guarded
against in the future by wearing a "lead-amulet."

There are many other superstitions in no way connected with
the treatment of the sick. Tree-worship and stone-worship still
exist in many parts of Arabia in spite of the so-called "pure
monotheism" of Islam. Both of these forms of worship date
back to the time of idolatry and remain as they were partly by
the sanction of Mohammed himself, for did he not make a
black-pebble in the Kaaba, the centre of his system of prayer?
Sacred trees are called *Manahil*, places where angels or jinn
descend; no leaf of such trees may be plucked and they are
honored with sacrifices of shreds of flesh, while they look gay
with bits of calico and beads which every worshipper hangs on
the shrine. Just outside of the Mecca gate at Jiddah stands
one of these rag-trees with its crowd of pilgrims; in Yemen they
are found by every wayside.[1]

[1] For on account of these ancient superstitions and idolatries still practiced, see W. Robertson Smith's "Religion of the Semites" and his "Kinship and marriage in Early Arabia." The mass of purely Mohammedan
superstition can be studied in books like the Arabian Nights and Lane's
"Modern Egyptians."

XXVIII

THE STAR-WORSHIPPERS OF MESOPOTAMIA [1]

"In a remote period of antiquity Sabeanism was diffused over Asia by the science of the Chaldeans and the arms of the Assyrians. They adored the seven gods or angels who directed the course of the seven planets and shed their irresistible influence on the earth. . . . They prayed thrice each day, and the temple of the moon at Haran was the term of their pilgrimage."—*Gibbon*.

IN the towns along the lower Euphrates and Tigris, especially at Amara, Suk es Shiukh, Busrah and Mohammerah, there dwell an interesting people, variously known as Sabeans, Nasorians, or St. John Christians. They call themselves Mandæans, and although numbering four or five thousand, they are and have always been entirely distinct from the Jews, Moslems and Christians among whom they have dwelt for centuries. Their origin is lost in obscurity although the few scholars who have studied the subject trace their history through the maze of their religion to ancient Babylonia and Chaldea. In this remnant of a race and religion we seem to have an example of the oldest form of idolatry, Star-worship, and many of their mysterious customs may throw a side-light upon the cult of ancient Babylonia. Mandæism is not only of deep interest as "the only existing religion compounded of Christian, heathen and Jewish elements,[2] but it affords another proof of the early spread of religious ideas in the East, and the Babylonian origin of much that is supposed to be Alexandrian Gnosticism in a semi-Christian, semi-pagan garb.

[1] This chapter is an enlargement of a paper on "The Star-Worshippers of Mesopotamia" read before the Victoria Institute, Adelphi Terrace, London, 1897.

[2] Kessler.

In the English Bible the name *Sabeans* is perplexing, and although used of three different tribes or peoples, none of these are any way related to the present Mandæans unless those mentioned in Job. Sabean is also the term used in the Koran, where it undoubtedly applies to the people and proves that when Islam arose their numbers and settlements were far from unimportant. The Koran recognizes them as distinct from idolaters, and places them with Jews and Christians as people of the book.[1] From this it is evident that the Sabeans[2] could not have been, as some allege, a minor Christian sect or identical with the Hemero-Baptists. Although giving special honor to John the Baptist, *they can in no sense be called Christians*.

Isolated by a creed, cult and language of their own, the Sabeans[3] love their isolation and do not intermarry with strangers nor accept a proselyte to their faith. Nearly all of them follow one of three trades. They raise the finest dairy produce of Mesopotamia ; they build a peculiar kind of light canoe, called *Mashhoof*, and all others are silver-smiths. No traveller should visit their villages without carrying away specimens of

---

[1] Surah ii. 59; v. 73; xxii. 17.

[2] According to Gesenius, Sabeans should be *Tsabians* from *tsabaoth*, the "host of heaven." Nöldeke and others say it comes from a root *subba* to wash, baptise, and refers to the manner of their worship. Gibbon is perhaps correct when, on the authority of Pocock, Hettinger, and D'Herbelot, he states the origin of their other name thus : "A slight infusion of the gospel had transformed the last remnant of the Chaldean polytheists into the Christians of St. John at Bussora."

[3] In regard to their name *Sabeans*, Lane's Arabic dictionary says that it comes from a root meaning "one who has departed from one religion to another religion." The Arabs used to call the prophet *as-Sabi*, because he departed from the religion of the Koreish to El-Islam. Nasoreans is the name given them by some authors. According to Petermann they themselves give this title only to those of their number who are distinguished for character or knowledge. It doubtless comes from Ναζωραῖοι, the early half-Christian sect of Syria.

their beautiful inlaid-work, black metal on silver and gold. A peaceful people they are, industrious, though mostly poor and seldom affording trouble to their Turkish rulers. Both men and women have a remarkably fine physique; tall, of dark complexion, good features, and with long black beards, some of the men are typical patriarchs, even as we imagine Abraham who left their present country for Haran. On ordinary days their dress does not distinguish them from Moslems or Jews, but on feast days they wear only white. Their women go about unveiled; they are rather taller and have a more masculine cast of features than Moslem women.

Specimens of MANDAITIC CURSIVE-SCRIPT *with transliteration and translation.*

	= Āssooda hāvilak	= peace be to you.
	= kethkŭm skawee	= how much is it?
	= ana libba kabeelak	= I love you much.
	= kasbah we dahwah	= silver and gold.
	= hofshaba rabba	= great day (Sunday)
	= atran hofshaba	= Monday.
„	= aklatha	= Tuesday.
„	= arba	= Wednesday
„	= hamsha	= Thursday.
„	= shitta	= Friday.
„	= shuvah	= Saturday.

The two great things that distinguish the Sabeans are their language and their religion. Both are remarkable. The former because of its long preservation among a dying people, and the latter as the most remarkable example of religious syncretism.

Naturally the bazaar-talk of all the river-country is Arabic; all Sabeans speak it and a goodly proportion read and write it; but beside this they have a household language of their own, the language of their sacred books, which is called Mandâitic. It is so closely related to Syriac that it might almost be called a dialect, yet it has an alphabet and grammar of its own, and their writing and speech is not fully intelligible to the Syriac-speaking Christians from Mosul. Wright says that their alphabet characters most resemble the Nabathean and their language that of the Babylonian Talmud.[1] One peculiarity is the naming of the letters with the ā vowel and not as in other Semitic languages by special names. The oldest manuscripts of the Mandâitic date from the sixteenth century, and are in European Libraries (Paris and Oxford). But according to Nöldeke the golden period of their literature, when their religious books received their final and present form, was 650–900 A. D. At present few can read or write their language, although all can speak it, and from religious motives they refuse to teach those outside of their faith even the first lesson, except secretly.

Although meeting Sabeans for years and being their guest on frequent journeys up and down the rivers, I could find no satisfactory answer to the question what their real faith and cult were. The popular story that they turn to the North Star when they pray and "baptise" every Sunday was all that Moslems or Christians could tell. Books of travel gave fragmentary, conflicting and often grossly erroneous statements. According

---

[1] The only grammars of the language are the *Sketch of a Sabean Grammar* by Captain Prideaux and the accurate and elaborate *Mandäische Grammatik* of the indefatigable scholar Nöldeke. One great drawback of the latter however is that the *Hebrew* character is used throughout and not the Mandâitic.

to some accounts they were idolaters, others classed them with Christians. An anonymous article in the London *Standard*, Oct. 19, 1894, entitled, "A prayer meeting of the Star-worshippers," curiously gave me the key to open the lock of their silence. Whoever wrote it must have been perfectly acquainted with their religious ceremonies, for when I translated it to a company of Sabeans at Amara they were dumbfounded. Knowing that I knew *something* made it easy for them to tell me more. The article referred to was in part as follows :

"It happens to be the festival of the Star-worshippers celebrated on the last day of the year and known as the *Kanshio Zahlo*, or day of renunciation. This is the eve of the new year, the great watch-night of the sect, when the annual prayer-meeting is held and a solemn sacrifice made to Avather Ramo, the Judge of the under world, and Ptahiel, his colleague ; and the white-robed figures we observe down by the riverside are those of members of the sect making the needful preparations for the prayer-meeting and its attendant ceremonies.

"First, they have to erect their *Mishkna*, their tabernacle or outdoor temple ; for the sect has, strange to say, no permanent house of worship or meeting-place, but raise one previous to their festival and only just in time for the celebration. And this is what they are now busy doing within a few yards of the water, as we ride into the place. The elders, in charge of a *shkando*, or deacon, who directs them, are gathering bundles of long reeds and wattles, which they weave quickly and deftly into a sort of basket work. An oblong space is marked out about sixteen feet long and twelve broad by stouter reeds, which are driven firmly into the ground close together, and then tied with strong cord. To these the squares of woven reeds and wattles are securely attached, forming the outer containing walls of the tabernacle. The side walls run from north to south, and are not more than seven feet high. Two windows, or rather openings for windows, are left east and west, and space for a door is made on the southern side, so that the priest when entering the edifice has the North Star, the great object of their adoration, immediately facing him.   An altar of beaten earth is raised in the centre of the reed-encircled enclosure, and the interstices of the walls well daubed with clay and soft earth, which speedily hardens.   On one side of the altar is placed a little furnace of dark earthenware, and on the other a little handmill, such as is generally used in the East for grinding meal, together with a small quantity of charcoal.   Close to the southern wall, a circular basin is now excavated in the ground, about eight feet across, and from the river a short canal or channel is dug leading to it.   Into this the water flows from the stream, and soon fills the little reservoir to the brim. Two tiny cabins or huts, made also of reeds and wickerwork, each just large enough to hold a single person, are then roughly put together, one by the side of the basin of water, the other at the further extremity of the southern wall, beyond the entrance.   The second of these cabins or huts is sacred to the *Ganzivro* or high priest of the Star-worshippers, and no layman is ever allowed to even so much as touch the walls with his hands after it is built and placed in position.   The doorway and window openings of the edifice are now hung with white curtains; and long before midnight, the hour at which the prayer-meeting commences, the little *Mishkna*, or tabernacle open to the sky, is finished and ready for the solemnity.

" Toward midnight the Star-worshippers, men and women, come slowly down to the *Mishkna* by the riverside.   Each, as he or she arrives, enters the tiny wattled hut by the southern wall, disrobes, and bathes in the little circular reservoir, the *tarmido*, or priest, standing by and pronouncing over each the formula, '*Eshmo d'haï, Eshmo d'manda haï madhkar elakh*' ('The name of the living one, the name of the living word, be remembered upon thee').   On emerging from the water, each one robes him or herself in the *rasta*, the ceremonial white garments peculiar to the Star-worshippers, consisting of a *sadro*, a long white shirt reaching to the ground; a *nassifo*,

or stole round the neck falling to the knees; a *hiniamo*, or
girdle of woollen material; a *gabooa*, square headpiece, reaching to the eyebrows; a *shalooal*, or white over-mantle; and
a *kanzolo*, or turban, wound round the *gabooa* headpiece, of
which one end is left hanging down over the shoulder. Peculiar sanctity attaches to the *rasta*, for the garments com-
posing it are those in which every Star-worshipper is buried,
and in which he believes he will appear for judgment before
Avather in the nether world *Materotho*. Each one, as soon
as he is thus attired, crosses to the open space in front of
the door of the tabernacle, and seats himself upon the ground
there, saluting those present with the customary *Sood Havilakh*,
'Blessing be with thee,' and receiving in return the usual
reply, *Assootah d'haï havilakh*, 'Blessing of the living one
be with thee.'

"The numbers increase as the hour of the ceremonial comes
nearer, and by midnight there are some twenty rows of these
white-robed figures, men and women, ranked in orderly array
facing the *Mishkna*, and awaiting in silent expectation the
coming of the priests. A couple of *tarmidos*, lamp in hand,
guard the entry to the tabernacle, and keep their eyes fixed
upon the pointers of the Great Bear in the sky above. As
soon as these attain the position indicating midnight, the priests
give a signal by waving the lamps they hold, and in a few moments the clergy of the sect march down in procession. In
front are four of the *shkandos*, young deacons, attired in the
rasta, with the addition of a silk cap, or *tagha*, under the
turban, to indicate their rank. Following these come four
tarmidos, ordained priests who have undergone the baptism of
the dead. Each wears a gold ring on the little finger of the
right hand, and carries a tau-shaped cross of olive wood to
show his standing. Behind the *tarmidos* comes the spiritual
head of the sect, the *Ganzivro*, a priest elected by his col-
leagues who has made complete renunciation of the world and
is regarded as one dead and in the realms of the blessed. He

is escorted by four other deacons.   One holds aloft the large
wooden tau-cross, known as *derashvod zivo*, that symbolizes his
religious office ;   a second bears the sacred scriptures of the
Star-worshippers, the *Sidra Rabba*, " the great Order," two-
thirds of which form the liturgy of the living and one-third the
ritual of the dead.   The third of the deacons carries two live
pigeons in a cage, and the last a measure of barley and of
sesame seeds.

    " The procession marches through the ranks of the seated
worshippers, who bend and kiss the garments of the *Ganzivro* as
he passes near them.   The *tarmidos* guarding the entrance to
the tabernacle draw back the hanging over the doorway and
the priests file in, the deacons and *tarmidos* to right and left,
leaving the *Ganzivro* standing alone in the centre, in front of
the earthen altar facing the North Star, Polaris.   The sacred
book *Sidra Rabba* is laid upon the altar folded back where the
liturgy of the living is divided from the ritual of the dead.
The high priest takes one of the live pigeons handed to him
by a *shkando*, extends his hands toward the Polar Star upon
which he fixes his eyes, and lets the bird fly, calling aloud,
'*Bshmo d'haï rabba mshabbah zivo kadmaya Elaha Edmen
Nafshi Eprah*,' ' In the name of the living one, blessed be
the primitive light, the ancient light, the Divinity self-created.'
The words, clearly enunciated within, are distinctly heard by
the worshippers without, and with one accord the white-robed
figures rise from their places and prostrate themselves upon the
ground toward the North Star, on which they have silently
been gazing.

    " Noiselessly the worshippers resume their seated position on
the ground outside.   Within the *Mishkna*, or tabernacle, the
Ganzivro steps on one side, and his place is immediately taken
by the senior priest, a *tarmido*, who opens the *Sidra Rabba*
before him on the altar and begins to read the *Shomhotto*,
' confession' of the sect, in a modulated chant, his voice
rising and falling as he reads, and ever and anon terminating

in a loud and swelling *Mshobbo havi eshmakhyo Manda d'haï,* 'Blessed be thy name, O source of life,' which the congregants without take up and repeat with bowed heads, their hands covering their eyes.

" While the reading is in progress two other priests turn, and prepare the *Peto elayat,* or high mystery, as they term their Communion.   One kindles a charcoal fire in the earthenware stove by the side of the altar, and the other grinds small some of the barley brought by the deacon.   He then expresses some oil from the sesame seed, and, mixing the barley meal and oil, prepares a mass of dough which he kneads and separates into small cakes the size of a two-shilling piece.   These are quickly thrust into or on the oven and baked, the chanting of the liturgy of the *Shomhotto* still proceeding with its steady singsong and response, *Mshobbo havi eshmakhyo,* from outside. The fourth of the *tarmidos* now takes the pigeon left in the cage from the *shkando,* or deacon, standing near him, and cuts its throat quickly with a very sharp knife, taking care that no blood is lost.   The little cakes are then brought to him by his colleague, and, still holding the dying pigeon, he strains its neck over them in such a way that four drops fall on each one so as to form the sacred *tau,* or cross.   Amid the continued reading of the liturgy, the cakes are carried round to the worshippers outside by the two principal priests who prepared them, who themselves pop them direct into the mouths of the members, with the words '*Rshimot bereshm d'haï,*' 'Marked be thou with the mark of the living one.'   The four deacons inside the *Mishkna* walk round to the rear of the altar and dig a little hole, in which the body of the dead pigeon is then buried.

" The chanting of the confession is now closed by the officiating *tarmido,* and the high priest, the *Ganzivro,* resuming his former place in front of the Sacred Book, begins the recitation of the *Massakhto,* or 'renunciation' of the dead, ever directing his prayers toward the North Star, on which the gaze of the worshippers outside continues fixed throughout the whole of the ceremonial observances and prayers. This star is the *Olma d'nhoora*, literally 'the world of light,' the primitive sun of the Star-worshippers' theogony, the paradise of the elect, and the abode of the pious hereafter. For three hours the reading of the 'renunciation' by the high priest continues, interrupted only, ever and anon, by the *Mshobbo havi eshmakhyo*, 'Blessed be thy name,' of the participants seated outside, until, toward dawn, a loud and ringing *Ano asborlakh ano asborli ya Avather*, 'I mind me of thee, mind thou of me O Avather,' cŏmes from the mouth of the priest, and signalizes the termination of the prayers.

"Before the North Star fades in the pale ashen grey of approaching dawn, a sheep, penned over night near the river, is led into the tabernacle by one of the four *shkandos* for sacrifice to Avather and his companion deity, Ptahiel. It is a wether, for the Star-worshippers never kill ewes, or eat their flesh when killed. The animal is laid upon some reeds, its head west and its tail east, the *Ganzivro* behind it facing the Star. He first pours water over his hands, then over his feet, the water being brought to him by a deacon. One of the *tarmidos* takes up a position at his elbow and places his hand on the *Ganzivro's* shoulder, saying *Ana shaddakh*, 'I bear witness.' The high priest bends toward the North Star, draws a sharp knife from his left side, and, reciting the formula, 'In the name of Alaha, Ptahiel created thee, Hibel Sivo permitted thee, and it is I who slay thee,' cuts the sheep's throat from ear to ear, and allows the blood to escape on to the matted reeds upon which the animal is stretched out. The four deacons go outside, wash their hands and feet, then flay the sheep, and cut it into as many portions as there are communicants outside. The pieces are now distributed among the worshippers, the priests leave the tabernacle in the same order as they came, and with a parting benediction from the *Ganzivro*, *Assootad d'hai havilakh*, 'The benison of the living one attend thee,' the prayer-meeting terminates, and the Star-worshippers quietly return to their homes before the crimson sun has time to peep above the horizon."

What a mosaic of ceremonies and what a mixed cult in this river-bank prayer-meeting! The Sabeans of Amara tell me that every minute particular is correctly described, and yet themselves do not furnish the clew to the maze. Here one sees Judaism, Islam and Christianity, as it were engrafted on one old Chaldean trunk. Gnosticism, star-worship, baptisms, love-feast, sacrifice, ornithomancy and what not in one confusion. The pigeon sacrifice closely corresponds outwardly to that of the Mosaic law concerning the cleansing of a leper and his belongings and is perhaps borrowed from that source.[1] But how Anti-Jewish is the partaking of blood and the star-worship.[2] The cross of blood seems a Christian element, as does also the communion of bread, but from a New Testament standpoint this is in discord with all that precedes.

Nevertheless a complete system of dogma lies behind this curious cult and one can never understand the latter without the former. Sabeanism is *a book religion;* and it has such a mass of sacred literature that few have ever had the patience to examine even a part of it. The *Sidra Rabba*, or Great Book, holds the first place. The copy I examined contains over five hundred large quarto pages of text divided into two parts, a "right" and a "left hand" testament; they begin at different ends of the book and they are bound together so that when one reads the "*right*," the "*left*" testament is upside-down. The other name for the Great Book is *Ginza*, Treasure. It is from this treasure-house that we chiefly gather the elements of their cosmogony and mythology.[3]

[1] Leviticus xiv. 4–7, 49–53.

[2] Cf. Job xxxi. 26–28.

[3] The first printed and translated edition of the *Sidra Rabba* was by Math. Norberg (Copenhagen, 1815-16), but it is said to be so defective that it is quite useless critically; Petermann reproduced the Paris MSS. in two volumes at Leipsic, 1867. Besides the *Sidra Rabba* there are:

First of all things was Pera Rabba the great Abyss.   With him " Shining ether "and the Spirit of Glory (*Mana Rabba*) form a primal triad, similar to the Gnostic and ancient Accadian triads.   Kessler goes so far as to say that it is the same. From Mana Raba who is the king of light, emanates *Yardana Rabba*, the great Jordan.   (This is an element of Gnosticism) Mana Rabba called into being the first of the æons, Primal Life, or *Hayye kadema*.   This is really the chief deity of the Sabeans, and all their prayers begin by invoking him.   From him again proceed secondary emanations, *Yushamim* (*i. e.*, Jah of heaven) and *Manda Hayye*, messenger of life.   This latter is the mediator of their system, and from him all those that accept his mediation are called *Mandäee*.   Yushamim was punished for attempting to raise himself above Primal Light, and now rules the world of inferior light.   Manda still " rests in the bosom of Primal light " (*cf.* John i. 18), and had a series of incarnations beginning with Abel (Hibil) and ending with John the Baptist ! Besides all these there is yet a third life called '*Ateeka*, who created the bodies of Adam and Eve, but could not give them spirit or make them stand upright.   If the Babylonian trinity or triad has its counterpart in the Mandäen *Pera, Ayar* and *Mana Rabba*, then *Manda Hayye* is clearly nothing but the old Babylonian Marduk (Merodach), firstborn, mediator and redeemer.   *Hibil*, the first incarnation of Manda, also has a contest with darkness in the underworld even as Marduk with the dragon Tiamat.

The Sabean underworld has its score of rulers, among others these rank first : *Zartay, Zartanay, Hag, Mag, Gaf, Gafan, Anatan* and *Kin*, with hells and vestibules in plenteous con-

---

Sidra d'Yaheya or Book of St. John, also called *Drasche d'Malek* (discourse of the King) ; The *Diwan ;* The *Sidra Neshmata*, or book of souls ; and last, but not least, the books of the zodiac called *Asfar Malwashee.* Except for the *small* portion of the *Sidra Rabba* found in Brandt's recently published *Mandäische Schriften* (1895) all of the above still await critical study and editing.

fusion. Hibil descends here, and from the fourth vestibule carries away the female devil *Ruha* the daughter of Kin. This Ruha, Kessler affirms, is really an anti-Christian parody of the Holy Spirit, but from conversation with the Sabeans I cannot believe this to be true. By her own son *Ur* Ruha becomes the mother of all the planets and signs of the zodiac. These are the source and controllers of all evil in the world and must therefore be propitiated. But the sky and fixed stars are pure and clear, the abode of Light. The central sun is the Polar Star, with jewelled crown standing before the door of Abathūr, or "father of the splendors." These "splendors," æons, or primary manifestations of deity, are said to number three hundred and sixty, (a Semitic way of expressing many), with names borrowed from the Parsee angelology (Zoroastrianism). The Mandæans consider all the Old Testament saints except Abel and Seth false prophets (Gnosticism).[1] True religion was professed by the ancient Egyptians, who, they say, were their ancestors. Another false prophet was *Yishu Mashiha* (Jesus Christ), who was in fact an incarnation of the planet Mercury. John the Baptist, *Yahya*, appeared forty-two years before Christ and was really an incarnation of Manda as was Hibil. He baptized at Jordan, and, by mistake also administered the rite to Jesus.

About 200 A. D., they say, there came into the world 60,000 saints from Pharaoh's host and took the place of the Mandæans who had been extirpated. Is not this a possible allusion to the spread of the Gnostic heresy and the coalescence of certain Gnostics with the then Sabean community? They say that their high priest then had his residence at Damascus ;

---

[1] See the history of Gnostic teaching, especially that of the Ophites and Sethians. All the evil characters in the Old Testament, with Cain at their head, were set forth as spiritual heroes. Judas Iscariot was represented as alone knowing the truth. I find no large account of the serpent in the Sabean system ; this may be otherwise accounted for.

that is, their centre of religion was between Alexandria and Antioch, the two schools of Gnosticism.

Mohammed, according to their system, was the last false prophet, but he was divinely kept from harming them, and they flourished to such an extent that at the time of the Abbasides they had four hundred centres of worship in Babylonia.

The Mandæan priesthood has three grades; *tarmida* or *ta'amida* ("disciple" or "baptism"), *shkanda* ("deacons"), and the *Ganzivra* ("high priest," literally the keeper of the Ginza or Great Book). The late Ganzivra was Sheikh Yahya, a man of parts and well-versed in their literature, who long lived at Suk-es-Shiukh. Their present high priest is called Sheikh Sahn and was at one time imprisoned at Busrah on charge of fomenting a rebellion of the Arab tribes near Kurna at the junction of the Tigris and Euphrates.

The Sabeans observe six great feasts beside their weekly sabbath (Sunday). One of the feasts celebrates the victory of Abel in the world of darkness, another the drowning of Pharaoh's army, but the chief feast, *Pantsha*, is one of Baptism. It is observed in summer, and all Sabeans are obliged to be baptized by sprinkling three times a day for five days. The regular Sunday baptisms by immersion in running water are largely voluntary and meritorious : these latter correspond to the Moslem laws of purifications and take place after touching a dead body, the birth of a child, marriage, etc.

The moral code of the Sabeans is that of the Old Testament in nearly every particular. Polygamy is allowed to the extent of five wives, and is even recommended in the Sidra Rabba but is seldom indulged in. They do not circumcise ; this is important, proving that they are not of Arab origin. They have no holy places or churches except those we have described which are built for a single night on the riverside.

The story that they go on pilgrimage to Haran[1] and visit the Pyramids as the tomb of Seth[2] is apparently a myth. They

[1] Gibbon.   [2] Sale's Koran.

are friendly to Christians of all sects and love to give the impression that because they honor the Baptist they are more closely related to us than are the Jews and Moslems. Of course they deny that they do not accept Jesus as a true Prophet, as they do all those other articles of their belief, which they deem wisest or safest to keep concealed.

All our investigations end as we began, by finding that the Sabeans " worship that which they know not," and profess a creed whose origin is hidden from them and whose elements, gathered from the four corners of the earth, are as diverse as they are incongruous. Who is able to classify these elements or among so much heterogeneous *débris* dig down to the original foundations of the structure? If we could, would we not, as in so many other cases, come back to Babylonia and the monuments?

XXIX

EARLY CHRISTIANITY IN ARABIA

"And some fell among thorns."—*Matthew* xiii. 7.

"But while men slept, his enemy came and sowed tares among the wheat and went his way. But when the blade was sprung up and brought forth fruit then appeared the tares also. So the servants of the householder came and said unto him, Sir, didst not thou sow good seed in thy field? from whence then hath it tares? He said unto them, An enemy hath done this."—*Matthew* xiii. 25–28.

IT is recorded in the Acts of the apostles that Arabians, or Arabian proselytes, were present at the Jewish feast of Pentecost. We must therefore go back to Apostolic times to find the beginnings of Christianity in Arabia. Whether these Arabians were from the northern part of the peninsula bordering on Syria, from the dominions of the Arabian king Hareth (Aretas), or came as Jewish proselytes from distant Jewish colonies of Yemen, must ever remain uncertain. In any case they doubtless carried back to their homes something of the Pentecostal message or blessing. The New Testament references to Arabia are not disconnected and unique, but stand in closest relation to the whole Old Testament revelation of God's dealings with Ishmael and his descendants.

In Paul's letter to the Galatians,[1] he writes, "Neither went I up to Jerusalem to them which were apostles before me; but I went to Arabia, and returned again unto Damascus." What did the great apostle to the Gentiles do in Arabia? A consideration of this question will give us a better standpoint to review the later rise of Christianity not only in North Arabia,

[1] Galatians i. 17.

but in Nejran and Yemen. "A veil of thick darkness," says
Lightfoot, "hangs over St. Paul's visit to Arabia." The particular part of Arabia visited, the length of his stay, the motive
of his going, the route taken and what he did there,—all is left
untold. We can draw the map and tell the story of all but the
first great journey of the apostle. Certainly the first journey
of the new Saul of Tarsus cannot have been without some great
purpose. The probable length of his stay, which is by some
put at only six months, but which may have been two years,[1]
would also indicate some importance in the event.

Visions and revelations to this Elijah and Moses of the new
dispensation there may have been while he tarried in the desert, but it is scarcely probable to suppose that at this critical
juncture in early church history so long a time should have
been occupied with these only. Therefore, we find the earliest
commentators of the opinion that Paul's visit to Arabia was his
first missionary journey, and that he "conferred not with flesh
and blood," but went into Arabia to preach the gospel.[2] "See
how fervent was his soul," says Chrysostom, "he was eager to
occupy lands yet untilled, he forthwith attacked a barbarous
and savage people, choosing a life of conflict and much toil."
The idea that Paul went to preach immediately after his conversion is natural; and that he should, as the Gentile apostle,
seek first that race which was also a son of Abraham and heir
of many Old Testament promises and whose representatives
were present at Pentecost, is not improbable.

But if Paul went to Arabia and preached the gospel, where
and to whom did he go? A certain reply to these questions is

[1] Gal. i. 18 ; Acts ix. 9, 25.

[2] Many others, including Hilary, Jerome, Theodoret and the Occumen-
ian commentators are stated by Rawlinson (St. Paul in Damascus and
Arabia, p. 128), to hold the same opinion. Porter, not alone of modern
writers, puts forth the same view in his "Five Years in Damascus," and
supposes that Paul's success was great enough to provoke the hostility of
Aretas and make him join the later persecution.

unattainable since revelation is silent, but (1)   The place was
most probably the Sinaitic peninsula, or the region east of Sinai
(Rawlinson).   (2)   There is more than one reason to hold
with Jerome and later writers that he went to a tribe where his
mission was unsuccessful as regards visible results.   (3)   The
only people of the desert then, as now, were Arab Bedouin,
and of the probability that Paul also knew their life and customs, Robertson Smith gives a curious illustration in an allusion
to Galations vi. 17, when speaking of tattoo marks in religion.[1]

Now was there an Arab tribe in the days of Paul, in the region southwest of Damascus, to whom a missionary came with
a new and strange message which was not favorably received,
and yet whom and whose message those Arabs could not forget?

We find a curious legend taken up with other nomad débris
into the maelstrom of Mohammed's mutterings that may help
to answer the question.   It is about the Nebi Salih or "good
prophet," who came to the people of Thamud,[2] and whose
person and mission is as much a mystery to Moslem commentators as Paul's visit to Arabia is to us.   European critics sug-
gest his identity with Shelah of Genesis xi. 13 ! but etymology
and chronology both afford the most meagre basis.   Palmer offers
a theory that Nebi Salih is none other than the "righteous
prophet" Moses;[3] but the difficulty is that this puts the
legend too far back in history.   It is not probable that the
people of Thamud "hewed out mountains into houses," such
as are found to-day as early as in the days of Moses.   Nor does
Old Testament indicate a time when Moses went to Arabs with
a Divine message.   Moreover, the legend is evidently a *local*
one that came to the knowledge of Mohammed, or it would
have been better known to him who borrowed so largely from
the former prophets; and if it is a *local* legend, it is not a
legend of Moses, for he is mentioned more than seventy-seven

[1] "Kinship and Marriage in Early Arabia," p. 214.

[2] Koran, Surah vii. 71.

[3] Desert of the Exodus, p. 50.

times in the Koran, and his story was well known in Arabia, at least as far as Yemen.

The pith of the legend underlies the bark ; what says the Koran ? Nebi Salih came as a " brother," [1] and said, " O, my people, worship God. Ye have no God but Him.[2] There has come to you an evident sign from your Lord.[3] . . . And remember how He made you vice-regents after 'Ad, and stablished you in the earth . . . and remember the benefits of God.[4] Said the chiefs of those who were big with pride *from amongst his people* (Pharisees or Jews from Damascus?) to those who believed amongst them : Do ye know that Salih is sent from his Lord ? (*i. e.*, his Lord is not your true God). They said, We do believe in that with which He is sent, (gospel?) " Said those who were big with pride, Verily, in what ye do believe we disbelieve." The passage is again significant : " And he turned away from them (back to Damascus?) and said, O, my people, I did preach unto you the message of my Lord,[5] and I gave you good advice, but ye love not sincere advisers." Does not this story have points of contact with what might have been the experiences of a man like Paul among such a people ?

The fact that there is a so-called tomb of Nebi Salih at El Watiyeh (Palmer) does not weigh much for or against any theory as to the identity of the prophet. Arabia has tombs of Job on the Upper Euphrates, of Eve at Jiddah, of Cain at Aden, and of other " prophets " where there is a demand for it. But it is interesting to learn from the learned author of *The Desert of the Exodus :* " The origin and history of Nebi Salih is quite unknown to the present Bedouin inhabitants, but they nevertheless regard him with more national veneration than even Moses himself." If revered more than Moses, why not was he later than Moses—greater than Moses—even *Saul of Tarsus ?* Whether this theory be only far-fetched or

[1] Acts xvii. 26.   [2] Acts xvii. 29.   [3] Acts xvii. 31.
[4] Acts xvii. 25.   [5] Acts xx. 20, 27.

whether it has confirmation in the early spread of Christianity in North Arabia the sequel may show.

Historical Christianity in Arabia had two centres, so that the study of its early rise and progress takes us first to the tribes furthest north, in the kingdoms of Hirah and Ghassan and then to fertile Yemen and Nejran.

Despite the growth of the Roman Empire eastward in the days of Pompey, the Arabs of Syria and Palmyra retained their independence and resisted all encroachment. Under Odenathus the Palmyrene kingdom flourished, and reached the zenith of its power under his wife and successor, the celebrated Zenobia. She was defeated by Aurelian, and Palmyra and its dependencies became a province of the Roman Empire. It is natural therefore to expect that Christianity was introduced into this region at an early period. Such was the case. Agbarus, so celebrated in the annals of the early church, was a prince of the territory of Edessa and Christianity had made some progress in the desert in the time of Arnobius.[1] Bishops of Bostra, in Northwest Arabia (not to be confounded with Busrah), are mentioned as having been present at the Nicene council (325 A. D.) with five other Arabian bishops.[2] The Arabian historians speak of the tribe of Ghassan as attached to the Christian faith centuries before the Hegira. It was of this tribe that the proverb became current: " They were lords in the days of ignorance and stars of Islam." They held sway over the desert east of Palestine and of Southern Syria. The name of Mavia or Muaviah is mentioned by ecclesiastical writers as an Arab queen who was converted to the faith and in consequence formed an alliance with the emperor and accepted a Christian Bishop, named Moses, ordained by the primate of Alexandria. Her conversion took place about A. D. 372. Thus we find that the progress of Christianity increased in proportion as the Arabs became more intimately connected with the Romans.

[1] Wright's " Early Christianity in Arabia," 1855.
[2] Buchanan's Christian Researches.

An unfortunate circumstance for the progress of Christianity in North Arabia was its location between the rival powers of Rome and Persia. It was a sort of buffer-state and suffered from both sides. The Persian monarchs persecuted the Christian Arabs and one of their Arab allies, a pagan, called Naaman, forbade all intercourses with Christians, on the part of his subjects. This edict we are told [1] was occasioned by the success of the example and preaching of Simeon Stylites, the pillar saint, celebrated in Tennyson's picture-poem. This desert-friar who was himself an Arab by birth, was a preacher after the heart of the stern, austere, half-starved Bedouin. His fame spread even into far-off Arabia Felix.[2] The stern edict of Naaman was withdrawn, however, and he himself was only prevented from embracing the faith by his fear of the Persian king.

Among the first monks to preach to the nomad tribes was Euthymius who seems to have been a medical missionary working miracles of healing among the ignorant Bedouins. One of the converted Arabs, Aspebetus, took the name of Peter, was "consecrated" by Juvenal, patriarch of Jerusalem, and became the first bishop of the tribes in the neighborhood of Southern Palestine.

The progress or even the existence of Christianity in the kingdom of Hirah seems to have been always uncertain as it was dependent on the favor of the Khosroes of Persia. Some of the Arabs at Hirah and Kufa were Christian as early as 380 A. D. One of the early converts, Noman abu Kamus, proved the sincerity of his faith by melting down a golden statue of the Arabian Venus, worshipped by his tribe, and by distributing the proceeds among the poor. Many of the tribe followed his example and were baptized.[3] To understand the im-

---

[1] Wright, p. 77.

[2] The latest version of his life is by Nöldeke in his "Sketches from Eastern History." (London, 1892.)

[3] Wright, p. 144.

portance of this spread of Christianity in North Arabia we
must remember that this was the age of caravans and not of
navigation. Palmyra, the centre of the trade from the Persian
Gulf, owed its importance and power to the trans-Arabian traffic
with Persia and the East. Irak and Mesopotamia were then
a part of Arabia and were ruled by Arabian dynasties.

It was in Southwestern Arabia, however, that Christianity exerted even greater power and made still larger conquests. We
cannot but wish that the story of its success, trials and extinction
had been given us in some purer form with more of the gospel
and less of ecclesiasticism. Had that early Christianity been
gold instead of glitter it would not have perished so easily in the
furnace of persecution or disappeared so utterly before the
tornado-blast of Islam.

The picture of the Christian church of this period (323–692
A. D.) as drawn by faithful historians is dark indeed. " More
and more the church became assimilated and conformed to the
world, church discipline grew lax, and moral decay made rapid
progress. Passionate contentions, quarrels and schisms among
bishops and clergy filled also public life with party-strife, animosity and bitterness. The immorality of the court poisoned
the capital and the provinces. Savagery and licentiousness
grew rampant. . . . Hypocrisy and bigotry took the place
of piety among those who strove after something higher, while
the masses consoled themselves with the reflection that every
man could not be a monk. . . . The shady side of this
period is dark enough but a bright side and noble personages
of deep piety, moral earnestness, resolute denial of self and the
world are certainly not wanting." [1] Not only was religious life
at a low level in all parts of christendom but heresies were
continually springing up to disturb the peace or to introduce
gigantic errors. Arabia was at one time called " the mother
of heresies." The most flagrant example was that of the Col-
lyridians, in the fourth century, which consisted in a heathen-

[1] Kurtz' " Church History," Vol. I., p. 386.

ish distortion of mariolatry. Cakes were offered to the Holy
Virgin, as in heathen times to Ceres.

At what time Christianity was first introduced into Arabia
Felix is uncertain. This part of Arabia was in a measure shut
off from the world of the Romans until the expedition of Ælius
Gallus. Before the coming of Christianity the Yemenites were
either idolaters or Sabeans. The large numbers of Jews in
Yemen was an additional obstacle to the early spread of the
faith as they were always bitterly hostile to the missionaries.
The legend that St. Bartholomew preached in Yemen on his
way to India need not be considered ; nor the more probable
one of Frumentius and his success as first bishop to Himyar.
In the reign of Constantius, Theophilus, the deacon of Nico-
media, a zealous Arian, was sent by the emperor to attend a
magnificent embassy to the court of Himyar and is said to have
prevailed on the Arabian king to embrace Christianity. He
built three churches in different parts of Yemen, at Zaphar,
Aden and Sana, as well as at Hormuz in the Persian Gulf. No
less than four bishoprics were established and the tribes of Rabia
Ghassan, and Kodaa were won to the faith. Ibn Khalikan, the
Arabian historian, enumerates as Christian tribes, the Bahrah,
Tanouch and Taglab. In Nejran, north of Sana, and Yathrib
there were also Christians.

Arabian idolatry was very tolerant and afforded throughout
the third and fourth centuries an equally safe asylum to the
persecuted Zoroastrians, Jews and Christians who settled in
various parts of the Peninsula. The kings of Himyar were
themselves idolaters but allowed every other sect great freedom,
including the Christians. But no sooner did the followers of
Judaism gain power than persecution began. About the year
560, Dzu Nowass, ruler of Himyar, revolted against his lord
the Abyssinian king, Elesbaan, and, instigated by the Jews,
began to persecute the Christians. All who refused to renounce
their faith were put to death without respect of age or sex, and
the villages of Nejran were given over to plunder. Large pits

were dug, filled with fuel, and many thousands of monks and virgins were committed to the flames.

Speedy punishment, however, overtook Dzu Nowass when the Abyssinian hosts invaded Yemen. The Christian conquerors avenged the massacre on its perpetrators, the Jews, with heathen fury. The whole fertile tract was once more a scene of bloodshed and devastation. The churches built before the days of Dzu Nowass were again rebuilt on the site of their ruins and new bishops were appointed in place of the martyrs. A short, though desperate, civil war, resulting in the proclamation of Abraha as king of Yemen, did not disturb the steady growth of Christianity. Paying tribute only to the Abyssinian crown, and at peace with all the Arab tribes, Abraha was loved for his justice and moderation by all his subjects and idolized by the Christians for his burning zeal in their religion. Large numbers of Jews, convinced by a public dispute and a miracle at Dhafar, were baptized. Many idolaters were added to the church; new schemes of benevolence were inaugurated; the foundations were being laid for a magnificent cathedral at Sana; in short Christian Yemen seemed on the eve of its Golden Age in the year 567 A. D.

What delayed its coming and how did the power of Abraha loose its prestige? The story is gleaned from Moslem and Christian writers; it is the last sad chapter in the short history of early Christianity in Arabia and the preface to the chronicles of Islam. So important is it considered that the synopsis of it is embodied in the Koran for the perpetual delight of Moslems.

In the early fall of the year 568, the caravans of Arabs, which came along the level road leading from Rhoda, bordered with rich vineyards and fig-orchards, stopped, on entering Sana, because of a crowd that stood gazing at a large piece of parchment nailed on the side wall of the entrance to the city. It was a royal proclamation written in large Himyaritic letters. A townsman in the long dress of a public teacher stood before it and read aloud to the motley crowd that paused as they came to morning market from the neighboring villages. Stately camels, bearing huge loads of dates, were urged by their drivers, who good-humoredly exchanged greetings with their Christian brethren ; donkeys, nearly hidden between baskets of luscious grapes, jostled a group of Jewish money-changers sitting in the gate ; a score of women, dark-eyed and in picturesque peasant dress, were carrying their empty gerbies to the wells—but one and all moved with curiosity, stood for a moment to listen.

The presbyter, for such he was, read as follows :

" I, Ibraha, by the grace of God and Jesus Christ our Saviour, king of Yemen, taking counsel and advice of the good Gregentius, bishop of Dhafar, and having completed the building of the cathedral to the glory of God and in memory of our victory over the idolaters, do now and hereby proclaim that all the Arab tribes who annually visit the heathen shrine at Mecca, are expected to cease going thither and to come with their caravans of merchandise to worship the true God, on a shorter and more convenient journey to our magnificent church at Sana, the capital, on penalty of a levy to be put by me on all caravans of tribes that refuse to obey this proclamation. And be it furthermore known to all the tribes of Koreish. . . ." The reader was rudely interrupted by a party of Bedouin who drove their dromedaries right through the gate and up the street with such fury that some of the crowd barely escaped being run over.

" It is a troop of those accursed Kenanehs," said Ibn Choza to his companion. " They were born without manners—wild asses of the desert." " Yes," answered the other ; " and who insult our good king with their nickname of El Ashram,—the split nosed,—because of the scar that remains since his encounter with the heathen Aryat." " If such as these, Abood, do not obey this latest order from our Christian king, we'll try the spears of my Modarites, and then woe betide their caravans of semn and their fertile palms. Not all the three hundred gods of the Kaabeh could save them from the righteous wrath of Abraha."

The new cathedral, whose ruined foundations yet testify as to its size and solidity, had been completed for some months, and on the morrow the good bishop was expected from Dhafar to preach to the crowds that thronged Yemen's capital at the feast. This year more strangers than ever before crowded the markets; many were come, in obedience to the proclamation, even from distant Yathrib and from beyond Nejran, to engage in commerce and religion at once,—the universal custom of the Arabs. The autumn rains were over and a fresh breeze from Jebel Nokum increased the cold, felt by such strangers especially, as came for the first time from the hot coast to an elevation of 9,000 feet.

Night fell on the towers and palaces of Sana, and there was no light in the streets except that of stars shining with northern brilliancy from between drifting clouds. Just before midnight, a solitary Arab hurried along one of the narrow paths, too narrow to be called a street, which led from the caravanseri to the church. His face and form were wrapped in a long sheepskin cloak, but his erect bearing, vigorous step, and the carved silver handle of the curved dagger, half hidden in his belt, betrayed one of the Kenaneh tribe. Stealthily looking around, he stopped before one of the windows of the cathedral; lifted himself to the granite ledge, dextrously used his dagger to remove one of the large panes of talc-stone (still used in all Sana), and jumped inside. He lingered only a few moments, came out as he went in, and hurried off toward the way of the North gate.

On the morrow a cry arose from the early worshippers, carried on the lips of every Christian in Sana, till it echoed through market and street: " *Abraha's church has been defiled!* Dung is on the altar, and the holy cross is smeared with ordure! 'Tis the work of the accursed Kenaneh—the signal of revolt for the idolaters of the North!" There was tumult in Sana. In vain Gregentius endeavored to quiet the populace by his

eloquence. Adding fuel to the flame, came the news on the
same day of the defeat of the Modarites and the death of Ibn
Choza, whom the king had sent on an expedition to a rebel-
lious tribe in Wady Dauasir. Abraha's wrath was doubly in-
flamed by the profanation of his church and the death of his
captain. He publicly vowed to annihilate the idolatrous
Koreish, as well as the Kenaneh, and to demolish their temple
at Mecca. Before nightfall that vow was the rallying-cry in the
soldiers' quarter and the toast in every Jewish wine shop of Sana.

The expedition was soon on its way. Abraha rode foremost,
seated on his milk-white elephant, caparisoned with plates of
gold. On his head was a linen cap covered with gold embroidery, and from which descended four chains. He wore a
loose tunic covered with pearls and Yemen akeek stone, over
his usual dress; while his muscular arms and short neck were
almost hidden with bracelets and chains of gold in the Abyssinian pattern; for arms he had a shield and spears. After him
came a band of musicians, and then the nobles and warriors,
under command of the valiant Kais. Than him no better
leader could have been chosen. Mourning the untimely death
of his brother, Ibn Choza, slain by the treacherous arrow of
Orwa, he sought a personal revenge even more than the honor
of his religion and his king, and was prepared to risk all in
fulfillment of the expedition. The army, increased by volunteers at every village on their route, by forced marches over
two hundred miles of mountain road, reached Jebel Orra, weary
and footsore. What is only a usual journey to the Bedouin of
the North, was a succession of hardships to the Yemen troops,
accustomed as they were to mountain air, plenty of water and
the rich fertility of their native valleys. No less did the herd
of elephants suffer from the fatigue of distance and the scarcity
of pasturage and water. Every day the advance was made
with increasing difficulty.

Meanwhile the Koreish had not been idle. Rumor never
runs faster than in the desert. All those who loved Mecca,

that oldest historic centre of all Western Arabia, rallied to the standard of the Koreish. It was the Kaaba, with its three hundred and sixty idols, against the Cross. No sooner was Abraha's approach known, than Dzu Neffer, Ibn Habib and other chiefs at the head of the tribes of Hamedan and Chethamah gathered to oppose the advance. A desperate conflict followed, but the camels were frightened at the sight of the elephants, nor could the desert Arabs withstand an assault of such large numbers.

The news of defeat struck the Koreish with the greatest consternation, and Abdulmuttalib, grandfather of the future prophet, who was guardian of the Kaaba, took counsel with all the chiefs of the allies. A swift messenger was sent to Abraha offering a third part of the wealth of all Hejaz as a ransom for the sacred Beit Ullah. The king, however, was inflexible, and his followers cried : " Vengeance for the desecrated Cross in our sanctuary ! No ransom from the idolaters ! Down with the Kaaba ! " Finally Abdulmuttalib himself came to seek audience. He was admitted to Abraha's presence and honored with a seat by his side ; but Arab tradition says he came only to ask about the loss of some camels, and told Abraha that the Lord of the Kaaba would defend it himself ! (Such sublime faith does Moslem tradition put into the mouth of the prophet's ancestors, even though the anachronism proves its falsehood.)

On the following day Kais led the advance through the narrow valley that leads into the city. Here a grievous surprise awaited the host of The Elephant. To supplement the faith of Abdulmuttalib, the Arabs laid in ambush, and before daydawn every one of the Koreish had occupied his place on the heights on either side of the pass, hidden behind the rough masses of boulder and trap that to this day make the whole hillside a natural battery. No sooner had the elephants and their riders entered the defile, than a shower of rocks and stones was incessantly poured upon them by their assailants. The unwieldly animals, mad with fright and pain, trampled the wounded to death, and confusion was followed by headlong flight, although the unequal contest lasted until sunset.   It was the Thermopylæ of Arabian idolatry, forever after celebrated in the Koran chapter of *The Elephant*. The battle affords a miracle, however, to the Moslem commentator by the easy change of a vowel, which makes "miraculous birds" with hell-stones in their beaks God's avengers, instead of the " camel-troops " of the Koreish.   Two months after the victory that prophet was born whose character and career sealed the fate of early Christianity in Arabia, already decided on the fatal day when Abraha mounted his elephant and left Sana for revenge.

The division of the Northern tribes between the Persians and Romans, followed by the defeat of the Yemen hosts, brought anarchy to all central Arabia.   The idolaters of Hirah and Ghassan overran the south, and the weak reign of Yeksoum, son of Abraha, could not stay the decay of the Christian state.   Even the Persian protectorate only delayed its final fall. The sudden rise of Islam, with its political and social preponderance, consummated the blow.   " With the death of Mohammed," says Wright, "the last sparks of Christianity in Arabia were extinguished, and it may be reasonably doubted whether any Christians were then left in the whole peninsula."

In 1888, Edward Glaser, the explorer, visited nearly every part of Yemen and among his discoveries were many ancient inscriptions.   From Mareb, the old Sabean capital, he brought back over three hundred, one of which dates from 542 A. D., and is considered by Professor Fritz Hommel the latest Sabean inscription.   It consists of one hundred and thirty-six lines telling of the suppressed revolt against the Ethiopic rule then established in Yemen.   The inscription opens with the words : " In the power of the All-merciful, and His Messiah and the Holy Ghost."   This and the scarcely recognizable ruins of the cathedral at Sana are the only remnants of Christianity that remain in Arabia Felix.

XXX

THE DAWN OF MODERN ARABIAN MISSIONS

"It surely is not without a purpose that this widespread and powerful race [the Arabs] has been kept these four thousand years, unsubdued and undegenerate, preserving still the vigor and simplicity of its character. It is certainly capable of a great future; and as certainly a great future lies before it. In may be among the last peoples of Southwestern Asia to yield to the transforming influences of Christianity and a Christian civilization. But to those influences it will assuredly yield in the fullness of time."—*Edson L. Clark.*

"Every nation has its appointed time, and when their appointed time comes they cannot keep it back an hour nor can they bring it on."—*The Koran.*

ISLAM dates from 622 A. D., but the first Christian missionary to Mohammedans was Raymund Lull, who was stoned to death outside the town of Bugia, North Africa, on June 30, 1315. He was also the first and only Christian of his day who felt the extent and urgency of the call to evangelize the Mohammedan world. His constant argument with Moslem teachers was : Islam is false and must die. His devotion and his pure character coupled with such intense moral earnestness won some converts, but his great central purpose was to overthrow the power of Islam as a system by logical demonstration of its error ; in this he failed. His two spiritual treatises are interesting, but his *Ars Major* would not convince a Moslem to-day any more than it did in the fourteenth century. His life is of romantic interest and his indefatigable zeal will always be a model and an inspiration to missionaries

314

among Moslems.[1] But he lived before his time and his age was unworthy of him.

Nothing was done to give the gospel to Arabia or the Mohammedans from the time of Raymund Lull to that of Henry Martyn, the first modern missionary to the Mohammedans. The histories of these two men contain all that there is to be written about missionary work for the Mohammedan world from 622 until 1812, so little did the Church of God feel its responsibility toward the millions walking in darkness after the false prophet.

To the Protestant Church of the eighteenth century Arabia and the Levant presented no attractions or appeal. The Turks, as representing the Mohammedan world, were remembered as early as 1549, it is true, by the English Book of Common Prayer, in the collect for Good Friday,[2] (which dates from the Sarum Missal). No effort was made, however, to carry the gospel to them or to any part of their empire, until long after other far more distant regions had been reached. Even Carey did not have the Moslem world on his large program. It was Claudius Buchanan who first aroused an interest in the needs of the Moslem world. On his return from India he told, on February 25, 1809, in his sermon at Bristol, the story of two Moslem converts, one of whom had died a martyr to Christ.

[1] See Smith's " Short History of Missions." Peroquet, Vie de Raymund Lull (1667). Low de Vita Ray. Lull (Halle, 1830). Helfferich Raymund Lull (Berlin, 1858). Dublin *Univ. Mag.*, Vol. LXXVIII., p. 43, " His Life and Work."

[2] O merciful God, who hast made all men, and hatest nothing that Thou hast made, nor wouldest the death of a sinner, but rather that he should be converted and live : have mercy upon all Jews, *Turks*, Infidels, and Heretics, and take from them all ignorance, hardness of heart, and contempt of Thy Word, and so fetch them home, blessed Lord, to Thy flock, that they may be saved among the remnant of the true Israelites, and be made one fold under one Shepherd, Jesus Christ our Lord, who liveth and reigneth with Thee and the Holy Spirit, one God, world without end. Amen.

In his *Christian Researches* he propounds a comprehensive
scheme for the evangelization of the Levant. The Church
Missionary Society sent out missionaries, and in 1819 the
American Board began work for Moslems by sending Pliny
Fisk and Levi Parsons to Syria.

This modern beginning of the gospel in Asia Minor had an
indirect bearing on the future evangelization of Arabia and
was a part of the Divine preparation. The journeys of Eli
Smith and H. G. O. Dwight brought the American churches
face to face with the whole problem of missions in that region.
The Syrian Mission through its press at Malta (1822) began
the assault on the citadel of Islam's learning. In 1833 the
press was removed to Beirut; and from that day until now it
has been scattering leaves of healing throughout all the Arabic-
speaking world. When in 1865 Dr. Van Dyck wrote the last
sheet of "copy" of the Arabic Bible translation and handed
it to the compositor, he marked an era of importance not only
to Syria and Asia Minor, but to the whole of Arabia, greater
than any accession or deposition of sultans. That Bible made
modern missions to Arabia possible; it was the result of seventeen
years of labor; "and herein is that saying true, One soweth,
and another reapeth . . . other men labored and ye are
entered into their labors." Whatever special difficulties and
obstacles missionaries to Arabia have met or will meet, the
great work of preparing the Word of God in the language of
the people and a complete Christian literature for every department of work, has already been accomplished by others; and
accomplished in such a way that the Arabic Bible of Beirut
will always be the Bible for Oman and Nejd and the most inland villages of Yemen and Hadramaut.

The history of direct effort to reach the great Arabian peninsula begins with Henry Martyn. It is deeply interesting to
follow the gradual unfoldings of the Divine Providence in the
reintroduction of the gospel into Arabia thirteen centuries after
Christianity had been blotted out in that land by the sword of

Mohammed and his successors. In more than one sense Henry
Martyn was the pioneer missionary to Arabia. He first came
into contact with the Arabs through his study of their language
and his employment of that remarkable character, Sabat, as
his munshee and co-worker. Sabat and his friend Abdullah
were two Arabs of notable pedigree, who, after visiting Mecca,
resolved to see the world. They first went to Cabul, where
Abdullah entered the service of the famous Ameer Zeman Shah.
Through the efforts of an Armenian Christian he abjured Islam
and had to flee for his life to Bokhara. " Sabat had preceded
him there and at once recognized him on the street. 'I had
no pity,' said Sabat afterward, 'I delivered him up to Morad
Shah, the king.' He was offered his life if he would abjure
Christ. He refused. Then one of his hands was cut off and
again he was pressed to recant. ' He made no answer, but looked
up steadfastly toward heaven, like Stephen, the first martyr,
his eyes streaming with tears. He looked at me, but it was
with the countenance of forgiveness. His other hand was then
cut off. But he never changed, and when he bowed his head
to receive the blow of death all Bokhara seemed to say, What
new thing is this?' Remorse drove Sabat to long wanderings,
in which he came to Madras, where the government gave him
the office of mufti or expounder of the law of Islam in the civil
courts. At Vizagapatam he fell in with a copy of the Arabic
New Testament as revised by Solomon Negri and sent out to
India in the middle of last century by the Society for Promot-
ing Christian Knowledge. He compared it with the Koran
and the truth fell on him like a flood of light. He
sought baptism in Madras at the hands of the Rev. Dr. Kerr
and was named Nathaniel. He was then twenty-seven years
of age. When the news reached his family in Arabia, his
brother set out to destroy him, and, disguised as an Asiatic,
wounded him with a dagger as he sat in his house at Vizagapatam. He sent him home with letters and gifts to his mother,
and then gave himself up to propagate the truth he had once

in his friend Abdullah's person, persecuted to the death." [1]
These two were doubtless the first fruits of modern Arabia to
Christ.

It was doubtless in a great degree Sabat who directed
Martyn's thoughts and plans toward Arabia and the Arabs.
On the last day of the year 1810 he wrote in his diary: "I
now pass from India to Arabia, not knowing what things shall
befall me there." His purpose in leaving India was partly his
broken health but more his intense longing to give the Mohammedans of Arabia and Persia the word of God in their own
tongues. On his voyage from Calcutta to Bombay he composed tracts in Arabic, spoke with the Arab sailors and studied
the Koran and Niebuhr's travels in Arabia. From Bombay he
sailed for Arabia and Persia in one of the ships of the old
Indian navy going on a cruise in the Persian Gulf. He reached
Muscat on April 20, 1811, and writes his first impressions in a
letter to Lydia Grenfell: "I am now in Arabia Felix; to judge
from the aspect of the country it has little pretensions to the
name, unless burning, barren rocks convey an idea of felicity;
but as there is a promise in reserve for the sons of Joktan, their
land may one day be blessed indeed." He attempted to go
inland for a short distance, but was forbidden by the soldiers of
the Sultan of Muscat.

Every word of Henry Martyn's journal regarding Arabia is
precious, but we can quote only one more passage: "April 24.
Went with one English party and two Armenians and an
Arab who served as guard and guide to see a remarkable pass
about a mile from the town and a garden planted by a Hindu
in a little village beyond. There was nothing to see, only the
little bit of green in this wilderness seemed to the Arab a great
curiosity. I conversed a good deal with him, but particularly
with his African slave, who was very intelligent about religion.
The latter knew as much about his religion as most mountaineers,

[1] "Life of Henry Martyn," by George Smith, C. I. E., LL. D., (1892)
p. 226.

and withal was so interested that he would not cease from his argument till I left the shore."

Martyn did not tarry long at Muscat but his visit was "a little bit of green in this wilderness" and the prayers he there offered found answer in God's Providence long afterward. On all his voyage to Bushire he was continually busy with his Arabic translation; the people of Arabia were still first in his heart for he expresses himself as desirous finally "to go to Arabia circuitously by way of Persia." His longing to give the Arabs the Scripture began in India and intensified his devotion to the study of Hebrew. Had Martyn's chief assistant in the Arabic translating, Sabat, been a better scholar their New Testament version would have proved abidingly useful. As Sabat's knowledge of the language proved very faulty their Arabic Testament did not remain in use. It was first printed at Calcutta in 1816, and although it accomplished a good work in common with other old translations, all have been superseded by the wonderfully perfect version of Eli Smith and Van Dyck. It was not due to Martyn, however, that the Arabic language had no worthy version of the Bible until 1860. In his diaries for September 8 and 9, 1810, we read these remarkable entries: "If my life is spared, there is no reason why the Arabic should not be done in Arabia, and the Persian in Persia as well as the Indian in India." . . . "Arabia shall hide me till I come forth with an approved New Testament in Arabic." . . . "Will government let me go away for three years before the time of my furlough arrives? If not I must quit the service, and I cannot devote my life to a more important work than that of preparing the Arabic Bible."

These facts about Martyn's life show at how many points it touched Arabia; his purposes, his prayers, his studies, his translations, his fellow-worker, and his visit to Muscat. But more than all these was the result for Arabia of Martyn's influence and the power of his spirit to inspire others.

> " O Eastern lover from the West !
>   Thou hast outsoared these prisoning bars ;
> Thy memory, on thy Master's breast,
>   Uplifts us like the beckoning stars.
> We follow now as thou hast led
> Baptize us, Saviour, for the dead."

In 1829 Anthony N. Groves, a dentist of Exeter, taking the commands of Christ literally, sold all he had and, in the spirit of Martyn, began his remarkable attempt at mission work in Bagdad.   His work was stopped twice, by the plague and by persecution, and the story of his life reveals how great were the obstacles which he vainly tried to surmount.[1]   From that day until long years after Northern and Eastern Arabia were waiting once more for the light.   The only effort made in the Gulf was by Dr. John Wilson of Bombay who, before 1843, sent Bible colporteurs once and again by Aden and up the Persian Gulf ; " he summoned the Church of Scotland to despatch a mission to the Jews of Arabia, Busrah and Bombay.   A missionary was ready in the person of William Burns who afterward went to China, the support of a missionary at Aden was guaranteed by a friend and Wilson had found a volunteer ' for the purpose of exploring Arabia ' when the disruption of the Church of Scotland arrested the movement."[2]   It was Henry Martyn's life that inspired John Wilson in 1824.   It was the Free Church of Scotland that afterward took up the work of Ion Keith Falconer the pioneer of Yemen.   So God's plans find fulfillment.   Even Muscat was not left without a witness in those years of waiting.   It appears that the captain of an American ship which called at Muscat every year for a cargo of dates was a godly man and used to distribute Arabic Bibles and Testaments, even before the Bible Society extended : work to this place.

[1] Journal of Mr. Anthony N. Groves, Missionary to and at Bagdä (London, 1831.)

[2] George Smith's Life of Martyn, p. 563.

As early as 1878 the British and Foreign Bible Society sent Anton Gibrail from Bombay to Bagdad on a colporteur-journey. And about the same time the South Russia agent of the Society, Mr. James Watt, visited Persia and Bagdad and pressed the needs of this field on the committee of the Bible Society. He was seconded in his efforts by Rev. Robert (now Canon) Bruce, a Church Missionary Society Missionary in India. Arrangements were made between the two societies by which Bible work was opened in Bagdad under the supervision of Mr. Bruce. In December, 1880, a Bible depot was opened. Since then the work has gone on continuously and extended, through the Arabian Mission, to the entire east coast of Arabia.

The first reference to the needs and opportunities for work in Western Arabia appears in the Annual Report of the British Bible Society for 1886, where the opening of a Bible depot at Aden is announced with the hope that it would lead to "the circulation of the Holy Bible on a larger scale and in a variety of languages." Ibrahim Abd el Masih was the first in charge of this depot, and his name was attached to the call for prayer from South Arabia issued after the death of Keith Falconer. Colporteurs from Egypt and from Aden of the British and Foreign Bible Society have once and again visited the Arabian Red Sea ports and penetrated to Sana, the capital of Yemen.

Between the years 1880 and 1890 more than one appeal went forth for Arabia's need. Old Doctor Lansing of the American U. P. Mission in Egypt who for over thirty years had labored there waiting for the dawn of a brighter day, when he heard of one of these appeals, was all on fire, to start for Yemen. "For some years," wrote an American minister in the far West, "I and my people have been praying for Arabia."

The Wahabi reformation in its time attracted the interest of those who studied the political horizon. The bombardment of Jiddah in 1858 compelled attention to Mecca and the pilgrimage, while from 1838, when England became mistress of Aden, until 1880 commerce and exploration was specially active on all the Arabian coast. It was during this period that the Anglo-Indian naval officers Morêsby, Haines, Elwon, Saunders, Carless, Wellsted and Cruttenden carefully surveyed the entire Arabian coast. What they did for commerce, Major-General F. T. Haig did for missions in Arabia. He it was who first made the extensive journey all around the coast of Arabia and into the interior of Yemen. His articles pleading for the occupation of the Peninsula reached Keith Falconer and finally decided his choice of a particular field, in the wide Mohammedan world, to which his thoughts were already turned. It was also the experience and counsel of this man of God that helped to determine the final location as well as the preliminary explorations of the American missionaries of the Arabian mission in 1890-92. The reports of General Haig are even to-day the best condensed statement of the needs and opportunities in the long neglected Peninsula while his account of the problems to be met and the right sort of men to meet them will always remain invaluable until the evangelization of Arabia is an accomplished fact.

In 1886 General Haig was asked by the committee of the Church Missionary Society to undertake an exploration of the Red Sea coast of Arabia and Somaliland with a view to ascertaining the openings for missionary effort. He set out from London on October 12th, 1886, reaching Alexandria on the 19th, and proceeded by way of the Red Sea coast in an Egyptian steamer to Aden, calling at Tor, Yanbo, Jiddah, Suakin, Massawa and Hodeidah. Dr. and Mrs. Harpur of the Church Missionary Society were already at Aden seeking an opening for mission work ; the former accompanied General Haig back to Hodeidah and occupied that place for a time as the first medical missionary in Arabia. General Haig then took the journey inland by the direct route to Sana with Ibrahim, the British and Foreign Bible Society colporteur and from Sana they went straight across Yemen to Aden. Shortly afterward General Haig proceeded to Muscat and up the Persian Gulf calling at all the ports. From Busrah he journeyed along the river to Bagdad and thence across the Syrian desert by the overland post route to Damascus. It was this long and difficult journey which formed the basis of two papers [1] entitled : " On both sides of the Red Sea," and " Arabia as a Mission Field." [2]

A few brief extracts from a paper contributed to the *Geographical Journal* [3] show the character of this first appeal to evangelize the land of the Arabs. Writing of Yemen he says : " We have in this southwestern part of Arabia a great mountainous country with a temperate climate, and a hardy laborious race. This hill-country and its races extend northward into Asir eastward into Hadramaut for an indefinite distance, while to the northeast they extend inland as far as the borders of the great desert. The finest and most war-like races are those to be found to the north and northeast of Sana. These have never yet submitted to the Turkish yokes; in fact the limits of the Turkish territory to the east of Sana are only a few miles distant from that place. Is it not of extreme importance in connection with the evangelization of all Southern Arabia that the gospel should be preached and the Word of God brought to these hardy mountaineers ? They are mostly Zeidiyeh, a sect akin to the Shiahs in doctrine, but I saw no trace of fanaticism among them, rather they seemed everywhere willing to listen to the truth. For the most part I suspect they are but poor observers of the prescribed religious practices of Islam. During the whole of my travels in Yemen I never once saw a man at prayer, and in only a few of the larger villages is there a mosque. The women are particularly accessible ; in the villages they wear no covering to the face, and those that we met at the khans, or inns, were always ready to come forward and talk. The little girls used frequently to

[1] *Church Missionary Intelligencer* for May and June, 1887.

[2] General also published an account of his journey in Yemen from a geographical standpoint in the *Geographical Journal*, Vol. IX., p. 479.

[3] See also *The Missionary Review of the World*, October, 1895.

run into our room, and, if invited, would come and sit down by our side.   Ignorance is, I should say, the predominant characteristic of the whole population—ignorance of their own religion, ignorance of the simplest elements of truth.   I believe that an evangelist, thoroughly master of the language, Arabic, might go from village to village all over Yemen preaching, or quietly *speaking* the gospel."

This testimony is true.   But the challenge has never yet been accepted and all the highlands are still waiting for the first news of the gospel.   Speaking of the capital of Yemen the report goes on :   " Sana is a most important point.   *It is impossible to exaggerate its importance from a missionary point of view.*   It is in the centre of the finest races of Southern Arabia, and if a mission could be established there, its influence would extend on all sides to a multitude of tribes otherwise shut out from the gospel."

After reviewing in detail the open doors in every part of Arabia, and speaking of the special obstacles at each point together with the best methods of inaugurating work, he writes toward the end of his report: " *In one degree or another then, all Arabia is, I consider, open to the gospel.*   It is as much open to it as the world generally was in apostolic times, that is to say, it is accessible to the evangelist at many different points, at all of which he would find men and women needing salvation, some of whom would receive his message, while others would reject it and persecute him.   In some parts of the country he would not be molested or interfered with by the ruling powers ; in others, as in Turkish Arabia, he might be arrested and even deported.   Dangerous fanatics are, I believe, seldom met with but occasionally the missionary might come across such, and then the consequences might be more serious.   But what if his lot were even worse than this, if he were hunted from village to village, and persecuted from city to city?   Our Lord contemplated no other reception for His disciples when He sent them forth.   This was in fact His ideal of the missionary life. . . . 'When they persecute you in this city (abandon the country? No.) flee ye into another.' The evangelist in Arabia need expect nothing worse than this and even this would probably be of rare occurrence. . . . There is no difficulty then about preaching the gospel in Arabia if men can be found to face the consequences. The real difficulty would be the protection of the converts. Most probably they would be exposed to violence and death. The infant church might be a martyr church at first like that of Uganda, but that would not prevent the spread of the truth or its ultimate triumph." The most remarkable thing about this report, which occupies only forty pages, is its prophetic character, its permanent value and the fact that it touches every phase of the problem still before us.

The immediate result of General Haig's report was the determination of the Church Missionary Society to leave Aden and Sheikh Othman to Keith Falconer and the Free Church of Scotland, while Dr. and Mrs. Harpur went to Hodeidah to try the possibilities of work in that city. There the skill of a Christian physician would have more of strategic power than in Aden itself which had two hospitals under government service. Everything was hopeful at the outset and the people flocked in large numbers to the dispensary. Evangelistic work was carried on, and Dr. Harpur wrote : " I try to read of the birth, death and resurrection of Christ including Isaiah liii., and the simplest parables." One or two of the Arabs became specially interested and read the Bible very eagerly. But the Turkish governor found objection and required a Turkish diploma from the missionary, or to have his diploma acknowledged at Constantinople. Work was at a standstill. Dr. Harpur was compelled to return to England on account of severe illness and Hodeidah was not again entered. In his letter to the *Church Missionary Intelligencer*, dated April 12th, 1887, we read :

"Should the way be closed *now*, we trust that God will

open it in His own time, and whenever that time may be, I want now to say that since I came here my great desire has been, and will continue to be, that I might be allowed to live and work among the people of Yemen. God knows best, wherever our work may be. Owing to the uncertainty that exists about my diplomas being ratified, and being in the meantime effectually stopped from any work, it seems advisable for us to go back to Aden, there to wait until we get directions from the Committee, using the time there for the study of the language. There is a door here, as far as the people themselves are concerned, and I trust we may not have to leave these poor people who have not rejected the gospel. What a cause there is for prayer for them to Him who is King of Kings and Lord of Lords.''

About the same time, a remarkable call to prayer was sent out by the little band of workers in South Arabia, who were left to mourn the sudden death of their spiritual leader, Ion Keith Falconer. It was the first call to prayer issued for Arabia and it did not remain unheeded :

PRAYER FOR THE SPREAD OF THE GOSPEL IN SOUTH ARABIA.

'' We earnestly invite united intercession to Almighty God for the people of this land, that He will open doors for the preaching of the gospel, and prepare the hearts of all to receive it.

We trust that many will respond to this request, and unite with us in setting apart a special time every Tuesday for prayer for the above object. We are, yours faithfully,

(Signed.)   F. I. HARPUR, M. B.,
Church Missionary Society.
ALEX. PATERSON, M. B. C. M.,
Free Church Mission.
MATTHEW LOCHHEAD,
Free Church Mission.
IBRAHIM ABD EL MESSIAH,
Yemen, S. Arabia.   B. and F. Bible Society.''

While the Church Missionary Society did not continue work at Hodeidah, they were already occupying the extreme northeast corner of Arabia and had begun work in Bagdad, the old city of the caliphs, with its commanding situation on the Tigris, and its large, Arab population. In 1882 Bagdad was occupied as an outpost of their Persia Mission on recommendation of Dr. Bruce. Rev. T. R. Hodgson was the first missionary there, but he afterward went into the service of the British and Foreign Bible Society and greatly extended its work in the Persian Gulf. He was succeeded by Dr. Henry Martyn Sutton and others. The mission has had hard struggles with the Turkish officials and its converts were compelled to flee. The medical work has had a vast and extensive influence in all the region round about, and at present the mission-staff is larger than ever before and the school recently opened is flourishing. Mosul has been taken over from the American Presbyterian Board by the Church Missionary Society, and in the words of one of their missionaries, "we are watching for an opportunity of carrying the gospel into the very heart of Central Arabia, where the independent Prince of Nejd holds rule, across whose territory runs one of the principal routes for pilgrims to Mecca."

As early as 1856 Rev. A. Stern made missionary journeys to Sana, Bagdad and other parts of Arabia to visit the Jews with the gospel. That remarkable missionary to the Jews, Joseph Wolff, the son of a Bavarian Rabbi and who was baptized by a Benedictine monk in 1812, also visited the Jews of Yemen and Bagdad in his wanderings.[1]

In 1884, Mr. William Lethaby, a Methodist lay-preacher from England, with his faithful wife, began a mission among the wild Arabs at Kerak in the mountains of Moab; so populous and important is this mountain fortress in the eyes of the nomads that they call it El Medina, "the city." This pioneer

[1] "The Missionary Expansion since the Reformation."—Graham, p. 19. "Life and Letters of Rev. A. Stern."

effort, after some years of struggle, was taken up by the Church
Missionary Society in connection with their Palestine mission.
Mr. Lethaby, after journeying in East Arabia, and attempting
in vain to cross the Peninsula from Bahrein westward (1892),
is now in charge of the Bible Society's depot at Aden.

As early as 1886 the North Africa Mission attempted to reach
the Bedouin tribes of Northern Arabia in the vicinity of Homs.
Mr. Samuel Van Tassel, a young Hollander, of New York,
trained at Grattan Guinnes's Institute, went out under their
direction and accompanied a Bedouin chief on his annual mi-
gration into the desert in 1890.   He found good opportunities
among the nomads for gospel-work, so that the door to him
seemed "wide-open," but Turkish official jealousy of all foreigners who have dealings with the Bedouin tribes, put an end
to his work and compelled its abandonment.   His experiences,
however, as the first one who lived and worked for Christ
among the nomads in the black tents of Kedar is valuable for
the future.   The door of access was not closed by the Bedouins
themselves, but by the Turks.   Mr. Van Tassel found the
Arabs very friendly, and willing to hear the Bible read, especially the Old Testament.   He found none of the fanaticism of
the towns, and even persuaded the sheikhs to rest their caravans on the Sabbath day.   It is interesting to note that the
North Africa Mission was led to enter North Arabia through
the representations of General Haig, then one of their council.
At present they have no workers in Arabia, although that name
still finds a place in their reports every month with the pathetic
rehearsal :[1]   "Northern Arabia is peopled by the Bedouin descendants of Ishmael ; they are not bigoted Moslems, like the
Syrians, but willing to be enlightened.   This portion of the
field is sadly in need of laborers."

In 1898 the Christian and Missionary Alliance of New York

[1] On Van Tassel's work and experiences see " North Africa " (21 Lin-
ton Road, Barking, London), Vol. for 1890, pp. 4, 21, 43, 59, 78 ; Vol.
for 1891, pp. 2, 14, 27, 31 and 50.

again called attention to the needs of Northern Arabia through Mr. Forder, formerly of the Kerak mission. He attempted to enter into the interior, by way of Damascus, but met with an accident, which prevented the undertaking.

Before sketching the lives of the two great pioneer missionaries to Arabia, we must chronicle the appeal for the dark peninsula that came from the heart of the Dark Continent. Not only because this appeal belongs to the early dawn of Arabian missions, but because of its remarkable character and its author. Henry Martyn in 1811 wrote at Muscat, "there is a promise in reserve for the sons of Joktan"; Alexander Mackay, from Uganda in 1888, took up the strain, and, in closing his long plea for a mission to the Arabs of Muscat, wrote: "May it soon be said, 'This day is salvation come to this house forasmuch as he also is a son of Abraham.'"

This plea, written only two years before Mackay's death, and dated, August, 1888, Usambiro, Central Africa, is a great missionary document for two reasons; it breathes the spirit of Christianity in showing love to one's enemies and it points out the real remedy against the slave-trade. And yet Mackay accompanied his carefully written article with this modest letter: "I enclose a few lines on a subject which has been weighing on my mind for some time. I shall not be disappointed if you consign them to the waste-paper basket, and shall only be too glad if, on a better representation on the part of others, the subject be taken up and something definite be done for these poor Arabs, whom I respect, but who have given me much trouble in years past. The best way by which we can turn the edge of their opposition and convert their blasphemy into blessing is to do our utmost for their salvation." [1]

In this article Mackay pleads for Arabia for Africa's sake and asks that "Muscat, which is in more senses than one the key to Central Africa," be occupied by a *strong* mission. "I do

[1] Mackay of Uganda, by his sister, (New York, 1897) pp. 417–430 gives the article in full.

not deny," he writes, "that the task is difficult; and the men
selected for work in Muscat must be endowed with no small
measure of the Spirit of Jesus, besides possessing such linguistic ability as to be able to reach not only the ears, but the
very *hearts* of men." He pleads for half a dozen men, the
pick of the English universities, to make the venture in faith.
His continual reason for the crying need of such a mission is
the strong influence it would exert in Africa because of the
Arab traders. "It is almost needless to say that the outlook
in Africa will be considerably brightened by the establishment
of a mission to the Arabs in Muscat." "The Arabs have
helped us often and have hindered us likewise. We owe them
therefore a double debt, which, I can see no more affective
way of paying than by at once establishing a strong mission at
their very headquarters—Muscat itself."

Mackay was not unaware of the great difficulties of work
among Mohammedans and in Arabia; he calls it "a gigantic
project" and terms Arabia "the cradle of Islam." But his
faith is so strong, that at the very beginning of his article he
quotes the remarkable resolution of the Church Missionary
Society passed on May 1st, 1888, regarding work for Mohammedans.[1]

The effect of Mackay's pleading was that the veteran Bishop
French took up the challenge and laid down his life at Muscat.
That life has "such linguistic capacity as to be able," ever-
more "to reach not only the ears but the very *hearts* of men"
in a way even far above the thought of Alexander Mackay of
Uganda.

[1] The text of this resolution is quoted at the head of chapter thirty-nine.

XXXI

" My sword I give to him that shall succeed me in my pilgrimage, and my courage and skill to him that can get it. My marks and scars I carry with me to be a witness for me, that I have fought His battles, who now will be my rewarder. . . . So he passed over and all the trumpets sounded for him on the other side."—*Bunyan's Pilgrim's Progress.* (Death of Valiant for Truth.)

ION KEITH FALCONER and Thomas Valpy French, both laid down their lives for Christ after a brief period of labor in the land they so dearly loved. Keith Falconer died at the age of thirty after having spent only *ten months*, all-told, on Arabian soil; Bishop French was sixty-six years old when he came to Muscat and lived only ninety-five days after his arrival. But both gave

" One crowded hour of glorious life,"

to the cause of Christ in Arabia and left behind them an influence, power and inspiration which

" Is worth an age without a name."

Ion Grant Neville Keith Falconer,[1] the third son of the late Earl of Kintore, was born at Edinburgh, Scotland, on the 5th of July, 1856. At thirteen years of age he went to Harrow to compete for an entrance scholarship and was successful. He was not a commonplace boy either in his ways of study or thoughts on religion. With a healthy ambition to excel and

---

[1] See " Memorials of the Hon. Ion Keith Falconer."—-Robert Sinker (6th Edition Cambridge 1890) and Ion Keith Falconer, Pioneer in Arabia by Rev. A. T. Pierson, D. D. (Oct. 1897, *Missionary Review of the World*).

yet with a kindly modesty he made friends of those whom he
surpassed and loved those who were his inferiors.   Manliness,
magnanimity, piety and unselfishness, rare traits in a lad, were
in him conspicuous.   He loved outdoor sports and excelled in
athletics as well as in his studies.   At twenty he was President
of the London Bicycle Club and at twenty-two the champion
racer in Great Britain.

One paragraph taken from the close of one of his letters
gives us a glimpse of the boy at school and throws light on his
future choice of a profession.   It is dated July 16th, 1873 :
" .   .   .   Charrington sent me a book yesterday which I
have read.   It is called *Following Fully*   .   .   . about a
man who works among the cholera people in London so hard
that he at last succumbs and dies.   But every page is full of
Jesus Christ, so that I liked it.   And I like Charrington because
he is quite devoted to Him, and has really given up all for His
glory.   I must go and do the same soon : how I don't know."
This same year he left Harrow, and, after spending a year with
a tutor exclusively in mathematics, entered Cambridge.   His
intentions were at first to compete for honors in mathematics
but after careful thought he changed his plans and began to
read for honors in the Theological Tripos.

During his college days he also distinguished himself as a
master in his two favorite pursuits, bicycling and shorthand.
On the later subject he wrote the article in the Encyclopedia
Britannica.   He had a fine intellect, tremendous power of application and a genius for plodding.   His knowledge of
Hebrew was extraordinary ; he wrote post-cards in that language to his professor on every conceivable subject, and translated the hymn, "Lead Kindly Light" as a pastime.   No
wonder that he received the highest honor in that language that
Cambridge can give and passed with ease the Semitic languages examination at the close of his course.

But in all his studies and pastimes he did not cease to show
that he was first of all a Christian and had the missionary

spirit. By evangelistic work at Barnwell and Mile-End, alone and with his friend, Mr. F. N. Charrington, he labored to reach the poor and down-trodden. For the work in London he became at once treasurer and contributor of $10,000 and his work at Mile-End Road is held in loving remembrance by the present workers. Here doubtless it was that his thoughts first turned to the regions beyond. For in a letter dated June 12th, 1881, from Stepney Green, he writes: "It is overwhelming to think of the vastness of the harvest-field when compared with the indolence, indifference and unwillingness on the part of most so-called Christians, to become, even in a moderate degree, laborers in the same. I take the rebuke to myself. . . . To enjoy the blessings and happiness God gives, and never to stretch out a helping hand to the poor and the wicked, is a most horrible thing. When we come to die, it will be awful for us, if we have to look back on a life spent purely on self, but, believe me, if we are to spend our life otherwise, we must make up our minds to be thought ' odd ' and ' eccentric ' and ' unsocial,' and to be sneered at and avoided. . . . The usual centre is SELF, the proper centre is GOD. If, therefore, one lives for God, one is *out of centre* or *eccentric*, with regard to the people who do not."

After his final examination at Cambridge, he turned his whole attention to Arabic ; why, he himself knew not, except that he loved the language ; it was God's plan in his life. To secure special advantages he went first to Leipzig in October, 1880, and afterward to Assiut, Egypt. The Semitic scholar was becoming an Arab and fell in love with the desert even then. He wrote from Assiut, after some months of study : "I am meditating a camel-ride in the desert. I mean to go from here to Luxor on a donkey, camping out every night, and from Luxor to Kossair, on the Red Sea, on a dromedary. . . . I shall learn two things by doing this journey, Arabic and cooking." An attack of fever prevented the journey, and Falconer returned to England. Even there his engrossing study was Arabic, in which he was now reading such difficult books as the Mo'allakat and Al Hariri; as he expressed it, "I expect to peg away at the Arabic dictionary till my last day."

In March, 1884, he married Miss Gwendolen Bevan; they took a journey to Italy, and then settled at Cambridge, where Keith Falconer lectured and studied. In the spring of 1885 he published his Kalilah and Dimnah, translated from the Syriac, with notes; a lasting monument to his Semitic scholarship and an example of his wide general learning.[1]

Toward the end of the year 1884 his thoughts first began to be definitely drawn to the foreign mission field, but as yet without any special choice of field. A summary of the papers written on Arabia, by General Haig, for the *Church Missionary Intelligencer* was published in *The Christian*, in February, 1885, and fell under the eyes of Keith Falconer. The idea of evangelizing Arabia took hold of him with Divine power. His whole soul answered, "Here am I, send me." The immediate outcome was a request for an interview with General Haig, whom he accordingly met in London on February 21st, 1885, "to talk about Aden and Arabia." He determined to go to Aden and see the field for himself. Only two questions did he stop to consider: First, as to the healthfulness of the place, and then whether he should go out as a free lance or should associate himself more or less closely with some existing society. Warmly attached to the Free Church of Scotland from his childhood, he met the Foreign Mission Committee of that church and his project was recognized by them. On October 7th he left, with his young wife, for Aden, and arrived there on October 28th. They remained until March 6th of the following spring.

The first missionary report of this pioneer in South Arabia indicates what he thought of the field; and why he decided to

[1] Kalilah and Dimnah, or The Fables of Bidpai, by I. G. N. Keith Falconer, Cambridge, 1885.

make Sheikh Othman, and not Aden, the centre of future work ; it also sets forth the methods which Keith Falconer proposed to adopt for the evangelization of Arabia. The following extracts are of especial interest :

"The population of Aden is made up of (1) Arabs, all Moslems, mostly Sunnis of the Shafii sect; (2) Africans, mostly Somalis who are all Shafii Moslems ; (3) Jews ; (4) Natives of India, mostly Moslems, the rest being Hindus, a few Parsis, and a few Portuguese from Goa. In 1872, for every five Arabs there were less than three Somalis ; but I am told that now they are numerically equal. The Arabs and Somalis together make up the great bulk—about four-fifths—of the whole. In 1872 the Jews numbered 1,435 ; they are now reckoned at more than 2,000. The Europeans, the garrison, and camp-followers number about 3,500. The climate of Aden is, for the tropics, unusually healthy. The port-surgeon, who has been here five years, assures me that a missionary need have no fear on the score of health. This is due to the scarcity of rain and vegetation, and to the constant sea-breezes. The summer heat is severe and depressing, but not unhealthy. There can be little doubt that Aden, from the fact of its being a British possession, from its geographical position, its political relations with the interior, its commerce with Yemen, its healthy climate, and its mixed Arab-Somali population, is, humanly speaking a good centre for Christian work among the Moslems of Arabia and Africa.

"The next question is, how and where precisely to begin ? My own notion is to establish a school, industrial orphanage, and medical mission at Sheikh Othman. The children are far more hopeful than the adults, and the power to give medical aid would be not only very useful in Sheikh Othman, but invaluable in pushing into the interior. There are numbers of castaway Somali children in Aden whose parents are only too willing that they should be fed and cared for by others. These, as well as orphans, might be gathered and brought up in the faith of Christ, *nemine contradicente.*   It would be necessary to teach the children to work with their hands, and I think that a carpenter or craftsman of some kind from home or from India should be on the mission staff.   But the chief object of the institution would be to train native evangelists and teachers; and a part of their training should be *medical.*   With a slight, rough-and-ready knowledge of medicine and surgery, they would find many doors open to them.   In the school, reading by means of the Arabic Bible and Christian books, writing, and arithmetic would be taught to all; and English, historical geography, Euclid, algebra, and natural science to the cleverer children.   A native teacher, procurable from Syria or Egypt, would be very valuable, and I think a necessity at first.   If it were known in the interior that a competent medical man and surgeon resided in Sheikh Othman, the Arabs who now come to Aden for advice would stop short at our mission-house; and the surgeon would have considerable scope both in Sheikh Othman, El-Hautah, and the little country villages, not to speak of the opposite African country.   Of course the treatment of surgical cases would involve the keeping of a few beds.   The medical missionary should be a thoroughly qualified man, as natives often delay to come for advice until disease has become serious and complicated.   The port-surgeon has impressed this upon me several times.   It should be mentioned that the native assistant at the Sheikh Othman dispensary often finds that Arabs come to Sheikh Othman to be treated, and, deriving no benefit, refuse to go on to Aden, and return home. The institution should stand in a cultivated plot or garden. This would render it far more attractive, and would greatly benefit the children.   It would be possible to arrange for this in Sheikh Othman, where there is plenty of water, and the soil is good; but not in Aden, where almost utter barrenness is everywhere found.

" My reasons, then, for perferring Sheikh Othman are:

" 1.   We should not be seriously competing with government institutions. In fact, I am told that the government would be glad to be relieved of the necessity of keeping up a dispensary at Sheikh Othman.

" 2. The climate is fresher and less enervating than that of Aden. From its position it has the benefit of any sea-breeze which may blow, and the soil absorbs heat without giving it out again. On the other hand, in Aden, the high, black, cinder-like rocks often obstruct the breeze, store heat in the day, and give it out at night. Thus the nights in Sheikh Othman are markedly cooler than in Aden.

" 3. There is abundance of water, and the soil is capable of cultivation—a fact proved by the two fine private gardens there, not to speak of the government garden. But at Aden the soil is utterly barren, and all water must be paid for. It is either condensed, or procured by an aqueduct, or from a well sunk 120 feet in the solid rock. The water from the latter is quite sweet, and sometimes handed round after dinner in wine-glasses !

" 4. I am told on the best authority that it would be very difficult to get a suitable site in Aden, whereas there are plenty in Sheikh Othman. Besides any number of building sites, two very large garden sites are vacant. The latter I have inspected, and the one I am recommended to take as having the best soil is admirably situated between the old village and the new set-tlement. It occupies the space between them. I can have the whole or the half of it *granted* to me at a nominal quit-rent.

" 5. Sheikh Othman is eight miles on the road to the in-terior, and so in closer contact with the tribes, and removed from the influence of the bad and unchristian example set by so many Europeans.

" On the other hand, it must be borne in mind that the population of Sheikh Othman—about 6,500—is comparatively small, though likely to increase somewhat ; and that it is very shifting, not more than some 1,500 being permanently resident. The last objection, however, applies to Aden as well."

In another portion of the same report, after telling of the importance of Aden as a missionary centre, he emphasizes the fact that "More than a quarter of a million camels, with their drivers, enter and leave Aden yearly with produce from all parts of Yemen. The great majority of these pass through Sheikh Othman, where they make a halt of several hours on the journey to Aden." No one acquainted with Aden and its vicinity and reading Keith Falconer's letters can fail to be struck with the fact that from the outset he had his plans made *for the interior*, and that Sheikh Othman was only the first stage which he intended to use as a base of operations. He wrote to General Haig about the same time as the date of his report: "I have made up my mind that the right place for me to settle at is Sheikh Othman, not Aden. This will leave Aden and Steamer Point open to the Church Missionary Society. Though I do not think that a medical missionary would have much scope in Aden, I think that a Bible and tract-room and preaching-hall might be started there. . . . I hope to visit Lahej soon, but fear I shall be unable to go to Sana. I should not know where to leave my wife. When I have a colleague at Sheikh Othman with a wife, the two ladies can be together while the husbands go to Sana and elsewhere. If the Church Missionary Society missionaries come here I trust we shall find ways and means of coöperating and helping one another."

In February, 1886, Keith Falconer went with a Scotch military doctor to Lahej, the first large village beyond Sheikh Othman, in the middle of an oasis, and then governed by an independent "Sultan." In March, having completed his preliminary survey of the field and decided on choice of a location, he sailed for England, not to tarry there, but to prepare for the final exodus to Arabia. "For," says his biographer, "the soldier of the Cross had counted the cost, had weighed with the utmost care every risk and had taken his final resolve. The manner in which he told his friends this was very charac-

teristic of the man . . . who goes forth to the fight ready
to spend and be spent in the cause of Christ." In May he met
the General Assembly of the Free Church and made his
famous address on Mohammedanism and missions to Mohammedans. In order to begin the work at Aden, a second missionary, a medical man, was desired. Although the man was
not yet found, Keith Falconer made the generous proposal to
pay the sum of £300 ($1,500) annually to the Free Church
for the new missionary's salary. He had already offered to
pay the expenses of himself and his wife, and had agreed to
take upon himself the whole cost of the building of the mission-
house. He laid on the missionary altar not only his talent of
learning but that of money, and was in truth "an honorary
missionary."

The time between Keith Falconer's arrival in England and
his return to Arabia was crowded full of life and activity, but
only the most important events can be narrated. He received
the gratifying but altogether unexpected offer of the post of
Lord Almoner's professor of Arabic at Cambridge, which he
accepted, becoming the successor of Edward H. Palmer and
Robertson Smith. He prepared the lectures required, choosing
for his subject "The Pilgrimage to Mecca." He read all the
books on the subject in many languages, even learning the
Dutch grammar in order to understand a work in that language.
He visited hospitals in search of an associate for Arabia. He
selected his library and furniture to take to Aden and disposed
of his house-lease. He acted as judge at the Young Men's
Christian Association Cycling Club races in Cambridge. He
went to Glasgow to meet Dr. Stewart Cowen who was appointed
his co-worker to Arabia. He tried to insure his life in favor
of the mission-work at Mile-End; but while the insurance
office declared him "First-Class," they refused to grant the
policy when they heard of his proposed place of residence.
He gave several farewell addresses in Scotland and delivered
his Cambridge lectures just on the eve of leaving for Arabia.

All this work was crowded into six months' time by the man who, like Napoleon, did not have the word *impossible* in his vocabulary.   How well the work was done is proved by his lectures, the article in the Encyclopedia and his farewell addresses. What could be finer and stronger than these last sentences from his farewell address at Glasgow which still ring with power :

"We have a great and imposing war-office, but a very small army . . . while vast continents are shrouded in almost utter darkness, and hundreds of millions suffer the horrors of heathenism or of Islam, the burden of proof lies upon you to show that the circumstances in which God has placed you were meant by Him to keep out of the foreign mission field."

Dr. Cowen arrived at Aden on December 7th, 1886, and Keith Falconer a day later, by the Austrian steamship "Berenice." He wrote, "We stopped at Jiddah, but to my great disappointment quarantine prevented me from going on shore.   I gazed long at the hills which hid Mecca from us."

Mrs. Keith Falconer arrived a fortnight later.   But the new missionaries were unfortunate at the outset in obtaining a suitable dwelling.   The stone bungalow, which they expected to occupy at Sheikh Othman until a mission-house was built, could not be rented ; after considerable difficulty they managed to secure a large native hut, about forty feet square, which, with certain changes, appeared suitable for the emergency.   A shed, erected by Keith Falconer, served them as a dispensary, and on January 11th, he wrote, "Our temporary quarters are very comfortable and the books look very nice." Everything went well for a time and arrangements were made to begin building the mission-house.   A tour was taken to Bir Achmed and the gospel was preached every day by word and work, although some of the party were down with fever nearly all the time.

Early in February, 1887, they were cheered by the visit of General Haig, returning from his Yemen journey ; but very soon after things began for the first time to be clouded over. On February 10th, returning from a tour inland, Keith Falconer was seized with a high fever which continued for three days and then began to abate, but did not leave him entirely. Mrs. Keith Falconer also had a severe attack of fever, and both went for a change to Steamer Point for three weeks, after which they returned to their " hut " at Sheikh Othman. On May 1st, Keith Falconer wrote to his mother, " You will be sorry to hear that I have been down with yet another attack . . . this makes my seventh attack. This rather miserable shanty, in which we are compelled to live, is largely the cause of our fevers . . . we expect to begin living in the new house about June 1st, though it will not be finished then." But this letter did not reach her until after the telegram had told the news that God had called His servant to Himself. On Tuesday, May 10th, after continued fevers and two restless nights, he went to sleep, and in the morning . . . " one glance told all. He was lying on his back with eyes half open. The whole attitude and expression indicated a sudden and painless end, as if it had taken place during sleep, there being no indication whatever of his having tried to move or speak." On the evening of the next day he was laid to rest, " In the cemetery at Aden by British officers and soldiers —fitting burial for a soldier of Chirist, who, with armor on and courage undaunted, fell with face to the foe. The martyr of Aden had entered God's Eden. And so Great Britain made her first offering—a costly sacrifice—to Arabia's evangelization."

Keith Falconer did not live long, but he lived long enough to do what he had purposed, (and to do it after God's plan not his own) "*to call attention to Arabia.*" The workman fell but the work did not cease. The Free Church asked for one volunteer to step into his place, and thirteen of the graduating class of New College responded. By the story of Keith Falconer's life ten thousand lives have been spiritually quickened to think of the foreign field and its claims.   He, " being dead, yet speaketh," and will continue to speak until Arabia is evangelized.   Every future missionary to Arabia and every friend of missions who reads Falconer's life will approve the appropriateness of the simple inscription on his grave at Aden :

TO

THE DEAR MEMORY OF

THE HON. ION KEITH FALCONER,

THIRD SON OF

THE EARL AND COUNTESS OF KINTORE,

WHO ENTERED INTO REST

AT SHEIKH OTHMAN, MAY 11, 1887,

AGED 30 YEARS.

" If any man serve Me, let him follow Me ; and, where I am, there shall also My servant be : if any man serve Me, him will My Father honor."

The influence of Keith Falconer's consecration was widely felt at the time of his death and has been felt ever since.   His biography has become a missionary classic, and has passed through six editions.   The Presbytery of the Scotch Church in Kafraria, South Africa, resolved in October, 1887, that " steps be taken to prepare a memoir of the late Hon. Ion Keith Falconer, to be printed in *Kafir* as a tract for circulation among the native congregations with a view to impress them with an example of self-sacrifice."

The mission at Sheikh Othman was continued.   Through the generosity of Keith Falconer's mother and widow stipends for two missionaries were guaranteed.   Dr. Cowen returned to England, but Rev. W. R. W. Gardner and Dr. Alexander Patterson came to the field.   For a time Mr. Matthew Lochhead, from the mission among the Kabyles in Morocco, also joined them.   A school for rescued slaves was started, but the children's health failing they were transferred to Lovedale in

Africa. In 1893, Rev. J. C. Young, M. D., was sent out as a
medical missionary to enforce the Rev. Mr. Gardner who with
Mrs. Gardner were then alone ; Dr. Paterson and Mr. Lochhead having left for reasons of health. Rev. and Mrs. Gardner went to Cairo in 1895, and the following year Dr. Young
was joined by Dr. and Mrs. W. D. Miller. In 1898 Mrs.
Miller died, and Dr. Miller returned home. At present the
mission staff consists of Rev. Dr. Young and Dr. Morris, who
joined the mission in 1898.

Despite these frequent changes and short periods of service,
the Keith Falconer mission has not been at a standstill. Each
of the faithful band used their special talent and individuality
in removing somewhat from the vast mountain of Moslem
prejudice and opposition " to make straight in the desert a
highway for our God." The immediate interior around Aden
has been frequently visited ; the mission dispensary is known
for hundreds of miles beyond Sheikh Othman. We record
with regret that Keith Falconer's wish to go to Sana remains
unfulfilled on the part of the mission. A school for boys has
been started, and the small "shanty" dispensary has grown
into a fully equipped mission hospital, which treated over
17,800 out-patients in 1898. A much needed and most hopeful work among the soldiers is carried on in Steamer Point
(Aden) and the Keith Falconer Memorial Church is filled
every Sabbath with those who love to hear the old gospel.

XXXII

IF it was Keith Falconer's life and death that sealed the missionary love of the church to Aden, it was the death of Thomas Valpy French[1] that turned many eyes to Muscat. Bishop French it was who signalized the completion of his fortieth year of missionary service by attacking, single handed, the seemingly impregnable fortress of Islam in Oman. He is called by Eugene Stock, "the most distinguished of all Church Missionary Society missionaries."

We are tempted to describe this man's early mission work in founding the Agra college and protecting the native Christians in the mutiny; his pioneer work in Derajat; his founding of the St. John Divinity School at Lahore; his controversies with the Mohammedans; and his manifold labors as the first Bishop of Lahore, but we can only chronicle here the closing years of his useful life. After forty years of "labors abundant" and "journeyings oft" he resigned his bishopric to travel among Arabic-speaking people and learn more of their language. He visited the Holy Land, Armenia, Bagdad and Tunis, everywhere diligently seeking to learn Arabic, and persuade the Moslems of the truth of Christianity. He became, as some one expressed it, a "Christian fakir" for the sake of the gospel and desired to end his life as he began it, in pioneer missionary-work.

As we have said it was Mackay of Uganda who riveted the bishop's attention to Muscat. Such a plea from such lips

[1] Life and Correspondence of T. V. French, First Bishop of Lahore, by Rev. Robert Birks, (Murray, London, 1895).

could not but touch the heart of such a veteran. No one else came forward, so how could he refuse? He knew that age and infirmities were coming upon him, but he wanted to die a missionary to Mohammedans. He had, to use his own words, "an inexpressible desire" to preach to the Arabs. He was willing to begin the work on his own account with the hope that the Church Missionary Society would take it up.

What was the character of this lion-heart who dared to lift his grey head high and respond *alone*, to Mackay's call for "half a dozen men, the pick of the English Universities to make the venture in faith"? One who was his friend and fellow-missionary for many years wrote: "To live with him was to drink in an atmosphere that was spiritually bracing. As the air of the Engadine is to the body, so was his intimacy to the soul. It was an education to be with him. To acquire anything approaching his sense of duty was alone worth a visit to India. He demanded implicit obedience from those whom he directed, and often the cost was considerable. If any were unwilling to face a risk, he fell grievously in the bishop's estimation. There was nothing that he thought a man should not yield—home, or wife, or health—if God's call was apparent. But then every one knew that he only asked of them what he himself had done, and was always doing. How shall I speak of his unworldliness? India is full of tales of this; of acts that often led to somewhat humorous results. There was no in season or out of season with him. He was always on his Master's business. No biography, it is said, will be complete that does not show this side of his character. To outsiders frequently it seemed to lead him into inconsistencies. It did not seem incongruous for him to turn to the lady next to him, at a large luncheon party, and begin to discuss the heavenly Bride of Christ; neither was it strange when hymn-books were distributed at a large reception he held at Government House (kindly lent for the bishop's sojourn there), and the evening party was closed with hymns and prayer."

Rev. Robert Clark of the Punjab Church Missionary Society, testifies : " When he first began his work in Agra, he studied about sixteen hours a day.   He taught in his school, he preached in the bazaars, he instructed inquirers for baptism, he prepared catechists for ordination, he was engaged in writing books, at the same time that he was learning Arabic, Persian, Urdu, Sanscrit, and Hindi with munshis.   Such excellence few can attain to, because few can safely follow in his steps in this respect.   But all can copy his example of prayerful labor.   When he spent his holidays in travels and in preaching excursions far and near, he showed us how to spend every hour of relaxation in the most profitable way.   When he refused to possess even a very ordinary conveyance, because he thought that a missionary should go on foot, and declined to use anything but the most common furniture for his house, he set us an example of self-abnegation, and showed us what, in his opinion, should be the attitude of the missionary before the world.   When he spent his earliest mornings with God, with his Hebrew Bible and Greek Testament before him, he often invited some friend to sit by him to share with him the rich thoughts which the Word of God suggested to his mind."

This was the man who in solitary loneliness, without one friend to stand at his side, planted and upheld till death the banner of the cross where it had never been planted before. In the hotest season of the year, with a little tent and two servants he was preparing to push inland when death interposed and gave rest to this veteran of sixty-six years.   " We fools accounted his life madness, but he is numbered among the children of God and his lot is among the saints."   (Wisdom of Solomon v. 4, 5.)   Only Judas can " have indignation saying to what purpose is this waste ? "   This broken box of exceeding precious ointment has given fragrance to the whole world.

We will let Bishop French tell his own brief story of the work at Muscat, beginning with the time when we travelled together down the Red Sea both in quest of God's plan for us in Arabia.[1]

Near Aden, Jan. 22d, 1891.

"Boisterous winds and turbulent seas have racked my brain sorely, and I have seldom had such torture in this line. But we are close to the Straits of Bab-el-Mandeb, and hope to reach Aden some twelve hours hence. I should have been sorry to miss Hodeidah, where I had a long day (spite of difficulty of reaching it by *sambuca* or small boat of broad and heavy build), returning to ship in the evening. I left my friends, Maitland and a young American missionary, and made my way straight out through a gate of one of the stout city walls, into the country beyond, where are palm-groves and some fairly imposing stuccoed country-houses of merchants and men of rank. Under an arcade (as the sun was to be feared) I got a little congregation together, some learned, others unlearned, and addressed them for over an hour, eliciting the opposition of one or two of the *ulumā*, or educated men. For the first time in this part of my journey, my mouth seemed a little opened and heart enlarged to witness for Christ, and a few seemed really struck and interested. I tried to get entrance into a mosque or two, as of old time into Afghan mosques with Gordon and others, but failed to find the proper Imams within. I secured the lower steps of a flight of steps leading up to the private residence of a high Turkish officer, in rich uniform, a general of army here, not knowing whose steps I was occupying. However, the old gentleman came down (as a Roman centurion in old time might have done) and took his seat, with a few others, on his own doorstep, and listened with singular docility and thankfulness, and begged my blessing on his office, and his fulfillment of its arduous duties. After first leave-taking, he sent down to me a beautiful walking-stick of lemon-wood, so I had to mount the steps to express

[1] The letters appeared in the *Church Missionary Intelligencer*, for May and July, 1891.

my gratitude and acknowledgment of his singular courtesy
and friendship.   Then came a still more enthusiastic and
affectionate leave-taking still, and warm kissing of hands, to
Maitland's astonishment.   I certainly never experienced such
kindness and friendship from any Turkish official before in any
quarter.   I trust the message may have struck his heart.
Anyhow, he gladly accepted a copy of the whole Bible—this
is one of the most bigoted of Arab cities.

"There was an excellent colporteur here this week, of the
Bible Society, Stephanos, a Jewish convert, I believe, and excellent Arabic scholar.   The Wali, or viceroy of the city, has
forbidden his carrying Arabic Bibles into the interior, though
the Hebrew ones for the Jews at Sennaa are passed, some six
days, into the mountains.   In Jidda itself, I had some small
measure of encouragement, but not nearly so much as in
Hodeidah, which has now outstripped Mocha as a thriving
trade centre in those parts."

Muscat, Gulf of Oman,
February 13th, 1891.

"I arrived here on Sunday last with Mr. Maitland, of the
Cambridge Delhi Mission, whom I met in Egypt, and who
spends a few weeks for his health's sake with me, perhaps until
Easter.   We did not like throwing ourselves on the British
Consul here, as we thought it might embarrass him to entertain
Christian missionaries on their first arrival here ; and we had
very great difficulty in finding even the meanest quarters for
the first day or two, but are now in quarters in an adjoining
village, more tolerable as regards necessary comforts, belonging to the American Consul, who is agent for a new York
house of business.   I have written to India for a Swiss-cottage
tent, as a resource in case of no possible residence being
available here, or anything approaching even the English village public-house, or Persian caravanserai.   In the adjoining
hills such a tent might give shelter during the hot weather, if
the Arabs will tolerate the presence of a Christian missionary.

" Of possibilities of entrance of a mission, I feel it would be premature to speak yet. We are pushing on our Arabic studies, and I am glad to find how much more intelligible my Arab teaching is than in Tunis and Egypt. I hope soon to find a Sheikh of some learning, to carry on translations in Arabic under his guidance, if life and health be spared. I feel most thankful to feel myself again in a definite temporary centre, at least of missionary effort. ' Patience and long-suffering with joyfulness ' I would humbly and heartily desire to cultivate, as most appropriate to my present condition and circumstances. The British Consul, a very polite and courteous and high principled man, is hopeless as to any effect being produced on the Oman Arabs, and feels his position precludes him from making common cause with any effort for making proselytes among them. So when Maitland goes I shall be pretty lonely here, not for the first time, however, and I only pray that the loneliness may help me to realize more fully the blessed Presence which fills, strengthens, animates, and supports."

His last letter written from Muscat to the Church Missionary Society is dated April 24th, 1891. A portion of it is as follows :

" Patience here, as elsewhere (and more than in most scenes I have visited), is a great prerequisite. I still live alone in a borrowed house, a spare one belonging to the American Consul here, and, rough as it is, it is amply sufficient for a missionary, and is in the heart of the town. I cannot get many—very few, indeed—to come to my house and read, which is naturally one of my great objects. They ask me into their shops and houses sometimes, to sit and discuss on the great question at issue between us and them, some Beluchees, mostly Arabs ; and the latter I vastly prefer, and consider more hopeful. There are some Hindus in the crowded bazaars, but I see little of them—partly because of the noise of narrow streets and traffic, and partly because I do not wish to be tempted away from the

Arabic.   Most of the few Hindu traffickers living here understand Arabic.

" There is much outward observance of religious forms ; there
are crowds of mosques; rather a large proportion of educated
men and women too ; the latter take special interest in religious
questions, and sometimes lead the opposition to the gospel.
They have large girls' schools and female teachers.   There is a
lepers' village nigh at hand to the town.   I occupied for the
second time this morning a shed they have allotted me, well
roofed over ; and those poor lepers, men and women, gathered
in fair numbers to listen.   Chiefly, however, I reach the educated men by the roadside or in a house-portico, sometimes
even in a mosque, which is to me a new experience.   Still
there is considerable shyness, occasionally bitter opposition ;
yet bright faces of welcome sometimes cheer me and help me
on, and I am only surprised that so much is borne with.   I
have made special efforts to get into the mosques, but most
often this is refused.   The Moolahs and Muallims seem afraid
of coming to help me on in my translations, or in encountering
with me more difficult passages in the best classics.   This has
surprised and disconcerted me rather ; but I have been saved
in the main from anything like depression, and have had happy
and comfortable proofs of the Saviour's gracious Presence with
me.   The Psalms, as usual, seem most appropriate and an-
swerable to the needs of such a pioneer and lonely work.   .   .   .

" If I can get no faithful servant and guide for the journey
into the interior, well versed in dealing with Arabs and getting
needful common supplies (I want but little), I may try Bahrein,
or Hodeidah and Sennaa, and if that fails, the North of Africa
again, in some highland ; for without a house of our own the
climate would be insufferable for me—at least, during the very
hot months—and one's work would be at a standstill. But I
shall not give up, please God, even temporarily, my plans for
the interior, unless, all avenues being closed, it would be sheer
madness to attempt to carry them out."

He never reached the interior, for he received a sunstroke on his way from Muscat to the neighboring village, Mattra, in an open boat.   He was removed to the Consulate but scarcely regained consciousness except to utter a " God bless you " to the Consul, Colonel Mockler.   He died on May 14th, 1891.   The very manner of his death fulfilled, more than he ever thought, his own words in one of his letters from Muscat :   " In memory of Henry Martyn's pleadings for Arabia, Arabs and the Arabic, I seem almost trying at least to follow more directly in his footsteps and under his guidance, than even in Persia or India, however incalculable the distance at which the guided one follows the leader ! "

The grave of Bishop French is in the bottom of a narrow ravine circled by black rocks and reached by boat, by rounding the rocky point to the south of Muscat.   Here are many graves of sailors of the Royal marine and others who died on this burning and inhospitable coast.   Here also rests the body of Rev. George E. Stone, the American Missionary, who was called home in the summer of 1899, after a short period of service.

IN MEMORY OF THOMAS VALPY FRENCH, BISHOP MISSIONARY.

Where Muscat fronts the Orient sun
  'Twixt heaving sea and rocky steep,
His work of mercy scarce begun,
  A saintly soul has fallen asleep:
Who comes to lift the Cross instead?
Who takes the standard from the dead?

Where, under India's glowing sky,
  Agra the proud, and strong Lahore,
Lift roof and gleaming dome on high,
  His " seven-toned tongue " is heard no more:
Who comes to sound alarm instead?
Who takes the clarion from the dead?

Where white camps mark the Afghan's bound,
   From Indus to Suleiman's range,
Through many a gorge and upland—sound
   Tidings of joy divinely strange:
But there they miss *his* eager tread;
Who comes to toil then for the dead?

Where smile Cheltonian hills and dales,
   Where stretches Erith down the shore
Of Thames, wood-fringed and fleck'd with sails,
   His holy voice is heard no more
Is it for nothing he is dead?
Send forth your children in his stead!

Far from fair Oxford's grooves and towers,
   Her scholar Bishop dies apart;
He blames the ease of cultured hours
   In death's still voice that shakes the heart.
Brave saint! for dark Arabia dead!
I go to fight the fight instead!

O Eastern-lover from the West!
   Thou hast out-soared these prisoning bars;
Thy memory, on thy Master's breast,
   Uplifts us like the beckoning stars.
We follow now as thou hast led;
Baptize us, Saviour, for the dead!

                              —Archdeacon A. E. Moule.

XXXIII

" Our ultimate object is to occupy the interior of Arabia."—*Plan of the Arabian Mission.*

" To such an appeal there can be but one reply. The Dutch Reformed Church when it took up the mission originally commenced on an independent basis as the Arabian Mission, did so with full knowledge of the plans and purposes of its founders, which, as the very title of the mission shows, embraced nothing less than such a comprehensive scheme of evangelization as that above described."—*Major-General F. T. Haig.*

" It is not keeping expenses down, but keeping faith and enthusiasm up, that gives a clear balance sheet. Give the Church heroic leadership, place before it high ideals, keep it on the march for larger conquests, and the financial problem will take care of itself. If the Church sees that we are not going to trust God enough to venture upon any work for Him till we have the money in sight, it will probably adopt the same prudence in making contributions, and our good financiering will be with heavy loss of income."—*The Christian Advocate.*

THE Arabian Mission was organized August 1st, 1889, and its first missionary, Rev. James Cantine, sailed for the field October 16th of the same year. In order to trace the steps that led this organization of this first American Mission to Arabia, we must go back a year earlier.

In the Theological Seminary of the Reformed (Dutch) Church at New Brunswick, New Jersey, the missionary spirit was especially active during the year 1888. This was fostered by members of the faculty who had a warm love for that work, by a missionary lectureship recently inaugurated, by the missionary alumni of the seminary, and by some of the students themselves who brought missions to the front. Among these students were James Cantine and Philip T. Phelps of the senior

353

class, and Samuel M. Zwemer of the middle class, who had individually decided to work abroad, God willing, and who used to meet for prayer and consultation regarding the choice of a field of labor. The first meeting of this band was held on October 31st, 1888, and the topic discussed was, "what constitutes a call to the Foreign field?" After that they met almost every week, and gradually the idea took shape of banding themselves together to begin pioneer work in some one of the unoccupied fields. Tibet and Central Africa were mentioned; but their thoughts generally seemed to unite on some Arabic-speaking country especially Nubia or the upper Nile. The Seminary library was ransacked for information on these fields, without definite results. At the end of November the band decided to consult with their Hebrew and Arabic professor, Rev. J. G. Lansing, D.D., who, being of missionary parentage and full of the missionary passion, warmly welcomed their confidence and from that time became associated with them in their plans. After some time it was mutually agreed that God called them to pioneer work in some portion of the Mohammedan world in or adjacent to Arabia.

Over against this Divine call there appeared a great human difficulty: the fact that the church to which they belonged and owed allegiance conducted no missions in the Mohammedan world. The Mission Board of that church was already burdened with a debt of $35,000, and therefore it was improbable that they would establish such a work in addition to their other mission work. In spite of these obstacles, however, it was decided, February 11, 1899, to make formal application to the Board, and on May 23d the following plan was drawn up, and presented to the Board of Foreign Missions:

"We the undersigned desiring to engage in pioneer mission work in some Arabic-speaking country, and especially in behalf of Moslems and slaves, do at the outset recognize the following facts:

1. The great need and encouragement for this work at the present time.

2. The non-existence of such mission work under the supervision of our Board of Foreign Missions at the present time.

3. The fact that hitherto little has been done in the channels indicated.

4. The inability of our Board to inaugurate this work under its present status.

Therefore, that the object desired may be realized, we respectfully submit to the Board, and with their endorsement to the church at large, the following propositions :

1. The inauguration of this work at as early a time as possible.

2. The field to be Arabia, the upper Nile or any other field, subject to the statement of the preamble, that shall be deemed most advantageous, after due consideration.

3. The expenses of said mission to be met (*a*) by yearly subscriptions in amounts of from five to two hundred dollars; the subscribers of like amounts to constitute a syndicate with such organization as shall be deemed desirable; (*b*) by syndicates of such individuals, churches and organizations as shall undertake the support of individual missionaries, or contribute to such specific objects as shall be required by the mission.

4. These syndicates shall be formed and the financial pledges made payable for a term of five years.

5. At the expiration of this period of five years the mission shall pass under the direct supervision of our Board as in the case of our other missions. Should the Board still be financially unable, syndicates shall be re-formed and pledges re-taken.

6. In the meantime the mission shall be generally under the care of the Board . . . through whose hands its funds shall pass.

7. The undersigned request the approval of the Board to this undertaking in general, and particularly in the matter of soliciting subscriptions.

(Signed.)   J. G. LANSING,
JAS. CANTINE,
P. T. PHELPS,
S. M. ZWEMER."

This plan was first presented to the Board on June 3d, when it was provisionally accepted to be referred to the General Synod. On June 11th, the Synod, after a long and ardent discussion, referred the whole matter back to the Board, asking them "carefully to consider the whole question and, should the Board see their way clear, that they be authorized to

inaugurate the mission proposed." On June 26th the Board
met and passed the following resolution :

> " *Resolved,* That, while the Board is greatly interested in the propo-
> sition to engage in mission work among the Arabic speaking peoples, the
> work in which the Board is already engaged is so great and so constantly
> growing, and the financial condition of the Board is such (its debt at that
> time being $35,000), that the Board feels constrained to decline to assume
> any responsibility in the matter.
>
> " If, however, during the next four months, such a degree of interest in
> Foreign Missions should be developed in the churches as to reduce the
> amount to which the treasury is now overdrawn to a small fraction, then
> the Board would feel inclined to favor that important enterprise."

Meanwhile the plan had been fully discussed in the church
papers, and although there were warm friends of the enterprise
who earnestly plead by pen and purse for its inauguration, the
current generally ran dead against the proposal, and much cold
water was thrown on the enterprise.[1]

How those felt who were most concerned in the decision was
expressed by Professor Lansing, on their behalf, in the following words : " The writer and the individuals named are
deeply grateful to General Synod for its hearty reception and
advocacy of the proposed mission. And, on the other hand,
they not only have no word of complaint to utter in regard to
the action of the Board, but are grateful to the Board for the
careful consideration they have given the matter, and deeply
sympathize with them in the sorrow which they and all must
feel in connection with the adverse action taken. But this does
not discharge the responsibility. A responsibility Divinely
imposed is not discharged by any admission of existing human
difficulty. . . . When God calls we must obey, not object.
And also when God calls to some specific work, then He must
have some way by which that work can be done."

[1] An able plea for the acceptance of the Missions by the Church was
made by Rev. J. A. Davis, in the *Christian Intelligencer,* N. Y., September 18, 1889.

After much thought and prayer a plan was adopted for conducting this work. The motto of the new mission appeared at the head : "Oh that Ishmael might live before Thee." After the preamble, similar to the original plan, there are the following sections :

" 1. This missionary movement shall be known as The Arabian Mission.

2. The field, so far as at present it is possible to be determined, shall be Arabia and the adjacent coast of Africa.

3. Selected by and associated with the undersigned shall be a Committee of Advice, composed of four contributors, to assist in advancing the interests of this mission.

4. In view of the fact that this mission is of necessity undenominational in its personnel and working, contributions are solicited from any and all to whom this may come, without reference to denominational adherence.

5. The amount required to carry on the work of this mission will be the sum necessary to meet the equipment and working expenses of the individuals approved of and sent to engage in the work of this mission. No debt shall be incurred and no salaries be paid to other than missionaries.

6. It is desired that the amount subscribed *shall not interfere with the individual's regular denominational contributions to foreign missions.* . . .

7. Of the undersigned the first party shall be Treasurer, and have general oversight of the interests of the mission at home and as such shall render an annual statement, while the missionaries in the field shall have the direction of those interests abroad. . . ."

The rough draft of this plan was drawn up at Pine Hill Cottage, in the Catskills, on August 1st. A few days later, while the band was at the old Cantine homestead, Stone Ridge, New York, Dr. Lansing composed the Arabian Mission hymn, which will always be an inspiration to those who love Arabia ; but it will never be sung with deeper feeling than it was for the first time, in an upper room, by three voices.

When the plan was published, the Rubicon was crossed, although not without the loss of one name from among the signers. Contributions began to come in, the Committee of

There's a land long since neglected
There's a people still rejected
But of truth and grace elected
     In his love for them.
Softer than their night winds fleeting
Richer than their starry tenting
Stronger than their winds protecting
     Is his love for them.
To the host of Islam leading
To the slave in bondage bleeding
To the desert dweller pleading
     Bring his love to them.
Through the promise on God's pages
Through His work in history's stages
Through the Cross that crowns the ages
     Show his love to them.
With the prayer that still availeth
With the power that prevaileth
With the love that never faileth
     Tell his love to them.

Till the deserts, ours now aliens
Till its tribes and their dominions
Till Arabia's captured millions
     Praise His love of them.

THE ARABIAN MISSIONARY HYMN.

Facsimile of the original copy composed by Prof. J. G. Lansing in 1889,
at Stone Ridge, N. Y.

Advice was selected, and the mission was incorporated. Among other tokens of favor the mission received at this juncture from Catherine Crane Halstead, a legacy, of nearly five thousand dollars—the largest gift, and the only legacy received by the Arabian Mission in the past decade. This unexpected and providential donation was encouraging and enabled the mission to begin work immediately.

On October 1st James Cantine was ordained by the Classis of Kingston in the Fair Street Reformed Church and he sailed for Syria on October 16th, stopping at Edinburgh to consult with the Free Church of Scotland Committee regarding co-operation with their mission at Aden. The proposition was cordially welcomed but was not acted upon since at Sheikh Othman, it was afterwards mutually agreed that more would probably be accomplished if the missions worked separately. The second member of the band to leave for the field was ordained by the Classis of Iowa, at Orange City, and sailed on June 28th, 1890.

The two pioneers left Syria for Cairo at the end of November to meet Professor Lansing who was in Egypt for his health. On December 18th Mr. Cantine left by direct steamer for Aden, and on January 8th, 1891, the writer followed in an Egyptian coasting steamer, desiring to call at Jiddah and Hodeidah, and to meet General Haig, who was then at Suakin in charge of rescue work for orphans after the war.[1] My journey down the Red Sea was made in company with the aged Bishop French, though neither of us ever heard of the other before we met on the train to take the same ship at Suez. We then learned for the first time that both were bound for the same point with the same object, to preach Christ to the Arabs.

From Aden the two American missionaries made it their first task to explore the points suggested by General Haig for missionary occupation. One, Mr. Cantine, journeyed north-

---

[1] This meeting with General Haig was described by him in an account in the London *Christian* (June, 1891).

ward to the country of the Sultan of Lahaj, while the other
sailed along the southern coast in company with Kamil, the
Syrian convert from Islam.   This earnest young disciple had
become acquainted with Mr. Cantine in Syria, and early expressed a desire to join in the work for Arabia.   He loved the
Scriptures and never shrank from obstacles which stood in the
way of faith or service.   His biography, by Dr. Henry Jessup,
shows what he surrendered for Christ; only the day of days
will show how much he accomplished for Arabia.   On May
26th, 1891, Mr. Cantine sailed to visit Muscat and the Persian
Gulf, with the understanding that his co-laborer should meanwhile attempt the journey to Sana and study the possible openings for work in Yemen.   The news of Bishop French's death
had already reached Aden.   Mr. Cantine tarried at Muscat a
fortnight, after which he visited Bahrein and other ports of the
Gulf, going on finally to Busrah and Bagdad.   The importance
of Busrah as a mission centre was evident.   In population,
accessibility and strategic location it was superior to other
places in Eastern Arabia.   Here seemed to be the place to
drive the opening wedge.

Meanwhile a twenty-days' journey to Sana and the villages
of Yemen on the Hodeidah route, had shown the importance
of Sana as a centre of operations, as is shown from the following written at that time :   " It has advantages of large population, central location, importance of position and healthfulness
of climate.   Mail comes weekly and a telegraph connects with
the outside world.   Its disadvantages are, a Turkish government and the consequent difficulties of open and aggressive
work.   Like the road from Hodeidah to Sana, it will be uphill
work, through mountains and strong places, but in both cases
you reach Arabia Felix."   On meeting Mr. Cantine at Busrah,
however, the arguments for Yemen were set aside, and it was
agreed that it was best to make Busrah the first headquarters.
It was never thought at the time that Yemen's highlands would,
after ten years, still be without a missionary.

THE OLD MISSION HOUSE AT BUSRAH

THE KITCHEN OF THE OLD MISSION HOUSE, BUSRAH

Dr. M. Eustace was then at Busrah, doing dispensary-work for the poor and acting as physician to the European community. He welcomed the missionaries and worked with them heartily until he was transferred to the Church Missionary Society hospital at Quetta. His departure emphasized the power of a medical missionary among Moslems, and the missionaries made a strong plea for a physician to join them. In January, 1892, the Board of Trustees sent out Dr. C. E. Riggs, a man with testimonials of his standing as a physician and a member of an Evangelical church, but who, shortly after reaching the field, avowed his disbelief in the divinity of Christ. His commission was revoked and he soon returned to America. After several strange adventures this singular yet lovable man reached Chicago, was converted under the preaching of D. L. Moody at the World's Fair, and died at his home in New Orleans about a year later. It was a long way to the Father's house but proves the power of prayer, and that God never forgets His own.

On June 24th of the same year faithful Kamil, rightly named Abd El Messiah (servant of Christ), was called to his reward. His illness was so sudden and the circumstances that attended his death so suspicious that we cannot but believe that he died a martyr by poison. He was the strongest man of the mission in controversy with Moslems, and a most lovable character, so that the report of that year truthfully states, "our loss in his death is unmeasured."

These two successive blows were very serious and now two other losses followed. Yakoob, another Moslem convert, who had been in mission employ, and whose wife received baptism at Busrah, was arrested and prevented from returning to our field. Also one of the two efficient colporteurs employed by the mission, left to seek his fortune in America. The continued illness of Dr. Lansing in the home land and a decrease in contributions likewise cast a shadow on the work. But faith grew stronger by trial. In the quarterly letter, near the close of this year, we read: "The experience of the missionaries ever since arriving at Aden, their tours along the coast and inland, the opportunities for work along the Euphrates, the Tigris and the Gulf, and the deep consciousness that our mission is called of God to carry the gospel into the interior of Arabia— all prompt us to make a special plea at this time for additional workers.   There are several points near Busrah where permanent work should be inaugurated without delay, and places like Bahrein, Muscat or Sana are equally, perhaps more, open to the gospel than Busrah itself. . . . *If the Arabian mission is to be true to its name and purpose, it must occupy Arabia.*"   This was followed by an appeal for five new men and the request that, should means be lacking to send them out, salaries be reduced, "confident that the best way to increase contributions is by extending our work and trusting that God will provide for the future."

The mission was at this time passing through a period of determined opposition and open hostility on the part of the Turkish local government.   Colporteurs were arrested; the Bible shop sealed up; books confiscated; and a guard placed at the door of the house occupied by the missionaries.   A petition was sent to the Sublime Porte to expel the mission.   But the opposition was short-lived and the petition never accomplished its purpose.   In December Rev. Peter J. Zwemer joined the mission in Busrah.   The difficulties in the way of securing a residence were at first very great and frequent change of abode was detrimental to the work.   Arrangements were likewise made during this year to carry on all the Bible work for the British and Foreign Bible Society in the region occupied by the mission.

The chief event of the next year was the occupation of Bahrein as a second station.   Although the first attempt to open a Bible shop and to secure a residence on the islands was fraught with exceeding difficulty and much opposition, the attempt was successful, and at the close of the first year over two hundred portions of Scripture had been sold. A journey was made into the province of Hassa and the eastern threshold of Arabia was thus crossed for the first time by a missionary. At Busrah the evangelistic work and Bible circulation made progress, but medical work was at a standstill. Cholera visited both stations and greatly interfered with the work ; many people fled from Busrah, and at Bahrein the total number of deaths was over five thousand. Peter Zwemer kept lonely watch on the islands at that time ; his only servant died of cholera and he himself could not get away as no ship would take passengers.

Early in 1894 the good news came that Dr. James T. Wyckoff had been appointed to join the mission. Sailing on January 6th, and going via Constantinople to secure his Turkish diploma he arrived at Busrah in March. But the joy of welcoming a medical missionary was short-lived, for after a brief stay at Busrah he went to Bahrein where a severe attack of chronic dysentery soon compelled him to return to Busrah and subsequently to Kerachi and America. Thus the mission lost its third medical missionary, and his successor did not come out until the following year.

Muscat was visited by Peter Zwemer as early as December, 1893, and his reports of this port as a prospective centre for work in Oman were so encouraging after several exploration journeys, that it was decided to allow him to occupy the station.

During the summer of 1894, the writer, at the request and expense of the Mildmay Mission to the Jews, made a journey to Sana, to distribute Hebrew New Testaments. It was also hoped that it would be possible for him to cross from Sana to Bahrein, by way of Wady Dauasir. But the theft of all his money even before reaching Sana and his arrest by the Turks, prevented the attempt.

After many trials and tribulations in the administration of the mission at home, negotiations were concluded in June,

1894, by which it was transferred to the management and care
of the Board of Foreign Missions of the Reformed Church.
The distinct existence of the corporation is still preserved, but
the trustees are chosen from among the members of the Foreign
Mission Board.   No other departures from former methods
were made, save that the administration was now in experienced hands and at less expense than formerly.   The change
was cordially accepted by nearly all the missionaries and the
contributors ; now no one questions its wisdom and benefit.

The year 1895 was another trying year to the mission, but
there were also blessings.   The departure of Rev. James Cantine to America on furlough, after nearly seven years in Arabia,
necessitated the transferral of the writer to Busrah and so left
Bahrein practically uncared for.   The missionaries and native
helpers suffered more than usual from the enervating climate,
and touring from both Muscat and Bahrein was made impossible for a large part of the year by tribal wars and troubles.
In February the Bedouins attacked Muscat and captured the
town ; the place was given over to pillage and over two hundred lives were lost ; the mission-house and shop were looted and
Peter Zwemer took refuge at the British consulate.   At Bahrein a similar trouble threatened for months and terror reigned,
but the disturbance never reached the islands and the unruly
Arabs were punished by English gunboats.   At Busrah the
Bible work was stopped by the Turkish authorities ; the shop
closed and colporteurs arrested.   The arrival of Dr. H. R.
Lankford Worrall at Busrah, on April 21st, with a Turkish
diploma, once more gave the mission the golden key to the
hearts of the people.   Dr. Worrall has used it faithfully, although his severe illness the first summer almost made the mission despair of the health of doctors.

Mr. Cantine visited the churches in America and greatly
stimulated interest, prayer and offerings, although no new missionaries were found willing and suitable for the field.

At the end of the year Amara was opened as an out-station

in the midst of much opposition but greater blessing. Even during this year earnest inquirers in this fanatical river village gladdened the hearts of the workers.

Work for the women of Eastern Arabia was begun in 1896 by Amy Elizabeth Wilkes Zwemer, who left the Church Mission Society mission at Bagdad to be married to Rev. S. M. Zwemer. First at Busrah, then at Bahrein and Kateef she inaugurated the work which only a woman can do in Moslem lands. Extensive tours were made by the colporteurs and by Peter Zwemer. The entire region north of Muscat as far as Someil and Rastak, even to Jebel Achdar, was penetrated by the missionary and colporteurs. One of the latter visited the so-called "pirate coast" south of Katar and sold over a hundred portions of Scripture. The following table shows the increase of Scripture sales by the mission at all of its stations. More than five-sixths of these copies were sold to Moslems:

1892	1893	1894	1895	1896	1897	1898	1899
620	825	1,760	2,313	2,805	1,779	2,010	2,464

At Busrah first fruits were gathered after these years of sowing in two remarkable cases. A soldier at Amara accepted Christ and came to Busrah for instruction; this man has since "suffered the loss of all things" and "witnessed a good confession" wherever he has been dragged as an exile or driven as an apostate. Another convert was a middle-aged Persian who was deeply convicted of sin by reading a copy of Luke's gospel in the dispensary at Busrah. He was a consumptive, and after finding peace in Christ, left Busrah for Shiraz.

In the autumn Mr. Cantine returned to the field, but the following February Mr. and Mrs. S. M. Zwemer departed on furlough, so that, with no reinforcements, the mission-staff remained insufficient. The work at Bahrein not only stood still, but, because of the unfaithfulness of a native helper, retrograded. Muscat was, on the contrary, increasing in importance.   A school was begun by Mr. P. J. Zwemer, when eighteen helpless African boys, rescued from a slave-dhow, were handed over to his care.   The little hand press in the mission-house sent forth its first message; a tract comparing Christ and Mohammed, which stirred thought as well as opposition.   It was the first Christian writing ever printed in Arabia and its simple message is prophetic :   " Mohammed or Christ, on whom do you rely ? "

At Busrah the medical work drew many within hearing of the gospel and Dr. Worrall was able to open work at Nasariyeh.   At Amara the seed once more fell on good soil, and a small band of inquirers came together for prayer, but the harvest is not yet.

At the close of 1897, Rev. F. J. Barny, supported by the young people of the Marble Collegiate Church, New York City, came to the field, and began language study.

The year 1898 is fresh in the memory of all those who are interested in the Arabian Mission.   During it Peter Zwemer, after having gone to America, was called to his reward and four new missionaries sent out into the harvest field to sow the seed of the kingdom.   Two of them, Miss Margaret Rice (now Mrs. Barny) and Rev. George E. Stone, sailed with Mr. and Mrs. S. M. Zwemer on their return in August.   The other two, Dr. Sharon J. Thoms and Dr. Marion Wells Thoms, of the University of Michigan, came to the field in December, 1898. Mr. Stone has now also gone to his reward—the third of the Arabian Mission to lay down his life for Arabia.

XXXIV

A SKILLFUL and loving hand has laid a wreath of immortelles on the unknown grave of Kamil ; his biography will live. We can only briefly record our love and admiration for those other two of the Arabian Mission, who " loved not their lives unto the death," but " hazarded their lives for the name of our Lord Jesus Christ."

PETER JOHN ZWEMER was born at South Holland, Illinois, near Chicago, on September 2d, 1868. His childhood was spent in a loving Christian home surrounded by gracious influences and the prayers of godly parents. In 1880 he entered the preparatory department of Hope College, Holland, Michigan, and was finally graduated from the college in 1888. He was the only one of his class to choose the foreign field, and for it he sought special preparation after graduation, by work as Bible colporteur in Western Pennsylvania and New York, and a year of teaching in Iowa. In 1892 he was graduated from the New Brunswick Theological Seminary, and on September 14th, of the same year, was ordained at Grand Rapids, Michigan, and sailed for Arabia on October 19th. From the day of his arrival on the field to the day of his death his first thought was gospel work for the Arabs. He was of a practical turn of mind, and had no visionary ideas nor desire for martyrdom, but a sturdy, steady purpose to make his life tell. He was eager to meet men, keen to grasp opportunities, a cosmopolitan in spirit always and everywhere. A student of character rather than of books, he preferred to make two difficult journeys than report on one. He loved to teach and knew how to do it. Sympathy for the weak and suffering and a

367

hatred for all shams were prominent traits. He endeared himself even to those from whom he differed in opinion or conduct by his whole-hearted sincerity and earnest advocacy of his views. Arabia was to him a school of faith ; his Christian character ripened into full fruitage through much suffering. Mr. Cantine wrote of him :

" Our personal relations were perhaps more intimate than those usually known by the missionaries of our scattered stations. I was at Busrah to welcome him when in 1892 he responded to our first call for volunteers, and was also the one to say good-bye a few months ago as he left behind him the rocks and hills of Muscat and Oman, among which the precious cruse of his strength had been broken for the Master's service. His course was more trying than that of the others of our company, as he came among us when the impulse and enthusiasm which attach to the opening of a new work were beginning to fail, and before our experience had enabled us to lessen some of the trials and discomforts of a pioneer effort. A thorough American, appreciating and treasuring the memory of the civilization left behind, he yet readily adapted himself to the conditions here found. Of a sensitive nature, he keenly felt any roughness from friend or foe, but I never knew him on that account to show any bitterness or to shirk the performance of any recognized duty.

" Of those qualities which make for success in our field he had not a few. His social instincts led him at once to make friends among the Arabs, and while his vocabulary was still very limited, he would spend hours in the coffee-shops and in the gathering-places of the town. His exceptional musical talents also attracted and made for him many acquaintances among those he was seeking to reach, besides proving a constant pleasure to his associates and a most important aid in all our public services. And many a difficulty was surmounted by his hopefulness and buoyancy of disposition, which even pain and sickness could not destroy."

Hon. Ion Keith Falconer

Rev. Peter J. Zwemer

Bishop Valpy French

Kamil Abdel Messiah,

FOUR MISSIONARY MARTYRS OF ARABIA

His short period of service in Arabia was longer than that of either Keith Falconer or Bishop French and although their lives have perhaps exerted a much wider influence, his has left larger fruitage on Arabian soil. Of his sickness and death the Rev. H. N. Cobb, D. D., Secretary of the mission wrote:

"When the station at Muscat was opened in 1893 it was assigned to him. From that time until May of the present year Muscat was his home. There he remained alone most of the time. Frequent attacks of fever prostrated him, unsanitary and unpleasant conditions surrounded him, the heat, constant and intense, often overwhelmed him; still he clung heroically to his post, uttering no word of complaint, and quitting it only when mission business made it necessary, or tours were to be undertaken along the coast or in the interior, or when prolonged attacks of fever and the preservation of life made a limited absence imperative. When one considers all that he endured, the wonder is not that he died, but that he lived as long as he did. No higher heroism fought, suffered and at last succumbed at Santiago. He had become so much reduced by repeated attacks of fever and rheumatism that it was thought wise last year that he should leave Arabia and come home. His desire was to remain until next year, 1899, but in the early part of this year it became evident that he must not remain. When in the latter part of May he left Arabia, his weakness was so great that he was carried on board the steamer. On the homeward way, though writing back cheerfully concerning his improvement to those whom he had left behind, he grew gradually worse, and when he arrived in this country on the evening of July 12, was taken immediately to the Presbyterian Hospital through the kind assistance of a student for orders in the Roman Catholic Church. Those who have visited him there, and they have been many, have been struck by his cheerfulness, his hopeful courage, his anxious desire to recover, that he might return to his field and work, and yet his willing submission to his Father's will."

He clung to life with a grip of steel and laughed at the idea the doctors had of his approaching death because he could not believe that his work was done. "I have done nothing yet and when I go back this time I will be ready to begin work," were his words. Yet he had no fear of death. His eye never turned away from Arabia; he longed to plant the plough once more in the stony soil of Oman and to teach the most ignorant the way of life. From his dying bed he sent to the committee a report regarding changes necessary in the house at Muscat. His hand, almost too weak to hold a pen, wrote on October 7th: "Dear father—I am slowly but surely improving and may be home soon. Now the board has authorized me to complete the building-fund. I have just secured $100 for a Muscat touring boat. Dr. and Mrs. Thoms sailed this morn- for Arabia, *laus Deo!* I felt sorry I could not divide myself and go with them . . . patiently longing I wait His time."

Even later than this, when he could no longer write, he dictated letters regarding the work at home and in the field. On the evening of Tuesday, October 18th, 1898, six weeks after his thirtieth birthday he quietly fell asleep. "His time" had come. After a brief service, the body was taken by loving hands to Holland, Michigan, and laid to rest in the sure and certain hope of a glorious resurrection. But his heart rests in Arabia and his memory will remain longest where he suffered most and where his fellowship was so blessed.

"O blest communion! fellowship divine!
We feebly struggle, they in glory shine
Yet all are one in Thee for all are Thine.
Hallelujah!

"And when the strife is fierce, the warfare long,—
Steals on the ear the distant triumph-song
And hearts are brave again and arms are strong.
Hallelujah!"

GEORGE E. STONE.

On the twenty-sixth of June, 1899, George E. Stone died of heat apoplexy at the coast town of Birka a few miles east of Muscat. On Thursday the twenty-second of that month, in company with a colporteur, he left Muscat, for a few days change. He was in fairly good health, although suffering from boils. Monday morning he had a little fever; in the afternoon it came again and in a few hours he had departed. His body was taken to Muscat by the colporteur and there buried near the grave of Bishop French whose death was from the same cause.

Rev. George E. Stone was born on September 2d, 1870, at Mexico, Oswego County, New York. He was graduated from Hamilton College in 1895, and from the Auburn Theological Seminary in 1898. Toward the close of his studies his thoughts were drawn to the foreign field and he became a "student volunteer." The reason for his decision was characteristic of the man. As he himself expressed it in his inimitable five-minute speech at the General Synod: "I tried in every possible way to avoid going to the foreign field but I had no peace. I go from a sense of obedience." He first heard of the special needs of Arabia through a former classmate who represented Union Seminary at the New Brunswick Inter-Seminary Conference in November, 1897. Shortly after he wrote for information about the field, and without further hesitancy he applied and was accepted. Ordained by the Presbytery of Cayuga at Syracuse, he sailed with the mission party in August, 1898.

George Stone was a man of much promise; altogether a character of one piece without seam or rent. Sturdy, manly, straightforward, humble and honest to the core. He was entirely unconventional and did not know what it was to try to make a good impression. He was simply natural. With native tact and Yankee wit was joined a keen sense of duty and a willingness to plod. Confessing that he was never in-

tended for a linguist he yet, by sheer application, made remarkably rapid progress in Arabic.   He made friends readily and
was faithful to sow beside all waters.   No one could travel
with him and not know that he was a fisher of men; yet he
was never obtrusive in his method.   He had a splendid constitution, and looked forward to a long life in Arabia, but God
willed otherwise.

He was at Bahrein from October 9th until February 14th,
when he left for Muscat to take the place of Rev. F. J. Barny,
who had been ill with typhoid and was going on sick-leave to
India.   He was the only person available at the time, although
it was not a pleasant task for a novice to be suddenly called to
take care of a station of which he knew little more than the
name.   Without a word of demur he left Bahrein at three
hours' notice and sailed for Muscat.   There he remained alone,
but faithful unto death, until June, when Rev. James Cantine
arrived to take charge of the work.   His letters were always
cheerful; he seemed to grasp the situation, and with all its
difficulties to see light above the clouds.   The following sentences from a few of his letters show what sort of man he was.
They were written in ordinary correspondence and with no idea
that the words would ever be treasured :

"I was pretty certain that I should be sent to Muscat later
on, but had no idea of going so soon.   However, it is all right.
Anything that has been prayed over as much as your decisions
at Busrah, must have been directed of God, and I have been
under His orders for some time.   .   .   .   I have had two or
three fevers, but they are small affairs, sick one day and well
the next.   No further news.   I can only add my thankfulness
to God for the way He has led me through the last two months
and for giving me a share from the beginning in actual mission-
work.   .   .   .   Many thanks for the report.   I can learn a
great deal from it to help out my ignorance.   I do feel like a
baby before this great work but, as the darkies used to sing,
the Lord is 'inching me along.'   .   .   .

"Pray for me that I may have wisdom and grace to carry this business through. I want it settled right."

To his Auburn friends he wrote this in a characteristic letter :

"You ask what I think of it now that I am on the spot. First : that the need has not been exaggerated, and that Mohammedanism is as bad as it is painted. Second : that we have a splendid fighting chance here in Arabia, and the land is open enough so that we can enter if we will. If a man never got beyond the Bahrein Islands he would have a parish of 50,000 souls. Third : that on account of the ignorance of the people they must be taught by word of mouth and therefore if we are to reach them all, we must have many helpers. Fourth : that I am glad I came to Arabia, and that to me has been given a part in this struggle. I do firmly believe that the strength of Islam has been overestimated, and that if ever the Church can be induced to throw her full weight against it, it will be found an easier conquest than we imagine—*not but what it will cost lives*, it has always been so, but I do believe that Islam is doomed."

Little did he think, perhaps, *whose* life it would first cost. Will his call be heeded and will the Church, will you, help to throw the whole weight of your prayers against Islam? "Except a corn of wheat fall into the ground and die it abideth alone, but if it die it bringeth forth much fruit."

> "The seed must die before the corn appears
> Out of the ground in blade and fruitful ears.
> Low have those ears before the sickle lain,
> Ere thou canst treasure up the golden grain.
> The grain is crushed before the bread is made ;
> And the bread broke ere life to man conveyed.
> Oh, be content to die, to be laid low,
> And to be crushed, and to be broken so,
> If thou upon God's table may be bread,
> Life-giving food for souls an hungered."

XXXV

PROBLEMS OF THE ARABIAN FIELD

"A word as to the task your mission attempts. It is to me the hardest in the whole mission-field. To conquer Mohammedanism is to capture satan's throne and I think it involves the greatest conflict Christianity has ever known. In attacking Arabia you aim at the citadel of supreme error occupied by the last enemy that shall bow to the kingship of Christ."— *Rev. W. A. Essery*, Hon. Secretary of the Turkish Mission Aid Society.

"While the difficulties in the way of missionary work in lands under Mohammedan rule may well appear to the eye of sense most formidable, this meeting is firmly persuaded, that, so long as the door of access to individual Mohammedans is open, so long it is the clear and bounden duty of the Church of Christ to make use of its opportunities for delivering the gospel message to them, in full expectation that the power of the Holy Spirit will, in God's good time, have a signal manifestation in the triumph of Christianity in those lands."—*Resolution of the Church Missionary Society*, May 1st, 1888.

THE problem of missionary work in Arabia is twofold : (1) the general problem of Mohammedanism as a political religious system which Arabia has in common with all Moslem lands ; and (2) the special problems or difficulties which pertain to Arabia in particular.

The general problem of missions to Moslems is too vast and important to be treated here. Dr. George Smith says that "the great work to which the providence of God summons the church in the second century of modern missions is that of evangelizing the Mohammedans." It is *the* missionary problem of the future. Dr. H. H. Jessup, who speaks of it as "a work of surpassing difficulty, which will require a new baptism of apostolic wisdom and energy, faith and love" gives the elements of the problem in his book.[1] As unfavorable features he enumerates,

[1] The Mohammedan Missionary Problem.—H. H. Jessup, D. D., 1879.

(1) the union of the temporal and spiritual power, (2) the divorce between morality and religion, (3) Ishmaelitic intolerance, (4) destruction of true family life, (5) the degradation of woman, (6) gross immorality, (7) untruthfulness, (8) misrepresentation of Christian doctrine, and (9) the aggressive spirit of Islam. Among the favorable features he names: (1) belief in the unity of God, (2) reverence for the Old and New Testament, (3) and for Christ, (4) hatred of idolatry, (5) abstinence from intoxicating drink, (6) the growing influence of Christian nations, (7) the universal belief of the Moslems that in the latter days there will be a universal apostasy from Islam. In some respects the problem has changed since Dr. Jessup's book was written but in its main outlines it remains the same.

The problem of Arabia as a mission-field can best be studied by considering in order: the land itself as regards its accessibility; the climate and other special difficulties; the present missionary force; the methods suited to the field; and the right men for the work. The chapters on the geography of the peninsula show how different are the various provinces and what are the strategic centres in each. It is generally considered both a good missionary policy and a true apostolic principle to work out from the *cities* as centres of population and influence. This is especially necessary in Arabia where the population is scattered and largely nomadic. All nomads come to some city or village for their supplies at frequent intervals or, if they are independent of a foreign market, they bring their produce to the cities. This by way of preface.

First, what parts of Arabia are really *accessible* to missionary operations? (1) The Sinaitic peninsula with the adjoining coast of Hejaz nearly as far as Yanbo; the population is mostly Bedouin but a good centre for work would be the Egyptian quarantine station of Tor in the Gulf of Suez. (2) Aden and the surrounding region under British protection, with a population of perhaps 200,000 souls. (3) The entire south coast from Aden to Makalla and Shehr with its *hinterland;* this region has been freely visited by explorers and travellers, men and women ; the people are quite friendly and the natural base of operations would be the town of Makalla. (4) Oman with its coast-towns and hill-country, everywhere accessible; wherever missionaries have tried to enter they have met with a welcome above all expectations. (5) The so-called "pirate-coast" in East Arabia between Ras el Kheima and Abu Thubi ; many villages, all under British subsidy and with resident native agents. (6) The islands of Bahrein.

All of these regions are outside of *Turkish* Arabia and are more or less under the influence of Great Britain so that every kind of missionary work is possible. No passports are required for travelling ; no special diplomas for the right to practice medicine ; no censorship of books ; no official espionage or prohibition of residence.

In Turkish Arabia the case is different, but it would be very incorrect to say that Turkish Arabia is inaccessible. "The Turks are no doubt," as General Haig remarks, "a great obstacle, but we must give them their due, and admit that they are not nearly so intolerant as some European States, including Russia." Only one portion of Turkish Arabia seems, at present, to be *absolutely* inaccessible, namely, the two sacred cities Mecca and Medina. At present, we say, for it does not seem possible that these twin-cities would long remain closed if the church had faith to approach their doors and were ready to enter.

Other portions of Turkish Arabia are accessible, at least to some extent. (1) The entire coast of Hejaz is accessible ; two cities, Jiddah, and Hodeidah, are specially suited for medical mission work ; while it is not at all improbable that with proper faith and kindly tact, the lovely town of Taif, that garden of Mecca, would harbor a medical missionary. Doughty's experiences seem to indicate that Taif is not considered holy ground.[1] (2) Yemen, the Arabia Felix indeed ; with a

[1] Vol. II., pp. 503-529.

splendid climate, a superior Arab population, numerous villages and cities, and with marvellous fertility of soil. Surely these highlands will not remain forever under the rod of oppression; when the hour of deliverance comes, every village should have a mission-school and every city a mission-station. Even now under the Turk work is possible for the large *Jewish* population. (3) Hassa with its capital Hofhoof and Katif on the coast. (4) The vilayets of Busrah and Bagdad. These four regions in Turkish Arabia are accessible with three limitations to missionary-work :—Every missionary must have proper passports; no medical missionary can practice without a Constantinople diploma; and no books or Bibles can be sold unless they have been examined by a censor of the press and bear the seal of the government. The passport matter is awkward at times but is not an insurmountable barrier; where the government considers travelling safe, passports are always given. The medical diploma requirement is not different from the law of France and other countries; once in possession of such a diploma, the leverage power of the Christian physician is increased rather than limited. The third restriction prevents the distribution of all controversial literature but admits the Bible and many other Christian books; it is rather burdensome and irritating to one's patience but does not shut the door to real missionary work. Every copy of the Arabic Scriptures printed at Beirut bears the *imprimatur* of the Ottoman Government— the sign and seal of the " Caliph " that the Word of God shall have free course in his tottering empire.

Finally there is the vast interior—Asir, Nejran, Yemama, Nejd, Jebel Shammar—is that too accessible? The whole region is free from Ottoman rule and, for the greater part, under one independent prince, Abd-ul-Aziz, the successor of Ibn Rashid. But for the rest the question must remain unanswered until a missionary has attempted to enter these regions and has brought back a report. For travellers the whole of the interior has proved accessible since the days of Palgrave; and

the presumptive evidence is that a missionary could also penetrate everywhere even if he were not at first allowed to settle in
any of the towns.   I have not the least doubt that a properly
qualified medical missionary with a thorough knowledge of the
language would find not only an open door but a warm welcome in the capital of Nejd or even at Riad.

Regarding the general accessibility of Arabia, General Haig
wrote in his report as follows : " There is no difficulty then
about preaching the gospel in Arabia if men can be found to
face the consequences.   The real difficulty would be the protection of the converts.   Most probably they would be exposed
to violence and death.   The infant church might be a martyr
church at first, like that of Uganda, but that would not prevent
the spread of the truth or its ultimate triumph."

The climate of Arabia is, at present, an obstacle to missionary work, but in the mountain ranges of Oman and Yemen as
well as in all the interior plateau of Nejd a healthful, bracing
climate prevails.   Now, alas, while all work is still confined to
the coast, we have perhaps one of the most trying climates in
the world.   The intense heat of summer (often 110° Fahrenheit
in the shade) is aggravated by the humidity of the atmosphere,
and the dust raised by every wind.   In the winter, from December to March, the winds in the northern part of the gulf
and the Red Sea, are often cold and cutting and although the
temperature is more suited at that time to Europeans and
Americans, it appears to be less healthy for natives.   The so-
called gulf-fever of the remittent type is very dangerous and
convalescence is at times only possible by leaving the gulf.
Cholera and smallpox are not uncommon.   Ophthalmia is rife.
Prickly heat in aggravated form, boils, and all the insect
plagues of Egypt are a cause of suffering in their season.

Moslem fanaticism is not peculiar to Arabia nor is it more
intense or universal here than in any other purely Mohammedan
land.   The fanaticism of the Arabs has been grossly exaggerated.   The Wahabis represent the extreme of exclusiveness

and prejudice, but even among them it is possible for a missionary to preach Christ and read the Bible.   Personal violence to the messenger of the gospel has proved in ten years experience, almost unknown in any part of Arabia visited by missionaries.   Sometimes Bibles and books are collected by a fanatical Mullah and consigned to the flames or the oblivion of an upper shelf in his house.   The fellows of the baser sort perpetrate insults and annoyances at times in village-work or refuse hospitality.   But we, in Arabia, have never met with the strong anti-foreign feeling such as seems to be prevalent, for example, in China.   The prejudice is seldom against the dress or manner or speech of the foreigner ; even his food is considered clean and no Arab would refuse to share his meal with a Christian traveller.   But there *is* often a strong prejudice against certain aspects of Christian doctrine, especially if crudely or unwisely put.   In an Arab coffee-shop it would be unsafe as well as unwise to use the words " Son of God," "death of Christ," " Trinity " etc., without a previous explanation.   Yet on the whole the Arabs are friendly to any stranger or guest and this friendliness is especially strong toward Englishmen and on the coast, because of the clear contrast between English and Ottoman or Arab rule.   Commerce too with its general integrity and " the word of an Englishman " has in a sense been the handmaid of missions by disarming prejudice and opening Arab eyes to the superiority of western civilization.

From a missionary standpoint the population of Arabia can best be divided into the illiterate and those who can read. The former class are in the vast majority and include all the Bedouins with exceedingly few exceptions.   Taking the population at eight million, to say that one half a million could read would be a large estimate.   On this account work for those who are able to read, by means of colportage and bookshops, may be too highly rated as to its *extensive* result ; its *intensive* value no one will question.

The problem of reaching the nomad population is a very serious

one. The data for a correct theory of work among them are
yet to be collected.   Experience of work among them has been
very limited ; indeed the only work of importance was that of
Samuel Van Tassel in North Arabia.   As a class they are less
religious than the town or agricultural Arabs.   One who has
studied the subject writes : "The Arabs [Bedouins] remain Mohammedans simply because they know of nothing better ; the
Bedouins are Moslems only in name observing the prescribed
forms in the neighborhood of the towns, but speedily casting

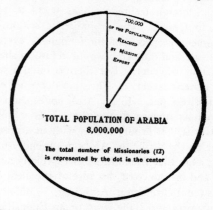

POPULATION TOUCHED BY MISSION EFFORT.

| Adan, etc., | . | 100,000. | Muscat | . | . | . | . | 20,000 |
| Bahrein | . | . | 60,000. | Busrah and Bagdad, | 520,000 |

them aside on regaining the desert.   Yet there are men among
them not without reverent thoughts of the Creator, derived
from the contemplation of His works, thoughts which, according to Palmer, take sometimes the form of solemn but simple
prayer."   The character of missionary work among this nomad
population (perhaps one-fourth or fifth of the population of the
peninsula) will be very similar to that of James Gilmour among
the Mongols ; and it will require men of his stamp to carry it
on successfully.

*The present missionary force in Arabia is utterly inadequate
to supply the needs even of that portion of the field which they
have occupied.* There are only *four* points on a coast of four
thousand miles where there are missionaries. There is not a single
missionary over ten miles inland from this coast. No missionary has ever crossed the peninsula in either direction. The
total number of foreign missionaries in Arabia, is less than a
dozen—twelve workers, men and women, let us say, for a population of 8,000,000 souls.

AREA OCCUPIED BY MISSIONARIES.

Adan, etc., 8,000 square miles.   Muscat . . . . . 600 square miles.
Bahrein .   400   "   "   Busrah and Bagdad, 71,000 "   "

The Keith Falconer Mission is not as strong in its numbers
as when Keith Falconer died. The Arabian Mission has only
recently received enough reinforcement to man its three stations
permanently. There has been too much of the spirit of ex-
periment instead of the spirit of enterprise ; a corporal's guard
went out to attack the chief citadel of the enemy. Bishop
French was *alone* when he died at Muscat. The Arabian
Mission waited years before they received reinforcements.
What is the spiritual need of Arabia to-day? Of the total area

of the peninsula only about *one-twelfth* is in any way reached by missionary effort.   This does not mean that one-twelfth of the area is covered by mission-stations and touring, but that in some way or other about one-twelfth of the peninsula is "occupied" by organized mission-work in its plan and purpose, day by day.   As to the proportion of missionaries to the population *ten men out of eleven have no opportunity in this neglected country to hear the gospel even if they would.*

The only part of Arabia that is fairly well occupied is the River-country—that is the two vilayets of Bagdad and Busrah. Here there are two stations and two out-stations on the rivers ; colporteurs and missionaries regularly visit the larger villages ; several native workers are in regular employ and the Bible Society is active.   Yet in these two vilayets nothing has ever yet been done for the large Bedouin population, and there are only six foreign missionaries, men and women, to a population (Turkish census) of 1,050,000 souls.

Looking at Arabia by provinces: Hejaz has no missionary ; Yemen (with the exception of Sheikh Othman and Aden) has no missionary ; Hadramaut has no missionary ; Nejd has no missionary ; Hassa has no missionary ; Jebel Shammar and all the northern desert has no missionary ; Oman has *one* missionary.   Again, the following towns and cities are accessible, but have not one witness for Christ: Sana, Hodeidah, Menakha, Zebid, Damar, Taiz, Ibb, with forty smaller towns in Yemen ; Makallah, Shehr, and Shibam in Hadramaut ; Rastak, Someil, Sohar, Sur, Abu Thubi, Dabai, Sharka and other important towns in Oman ; not to speak of the important towns of Nejd and in Mesopotamia, still without any missionaries and never visited by an evangelist.

Arabia is in truth a neglected field, even now.   Thus far the work has been really preliminary ; the evangelization of Arabia must yet begin ; not until every province is entered and every one of the strategic points specified is occupied can we truly speak of Arabia as a mission-field.   Nor is the project visionary. Given the men and the means there is not the slightest reason why the next decade should not see the entire peninsula the field for some sort of missionary effort. The doors are open, or they will open to the knock of faith. God still lives and works.

Regarding the best methods of mission-work in Arabia the experience of missionaries in other Moslem lands is of the greatest value. The story of the Church Missionary Society in the Punjab, that of the North Africa Mission, and above all the work of the Rhenish Society in Sumatra should be thoroughly familiar to every Arabian missionary. Medical missions have their special place and power, but also their special difficulties in pioneer work like that in Arabia. Surgery is worth infinitely more than medicine among a people like the Arabs, where fatalism and neglect of the sick make the science of medicine of doubtful result in so many cases. "Kill or cure" rather than prolonged treatment, suits the Moslem palate. But a skillful surgeon with a Turkish diploma holds the key to every door in the entire peninsula. There is not one mission-hospital in Arabia! Surely such centres as Bagdad, Busrah, Bahrein, Sana, Jiddah, Hodeidah and Hofhoof should have these acknowledged powerful methods of evangelization. At Aden and Muscat there are Indian Government hospitals.

Educational work is still absent or in its infancy as regards the Moslem population, so that there are no data from which to formulate theories as to their success. In some parts of Arabia schools might not be permitted by the government; everywhere they would necessaily at the outset be very elementary.

Christian women, as experience has proved both in Yemen and East Arabia, are welcomed everywhere. With or without medical qualifications, but with hearts of love and sympathy for the poor, the suffering and the miserable, they can enter every house or hut. Even in the black tents of Kedar there are aching hearts and wretched homes to which the gospel of peace and love can alone bring relief. Lady Ann Blunt and

Mrs. Theodore Bent have proved what women can do in Arabia for the sake of science; will there be no Christian women who will penetrate as far inland for the sake of their Saviour?

Colportage is an approved mission-method especially in Arabia, since the Bible and a full line of educational and religious literature is ready to our hand from the Syrian and Egyptian missions. In Yemen this work would be especially useful and practicable, but there it has scarcely been attempted systematically. The problem is to find men of the right stamp for the work. Men who are "willing to endure hardness as good soldiers of Jesus Christ," with tact and good temper and the ability to talk with the simple-minded. Love is worth more than learning in a colporteur. Good health and a clean Turkish passport are two other requisites. Even this method of work is in its infancy; there are many open doors for the Word of God that have never yet been entered.

Under evangelistic work come the problems of street-preaching, touring, and the use or abuse of controversy. The best place for preaching at stations is the mission-house itself, after the example of Paul (Acts xxviii. 30, 31). On tours or in village-work the *mejlis* of the sheikh or the public coffee-shop makes a capital pulpit. In a small hand-book for missionaries to Moslems by Rev. Arthur Brinckman, now out of print,[1] I find the following admirable hints on public preaching to Moslems which apply to Arabia also:

"If possible always address your audience from above. Sitting down is sometimes better than standing; you are not so likely to get excited, the attitude is less war-like in appearance. Be with your back to a wall if possible; there are many reasons for this.

"When drawn into argument, keep on praying that you may speak slowly, and with effect. When asked a question do not answer quickly—if you do, you will be looked on as a sharp

[1] Notes on Islam: A Hand-book for Missionaries.—Rev. Arthur Brinckman, London, 1868.

THE BIBLE SHOP AT BUSRAH

INTERIOR OF A NATIVE SHOP

controversialist only; think over your answer first, and give it most kindly and slowly. If possible always quote a passage near the beginning or end of a Koran chapter and there will be less delay in finding it."

The question of the right place of *controversy* or whether it should have a place at all in mission-work among Moslems is of the highest importance. Opinions differ decidedly among those who are pillars of the truth. The best and briefest argument *against* the use of controversy is that given by Spurgeon in one of his early sermons at New Park Street Chapel.[1] He argues in brief that a missionary is a witness, not a debator, and is only responsible for proclaiming the gospel by his lips and by his life.

There is truth in this, but on the other hand even the apostles "disputed" in the synagogues with the Jews, and from the days of saintly Martyn (not to say Raymond Lull), until now, the Christian missionary has been compelled by the very force of circumstances to vindicate the honor of Christ and establish the evidences of Christianity by means of controversy. When, in July, 1864, the Turkish government persuaded Sir Henry Bulwer to sign the death-warrant to all missionary work among Moslems in the Turkish empire by the memorandum that made controversy a crime, the fact was immediately recognized. Rev. J. Ridgeway, then the editorial secretary of the Church Missionary Society, wrote an able paper in the *Church Missionary Intelligencer* on the theme : " *Missionary work as regards Mohammedans impossible if controversy be interdicted.*" " By controversy," he wrote, " we understand not acrimonious and irritating recriminations, which, well aware how unbecoming and injurious they are, the missionaries have always eschewed, but that calm investigation of conflicting religious systems that is indispensable to the decision of the important question—which is true and which is false? "[2]

[1] Reprinted in " North Africa " (April, 1892), under the title: *Preaching, not Controversy.*

[2] History of the Church Missionary Society, Vol. II., p. 155.

It is only in this sense that controversy is justifiable ; and this kind of controversy, whether by the printed page or word of mouth, has not proved unfruitful of good results. Sir William Muir gives a complete synopsis of all Mohammedan attacks on the Christian faith and the replies made in defence of Christianity; his criticisms of the books in question are also of great interest. Since that date there have been new attacks and new apologies both from the Moslem side and from that of the missionary. As a plough breaks up the soil before the seed is sown so this kind of literature and argument will often break up the fallow ground of Moslem hearts for the seed of God's Word. Even awakened fanaticism or active opposition is more hopeful than absolute stagnation of thought and petrifaction of feeling. How to awaken the Moslem conscience is the real problem.

It is less important to consider the attitude of the Turkish empire toward Christians than the attitude of the Moslem mind toward Christianity, as regards Arabia's evangelization.[1] The prevailing attitude of the Moslem mind, in any particular part of Arabia, toward Christianity practically decides the fate of a convert. Were Moslems all strictly adherent to their traditions and the law regarding renegades from Islam, every convert would be a martyr and every inquirer would disappear. The Ottoman code of Moslem law gives specific directions for the trial and execution of the renegade from the faith. " He is to have three distinct offers of life if he will return to the faith and time for reflection, after each offer, is to be given him. If he remains obdurate he is to be executed by strangulation and then his head is to be cut off and placed under his arm. His body is thus to be exposed three days in the most public place." [2] But, thank God, Moslems do not strictly adhere to this law. In this, as in other respects, many are better than

[1] The Mohammedan Controversy and other articles.—Sir Wm. Muir, Edinburgh, 1897.

[2] *Missionary Review,* October, 1893, p. 727, in article by " C. H."

their religion and superior to their prophet. Converts in that part of Arabia which is under English rule or protection are as safe as they are in India; which does not mean that they are entirely free from persecution. In Turkish Arabia the law is carried out by secret murder, or by banishment; yet not in every case, for even there inquirers and converts, if not active or prominent, have remained for a time unmolested. What the result would be in the independent Moslem states of Arabia we do not know.

The Berlin Treaty was intended to be the Magna Charta of Christian liberty in the Turkish empire, but the Turk has not kept the compact. Its provisions were too galling to Moslem pride and prestige; reforms never got beyond the paper stage. The massacres of 1894 to 1896 proved that the Sultan is still the Pope of a religious fraternity and king of a political empire based on the forty-seventh chapter of the Koran: "When ye encounter the unbelievers strike off their heads until you have made a great slaughter of them." And the inaction of all the Christian powers at that time proved that it is vain to put confidence in princes. But in spite of all possible government opposition or even the martyrdom of every individual convert "so long as the door of access to individual Mohammedans is open, so long it is the clear and bounden duty of the church of Christ to make use of its opportunities for delivering the gospel message to them."

The attitude of the Arab mind is not universally hostile to Christianity. The vast majority are indifferent to religion in any form. "What shall we eat and what shall we drink and wherewithal shall we be clothed,"—is the sum of all their thoughts. The Arab merchant serves Mammon with all his heart seven days a week. Religion is an ornament and a conventionality; he wears it like his flowing overgarment and it fits him just as loosely. He thinks it scarcely worth while to discuss questions of belief. Every one has their own religion, is a remark one often hears in Arabia. It is a faint echo of the

all-embracing tolerance of the days of ignorance when three
hundred and sixty idols, including an image of Christ and the
virgin, filled the Kaaba!

Then there are some thoughtful men who know better,—
seekers after truth,—and who feel that there are strong points
in Christianity and weak points in Islam which have not been
duly considered.   One meets examples of this class everywhere in all stations of life and in most unexpected quarters.
In the heart of Yemen I met a Mullah who had a wonderful
knowledge of the Arabic Bible; and the copy he showed me
was an imperfect translation by Richard Watson dated 1825!
Another prominent Mohammedan in Eastern Arabia recently
expressed his opinion that the Christ of the New Testament
never intended to found a new religion, but to introduce
everywhere *spiritual* worship of the God of Abraham; he said
that a long and independent study of the Bible had led him
to this opinion.

The steady increase of the circulation of Scriptures in Arabia
is also an indication which way the current is drifting.   Rev.
George E. Stone, a few weeks before his death, writing of the
Bible circulation at Muscat said, " I don't know when the ex-
plosion is coming but we are getting the dynamite under this
rock of Islam and some day God will touch it off."   The
Bible in Arabia will indeed prove its power in changing the entire attitude of the Moslem mind.   " Is not my word like as
a fire? saith the Lord; and like a hammer that breaketh the
rock in pieces? ——"

Finally there is the problem of securing the right men for
the work.   So hard is the field in many ways and so hard are
Moslem hearts that the description of Aaron Matthews' ideal
missionary for the Jews would apply to the Arabs as well, (the
last clause omitted).   He wrote :   " A Jewish missionary requires Abraham's faith, Job's patience, the meekness of Moses,
the strength of Samson, the wisdom of Solomon, the love of
John, the zeal of Paul, the knowledge of the Scripture of Timo-

thy, and a little bit of Baron Rothschild's pocket." The financial part of the equipment is not essential on the part of the missionary; he should be content with food and raiment. The less display of Baron Rothschild's pocket the better, in a land where people go to bed hungry and where all live in the greatest simplicity.

The candidate for missionary work in Arabia should have a strong and sound constitution. He should know how to "rough it" when necessary; the more of the Bohemian there is in his nature the better. He should have both ability and dogged determination enough to acquire the Arabic language. Other scholarship is useful but not necessary. To get along well with the Arabs he should have patience. And to avoid wearing himself out, a good temper; a man with a very hot temper could never stand three seasons in the Persian Gulf. Regarding spiritual qualifications I cannot do better than quote the solemn words at the close of General Haig's paper on "Arabia as a mission-field." I believe they deserve to be repeated not only for the sake of those who *send* missionaries to Arabia, but for the sake of those who *are* missionaries to Arabia. It is a high ideal.

"Given the right men, and Arabia may be won for Christ; start with the wrong men, and little will be accomplished. But what qualifications are needed! what enthusiasm, what fire of love, what dogged resolution, what uttermost self-sacrificing zeal for the salvation of men and the glory of Christ! But upon this point I prefer to quote here the words of a man who is preëminently qualified to speak upon the subject. Three years ago he wrote to me:

"'Unless you have missionaries so full of the spirit of Christ that they count not their own lives dear to them, you will probably look in vain for converts who will be prepared to lose their lives in the Master's service. In a relaxing tropical climate, like that of Aden, circumstances are very unfavorable for the development of self-denying character, or of energetic service.　No small amount of grace would be needed to sustain it ; for we are compound beings, and there is a wonderful re-action of the body upon the soul, as well as of the soul upon the body.　It is supremely important, then, in an enterprise like yours, to have the *right stamp* of men—men who have made some sacrifices, and who do not count sacrifice to be sacrifice, but privilege and honor—men who do not know what *discouragement* means, and men who expect great things from God.　Such alone will prove really successful workers in a field so replete with difficulty.　Unless Eternity bulks very largely in the estimation of a man, how can he encourage a native convert to take a step that will at once destroy all his hopes and prospects of an earthly character, and possibly re-sult in imprisonment, and torture, and death itself ? and unless you have men who are prepared, should God seem to call for it, to lead their converts into circumstances of such danger and trial, it is not very likely that they will find converts who will go very much in advance of themselves.　Men of this stamp are not to be *manufactured ;* they are God-made.　They are not to be *found;* they must be God-sought and God-given.　But the Master who has need of them is able to provide them. Nothing is too hard for the Lord.' "

" *Pray ye therefore the Lord of the harvest that He would thrust forth laborers into His harvest.*"

XXXVI

THE OUTLOOK FOR MISSIONS TO MOSLEMS

" Take it at its very worst. They are dead lands and dead souls, blind and cold and stiff in death as no heathen are; but we who love them see the possibilities of sacrifice, of endurance of enthusiasm of *life*, not yet effaced. Does not the Son of God who died for them see these possibilities too ? Do you think He says of the Mohammedan, ' There is no help for him in his God ' ? Has He not a challenge too for your faith, the challenge that rolled away the stone from the grave where Lazarus lay ? ' Said I not unto thee, that, if thou wouldst believe thou shouldst see the glory of God ? Then they took away the stone from the place where the dead was laid.' "—*I. Lilias Trotter,* (missionary to Algiers).

TWO views are widely prevalent regarding the hopelessness of missionary work among Moslems generally, and although these views are diametrically opposite they are agreed that it is waste of time and effort to go to Mohammedan lands, that it is a forlorn hope at best. The first view is that of those who are themselves outside of the kingdom, and who shut its doors against the Moslem, saying : Experience has proved it to be not only useless but dangerous to meddle with the Moslem and his religion. Their faith is good enough for them ; it is suited to their ways. They do not worship idols and have a code of morality suitable to the Orient. Mohammed was a prophet of God and did all that could be done for these kind of people. Every attempt to convert them ends in failure. Let them alone. Islam will work out its own reformation. Some, like Canon Taylor and Doctor Blyden, who profess to be Christians, even consider Islam the handmaid of Christianity and specially fitted for the whole Negro race.[1]

[1] Christianity, Islam and the Negro Race, by E. W. Blyden, London, 1888.

391

The opposite view is that Mohammedanism is not too hopeful to be meddled with but too hopeless ! They who hold it profess to believe in the Holy Ghost as the Lord and Life-Giver for the *heathen* world, but hesitate when it comes to Islam. The Moslem is, they say, wrapped up in self-righteousness and conceit ; even those whose fanaticism is overcome dare not accept Christ. It is better to go to the heathen who will hear. Missions to the Moslem world are hopeless, fruitless, useless. It is impossible to Christianize them and there have been few, if any, converts.

That both of these views cannot be correct is evident, since they are contradictory. That the first is false the whole history of Islam demonstrates. " By their fruits ye shall know them." But what of the other view, held by so many, that we need not expect large results where there is so little promise ?

Professor J. G. Lansing, one of the founders of the Arabian mission, wrote in 1890 : " If the smallness of the number of converts from Islam to Christianity be pointed out, this argues not so much the unapproachability of Moslems as the indifference and inactivity of Christians. The doctrine of fatalism commonly accredited to Islam, is not one-half so fatalistic in its spirit and operation as that which for thirteen centuries has been practically held by the Christian Church as to the hope of bringing the hosts of Islam into the following of Jesus Christ." Is it possible that the lack of results complained of has been really a *lack of faith ?* Hudson Taylor remarked a few years ago, " I expect to see some of the most marvellous results within a few years in the missions to Islam, because of this work especially the enemy has said : It is without result. God is not mocked." Has the apostle to China read the signs of the times aright ?

Neither God's Providence nor His Word are silent in answer to that question. First we have the exceeding hopefulness of results of recent missionary work in many Moslem lands ; then the sure promises of God to give His Church the victory over

Islam ; and lastly the many exceeding great and precious promises for Arabia the cradle of Islam in particular.

1. It is not true that there have been no conversions among Moslems. In India alone there are hundreds who have publicly abjured Islam and been received into the Christian Church. The very first native clergyman of the Northwest Provinces was a converted Mohammedan. Sayad Wilayat Ali of Agra suffered martyrdom at Delhi for Christ. Mirza Ghulam Masih of the royal house of Delhi became a Christian and Abdullah Athim, the valiant-hearted of Amballa embraced the faith. At the Chicago Parliament of Religions Dr. Imad-ud-Din, himself a convert from Islam and a voluminous controversial writer, read a paper on Christian efforts among Indian Mohammedans·; this paper gives the names of one hundred and seventeen prominent converts from Islam, mostly from the Punjab. Beside these, the author says, " there are all sorts and conditions of men, rich and poor, high and low men and women, children, learned and unlearned, tradesmen, servants, all kinds and classes of Mohammedans whom the Lord our God hath called into His Church." It is officially stated that quite one-half of the converts from among the higher classes in the Punjab are from amongst Moslems.

In Persia there have been martyrs for the faith in recent years and several have been baptized. In the Turkish empire there have been scores of converts who have been obliged to flee for their lives or remain believers in secret. At Constantinople a congregation of converted Moslems was gathered by Dr. Koelle, but man after man disappeared—no doubt murdered for his faith. In Egypt there have been scores of baptisms and among others a student of Al Azhar University and a Bey's son confessed Christ. One has only to turn over the leaves of the Church Missionary Society annual reports to read of Mohammedans being baptized in Kerachi, and Bombay, Peshawar, Delhi, Agra, and on the borders of Afghanistan. In North Africa where the work is very recent there have been conversions and in one locality a remarkable spiritual movement is in progress among the Moslems.

In Java and Sumatra the Dutch and Rhenish missionary societies have labored with remarkable success among the Mohammedan population. At four stations of the Rhenish Mission is Sumatra where the work is practically altogether among Moslems, (namely, Sipirok-Simangumban, Bungabonder, Sipiongot, and Simanasor) the total number of church members according to the *Bombay Guardian*, is three thousand five hundred and ten. The total number of baptisms from Islam in these stations was during 1897 sixty-nine, and during the first half of 1898 already ninety-seven baptisms were reported. In some of the villages where formerly Islam was predominant it has been expelled altogether. The total number of Battak Christians amount to thirty-one thousand, the largest part of whom were formerly Moslems.[1] In some parts of Java still larger results are claimed.

In most Moslem fields it is absolutely impossible to obtain accurate statistics of the number of conversions for obvious reasons. The threatened death-penalty demands great caution in exposing a convert by freely publishing the fact of his conversion. Everywhere there are multitudes of secret believers whose names are sometimes not known even to the missionaries. Any one who has read the lives of Moslem converts such as that of Kamil or Imad-ud-Din or who knows from books like " Sweet First Fruits " what it means for a Moslem to forsake the faith of his fathers, knows that work in Moslem lands must not be judged by baptismal statistics.

There are other indications of spiritual life entering the Moslem world. There are thousands of Mohammedan youth receiving instruction in Christian mission schools ; in Egypt, one mission has twenty-four hundred and sixty-four Moslem pupils enrolled. The permeating power of spiritual Christianity is again at work in the Levant as when Paul and Silas made

[1] Missions in Sumatra, Dr. A. Schreiber, " North Africa," May, 1896.

their missionary journeys. The old churches of the East by their unfaithfulness were the occasion of the great apostasy of Islam; *their revival is the pledge of its downfall.* There is now an Evangelical Church in Persia, Egypt, Palestine, Syria and Asia Minor. Bodies of living Christians in the midst of Islam; no wonder that their power is beginning to be felt. The devil takes no antiseptic precautions against a non-contagious Christianity. But Evangelical Christianity *is* contagious, and the whole lurid horizon proclaims in persecutions and massacres and raging oppositions everywhere that Islam feels the power of Christian missions, even although they have only begun to attack in a miserly and puny way this stronghold of Satan.

Regarding the character of Moslem converts Bishop Thoburn says: " I believe that when truly converted the Mohammedan makes not only a devoted Christian but in some respects will make a superior leader. Leadership is a great want in every mission-field and the Mohammedans of India have the material, if it can only be won for Christ and sanctified to His service, out of which splendid workers can be made in the Master's vineyard." Doctor Jessup voices the same opinion, " It is not easy for a Mohammedan to embrace Christianity but history shows that when he is converted the Moslem becomes a strong and vigorous Christian."

2. In the work of missions among Mohammedans as well as in that among the heathen we have the assurance of final victory in the abundant testimony of God's Word. God's promises never fail of fulfillment; and those world-wide promises never are put in such a form as to exclude the Mohammedans. The Bible tells us that many false prophets shall arise and deceive many; but it does not for a moment allow that the empire of Christ shall divide rule with any of them. " It pleased the Father that in Him [Jesus not Mohammed] should all fullness dwell." " The Father loveth the Son and hath given all things into His hands "—not into the hands of

Mohammed. "God hath exalted Him and given Him a
name which is above every name . . . far above all
principality and power and might and dominion and every
name that is named not only in this world but also in that
which is to come." "That at the name of Jesus every" Mohammedan "knee should bow and every" Moslem "tongue
confess that Jesus Christ is Lord to the glory of God the
Father." The present may see Islam triumphant, but the
future belongs to Christ. Over against the lying truth "there
is no God but God and Mohammed is His prophet," Christianity lifts the standard, "Who is he that overcometh the
world but he that believeth that Jesus Christ is the Son of
God?" The Divinity of Christ, which Moslems deny, decides the destiny of all world-kingdoms.

Witness the present governments of the Moslem world. "Be
wise now therefore O ye kings, be instructed ye judges of the
earth . . . kiss the Son lest He be angry and ye perish
from the way when His wrath is kindled but a little." There
is a general failure among Christians to realize the number and
importance of the missionary promises in the Old Testament.[1]
The Great Commission was based on these exceeding great
promises. The nations were God's plan before they were on
Christ's program. And is it not remarkable that nearly all of
these Old Testament promises are grouped around the names
of countries which now are the centre and strength of the Moslem world? "Known unto God are all His works from the beginning of the world." Or will these promises of world-wide
import only stretch beyond Egypt, Mesopotamia, Syria and
Arabia, not including those lands in God's plan of redemption
and dominion? Is there not a special blessing in store for the
lands that border Palestine, when the Lord shall comfort Zion

---

[1] Gen. xii. 3, xviii. 8, xxii. 18, xxvi. 4, xxviii. 14; Num. xiv. 21;
Forty-three of the Psalms; Isaiah ii. 2, 18, etc., etc.; Jeremiah iii. 17;
Dan. vii. 13, 14; Joel ii. 28; Jonah. iii., iv.; Micah v. 4; Hab. ii. 14;
Zeph. ii. 11; Hag. ii. 6, 7; Zech. ix. 10, xiv. 9; Mal. i. 11.

and restore all her waste places ? "In that day shall Israel be the third with Egypt and with Assyria even a blessing in the midst of the earth.   Whom the Lord of hosts shall bless, saying, Blessed be Egypt My people and Assyria the work of My hands and Israel My inheritance."

The Moslem world is in no *better* condition and in no *worse* condition than the heathen world as portrayed in the New Testament.   The need of both is the same ; and the same duty to evangelize them ; and the same promise of God's blessing on our work of witness.   The Mohammedan world is also without excuse (Rom. i. 20, 32), without hope (John iii. 36 ; Eph. ii. 12), without peace (Isaiah xlviii. 22), without feeling (Eph. iv. 19), without Christ (Rom. xiii. 13, 14) as is the heathen world.   But no less is our responsibility toward them nor the power of God's love to win them.

It is the rock of Christ's *Sonship* which is the stone of stumbling and the rock of offence to the Moslem mind.   But it is this very rock on which Christ builds His church ; and the foundation of God standeth sure.   Writing on this subject Mr. Edward Glenny, the Secretary of the North Africa Mission, well says :

"Blessed be God, we are not left to carry on this warfare at our own charges ! 'He that sent Me is with Me,' said the Master ; and He who sends His servants now is surely with them also, for the promise stands, 'Lo ! I am with you alway, even unto the end of the age.'   In all our efforts for the salvation of men, we are dependent upon the power of the Spirit of God ; for no man can say that Jesus is the Lord, but by the Holy Ghost.   But if those of us who work at home are conscious of this, those who labor in Mohammedan countries realize it most intensely.   Amongst the masses at home, what we have to contend against mostly is indifference ; but there it is deeply-rooted prejudice, aye, even in many cases, hatred to Jesus as the Son of God.   But the battle is the Lord's, not ours ; we are but instruments to carry out His purposes.   The

Spirit has been sent forth from the Father to 'convict THE WORLD of sin,' and we are not justified in making any reservation in the case of Mohammedans—yea, may we not expect that if there be a nation or race on the earth more inaccessible than another, more averse to the gospel, more hardened against its teachings, that there the Lord will show 'the exceeding greatness of His power' by calling out some from their midst whom He may make 'chosen vessels' to bear His name to others? Has not that been His mode of working in time past?"

3. There is no land in the world and no people (with the exception of Palestine and the Jews) which bear such close relation to the Theocratic covenants and Old Testament promises as Arabia and the Arabs. The promises for the final victory of the Kingdom of God in Arabia are many, definite and glorious. These promises group themselves around seven names which have from time immemorial been identified with the peninsula of Arabia: *Ishmael, Kedar, Nebaioth, Sheba, Seba, Midian* and *Ephah.* We select these names only, omitting others which have an indirect reference to Arabia or the Arabs, as well as those promises, so numerous and glorious, concerning the wilderness and desert-lands. The latter would surely, for the dwellers of Palestine, have primary reference to Northern Arabia; but our argument is strong enough without these special promises.[1]

In order to understand the promises given to the sons of Ishmael, Kedar and Nebaioth, we need first to know the relation which Ishmael bears to the Abrahamic covenant and the place he occupies in God's plan for the nations as outlined in the book of Genesis.

Hagar, the mother of the Arabian patriarch, seems to have occupied a prominent place in Abraham's household and appears to have brought to that position not only mental gifts but

[1] See Isaiah xxxv. 1–3, xl. 3, xli. 19, xliii. 19, li. 3; Ezekiel xxxiv. 25, xlvii. 8; Ps. lxxii. 9, etc.

also an inward participation in the faith of the God of Abraham. She was probably added to the family of faith during Abraham's sojourn in Egypt and occupied the same position toward the female servants that Eliezer of Damascus did to the male servants. It is when she was driven forth into the wilderness by the jealous harshness of Sarah that we have the first revelation of God regarding her seed. " The angel of the Lord found her by a fountain of water in the wilderness, by the fountain in the way to Shur." [2] And He said, Whence camest thou? and whither wilt thou go? And she said, I flee from the face of my mistress Sarai. And the angel of the Lord said unto her, Return to thy mistress and submit thyself under her hands. And the angel of the Lord said unto her, . . . " I will multiply thy seed exceedingly that it shall not be numbered for multitude. And the angel of the Lord said unto her, Behold thou art with child, and shalt bear a son and shalt call his name Ishmael [God will hear] ; because the Lord hath heard thy affliction. And he will be a wild man, his hand will be against every man, and every man's hand against him ; and he shall dwell in the presence of all his brethren. And she called the name of the Lord that spake unto her, Thou God seest me : for she said, Have I also here looked after Him that seeth me."

It is plain from the context that the angel of the Lord and the Lord Himself are here identified ; it was the angel of Jehovah, the angel of the covenant of the Christ of the Old Testament. Why should this " angel " first appear to the Egyptian bondwoman ? Is it according to the law that the Lord always reveals Himself first to the poorest, most distressed and receptive hearts or was it the special office of the covenant angel to seek " that which was lost " from the patriarchal church at its very beginning ? Lange suggests in his commentary that the " Angel of Jehovah, as the Christ who was

[2] According to Gesenius this is Suez, while Keil identifies it with Jifar, a site in the northwestern part of Arabia near Egypt.

to come through Isaac had a peculiar reason for assisting Hagar, since she for the sake of the future Christ is involved in this sorrow." In any case the special revelation and the special promise was given to Hagar not only but to her seed. Christ, if we may so express it, outlines the future history and character of the Ishmaelites as well as their strength and glory; but He also gives them a spiritual promise in the God-given name, *Ishmael*, Elohim will hear. Without this the theophany loses it true character. Ishmael as the child of Abraham could not be left undistinguishable among the heathen. It was for Abraham's sake that the revelation included the un-born child in its promises.

The fulfillment of the promise that Ishmael's seed should multiply exceedingly has never been more clearly stated than by the geographer Ritter : "Arabia, whose population consists to a large extent of Ishmaelites, is a living fountain of men whose streams for thousands of years have poured themselves far and wide to the east and west. Before Mohammed its tribes were found in all border-Asia, in the East Indies as early as the middle ages; and in all North Africa it is the cradle of all the wandering hordes. Along the whole Indian ocean down to Molucca they had their settlements in the middle ages; they spread along the coast to Mozambique; their caravans crossed India to China, and in Europe they peopled Southern Spain and ruled it for seven hundred years." Where there has been such clear fulfillment of the promise of natural increase, is there no ground that *God will hear* and give spiritual blessing also and that Ishmael "shall dwell in the presence of all his brethren" in the new covenant of grace?

Thirteen years after the first promise to Ishmael we hear the promise renewed just after the institution of circumcision, the sign of the covenant of faith. "And Abraham said unto God, O that Ishmael might [even yet] live before Thee. And God said, Sarah thy wife shall bear thee a son indeed; and thou shalt call his name Isaac: and I will establish my covenant

RESCUED SLAVE BOYS AT MUSCAT

THE ARABIAN MISSION HOUSE AT MUSCAT

with him for an everlasting covenant, and with his seed after him. And as for Ishmael, I have heard thee. . . . " What is the significance of Abraham's prayer for Ishmael? Is it probable that he merely asks for temporal prosperity and for length of life? This is the idea of some commentators but none of them explain why the prayer asks that Ishmael may live "*before God.*" Keil and others, more correctly we think, regard the prayer of Abraham as arising out of his anxiety lest Ishmael should not have *any* part in the blessings of the covenant. The fact that the answer of God contains no denial of the prayer of Abraham is in favor of this interpretation.

In the prayer Abraham expresses his anticipation of an indefinite neglect of Ishmael which was painful to his parental heart. He asks for him, therefore, a life from God in the highest sense. Else what does the circumcision of Ishmael mean? The sealing or ratifying of the covenant of God with Abraham *through Isaac's seed*, embraces not only the seed of Isaac, but all those who in a wider sense are sharers of the covenant, Ishmael and his descendants. And however much the Arabs may have departed from the *faith* of Abraham they have for all these centuries remained faithful to the *sign* of the old covenant by the rite of circumcision. This is one of the most remarkable facts of history. *Circumcision is not once alluded to in the Koran,* and Moslem writers offer no explanation for the omission. Yet the custom is universal in Arabia, and from them it passed over with other traditions to all the Moslem world. The Moslems date circumcision from Abraham and circumcise at a late period. The Arabs in "the time of ignorance" also practiced the rite; an uncircumcised person is unknown even among those Bedouins who know nothing of Islam save the name of the prophet.[1]

"As for Ishmael I have heard thee." For the third time we read of a special revelation to prove God's love for the son of the bondmaid. In the pathetic story of Hagar's expulsion,

[1] Compare Rom. iv. 11, and Gal. iii. 17.

Ishmael is the centre figure.[1] His mocking was its cause; for *his* sake it was grievous in Abraham's sight to expel them. To Ishmael again is there a special promise, "because he is thy seed." When the water is spent in the bottle and Hagar turns away from seeing the death of the child, it was not her weeping but the lad's prayer that brought deliverance from heaven. "And the angel of God called to Hagar out of heaven and said unto her, What aileth thee, Hagar? fear not; for God hath heard the voice of the lad where he is. Arise, lift up the lad and hold him by thine hand; for I will make of him a great nation. And God opened her eyes, and she saw a well of water; and she went and filled the bottle with water and gave the lad drink. And God was with the lad."

No less does this history show the moral beauty of Hagar's character, her tender mother love and all the beautiful traits of a maternal solicitude than the repentance of Ishmael. God heard his voice; God forgave his sinful mocking; God confirmed his promise; God saved his life; God was with the lad. The Providence of God watched over Ishmael. Long years after he seems to have visited his father Abraham, for we read that when the patriarch died in a good old age "his sons Isaac and Ishmael buried him in the cave of Machpelah." No mention is made here of the sons of Keturah. And twice in the Bible the generations of Ishmael are recorded in full[2] in order to bind together the prophecies of Genesis with the Messianic promises of Isaiah for the seed of Ishmael.

The twelve princes, sons of Ishmael, whose names are recorded "by their towns and their castles" were undoubtedly the patriarchs of so many Arab tribes. Some of the names can be distinctly traced through history and others are easily identified with modern clans in Arabia. Mibsam, *e. g.*, seems to correspond with the Nejd clan of *Bessam* some of whom are merchants at Busrah; Mishma is surely the same as the

[1] Gen. xxi. 9–22.

[2] Gen. xxv. 11–18, and 1 Chron. i. 28.

Arabic *Bni Misma;* while nearly all commentators agree that
Duma is *Dumat el Jendal* in North Arabia, one of the oldest
Arabic settlements. Aside from conjecture two names stand
prominent and well-known in profane history; *Nebajoth* and
Kedar. Pliny in his natural history mentions them together
as the Nabatœi et Cedrei and the Arab historians are familiar
with the names. Undoubtedly the Nabatans are related to
Nebajoth; although this is denied by Quartermere it is affirmed
by M. Chwolson and is the universal opinion of the Arabs
themselves.

Now it is these very two names, whose identity no one
questions, that are the centre of glorious promises. It is generally known that the sixtieth chapter of Isaiah is the gem of
missionary prophecy in the Old Testament; but it does not
occur to every one that a large portion of it consists of special
promises for Arabia. " The multitude of camels shall cover
thee, the dromedaries of Midian and Ephah, (Sons of Keturah,
Gen. xxv. 1–5); all they from Sheba (South Arabia or
Yemen) shall come; they shall bring gold and incense; and
they shall show forth the praises of the Lord. All the flocks
of Kedar shall be gathered together unto thee; the rams of
Nebaioth shall minister unto thee: they shall come up with
acceptance upon mine altar and I will glorify the house of my
glory. Who are these that fly as a cloud and as doves to their
windows?"

These verses read in connection with the grand array of
promises that precede them leave no room for doubt that the
sons of Ishmael have a large place in this coming glory of the
Lord and the brightness of His rising. It has only been delayed by our neglect to evangelize Northern Arabia but God
will keep His promise yet and Christ shall see of the travail
of His soul, among the camel-drivers and shepherds of Arabia.
And then shall be fulfilled that other promise significantly put
in Isaiah xlii. for this part of the peninsula: " Sing unto the
Lord a new song and His praise from the end of the earth

. . . let the wilderness and the cities thereof lift up their
voice, the villages that Kedar doth inhabit : let the inhabitants
of the rock sing, let them shout from the top of the mountains." It is all there, with geographical accuracy and up-to-
date ; "*cities in the wilderness*" that is Nejd under its present
government; Kedar forsaking the nomad tent and becoming
villagers; and the rock-dwellers of Medain Salih ! "And I
will bring the blind by a way they knew not ; I will lead them
in paths that they have not known : I will make darkness light
before them and crooked things straight." The only proper
name, the only geographical centre of the entire chapter is
Kedar. In two other prophecies,[1] which have no Messianic
character, Kedar is referred to *as synonymous with Arabia*.

Another group of missionary promises for Arabia cluster
round the names *Seba* and *Sheba*. "All they from Sheba shall
come ; they shall bring gold and incense and they shall show
forth the praises of the Lord." (Is. lx. 6.) "The kings of
Sheba and Seba shall offer gifts. Yea all kings shall fall down
before Him, all nations shall serve Him. . . . He shall
live and to Him shall be given of the gold of Sheba ; prayer also
shall be made for Him continually and daily shall He be
praised." The Messianic character of this psalm is generally
acknowledged.

Where are Seba and Sheba? Who are they? Three
Shebas are referred to in genealogy and prophecy. 1. A son
of Raamah, son of Cush ; 2. A son of Joktan ; 3. A son
of Jokshan son of Keturah. But all of these find their dwell-
ing-place in what is now Southern Arabia. The Joktanite
Sheba is the kingdom of the Himyarites in Yemen.[2] The
kingdom of Sheba embraced the greater part of Yemen ; its
chief cities and probably its successive capitals were Seba,
Sana (Uzal), and Zaphar (Sephar). Seba, the oldest capital, is
identical with the present *Marib*, northeast of Sana ; for Ez-

---

[1] Isaiah xxi. 13–17 and Jer. xlix. 28–33.
[2] See Smith's Bible Dictionary.

Zejjaj in the Taj El Aroos dictionary says, " Seba was the city of Marib or the country in the Yemen of which the city was Marib." Ptolemy's map makes plain what the Romans and Greeks understood by Seba and Sheba. The Cushite Sheba settled somewhere on the shores of the Persian Gulf. In the *Marasid* Stanley-Poole says he found " an identification which appears to be satisfactory—that on the island of Awāl, one of the Bahrein islands are the ruins of an ancient city called Seba."

The same authority holds that the Keturahite Sheba formed one tribe with the Cushite Sheba and also dwelt in Eastern Arabia. Sheba has always been a land of gold and incense and we are only beginning to know a little of the opulence and glory of the ancient Himyarite kingdom in Yemen from the lately discovered inscriptions and ruins.

In the same psalm that gives these promises to Southern and Eastern Arabia we have this remarkable verse : " He shall have dominion also from sea to sea and from the river unto the ends of the earth. They that dwell in the wilderness shall bow before Him and His enemies shall lick the dust." *The* river referred to is undoubtedly the Euphrates [1] and the boundaries given are intended to include the ideal extent of the promised land. Now it is, to say the least, remarkable that modern Jewish commentators interpret this passage together with the forty-eighth chapter of Ezekiel so as to include *the whole peninsula of Arabia* in the land of promise. I have seen a curious map, printed by Jews in London, on which the twelve restored tribes had each their strip of territory right across Arabia from the Red Sea to the Gulf and including Palestine and Syria.

Isaac Da Costa, the great Dutch poet, who was of Jewish descent gathers together in his epic, " Hagar," some of these Bible promises for the sons of Ishmael. [2]

---

[1] Cf. Exodus xxiii. 31 and Deut. xi. 24.
[2] *The Christian Intelligencer* (N. Y.), March 15, 1899.

" Mother of Ishmael !   The word that God hath spoken
Never hath failed the least, nor was His promise broken.
Whether in judgment threatened or as blessing given ;
Whether for time and earth or for eternal heaven,
To Esau or to Jacob.   .   .   .
The patriarch prayed to God, while bowing in the dust:
' Oh that before thee Ishmael might live ! '—His prayer, his trust.
Nor was that prayer despised, *that* promise left alone
Without fulfillment.   For the days shall come
When Ishmael shall bow his haughty chieftain head
Before that Greatest Chief of Isaac's royal seed.
Thou, favored Solomon, hast first fulfillment seen
Of Hagar's promise, when came suppliant Sheba's queen.
Next Araby the blest brought Bethlehem's newborn King,
Her myrrh and spices, gold and offering.
Again at Pentecost they came, first-fruits of harvest vast ;
When, to adore the name of Jesus, at the last
To Zion's glorious hill the nation's joy to share
The scattered flocks of Kedar all are gathered there,
Nebajoth, Hefa, Midian.   .   .   .
Then Israel shall know Whose heart their hardness broke,
Whose side they pierced, Whose curse they dared invoke.
And then, while at His feet they mourn His bitter death,
Receive His pardon.   .   .   .
Before Whose same white throne Gentile and Jew shall meet
With Parthian, Roman, Greek, the far North and the South,
From Mississippi's source to Ganges' giant mouth,
And every tongue and tribe shall join in one new song,
Redemption ! Peace on earth and good-will unto men ;
The purpose of all ages unto all ages sure.   Amen.
Glory unto the Father !   Glory the Lamb, once slain,
Spotless for human guilt, exalted now to reign !
And to the Holy Ghost, life-giver, whose refreshing
Makes all earth's deserts bloom with living showers of blessing ! "

.   .   .   .

" Mother of Ishmael !   I see thee yet once more,
Thee, under burning skies and on a waveless shore !
Thou comfortless, soul storm tossed, tempest shaken,
Heart full of anguish and of hope forsaken,

Thou, too, didst find at last God's glory all thy stay!
He came. He spake to thee. He made thy night His day.
As then, so now. Return to Sarah's tent
And Abraham's God, and better covenant,
And sing with Mary, through her Saviour free,
' God of my life, Thou hast looked down on me.' "

But Arabia, although it has all this wealth of promise, is not a field for *feeble* faith. Yet we can learn to look at this barren land because of these promises with the same reckless, uncalculating, *defiant* confidence in which Abraham " without being weakened in faith, he considered his own body now as good as dead " (R. V.) " but waxed strong through faith giving glory to God." The promises are great because the obstacles are great ; that the glory of the plan as well as the glory of the work may be to God alone. Arabia needs men who will believe as seeing the Invisible. Six hundred years ago Raymond Lull wrote : " It seems to me that the Holy Land cannot be won in any other way than that whereby Thou, O Lord Jesus Christ, and Thy Holy Apostles won it, by love and prayer, and the shedding of tears and blood."

A lonely worker among Moslems in North Africa recently wrote : " Yes it is lives poured out that these people need—a sowing in tears—in a measure that perhaps no heathen land requires ; they need a Calvary before they get their Pentecost. Thanks be unto God for a field like this : in the light of eternity we could ask no higher blessedness than the chance it gives of fellowship with His Son."

The dumb spirit of Islam has possessed Arabia from its childhood for thirteen hundred years; " he teareth and he foameth and gnasheth with his teeth and pineth away." " And He said unto them this kind can come forth by nothing but by prayer and fasting." *"If thou canst believe, all things are possible to him that believeth."* (Mark ix. 14–29.)

Life for Arabia must come from the Life-Giver. " I believe in the Holy Ghost," therefore mission-work in Arabia will prove the promise of God true in every particular and to its fullest extent. " O that Ishmael might live . . . as for Ishmael I have heard thee."

" Speed on, ye heralds, bringing
    Life to the desert slain;
Till in its mighty winging,
    God's spirit comes to reign
From death to new-begetting,
    God shall the power give,
Shall choose them for crown-setting
    And Ishmael shall live.

" So speaks the promise, bringing
    The age of Jubilee
To every home and tenting,
    From Tadmor to the sea.
The dead to life are risen,
    The glory spreads abroad,
The desert answers heaven,
    Hosannas to the Lord!"

Appendix I

A CHRONOLOGICAL TABLE

Circa 1892 B. C.—Birth of Ishmael.
   "   1773 " —Death of Ishmael.
   "   992 " —Bilkis, queen of Yemen (Sheba) visits Solomon.
   "   700 " —Amalgamation of Cushite and Sabean clans in Yemen.
   "   754 " —All Yemen and Oman under rule of Yaarüb.
   "   588 " —First Jewish settlements in Arabia.
A. D   33—Arabians present at Pentecost.
   "   37—The Apostle Paul goes to Arabia.
   "   60—Second Jewish immigration into Arabia.
   "   105—Roman Emperor Trajan under his general Palma subdues Northwestern Arabia.
   "   120—Destruction of great dam at Marib and the beginning of Arab migrations northward.
   "   297—Famine in Western Arabia. Migrations eastward.
   "   326—Nearchus, admiral of Alexander, surveys the Persian Gulf.
   "   325—Nicene Council—Arabians present.
   "   342—Christianity already extending in Northern Arabia. Churches built in Yemen.
   "   372—Mavia, queen of North Arabia, converted to Christianity.
   "   525—Abyssinian invasion of Yemen.
   "   561—Mohammed born at Mecca.
   "   575—Persians under Anosharwan expel the Abyssinians from Yemen.
   "   595—Mohammed marries Khadijah.
   "   595—Yemen passes under Persian Rule.
   "   610—Mohammed begins his prophetic career.
   "   622—(A. H. 1)—Mohammed flees from Mecca to Medina. The era of the *Hegira*.
   "   623—Battle of Bedr.
   "   624—Battle of Ohod.
   "   630—Mecca overcome. Embassy to Oman, etc.
   "   632—Death of Mohammed. Abubekr caliph. All Arabia subjugated by force of arms.
   "   634—Omar caliph. Expulsion of Jews and Christians from Arabia.
   "   638—Kufa and Busrah founded.

A. D.   644—Othman caliph.
"   655—Dissensions regarding caliphate. Medina attacked. Ali
            chosen caliph.
"   656—Battle of the Camel. Capital transferred to Kufa.
"   661—Ali assassinated. Hassan becomes caliph.
"   750—Beginning of Abbaside Caliphate (Bagdad).
"   754—Mansur.
"   786—Haroun el Rashid.
"   809—Amin.
"   813—Mamun.
"   833—Motasim.
"   847—Motawakkel.
"   889—Arise of Carmathian sect.
"   905—Yemen comes under Karamite caliphs.
"   932—Rebellion in Yemen. It becomes independent under
            Imams of Sana as rulers.
"   930—Carmathians take Mecca and carry away the black-stone to
            Katif.
"   1055—Togrul Beg at Bagdad.
"   1096-1272—The Crusades. Arabia in touch with European civil-
            ization through its bands of warriors.
"   1173—Yemen subdued by sultans of Egypt.
"   1240—Rise of Ottoman Turks.
"   1258—Fall of Bagdad.
"   1325—Yemen again independent.
"   1454—Imams of Yemen take Aden and fortify it.
"   1503—Portuguese under Ludovico Barthema, make voyages on
            Arabian coast and visit Aden and Muscat.
"   1507—Portuguese take Muscat.
"   1513—Portuguese under Abulquerque are repulsed at Aden. Visit
            Mokha and the Persian Gulf.
"   1516—Suleiman by order of Mameluke Sultan attacks Aden and is
            repulsed.
"   1538—Suleiman the Magnificent sends a fleet and takes Aden by
            treachery. Arab garrison butchered.
"   1540—Beginning of Turkish rule in Yemen.
"   1550—Arabs hand over Aden to the Portuguese.
"   1551—Aden recaptured by Peri Pasha.
"   1624-1741—Imams established rule over all Oman with capital
            at Rastak; then at Muscat.
"   1609—First visit to Aden by English captains.
"   1618—English establish factories at Mokha.
"   1622—Portuguese expelled from Bahrein and Arab coast by the
            Persians.
"   1630—Arabs drive out Turks from Yemen and *Imams* take the
            throne at Sana.
"   1740-65—Dutch East India Company in Persian Gulf and Red
            Sea ports.
"   1765—English East India Company in Persian Gulf and Red Sea
            ports.
"   1735—Abdali Sultan of Lahaj takes Aden.

A. D. 1741—Ahmed bin Said drives out Portuguese from Muscat and founds Dynasty of Imams, anew.

"   1765—Mohammed bin Abdul Wahab dies and his political associate Mohammed bin Saud propagates Wahabiism in Arabia.

"   1780—Spread of Wahabi doctrine over all of Central Arabia.

"   1801—Wahabis conquer Bahrein and hold it for nine years.

"   1803—Abd-ul-Aziz the Wahabi chief assassinated by a Persian fanatic.

"   1803—Wahabis take Mecca and lay seige to Jiddah.

"   1804—Wahabis take Medina.

"   1804—Said bin Sultan ruler of Oman and Zanzibar.

"   1809—Aden visited by Captain Haines of British Navy.

"   1818—Ibrahim Pasha captures Wahabi capital and sends Amir in chains to Constantinople where he is beheaded.

"   1805–1820—British suppress piracy in Persian Gulf.

"   1820—Son of Amir, Turki, proclaimed Sultan of Nejd and Oman coast.

"   1821—British make treaty with tribes on Oman coast called the " Trucial League."

"   1820–1847—British treaties with Bahrein chiefs to suppress slave-trade and piracy.

"   1831—Turki, ruler of Nejd, murdered.

"   1832—Feysul bin Turki, succeeds him.

"   1835—Abdullah bin Rashid becomes a powerful chief in Jebel Shammar.

"   1835—Aden again visited by British to avenge cruelty to sailors shipwrecked off its coast.

"   1839—Aden bombarded by British fleet and taken. Treaties made with surrounding tribes.

"   1840–1847—Aden attacked by Arabs.

"   1846—Tilal bin Abdullah bin Rashid succeeds to rulership of Jebel Shammar and becomes independent of Wahabi power.

"   1851–1856—Abdullah bin Mutalib Sherif of Mecca.

"   1854—Sultan of Oman makes treaty with England and cedes Kuria Muria Islands.

"   1856—Thuwani bin Said ruler of Oman.

"   1857—Perim occupied by British.

"   1858–1877—Abdullah bin Mohammed Sherif of Mecca.

"   1858—Cable laid in Red Sea from Suez to Aden, but proved defective (cost £800,000).

"   1858—Bombardment of Jiddah by British.

"   1865–1886—Abdullah bin Feysul ruler of Nejd with capital at Riad.

"   1867—Mitaab bin Abdullah succeeds Tilal.

"   1867—Menamah (Bahrein) bombarded by British because of broken treaty. Isa bin Ali made ruler.

"   1866—Sultan bin Thuwani ruler of Oman.

"   1868—Mohammed bin Rashid assumes power and rule at Hail as Amir of Nejd.

412 *APPENDIX I*

A. D. 1869—Cable laid from Bombay to Aden and Suez.
" 1870—Turkish invasion of Yemen.
" 1871—Turkish invasion of Hassa and occupation of Katif.
" 1871—Seyyid Turki ruler of Oman (Muscat).
" 1875—Busrah made a separate vilayet.
" 1877—Beginning of Turkish bureaucracy at Mecca.
" 1878—Treaty of Berlin. Reforms promised in Turkish Provinces.
" 1880—Hasein, Sherif of Mecca, is murdered.
" 1881–82—Abd el Mutalib again Sherif of Mecca.
" 1882—Aun er Rafik made Sherif of Mecca.
" 1886—Mohammed Ibn Rashid takes Riad overturning Saud government and becomes ruler of all Central Arabia.

Appendix II

TABLE OF THE ARAB TRIBES OF NORTHERN ARABIA

I. THE ANAEZE:

- *Walid Ali*
  - El Meshadaka.
  - El Meshatta.
  - El Hammamede.
  - El Jedaleme.
  - El Toluh.
- *El-Hessene*
  - El Hessene (proper).
  - Messalih.
- *Er-Ruwalla* (or Jilas)
  - El Ruwalla (proper).
  - Um Halif.
- *El-Beshr*
  - Tana Majid
    - Fedan.
    - Sebaa.
  - Selga
    - Medeyan.
    - Metarafe.
    - Aulad Suleiman.

II. AHL ES-SHEMMAL: (Northern tribes)

- El Mowaly.
- El Howeytat.
- El Hadedin.
- Es-Soleyb.
- (also) Arabs of the Hauran
  - El Feheily.
  - Es-Serdye.
- Bni Sokhr.
- Bni Heteym.

III. AHL EL-KIBLY: (Southernly tribes)

- Arabs of Kerak.
- Esh-Sherarat.
- Bni-Shammar
  - El Temeyat.
  - El Menjat.
  - Ibn Ghazy.
  - Bayr.
  - El-Fesyani.
- El-Jerba.
- El Jofeir.
- El Akeydat.
- Bni Sayd.
- El-Wouled.
- El-Bakara.

413

Appendix III

AN ARABIAN BIBLIOGRAPHY

A. The Geography of Arabia

Andrew, (Sir W. P.)—The Euphrates Valley Route (London, 1882).

Barthema, (Ludovico.)—Travels in Arabia translated by Richard Eden (1576).
Begum of Bhopal—Pilgrimage to Mecca (London, 1870).
Blunt, (Lady Ann.)—A pilgrimage to Nedj, 2 vols. (London, 1883).
"   "   "   —The Bedouins of the Euphrates (London, 1879).
Buist, (Dr.)—Physical Geography of the Red Sea (no date).
Burckhardt, (John Lewis.)—Notes on the Bedouins and Wahabis, 2 vols. (London, 1830; in German, Weimar, 1831).
Burckhardt, (John Lewis.)—Travels in Arabia, 2 vols. (London, 1830).
Burton, (Richard.)—Personal Narrative of a pilgrimage to El Medina and Mecca (London, 1857).

Chesney—Survey of the Euphrates and Tigris, 4 vols. (London, 1850).
Cloupet—Nonveau Voyage dans l'Arabie Heureuse en 1788 (Paris, 1810).
Constable, (Capt. C. G., and Lieut. A. W. Stiffe.)—The Persian Gulf Pilot (London, 1870, 1893).
Cruttenden, (C. J.)—Journal of an excursion to Sana'a the capital of Yemen (Bombay, 1838).

Doughty, (C. M.)—Arabia Deserta, 2 vols. (Cambridge, 1888).

Fogg, (W. P.)—Arabistan (London, 1875).
Forster—Geography of Arabia, 2 vols. (London).
Frede, (P.)—La Peche aux Perles en Perse et a Ceylan (Paris, 1890).
Fresnel—Lettres in Journal Asiatique iii. Series v. 521.

Galland—Recueil des Rites et Ceremonies du Pelerinage de la Mecque (Amsterdam, 1754).

Haig, (F. T., Maj. Gen.)—A Journey through Yemen. Proceedings of the Roy. Geog. Soc. of London, vol. ix., No. 8.
Harris, (W. B.)—A Journey through Yemen (London, 1893).
Hunter, (F. M.)—Statistical Account of the British Settlement of Aden (London, 1877).
Hurgronje, (Snouck.)—Mekka, mit bilder atlas, 2 vols. (Hague, 1888).

414

Irwin, (Eyle.)—Adventures in a voyage up the Red Sea on the coasts of Arabia, etc., in 1777 (London, 1780).

Jaubert—Geographie d'Edresi (in Arabic and French, Paris, 1836).
Jomard—Études Geog. et Hist. sur l'Arabie (in vol. iii. Mengin's History of Egypt.

King, (J. S.)—Description of the island of Perim (Bombay Government Records No. 49).

La Roque—A voyage to Arabia the Happy, etc. (London, 1726).

Makramah, (Aboo Abd Allah ibn Achmed.)—A Manuscript History of Aden (see Hunter's account).
Manzoni—El Yemen; Tre anni nell'Arabia felicè (Rome, 1884).
Michaelis—Receuil de Questiones proposeès a une Societé de Savants qui par ordre de Sa Majestie Danoise font le voyage de l'Arabie (Amsterdam, 1774).

Niebuhr, (Carsten.)—Original edition in German (Copenhagen, 1772).
  "   "   —In French edition (Amsterdam, 1774).
Niebuhr, (Carsten.)—Travels through Arabia trans. into English by Robert Heron, 2 vols. (Edinburgh, 1792).

Ouseley, (Sir W.)—Oriental Geography of Ibn Haukal.
  "   "   "   —Travels in Persia and Arabia, 3 vols. (London, 1800).

Palgrave—Travels in Eastern Arabia (London, 1863).
Parsons, (Abraham.)—Travels in Asia . . . including Mocha and Suez (London, 1808).
Phillips—Map of Arabia and Egypt with index (London, 1888).
Prideaux—Some recent discoveries in Southwest Arabia (Proceedings Soc. Bib. Archaelogy, London).

Schapira—Travels in Yemen (1877).
Seetzen—Travels in Yemen (1810).
Sprenger, (A.)—Die alte Geographie Arabiens als Grundlage der Entwicklungsgeschichte des Semitismus (Berne, 1875).
Sprenger, (A.)—Die Post- und Reiserouten des Orients (1864).
Stanley, (Dean.)—Sinai and Palestine.
Stern, (Rev. A.)—A journey to Sana'a in 1856 (Jewish Intelligencer, vol. xxiii., pp. 101 seq.
Stevens—Yemen (1873).

Taylor, (Bayard.)—Travels in Arabia (New York).
Tuck—Essay on Siniatic Inscriptions in the Journal of German Oriental Society, vol. xiv., pp. 129 seq.

Van den Berg, (L. W. C.)—Hadramaut and the Arabian colonies in the Indian Archipelago. Translated from the Dutch by Major Seeley (Bombay Govt. Records No. 212 new series).

Van Maltzen, (H. I.)—Reisen in Arabien (Braunschweig 1873).
Vincent's—Periplus of the Erythrean Sea.
Von Wrede, (Adolph.)—Reise in Hadramaut.

Wellstead, (Lieutenant.)—Travels in Arabia (London, 1838).
"   "   —Narrative of a journey to the ruins of Nakeb
    el Hajar (Journal Roy. Geo. Soc. vii. 20).
Whish—Memoir on Bahrein (1859).
Wüstenfeld (F.)—Baherein und Jemameh.

B. Manners and Customs[1]

Arabian Nights—(Various editions).

Baillie, (N. B. E.)—The Mohammedan law of sale (London, 1850).
"   "   —Mohammedan Law Hanifi code (London, 1865).
"   "   —Mohammedan Law Imamia code (London, 1869).
Boyle, (J. B. S.)—Manual of Mohammedan Laws (Lahore, 1873).
Burckhardt's—Arabic Proverbs (London).
"   —Notes on the Bedouins and Wahabis, (London, 1831).

Grady, (S. G.)—The Mohammedan Law of inheritance (London, 1869).

Hamilton, (Charles.)—Hedaya or Guide; a commentary on the Mussul-
    man Laws (London, 1886).

Jessup, (H. H.)—Women of the Arabs (New York, 1874).

Kremer, (Alfred Von.)—Kultur Geschichte des Orients, 2 vols. (Wien,
    1875–77).

Lane's—Manners and Customs of Modern Egyptians, 2 vols. (London).
"   —Arabian Nights, with Notes, 4 vols. (London).

Meer, (Mrs. Hassan Ali.)—Observations on the Mussulmans (London,
    1832).

Rumsey, (Almaric.)—Mohammedan law of Inheritance (London, 1886).

Smith, (Robertson.)—Kinship and Marriage in early Arabia (Cambridge).
Syeed, (Ameer Ali.)—Personal law of Mohammedans (London, 1880).

Tornauw—Das Moslemische Recht (1885).
Trumbull's, H. C.)—The Blood Covenant (Philadelphia, 1891).

Von Hammer, (Purgstall.)—Die Geisterlehre der Moslimen (Wien, 1852).

[1] Consult Bibliographies of Palestine and Syria with reference to Nomad life.

C. History of Arabia[1]

Abu Jaafer Muhammed et Tabbari—Tareek el mulook; Arabic and
   Latin. Edit. Kosegarten (Leipsic, 1754).
Abulfida—Annales Muslemici. Arab. et Latin. Various editions.

Badger, (George Percy.)—History of the Imams and Seyyids of Oman
   by Salil Ibn Razik from A. D., 661–1856. Trans. with intro. and
   notes (London, 1871).

Blau, Otto—Arabien im Zechsten jaarhundert. Zeitschift des Deutsch.
   Morgenland. Gezel. xviii. B.

Clark, E. L.—The Arabs and the Turks (Boston).
Crichton—History of Arabia and its people (London, 1844).

D'Herbelot—Bibliotheque Orientale (Maestricht, 1776).
Doughty, (C.)—Documents epigraphiques recueillis dans le nord de
   l'Arabie (avec préface et traduction des inscriptions nabatéennes de
   Medaln-Salih par E. Renan). With 57 plates 4to. (Paris, 1884.)
Dozy, R.—De Israeliten te Mekka (Leyden, 1864).
   "   " —Essai sur l'Histoire del' Islamisme (Paris, 1879).

Eichhorn—Monumenta Antiquissima Hist. Arabum (Gotha, 1775).

Faria y Souza—Manuel de Asia Portuguesa (Lisbon, 1666).
Flugel, Gustav—Geschichte der Araber bis auf den sturtz des Chalifats
   von Bagdad, 2 vols. (Leipzig, 1864).
Foster, Rev. C.—The historical geography of Arabia (London, 1844).
Freeman—History of the Saracens.
Fresnel—Lettres sur hist. des Arabes avant l'Islamisme. Journal Asi-
   atique (1838–1853).

Gibbon's—Decline and fall of the Roman Empire (Chaps. l., li., lii.).
Gilman, A.—The Saracens (Story of Nations) (London, 1891).

Haji Khalifah—Hist. of the Maritime wars of the Turks. Translated
   from the Turkish by James Mitchell (London, 1831).
Hallam's—History of the Middle Ages (Chapter vi.).
Hammer-Purgstall—Gemäldesaal der Lebensbeschreibungen grosser Mos-
   limischer Herscher (Leipzig, 1837).
Hamza Ispahaneusis—Tarikh Saniy Mulook el Ardh, Arab. Lat. ed.
   Gottwaldt (St. Petersburg, 1844).

Jergis El Mekin—Hist. Saracenica Arab. et Lat. (Leyden, 1625).

Khuzraji, Ali bin Hoosain El—History of Yemen (*MSS.* in Records of
   Residency at Aden).

Milman's—Latin Christianity Bk. iv. chaps. i., ii.
Muir—Annals of Early Caliphate (London, 1883). (See under Religion).
   " —The Caliphate, its Rise, Decline and Fall (London, 1891).

[1] Consult also list in Gilman's Saracens.

Ockley, S.—History of the Saracens (London, 1708).

Perceval, A. P. Caussin de—Essaisur l'Histoire des Arabes avant
    Islamisme (Paris, 1836).
Playfair, R. L.—History of Arabia Felix (Bombay, 1859).
Pocock, Eduardo—Specimen Hist. Arab. ex Abul Feda (Oxford 1650).

Quartermere—Memoire sur les Nabatheen.

Rasmussen—Addimenta ad Hist. Arab. ante Islam.
Redhouse, J. W.—A Tentative Chronological Synopsis of the history of
    Arabia and its neighbors from B. C. 500000 [!] to A. D. 679
    (London, 1890).
Roesch, A.—Die Koningen von Saba als Konigin Bilqis (Leipzig, 1880).
Rycant—The present state of the Ottoman Empire (London, 1675).

Sachan, C. Edward—The Chronology of Ancient Nations; an English
    version of Arabic " Vestiges of the past," A. H. 390–1000
    (London, 1885).
Schmölder—Sur les Ecoles Philosophique chezles Arabes (Paris, 1842).
Schulten—Hist. Imperii vetus Joctanidarum (Hard. Gelderland, 1786).
    "   —Monumenta Vetustiora Arab (Leyden, 1740).
Sedillot—Hist. gen. des Arabes (Paris, 1877).
Souza—Documentos Arabicos para a hist. Portuguesa (Lisbon, 1790).

Weil, Gustav—Geschichte der Chalifen, 3 vols. (Mannheim, 1846–51).
    "   "   —Geschichte der Islamisher Völker von Mohammed bis zur
    zeit des Sultan Selim (Stuttgart, 1866).
Wüstenfeld, F.—Die Geschichtschreiber der Araber und ihrer Werke
    (Gottingen, 1882).
Wüstenfeld, F.—Vergleichungs Tabellen der Muh. und Christ. Zeitrech-
    nung (Leipzig, 1854).
Wüstenfeld, F.—Die Chroniken der stadt Mekka gesammelt, und her-
    ausgegeben, Arab. Deutsch, 4 vols. (Leipzig, 1857).
Wüstenfeld, F.—Genealogische Tabellen der Arabische Stämme (Got-
    tingen, 1852).

D. Islam

Addison, Lancelot—State of Mahumedism (London, 1679).
Akehurst, Rev. G.—Impostures instanced in the life of Mohammed
    (London, 1859).
Alcock, N.—The rise of Mohammedanism accounted for (London,
    1796).
Anonymous—Life of Mohammed (London, 1799).
    "   —Reflections on Mohammedanism! (London, 1735).
    "   —The morality of the East as extracted from the Koran
    (London, 1766).
Arnold, Matthew—Essay on Persian Miracle Play (London, 1871).
    "   Edwin—Pearls of the Faith (Boston, 1883).
    "   J. M.—Ishmael, or the natural aspect of Islam (London, 1859).

Arnold, J. M.—Islam and Christianity (London, 1874).
" T. W.—The Preaching of Islam : A history of the Propagation of
the Muslim faith (London, 1896).

Bate, J. D.—Claims of Ishmael (Benares, 1884).
Bedwell, W.—Mahomet's Imposture (London, 1615).
" " —Mahomet unmasked (London, 1642).
Beverly, R. M.—A reply to Higgins [See Higgins,] 1829.
Blochman, H.—'Ain i Akbari of Abdul Fazl, (Eng. trans.) (Calcutta,
1868).
Blunt, W. S.—The Future of Islam (London, 1881).
Blyden—Islam, Christianity and the Negro Race.
Bonlainvilliers, Count—Life of Mohammed. Translation. (London,
1731).
Brinckman, A.—Notes on Islam (London, 1868).
Brydges, H. J.—History of the Wahabis (London, 1834).
Burton, R. F.—The Jew, the Gipsey and El Islam (London, 1898).
Bush, Rev. George—Life of Mohammed (New York, 1844).

Carlyle, Thos.—Heroes and Hero-Worship (London, 1840).
Cazenhove, Dr.—Mahometanism (Christian Remembrancer, Jan., 1855).

Daumer, G. F.—Mahomed und sein Werk (Hamburg, 1848).
Davenport, John—Apology for Mohammed (London, 1869).
De Goeje—Memoire sur les Carmathes de Baherein (Leyden, 1863).
Deutsch, Emanuel—Essay on Islam (London, 1874).
De Worde—A Lytell Treatyse of the Turkes Law called Alcoran
(London).
Dods, Marcus—Mohammed Buddha and Christ (London, 1878).
Döllinger—Mohammed's Religion nach ihrer Inneren Entwicklung und
ihrem Einflüsse (Ratisbon, 1838).
Dozy—L'Histoire d Islamisme (Leyden, 1879).
" —Het Islamisme (Leyden, 1879).
Dugat, Gustave—Histoire des philos. et des theol. Musulmans de 632–
1258 J. C. (Paris, 1878).
Duveyrier, H.—La conferie Musulmane de Sidi Moh. bin Ali Es-
Senonsi (Paris, 1886).

Falke R.—Budda, Mohammed, Christus ; ein vergleich u. z. w. (Güter-
sloh, 1897).
Forster, Rev. C.—Mahometanism unveiled, 2 vols. (London, 1829).

Gagnier, J.—Ismael Abulfeda, De Vita et Rebus gestis Mohammedis
(Oxford, 1723).
Galland—Recueil des Rites et Ceremonies du pelerinage de la Mecque
(Amst., 1754).
Garnett, L. M. J.—The Women of Turkey and their folk-lore (London,
1891).
Geiger Rabbi—Judaism and Islam [translation of the above] (Madras,
1898).
Geiger Rabbi—Was hat Mohammed aus das Judenthume aufgenommen ?
(Wiesbaden, 1833).

Georgens, E. P.—Der Islam und die moderne Kultur (Berlin, 1879).
Gerock—Versuch einer Darstellung der Christologie des Korans (Hamburg, 1839).
Gibbon—Decline and Fall of Roman Empire (in loco).
Gmelin, M. F.—Christenschlaverei und de Islam (Berlin, 1873).
Guyard, S.—La civilization Musulmane (Paris, 1884).

Haines, C. R.—Islam as a Missionary Religion (London, 1888).
Hamilton, C.—The Hedayah, a commentary on Moslem law Trans. (London, 1791.) (Edition by Grady, 1890).
Hauri, Johannes—Der Islam in seinem Einfluss auf das leben seiner bekenner (Leyden, 1880).
Herclots, Dr.—Qanoon-el-Islam (London, 1832).
Higgins, G.—An Apology for the life of Mohammed (London, 1829).
Hughes, F. P.—Notes on Mohammedanism (London, 1875).
"   " " —Dictionary of Islam (New York and London, 1885).
Hurgronje, C. Snouck—Het Mekkaansche Feest (Leyden, 1880).
"   "   " —Mekka : mit bilder atlas, (The Hague, 1880).

Inchbald, Rev. P.—Animadversions on Higgins, (Doncaster, 1830).
Irving, Washington—Life of Mahomet (London, 1850).
"   "   —Successors of Mahomet (London, 1852).

Jansen, H.—Verbreitung des Islams, u. z. w., in den verschiedeuen, Landern der Erde, 1890-1897 (Berlin, 1898).
Jessup, H. H.—The Mohammedan Missionary Problem (Phila., 1889).

Keller, A.—Der Geisteskampf des Christentums gegen den Islam bis zur Zeit der Kreuzzüge (Leipzig, 1897).
Koelle, S. W.—Mohammed and Mohammedanism critically considered (London, 1888).
Koelle, S. W.—Food for Reflection (London, 1865).
Koran : (Editions and translations).
    —English versions: Alexander Ross (from French, 1649-1688), Sale (1734), Rodwell (1861), Palmer (1880).
    —First Arabic, *printed text*, at Rome, 1530 (Brixiensis).
        Arabic text, Hinkelmann (Hamburg, 1649).
        "   and Latin text,—Maracci (Padua, 1698).
        "   text—Empress Catherine II. (St. Petersburg, 1787).
        "   "   "   "   ("   "   1790, 1793, 1796, 1798).
        "   "   Empress Catherine, II. (Kasan, 1803, 1809, 1839).
        "   (critical edition) G. Flügel, (Leipzig, 1834, 1842, 1869).
    —French, Savary (1783) and Kasimirski (Paris, 1840, 1841, 1857).
    —French version, Du Ryer (Paris, 1647).
    —German versions: Boysen (1773), Wahl (1828), Ullmann (1840, 1853).
    —German version, Schweigger (Nurnberg, 1616).
    —Latin version, Robert and Hermann (Basle, 1543).
    —Russian version (St. Petersburg, 1776).
Translations exist also in the other European languages; and in

Persian, Urdu, Pushto, Turkish, Javan, and Malayan made by Moslems.

KORAN COMMENTARIES:—(" There are no less than 20,000 in the library at Tripolis alone "—Arnold's Islam and Christianity, p. 81).
The most important are,—(Sunni)—

Al Baghawi, A. H. 515.	At-Tafsir 'l Kebir, A. H. 606.
Al Baidhawi, A. H. 685.	Azizi, A. H. 1239, (and Shiah).—
Al Jalalan, A. H. 864 and 911.	Az-Zamakhshari, A. H. 604.
Al Mazhari, A. H. 1225.	Hussain, A. H. 900.
Al Mudarik, A. H. 701.	Ibn u'l Arabi, A. H. 628.
Ar-Razi (30 vols.), A. H. 606.	Mir Bakir, A. H. 1041.
As-Safi, A. H. 668.	Saiyid Hasham, A. H. 1160.
As-sirru'l wajiz, A. H. 715.	Sheikh Saduk, A. H. 381.

Krehl, C. L. E.—Das leben des Moham. (Leipzig, 1884).

Kremer, Von Alfred—Geschichte der Heerschende Ideen des Islams: Der Gottsbegriff, die Prophetie und Staatsidee (Leipzig, 1868).

La Chatelier, A.—L'Islam an XIX*e* siecle (Paris, 1888).
Lake, J. J.—Islam, its origin, genius and mission (London, 1878).
Lamairesse, E., (et G. Dujarric.)—Vie de Mahomet d'apres la tradition, vol. i. (Paris, 1898).
Lane-Poole, Stanley—Studies in a Mosque (London, 1883).
"   "   "   —Table-talk of Mohammed (London, 1882).
Lane—Selections from the Koran (London, 1879).

MacBride, J. D.—The Mohammedan Religion Explained (London, 1859).
Maitland, E.—England and Islam (London, 1877).
Marracio, L.—Refutatio Al Coran (Batavii, 1698).
Marten, Henry—Controversial Tracts on Christianity and Islam, by the Rev. S. Lee (edited Cambridge, 1824).
Matthews—The Mishkat (traditions) translation (Calcutta, 1809).
Merrick, J. L.—The life and religion of Mohammed from Sheeah traditions (translated from Persian) (Boston, 1850).
Mills, C.—The History of Muhammedanism (London, 1817).
Mills, W. H.—The Muhammedan System (— 1828).
Mochler, J. A.—The relation of Islam to the Gospel (translation) (Calcutta, 1847).
Mohler, J. A.—Ueber das Verhaltniss des Islams zum Evangelium (1830).
Morgan, Joseph—Mohammedanism Explained (London, 1723).
Muir, Sir William—Life of Mahomet, 4 vols. (London, 1858 and 1897).
"   "   "   —Rise and Decline of Islam (in Present Day Tracts, London, 1887).
Muir, Sir William—Mahomet and Islam (London, 1890).
"   "   "   —Sweet First Fruits. Translated from Arabic. (London, 1896).
"   "   "   —The apology of Al Kindy, translated from Arabic (London, 1887).
Muir, Sir William—The Coran: Its composition and teaching and the testimony it bears to the Holy Scriptures (London, 1878).
Muir, Sir William—The Beacon of Truth (from Arabic) (London, 1897.)

Muir, Sir William—The Caliphate (London, 1897).
"   "   "   —The Mohammedan Controversy (Edinburgh, 1897).
Müller, F. A.—Der Islam im Morgen und Abendlanden (Berlin, 1885).
Murray, Rev. W.—Life of Mohammed, according to Abu El Fida (Elgin, no date).

Neale, F. A.—Islamism, its Rise and Progress (London, 1854).
Niemann, G. K.—Inleiding tot de keunisvanden Islam (Rotterdam, 1861).
Nöldecke, T.—Geschichte des Qurans (Göttingen, 1860).
"   "   —Das Leben Muhammeds (Hanover, 1863).

Oelsner, C. E.—Des effets de la religion de Mohammed (Paris, 1810).
Osborn, Major—Islam under the Arabs, (London, 1876).
"   "   —Islam under the Caliphs (London, 1878).

Pfander, Doctor—The Mizan El Hak (translated from Persian) (London, 1867).
Pfander, Doctor—Miftah ul Asrar (Persian) (Calcutta, 1839).
"   "   —Tarik ul Hyàt, Persian (Calcutta, 1840).
Palgrave, W. G.—Essays on Eastern Question (London, 1872).
"   "   " —Travels in Central and Eastern Arabia.
Palmer, E. H.—The Koran translated, 2 vols. (Oxford, 1880).
Pelly, Lewis—The Miracle Play of Hasan and Hussain (London, 1879).
Perron—L'Islamisme, Son Institutions, etc. (Paris, 1877).
"   —Femmes Arabes avant et depuis l'Islamisme (Paris, 1858).
Pitts, Joseph—Religion and manners of Mahometans (Oxford, 1704).
Prideaux, H.—The True Nature of the Imposture fully explained (London, 1718).

Rabadan—Mahometanism (Spanish and Arabic) 1603.
Reland (and others)—Four Treatises (on Islam) (London, 1712).
Rodwell, J. M.—The Koran, Translated (London, 1871).
Roebuck, J. A.—Life of Mahomet (London, 1833).
Ross, Alexander—The Koran (London, 1642).
Rumsey, A.—Al Sirajiyeh. Translated (London, 1869).
Ryer, Andre du—Life of Mahomet (London, 1718).

Sale—Translation of the Koran with preliminary discourse (London, 1734).
Scholl, Jules Charles—L'Islam et son fondateur: Étude morale (Neuchatel, 1874).
Sell, Rev. E.—The Faith of Islam (Madras, 1880 and London, 1897).
"   "   " —The Historical Development of the Quran (Madras, 1898).
Smith, Bosworth—Mohammed and Mohammedanism (London, 1876).
Smith, H. P.—The Bible and Islam (New York and London, 1897).
Sprenger, Aloys—Das leben und die Lehre des Mohammed, 3 vols. (Berlin, 1865).
Sprenger, A.—Life of Mohammed from original sources (Allahabad, 1851).
Steinschneider, Moritz—Polemische Literatur in Arabischer Sprache (Leipzig, 1877).
Stevens, W. R. W.—Christianity and Islam (London, 1877).

St. Hilaire, T. Bartholomew de—Mahomet et le Coran (Paris, 1865).
Stobart, J. W. H.—Islam and its Founder (London, 1876).
Syeed, Ahmed Khan—Essays on the life of Mohammed (London, 1870)·
Syeed, Ameer Ali—A critical examination of the life and teachings of
    Mohammed (London, 1873).

Tassy, Garcin de—L'Islamisme d'apres le Coran (Paris, 1874).
Taylor, W. C.—The Hist. of Mohammedanism (London, 1834).
Thiersant, P. Dabry de—Le Mahometisme en Chine (Paris, 1878).
Tisdall, W. St. Clair—The Religion of the Crescent (London, 1896).
Turpin, F. H.—Hist. de la vie de Mahomet, 3 vols. (Paris, 1773).

Wallich, J.—Religio Turcia et Mahometis Vita (1659).
Weil, Gustav—Das leben Mohammed; nach Ibn Ishak bearbeit von Ibn
    Hisham, 2 vols. (Stuttgart, 1864).
Weil, Gustav—Historische-Kritische Einleitung in den Koran (Biele-
    feld, 1844).
Wherry, E. M.—Commentary on the Quran, 5 vols. (London, 1882).
White, J.—Bampton Lectures (on Islam) (Oxford, 1784).
Wollaston, Arthur N.—Half Hours with Mohammed (London, 1890).
Wortabet, John—Researches into Religions of Syria, (London, 1860).
Wüstenfeld, H. F.—Das leben Muhammeds, 3 vols. (Gottingen, 1857.)
    "   "   " —Geschichte der Stadt Mekka, 4 vols. (Leipzig,
    1857–61).

Zotenberg—Tareek-i-Tabari. Translated.

E. Christianity and Missions [1]

Birks, Herbert—Life and Correspondence of Bishop T. V. French (Lon.
    (don, 1895).
Jessup, H. H.—The Setting of the Crescent and the Rising of the Cross or
    Kamil Abdul Messiah (Philadelphia, 1898).
Jessup, H. H.—The Mohammedan Missionary Problem (Phila., 1879).
Sinker, Robert—Memoir of Ion Keith Falconer (Cambridge, 1886).
The Arabian Mission. Quarterly Letters and Annual Reports, special
    papers on missionary journeys from 1890–1899 (New York.)
Wright, Thomas—Early Christianity in Arabia; a historical essay (Lon-
    don, 1855). This book gives a complete account of the early spread
    of Christianity and cites authorities, which being mostly in Latin, are
    omitted here.

F. Language and Literature

Abcarius—English–Arabic Dictionary (Beirut, 1882).
Ahlwardt, W.—The Divans of the six ancient Arabic Poets (London,
    1890).

[1] Consult British and Foreign Bible Society Reports for account of Scripture circulation; the *Free Church of Scotland Monthly* for reports of Keith Falconer Mission;
the *Church Missionary Intelligencer*, 1887, vol. xii., pp. 215, 273, 346, 408; *Missionary Review of the World*, 1892–1899, October numbers.

Ahlwardt, W.—Über die Poesie und Poetiek der Araber (Gotha, 1856).
"   "—Bemerkungen über die ächtheid der Alten Arab. Gedichten (Griefswald, 1872).
Arnold, F. A.—Arabic Chrestomathy, 2 parts (Halis, 1853).
Arnold, F. A.—Septem M'oallakat (Leipzic, 1850).

Badger, G. P.—English–Arabic Lexicon (London, 1881).
Birdwood, Allan B.—An Arabic Reading Book (London, 1891).

Cadri, Moh.—Guide to Arab. Conversation (Alexandria, 1879).
Caspari, C. P.—Arab. Grammatik (Halle, 1876).
Caussin de Perceval—Grammaire Arabe. (Paris, 1880).
Cheikho, P. L.—Chrestomathia Arabica cumlexico variisque notis (Beirut, 1897).
Clodius, J. C.—Gram. Arabica (Leipzig, 1729).
Clouston—Arabic Poetry for English Readers (Glasgow, 1889).

De Goeje, Prof.—A complete account of the authorship, etc., of the Arabian Nights (" De Gids," Amsterdam, Sept., 1886).
Derenbourg, H. and Spiro J.—Chrestomathy (Paris, 1885).
Dieterici, Fr.—Thier und Mensch vor dem koning der Genien u. z. w. (Leipzig, 1881).
Dieterici, Fr.—Arabisches-Deutsch Wortenbuch zum Koran und Thier und Mensch (Leipzig, 1881).
Dieterici, Fr.—Die Arabische Dicht-Kunst (Berlin, 1850).
Dombay, Fr. de—Gram. Mauro-Arab. (Vindob., 1800).
Dozy, R. P. A.—Supplément aux dictionnaires Arabes., 2 vols. (Leyden, 1877).
Dozy, R. P. A.—[And many other monographs on the language.]

Erpenius, Th.—Grammatica, etc. (Leyden, 1767).
Erpenius, Th.—Rudimenta Linguae Arabicae, Ed. A. Schultens (Leyden, 1770).
Euting—Katalog der Arabische Literatur (Strassburg, 1877).
Ewald, G. H. A.—Gram. Criticalinq. Arab., 2 vols. (Lips., 1831).

Farhat, G.—Dict. Arabe-Française (Marseilles, 1849).
Faris Es Shidiac—Arab. Gram. (London, 1856).
Fleischer, H. L.—Tausend und eine Nacht (text and notes, 12 vols.) (Breslau, 1825–43).
Fleisher, M. H. L.—Arabische Sprüche u. z. w. (Leipzig, 1837).
Flügel, G.—Die Grammatische Schulen der Araber nach den Quellen bearbeidt (Leipzig, 1862).
Flugel—Kitab El Fihrist, with German notes (Leipzig, 1871–72).
Flügel, Gustav—Lexicon Bibliographicum Arab., 7 vols. 4to. (Leipzig, 1835-58).
Forbes, Duncan—Arabic Grammar.
Freytag—Einleitung in das studium der Arabische Sprache (Bonn, 1861).
"   —Lexicon, Arab. Lat., 4 vols. (Halis, 1830).
"   —   "   "   (abridged Halis, 1837).
"   —Arabum Proverbia (3 vols.) (Bonn, 1838).

Giggejus, A.—Thesaurus linq. Arabicae, 4 vols. (Medioland, 1632).
Gies, H.—Zur kentniss sieben Arabischer Versarten (Leipzig, 1879).
Girgass and De Rosen—Chrestomathy (German ed. 1875. Russian, St. Petersburg, 1876).
Goeje, De M. J.—Debelangryhheid van de bevefening d. Arab. taal en letterkunde (Hague, 1866).
Golius, J.—Lexicon Arab. Lat. (Leyden, 1653).
Green, A. O.—A Practical Arabic Grammar (Oxford, 1887).

Hammer Van Purgstall—Literaturgeschichte der Araber: Von ihren be-ginne bis zum ende des Zwölfte Jaluhunderts der Hidschret, 7 vols. (Wein, 1850–56).
Heury, J.—Vocab. French-Arab. (Beyrout, 1881).
Hirth, J. Fr.—Anthologia Arab. (Jenae, 1774).
Hoefer's Zeitschrift—Ueber die Himyarische Sprache (vol. i., 225 sq).

Jahn, J.—Arabische Chrestomathie (Wien, 1802).
Jayaker, A. S. G.—The Omanese Dialect of Arabic, 2 parts (In Journal R. A. S., of Gt. Britain).

Kosengarten, J.—Arab. Chrestomathy (Leipzig, 1828).
Kremer, A. von—Lexikographie Arab. (Vienna, 1883).

Lane, E. W.—An Arabic English Dictionary (i.–viii.) (London, 1863–89).
    "   W.—The Thousand and One Nights, with notes, edited, 3 vols. (London, 1841).
Lansing, J. G.—Arabic Grammar (New York, 1890).

Mac Naghten, W. H.—Thousand and One Nights literally transl., 4 vols. (Calcutta, 1839).

Newman, F. W.—Dictionary, 2 vols. (London, 1890).
    "   "   " —Handbook of Modern Arabic (London, 1890).
Nöldeke, Th.—Beitrage zur Kentniss d. Poesie d. alten Araber, (Hanover, 1864).

Oberleitner, A.—Chrestomathia Arab. (Vienna, 1824).

Palmer, E. H.—Arabic Grammar (London, 1890).
    "   " " —Arabic Manual (London, 1890).
Perowne, J. J. S.—Adjrumiah, translated with Arabic voweled text (Cambridge, 1852).

Richardson—Arab. Persian English Dictionary (London, 1852).
Richardson, J. A.—Gram. of Arabic Language (London, 1811).
Rosenmüller, E. F. C.—Grammar (Leipzig, 1818).

Sacy, A. J. Sylvestre de—An Arabic Grammar.
    "   "   "   "   " —Arabic Chrestomathy, 4 vols. (Paris, 1829).
Socin, A.—Arabische Grammatik (Berlin, 1889).
Steingass, F.—Arab.-Eng. and Eng.-Arab. Dict. (London, 1890).

Tien, A.—Handbook of Arabic (London, 1890).
"   " —Manual of Colloquial Arab. (London, 1890).
Trumpp, E.—Einleitung in das Studium der Arabischen Grammatiker (Münich, 1876).
Tychsen, O. G.—Elementale Arabicum (1792).

Van Dyck, C. C. A.—Suggestions to beginners in the study of Arabic (Beirut, 1892).
Vollers—Ægypto-Arab. Sprache (Cairo, 1890).
Vriemoet, E. L.—Grammar (Franeker, 1733).

Wahrmund, A.—Arab. Deutsch Handworter buch, 2 vols. (Giessen, 1887).
"   " —Handbuch der Arab. Sprache (Giessen, 1866).
Winckler, J. L. W.—Arab. Sprachlehre nebst Wörterbuch (Leipzig, 1862).
Wright, W.—Arabic Reading Book (London, 1870).

Index

Bedouin tribes, Mission to, 328.
 " warfare, 203, 364.
Beit Allah, 34, 35.
Bent, Theodore, 73.
Bible, Arabic, 256, 316.
 " depot in Bagdad, 321.
 " distribution in Arabia, 320, 365, 377, 384, 388.
Black stone of Mecca, 31, 36.
Blood covenants, 166.
 " revenge, 155, 265.
Blunt, Lady Ann, 269.
British and Foreign Bible Society, 321.
British influence in Arabia, 218.
Bruce, Robert, 321.
Buchanan, Claudius, 314.
Bunder, Abbas, 235.
 " Jissa, 84.
Burckhardt (quoted), 269.
Burial place of Mohammed, 47.
Burns, William, 320.
Burton (quoted), 282.
Busrah, 124, 129, 361.
 " mission, 365.

CAMEL, Land of the, 88.
 " Use and character, 90.
Cantine, James, 353, 359, 360.
Caravan journey from Bagdad, 136.
 " routes of Oman, 94.
Carmathian princes, 115.
Castles in Hadramaut, 75.
Cave-dwellers, Gharah, 86.
Certificate, The Mecca, 40.
Charms used by women of Mecca, 42.
Child life among Arabs, 265.
Christian Church in Aden, 54.
 " " " Arabia, 306.
 " coins used as amulets, 43.

Christian and Missionary Alliance, 328.
Christianity in Arabia, 159, 300.
Christians, Hatred of, 30, 267.
 " St. John, 285.
Christ's Sonship, The Rock of, 397.
Church Missionary Society, 322, 327, 344.
Circumcision, 399.
Climate of Arabia, 20, 378.
 " " Bahrein, 106.
 " " Nejd, 147.
 " " Oman, 79, 80, 93.
Cobb, H. N. (quoted), 369.
Coffee trade in Yemen, 70.
Coins, Carmathian, 115.
Colportage work (see Bible Distribution), 384.
Commerce, English, in Arabia, 225.
 " in the Nejd, 151.
 " of Busrah, 126.
Consulates, British, 231.
Converts from Islam, 391.
Cosmogony, Sabean, 296.
Covenants, 166.
Cradle of the Human Race, 119.
Ctesiphon, Arch of, 133.
Cufic characters, 243.
Customhouse, Turkish, 58.
Customs, Arab, 166.

DA COSTA, ISAAC, 405.
Damar, 66.
Date culture, 124.
 " palm, 121.
Dauasir, Wady, 22, 145.
Dedan, 97.
Desert dwellers and the camel, 90.
Deserts of Arabia, 24, 144.
Difficulties of Arabian missions, 374.